Sexual
Dysfunction

Sexual Dysfunction

A behavioural approach to causation, assessment, and treatment

Derek Jehu
University of Manitoba

JOHN WILEY & SONS
Chichester • New York • Brisbane • Toronto

British Library Cataloguing in Publication Data:

Jehu, Derek
   Sexual dysfunction.
   1. Sex therapy
   2. Behavior therapy
   I. Title
   616.6'92'0651   RC556   79–40582

   ISBN 0 471 99756 0 (Cloth)
   ISBN 0 471 27597 2 (Paper)

Photosetting by Thomson Press (India) Ltd., New Delhi
and printed in Great Britain by The Pitman Press, Bath

To Kit

Contents

Chapter 1 A Behavioural Approach to Sexual Dysfunction:
An Introduction 1
General features 1
Definition 3
Causation 4
Assessment 5
Treatment 7

PART 1 AN OVERVIEW OF CAUSATION

Chapter 2 Organic Factors 11
Sexual stimulation 11
Sexual response 12
Aging 17
Illness 18
Surgery 27
Drugs 28
Conclusion 30

Chapter 3 Previous Learning Experiences 31
Learning conditions 31
Learning processes 36
Conclusion 40

Chapter 4 Contemporary Conditions 41
Psychological stresses 41
Partner discord 49
Psychological reactions to organic factors 54
Psychiatric syndromes 61
Deficient or false information 63
Deficient or inappropriate stimulation 64

PART 2 THE DYSFUNCTIONS

Chapter 5 Definition and Classification 69
Definition 69

Classification 75

Chapter 6 Male Dysfunctions 77
Inadequate sexual interest 77
Inadequate arousal or intromission 81
Inadequate orgasm or ejaculation 87
Inadequate sexual pleasure or painful intercourse 98

Chapter 7 Female Dysfunctions 103
Inadequate arousal or intromission 103
Inadequate orgasm 109
Inadequate sexual pleasure or painful intercourse 115

PART 3 AN OVERVIEW OF TREATMENT

Chapter 8 Therapeutic Interviews 119
Provision of information 119
Modification of attitudes 125
Management of sexual assignments 135

Chapter 9 Sexual Assignments 137
General pleasuring 138
Genital stimulation 141
Sexual intercourse 149

**Chapter 10 Specific Behavioural Procedures and Ancillary Physical
Treatment** 152
Relaxation training 152
Desensitization 154
Flooding 159
Vaginal dilatation 160
Classical conditioning 161
Biofeedback 162
Phantasy training 163
Hypnosis 164
Ancillary physical treatment 166
General conclusion 170

PART 4 ASSESSMENT AND PLANNING TREATMENT

Chapter 11 Assessment of Problems and Resources 175
Assessment of problem(s) 175
Assessment of resources 179
Behavioural formulation 192

Chapter 12 Selecting Goals and Planning Treatment 194
Goals of treatment 194

Planning treatment 196
Assessment of treatment 209

Chapter 13 Methods of Data Collection 211
Assessment interviews 211
Questionnaires 214
Self-monitoring 222
Physiological techniques 223
Medical examination 225

PART 5 OUTCOME OF TREATMENT

Chapter 14 Programmes for Male and Female Dysfunctions 229
Masters and Johnson (1970) 230
Mathews *et al.* (1976) 231
Obler (1973) 234

Chapter 15 Programmes for Male Dysfunctions 237
Erectile dysfunction 237
Premature ejaculation 243
Retarded or absent ejaculation 246

Chapter 16 Programmes for Female Dysfunctions 248
Vaginismus 248
Orgastic dysfunction 249
General conclusions 256

Appendix 261
Checklist of topics for assessment interviews with sexually dysfunctional clients and partners 261

References 265
Author Index 289
Subject Index 297

1

A Behavioural Approach to Sexual Dysfunction: An Introduction

To start on a personal note, this author does not regard himself as a 'sex therapist' who practises some distinct form of treatment called 'sex therapy' that is applicable only to problems of sexual dysfunction. Instead, the book is written from the viewpoint of a behaviour therapist who believes that the approach he uses is essentially similar whether it is directed towards sexual dysfunction or any other psychological problem. This is because the behavioural approach has certain fundamental characteristics that transcend its application to particular problems. Some of these characteristics are discussed below in sections introducing the definition, causation, assessment, and treatment of sexual dysfunction, but consideration is given first to certain characteristics of a more pervasive nature that influence all aspects of the approach.

GENERAL FEATURES

One of these very broad features of the behavioural approach is an attempt to apply general psychological principles to the explanation, assessment, and treatment of psychological problems. These principles are drawn from many areas of psychology and its related disciplines, including learning and cognition, developmental and social psychology, neurophysiology and the sociology of deviance. Thus, a large body of empirical, systematic, and cumulative knowledge from these sources may be a continuing source of profit for the understanding and treatment of psychological difficulties, just as anatomy, physiology, and biochemistry contribute to clinical medicine.

Of course, while the contribution of general psychology and its related disciplines to therapeutic activities may be considerable, it is important to recognize the inevitable incompleteness and inadequacy of this knowledge, as well as the practical problems of converting it into feasible therapeutic interventions. Moreover, such interventions can never be based entirely and exclusively upon the derived psychological principles. Rather, these constitute a flexible guide to understanding and treatment, leaving much need and scope for the personal spontaneity, experience, judgement, and inventiveness of the individual therapist.

A second general characteristic of behaviour therapy is its empirical stance. There is great respect for observational data, and a strong emphasis on using valid, reliable and quantifiable methods of data collection, together with research designs that are as rigorous as the circumstances permit. This empirical stance is essential for the proper evaluation and development of behaviour therapy and it promises cumulative improvement in the help given to clients. However, in no way does it prevent the derivation or innovation of new therapeutic procedures from any source, providing that these are empirically investigated and found to be relatively effective before they become an accepted part of the behavioural repertoire. The fact that the approach contains such a self-corrective mechanism perhaps constitutes the greatest hope for its long term viability and efficacy.

An attempt is made to adhere to this data oriented perspective throughout the book, and it is particularly apparent in Part 5 on the outcome of treatment. However, on the very many occasions when empirical data is not available, then the discussion is based upon clinical impressions and reports, although it is well recognized that these may prove to be entirely erroneous in the light of subsequent systematic investigation.

Finally, the behavioural approach is characterized by its operationism. Whether a behaviour therapist is dealing with the actions, thoughts, or feelings of his clients, he will attempt to provide operational definitions for these events, with publically observable anchors of a concrete and specific kind. For instance, the act of premature ejaculation might be defined as the expulsion of seminal fluid, before, during, or after intromission, together with a verbal report from the client that he was unable to control this ejaculation although he would have preferred to have delayed it for a longer period of time. Similarly, a client's false belief about some aspect of sexual anatomy or functioning might be defined in terms of his incorrect answers to questions concerning this matter, perhaps accompanied by his failure to locate an organ correctly on a diagram. Lastly, an emotional feeling such as anxiety could be specified in terms of the client's verbal description of his apprehension; his physical avoidance of those situations that he reports as anxiety-evoking for him; and certain physiological changes, perhaps in heart and respiration rates, blood pressure and sweating, when he imagines or confronts these feared situations.

There are several reasons for the stress in behaviour therapy on such operational definitions with anchors in publicly observable behaviour. First, this is the only client behaviour that is directly accessible to the therapist. 'Public events' like verbal reports of apprehension, the physical avoidance of feared situations, and increased sweating are open to observation by the therapist. In contrast, the client's thoughts and feelings are 'private events' open to observation only by himself, and the therapist can only infer them from the client's observable behaviour, including his verbal descriptions of his own thoughts and feelings. Similarly, there are therapeutic and ethical objections to the direct observation by a therapist of the client's sexual behaviour, so that this can only be inferred from the verbal reports of the client and his partner.

A second reason for emphasizing operationism is that it promotes more precise specification of a client's experiences. These are often described by clients in rather vague terms, such as being 'frigid' or feeling 'unhappy', which are used idiosyncratically and inconsistently. Thus, the specification of such experiences in terms of publicly observable behaviour will enhance the precision and consistency of assessment. It also permits some estimate of the reliability of assessment, for the occurrence of well defined and publicly observable behaviour can be checked by more than one observer, and this constitutes a further reason for espousing operationism in the behavioural approach.

We turn not to some features of this approach that are especially relevant in the tasks of defining, explaining, assessing and treating various psychological problems, including sexual dysfunction.

DEFINITION

In the behavioural approach, psychological problems are conceptualized as ways of responding in certain situations that are unacceptable to the client or other people. More particularly, as far as the sexual dysfunctions are concerned, these are defined as responses to sexual stimulation that the clients and/or their partners consider to be inadequate.

The responses involved might be sexual interest, arousal, intromission, orgasm or pleasure, and these can be adversely affected in different ways, yielding the various dysfunctions that are discussed in this book. These are described at length in Chapters 6 and 7, but in outline they comprise erectile dysfunction, premature ejaculation, retarded or absent ejaculation, and retrograde ejaculation in the male; vasocongestive dysfunction, vaginismus, and orgastic dysfunction in the female; and inadequate sexual interest, inadequate sexual pleasure, and dyspareunia in both sexes.

Erectile dysfunction involves some impairment of vasocongestion in the penis, so that the client is persistently unable to obtain a sufficiently firm erection, or to maintain this during insertion and intercourse. A persistent lack of adequate voluntary control over the orgastic and/or ejaculatory reflexes constitutes premature ejaculation. In contrast, retarded or absent ejaculation can be defined as a persistent delay or failure in the occurrence of orgasm and ejaculation despite the presence of an adequate erection. Finally among the male dysfunctions, retrograde ejaculation is the involuntary discharge of semen backwards into the bladder rather than forwards through the urethra, so that the client still has erections and orgasms but there is no visible ejaculate.

Turning to the female problems, as the name implies vasocongestive dysfunction consists of a persistent absence of lubrication and swelling in the genital and pelvic areas due to some impairment of the vasocongestive process during sexual stimulation. In cases of vaginismus there is a spastic contraction of the muscles at the outer third of the vagina and the perineum, which occurs as an involuntary reflex response to a threat of vaginal penetration, and makes intromission either impossible or at best difficult and painful. Lastly, the problem of orgastic dysfunction involves some persistent difficulty or failure in releasing the reflex contractions of the vaginal and pelvic musculature that comprise the female orgasm.

Inadequate sexual interest occurs in both men and women whenever they or their partners consider the level of interest to be lower than they would like it to be. Similarly, a member of either sex may complain of an absence of feeling during intercourse, or that this is insufficiently pleasurable or satisfying for them, and such complaints are referred to as inadequate sexual pleasure in this book. When intercourse is accompanied by pain in a male or female client, this constitutes a problem of dyspareunia.

It will be apparent from this outline of the dysfunctions discussed more fully later, that their definition involves subjective judgements of inadequacy as well as a description of the actual behaviour concerned, for there are no absolute standards of sexual competence or gratification. To take just one example, an erectile dysfunction involves not only some impairment of vasocongestion in the penis, but also a judgement that this is occurring too persistently despite appropriate sexual stimulation, for it would be unrealistic to expect erection to occur at any time and in any circumstances. Similar subjective judgements of inadequacy are involved in the definition of all the other sexual dysfunctions, and some of the possible factors influencing such judgements are discussed in Chapter 5.

CAUSATION

An overview of a behavioural approach to the causation of sexual dysfunction is offered in Part 2 of this book, and the possible causes of particular dysfunctions are discussed in Chapters 6 and 7. These causes are considered in the general categories of organic factors, previous learning experiences, and contemporary conditions, and causes from any of these categories may operate singly or in combination in particular cases of dysfunction.

The organic causes of sexual dysfunction include various illnesses as well as the side effects of certain surgical interventions and drugs. In comparison with other causes of a psychological nature, such organic factors are generally held to be less prevalent, although this varies across different dysfunctions. Moreover, when organic factors are operative, their adverse effects may arise either directly from damage to the physiological systems involved in sexual behaviour, or indirectly from the client's psychological reactions to the organic factor concerned.

The category of previous learning experiences comprehends both the learning conditions to which a client has been exposed, and the learning processes through which these conditions exercise their influence on his later behaviour. Certain conditions of a traumatic, restrictive, or interpersonal nature may adversely affect the adequacy of a client's later responses to sexual stimulation, and the evidence available on the influence of these conditions is reviewed in Chapter 3. Unfortunately, no similar evidence exists on the learning processes involved in the acquisition of sexual dysfunction. An assumption is made in the behavioural approach that these processes are essentially the same as those involved in the acquisition of any other kind of behaviour, but their respective contributions to sexual dysfunction remain to be investigated empirically, and until this is done one can only offer the speculations contained in Chapter 3.

In the subsequent chapter, various contemporary conditions that may contribute to sexual dysfunction are considered under the headings of psychological stress, partner discord, psychological reactions to organic factors, psychiatric syndromes, deficient or false information, and deficient or inappropriate stimulation. Conditions from any of these groups may serve to initiate and maintain sexually dysfunctional behaviour. For instance, if some aspect of a sexual encounter is stressful to a client, then this may evoke an anxiety reaction that initiates a failure of sexual response in this situation. Similarly, if a consequence of the failure is a humiliating, critical, or angry reaction from the partner, then this is likely to maintain the client's anxiety and the dysfunction it entails.

It is in part because of these initiating and maintaining functions of the contemporary conditions that their importance is emphasized in the behavioural approach. Although a client's inadequate sexual responses might have originated from an earlier illness or a previous learning experience of an adverse nature, these responses are triggered off by certain conditions in the client's current environment or in his own thoughts and feelings at the present time, and such contemporary conditions also determine the maintenance of the responses on future occasions.

Another related reason for the strong behavioural interest in contemporary conditions is their importance in defining sexually dysfunctional behaviour. Again, although this may have originated in an earlier illness or learning experience, it constitutes a dysfunction only when it is judged inadequate in the current situation. For instance, a man's erectile capacity might have been impaired by an earlier spinal injury or by severe punishment for masturbation, but he may only complain of this inadequacy after he enters a marriage relationship.

A third reason for emphasizing contemporary conditions is because they are the focus for behavioural treatment. It is impossible to alter events that have happened in the past, whether they are of an organic nature or a previous learning experience, but it is possible to try to modify any contemporary conditions that are contributing to a client's problem, and this is the strategy pursued in behaviour therapy.

ASSESSMENT

The assessment of a problem situation and the resources available for its remediation, together with the consequent planning of a treatment programme, probably require more knowledge and skill than any other aspect of the behavioural approach, and yet until quite recently they were grossly neglected in the literature. Fortunately, this deficiency is now being corrected (e.g. Ciminero *et al.*, 1977a; Cone and Hawkins, 1977; Hersen and Bellack, 1976; Keefe *et al.*,

1978). These important aspects of the behavioural approach to sexual dysfunction are discussed in Part 4 of this book.

As assessment of the problem situation requires a comprehensive and detailed description in operational terms of those aspects of the client's sexual functioning that are judged to be inadequate, together with a thorough exploration of the contemporary conditions that may influence the occurrence of the dysfunctional behaviour. These conditions are emphasized for the reasons discussed above, but this does not mean that the client's history is ignored. On the contrary, it may provide valuable clues to the more contemporary influences on his difficulties.

In assessing the available resources that may assist or impede treatment, consideration is given to those in the client's environmental situation, such as the availability of a regular partner and the quality of the relationship between them; to the client's personal resources, such as his degree of motivation and religious or moral beliefs; and to the resources relating to the professional therapist and the services at his disposal.

This assessment process should provide the necessary information for a behavioural formulation of the client's problem situation that includes a specification of his dysfunctional behaviour, some hypotheses about the contemporary conditions that influence its initiation and maintenance, and an appraisal of the available therapeutic resources. This formulation is discussed with the client and his partner, and it forms the basis for the negotiation of therapeutic goals with them and the planning of an agreed treatment programme.

A preliminary decision has to be made concerning the appropriateness of a programme of behavioural treatment focused upon the sexual dysfunction, rather than some other form of intervention with a different therapeutic target, perhaps some kind of medical treatment to alleviate a relevant organic problem or marital therapy to reduce partner discord. Subject to this decision, the goals of behaviour therapy for sexual dysfunction are formally conceptualized as the reduction of inadequate responses and the promotion of more adequate alternatives in specified sexual situations. The more precise nature of the goals in particular cases is determined by the client and partner according to their own wishes and values, but in consultation with the therapist. After the goals have been selected, the next step is to define them operationally in terms of the specific responses desired in particular situations, for this serves to clarify the goals for all concerned, to guide the planning of treatment, and to facilitate the assessment of its progress and outcome.

The planning of treatment calls for decisions concerning the therapists to be involved, the settings where it is to take place, the timing of its delivery, and the procedures to be employed. In the behavioural approach these procedures are selected and implemented so that they constitute a unique treatment programme which is individually tailored to suit a particular client. This strategy is a major feature of the approach, and it is in strong contrast to the provision of standardized programmes for particular dysfunctions.

After a suitable programme has been planned, it is systematically monitored during the treatment and follow up periods. In this way, the progress of the client can be assessed and any necessary revisions made to the treatment plan. More generally, such assessments of the progress of individual clients may provide information about the efficacy of the programmes and their component parts, so that the behavioural approach to sexual dysfunction can become more effective and efficient.

So far in this section, it is the process of assessment and treatment planning that has been outlined, on the basis of their fuller discussion in Chapters 11 and 12. It remains to indicate the methods of assessment that are examined at greater length in Chapter 13. At that point in the book these methods are considered under the headings of assessment interviews, questionnaires, self-monitoring, physiological techniques, and medical examination. The desirability of employing some suitable combination of methods from these various categories is emphasized, in order to achieve a balanced and comprehensive assessment.

TREATMENT

Essentially behaviour therapy is an educational process in the broadest sense, that is it provides the client with opportunities for new learning experiences. These experiences include a wide range of treatment procedures, from which an individualized programme is constituted for each client. A number of these procedures that may be drawn upon in the treatment of sexually dysfunctional clients are described in Part 3 of the book, while the available evidence on the outcome of such treatment is examined in Part 5.

In Part 3, the procedures concerned are considered under the general headings of therapeutic interviews, sexual assignments, specific behavioural procedures, and ancillary physical treatment. Among the major functions of the therapeutic interviews are the provision of information, the modification of attitudes, and the management of the sexual assignments. These assignments are undertaken by clients in the privacy of their homes, and they may involve general pleasuring, genital stimulation or sexual intercourse. The behavioural procedures are relatively specific to this approach, and examples would include desensitization and biofeedback. Finally, the implementation and efficacy of any of the psychological procedures outlined in this paragraph, may be enhanced by some form of ancillary physical treatment, such as vaginal muscle exercises, the administration of drugs or hormones, and various prosthetic or mechanical aids.

It will be aparent that some of these procedures have ingredients that are relatively specific to the behavioural approach, while there are certain other non-specific factors that operate not only in this but also in most other forms of treatment. The latter factors include the relationship between therapist and client, some understanding between them concerning the causation of the dysfunction, and the client's expectation of receiving effective help. All these non-specific factors are discussed in Chapter 8, and it is important to note that their importance is not denied or ignored in the behavioural approach, instead every effort is made to enhance the effectiveness of their contribution to the progress and outcome of treatment.

Part 1

An Overview of Causation

2

Organic Factors

This chapter opens with an outline of the physiological aspects of sexual behaviour as a necessary basis for discussion of the causation, assessment, and treatment of sexual dysfunctions. First, the kind of stimulation that elicits a sexual response is discussed, and this is followed by consideration of the nature of the sexual response and the effects upon it of aging, illness, surgery, and drugs.

SEXUAL STIMULATION

In human beings, sexual responses can be elicited by stimulation of several different kinds, of which touch is probably the most important. It is the only form of stimulation that can evoke arousal as a spinal reflex, independently of the brain. As we shall see below, a man with an injury that transacts the nervous pathways between the brain and the erection centre in the lowest portion of the spinal cord, is still able to obtain an erection if his genital area is stroked. In the neurologically intact person, the impulses from the tactile receptors are transmitted to the brain, where they are identified and evaluated as sexual stimulation in the light of the prevailing circumstances and the person's previous experiences. For instance, a woman is more likely to identify the touching of her genitals as sexual stimulation if it occurs during petting rather than a gynaecological examination, although the physical act of touching may be similar in each case. Likewise, most people find it pleasurable to have the glans penis, the clitoris, or the entrance to the vagina touched, but there are some who do not feel anything, while for others it may actually be painful. These atypical reactions may reflect the previous experiences of the individuals concerned, through which anxiety, guilt, or discomfort has become associated with sexual activities.

The sexual response can also be evoked by visual, auditory, olfactory, and gustatory stimuli. For instance, a man may respond to seeing a partner in the nude, to hearing her voice or listening to certain music, to smelling her bodily odours or the perfume she wears, and perhaps to tasting the secretions from her mouth or vagina. Unlike touch, these other forms of sensory stimulation can only evoke sexual responses through the mediation of the brain, where they are interpreted and evaluated to determine whether or not a particular pattern of stimulation will evoke sexual arousal. For instance, it is said to be unusual for a man to get an erection when he sees a naked woman in a nudist camp. Presumably, this is because the visual stimulation is not interpreted as sexual, whereas the same stimulus seen in a bedroom situation is more likely to result in a sexual interpretation and response. Similarly, a man will probably respond to the sight of the female bosom with indifference rather than arousal if his previous experience has been in a culture where it is customary for women to expose their breasts and where these are not invested with sexual significance.

In addition to sensory stimulation, sexual responses can also be evoked by a person's own erotic phantasies. Past experiences can be recalled and other sexually exciting situations can be imagined. These phantasy activities are clearly important in erotic dreams, during which they may produce orgasms in either sex (Henton, 1976), but in other circumstances there are probably very few people who are able to reach orgasm by phantasy alone. Many, however, do utilize phantasies during masturbation, and they are commonly employed to enhance arousal during coitus, for instance, a woman may imagine that she is being raped or a man that he is making love with another partner to whom he is sexually attracted. Thus, sexual responses are very often elicited by combination of sensory and phantasy stimulation.

SEXUAL RESPONSE

Although different kinds of sexual stimulation may produce very different psychological experiences at a physiological level the sexual response is essentially the same. There is some variation in intensity and duration according to the nature of the stimulation, for example, many women are reported to have their most intense orgastic responses to self-stimulation, the next most intense to manipulation by a partner, and the least intense during coitus (Masters and Johnson, 1966). Basically however, the nature and sequence of the bodily reactions are the same regardless of the kind of stimulation that evokes them.

This is just one of the many fundamentally important findings from the pioneer research by Masters and Johnson which is reported in their book *Human Sexual Response* (1966) and summarized in an authorized popular version edited by Brecher and Brecher (1968). The aim of the investigation was to discover what physical reactions develop as the human male and female respond to effective sexual stimulation. Over almost a decade, more than 10,000 orgasms were studied in 694 volunteers of both sexes, aged 18–89 years, and not exhibiting any sexual dysfunction. Their reactions during sexual arousal and orgasm were observed, monitored physiologically, and sometimes filmed. A variety of stimulation was used, including masturbation and sexual intercourse, as well as artificial coitus with a penis-like instrument made of transparent plastic through which internal vaginal reactions could be observed and filmed.

In the course of this work, Masters and Johnson identified two basic physiological reactions during the sexual response. Initially, blood flows into the sexual organs and other areas of the body, without a corresponding outflow, so that engorgement or *vasocongestion* occurs. This process is most clearly demonstrated by the male erection. The second reaction is increased muscle tension or *myotonia* throughout the body, which culminates in the muscular contractions of orgasm for both sexes. For descriptive purposes, Masters and Johnson divided the operation of these two processes in the sexual response cycle into four phases, as shown in Table 1. The main features of each phase are discussed below, but it should be noted that they are not proposed as standards of normality or healthiness, only as a scheme for describing a usual sequence of events. Within this sequence there is considerable variation in the intensity and duration of each phase, both between individuals and in the same person on different occasions.

More recently, Kaplan (1974) has offered an alternative conceptualization of the sexual response cycle in terms of two rather than four phases (Table 1). She prefers this biphasic cycle because the two phases have different anatomical and neural bases, and they vary in their vulnerability to the influence of aging, illness, surgery, and drugs. There are also different forms of sexual dysfunction associated with each phase, which respond to different treatment procedures. These reasons for advocating a biphasic cycle make a great deal of sense clinically, and it is utilized in the following summaries of the male and female sexual responses based on the original findings by Masters and Johnson.

Table 1. Phases of sexual response

Masters and Johnson (1966)	Kaplan (1974)	
	Male	Female
1. Excitement	1. Erection	1. Lubrication–swelling
2. Plateau		
3. Orgasmic	2. Ejaculation	2. Orgasm
4. Resolution		

Male response cycle

Erection phase

The major feature of the first phase of the male response is the erection of the penis due to local vasocongestion. This usually occurs rapidly, especially in younger men who tend to become erect within a few seconds. During their earlier stages, erections are often lost and regained with fluctuations in stimulation, and they are quite vulnerable to distractions such as extraneous noise. Later they become more persistent and resistant to distraction as engorgement reaches its peak. Other reactions in the sexual organs during the erection phase include contraction and thickening of the skin of the scrotal sac so that it loses its baggy appearance, and progressive raising of the testicles within the scrotum together with their enlargement by vasocongestion to between 50% and 100% of their usual size. Sometimes, at an advanced stage of erection, a small amount of clear fluid is exuded from the penis, and this is probably produced by Cowper's gland. In addition to these changes in the sexual organs there are some more general bodily reactions. Muscular tension, blood pressure, and heart and respiration rates all increase, and nipple erection and skin flushing may occur.

Ejaculation phase

These general reactions increase to a peak during the ejaculation phase of the male response. This normally follows the erection phase but not necessarily so, for the two are separate and distinct. Thus, full arousal can occur during the erection phase without ejaculation resulting, as happens in prepubertal boys as well as in severe cases of retarded or absent ejaculation. Conversely, it is quite possible for ejaculation to occur when the penis is flaccid.

Moreover, there is some very recent preliminary evidence to suggest that orgasm and ejaculation do not necessarily always occur together in some males who are capable of having multiple orgasms, a capacity that is usually thought to be restricted to women. These new findings are reported by Robbins and Jensen (1978) mainly on the basis of carefully conducted interviews with 13 selected men, and some physiological recordings from 1 of these subjects. All of them apparently were able to exercise voluntary control over ejaculation, so that they could experience 3 to 10 orgasms during a single session of lovemaking, before ejaculating with a final orgasm.

Within the ejaculation phase there are two components, emission and expulsion. The former comprises contractions of the internal sexual organs (the prostate gland, seminal vesicles, vas deferens and testes) as they collect the semen and deposit it at the entrance to the urethra. This process is accompanied by a feeling that ejaculation is inevitable, and indeed it is difficult for a man to delay his climax once emission has occurred. The expulsion component consists of rhythmic contractions of the penile urethra and the muscles at the base of the penis, which begin at intervals of 0.8 second but become less regular and frequent. They force the semen to spurt out of the penis and are accompanied by the intense pleasure of orgasm. Once this has happened, there is a refractory period during which the male is physiologically unresponsive to further sexual stimulation. He cannot attain a full erection or ejaculate again within a variable interval of time, which increases with age as we shall see later.

Resolution phase

The refractory period extends into what Masters and Johnson call the 'resolution phase'. The penis returns to its unstimulated state in two stages.

Usually, about half the erection is lost very soon after ejaculation, although this may not happen if the erection has been maintained for a long time. The remainder of the erection detumesces more slowly over a period of about half an hour. The scrotal sac regains its baggy appearance and with it the testicles resume their usual size and position. The general bodily reactions subside, and some men perspire whether or not they have been physically active. The sweating may be restricted to the palms of the hands and soles of the feet, or less commonly may be more widespread.

Female response cycle

Lubrication-swelling phase

The initial lubrication-swelling phase in women is a local vasocongestive reaction, analogous to erection in the male. Lubrication of the vagina occurs within 10 to 30 seconds of sexual stimulation and is probably due to engorgement of the vaginal blood vessels. This also causes the inner two thirds of the vagina to lengthen and expand. Subsequently, the outer third becomes so engorged and swollen that the entrance to the vagina is considerably narrowed, to form what Masters and Johnson call the 'orgasmic platform'. Concurrently, venous congestion produces a colour change in the labia minora, from pink to bright red in women who have never given birth, and from red to a deep wine colour in those who have. This 'sex skin' reaction (Masters and Johnson, 1966) always appears before orgasm is attained. Furthermore, in premenopausal women, once the colour change has occurred then orgasm follows inevitably providing that sexual stimulation is continued. At a fairly late stage of arousal the clitoris becomes engorged, but just prior to orgasm it is retracted to a relatively inaccessible position under the clitoral hood and behind the pubic bone. The uterus also becomes enlarged through vascular engorgement and rises from its usual position in the pelvic cavity. As in the male, there are increases in muscle tension, blood pressure, heart rate, and respiration, but nipple erection and skin flushing are usually much more marked in women. Masters and Johnson call the latter a 'sex flush' and describe a measles like rash they observed in about three quarters of their female subjects. This appeared under the ribs, quickly spread to the breasts and then to other areas of the body.

Orgasm phase

These general bodily reactions reach their peak during the orgasm phase of the female response cycle. The local muscular contractions that characterize this phase are analogous to those occurring in the male during the expulsion component of ejaculation. It is usually believed that there is no female equivalent to the emission component, and that women do not produce an ejaculate. However, Lowndes Sevely and Bennett (1978) have recently reviewed some anatomical, physiological, and anecdotal evidence, from which they conclude that women can discharge prostatic fluid through the urethra during orgasm, although this ejaculate does not of course contain spermatozoa as in the case of the male. The arguments these writers present clearly state a case for more rigorous investigation of this topic.

What triggers off orgasm in women is not known definitely, but it is highly probably that stimulation of the clitoris plays an important role. For instance, it seems likely that orgasm is produced during coitus through pressure from the pubic bone on the clitoris, and by movement of the clitoral hood arising from traction of the labia minora. Regardless of the form of stimulation that triggers it off, the orgastic response always follows an essentially similar physiological pattern. It consists of a series of rhythmic contractions of the orgasmic platform, the pelvic musculature and the uterus. There may be from 3 to 15 contractions commencing at intervals of 0.8 seconds and decreasing in intensity and frequency. These contractions are accompanied by feelings of pleasure which may vary considerably in intensity according to the nature of the stimulation and other circumstances (Clifford, 1978; Singer and Singer, 1978). Thus, the subjective experience of orgasm during coitus with a loved partner might be very different from that accompanying an orgasm produced by masturbation, although physiologically both orgasms are essentially the same. There is no refractory period following orgasm in women, they are physically capable of having a series of orgasms with intervals of only a few seconds between them which can continue until the woman is exhausted or no longer motivated.

Resolution phase

Thus, women can be brought to orgasm again at any time during the resolution phase if they are suitably stimulated, otherwise the body returns to its normal resting state. Decongestion of the orgasmic platform and the 'sex skin' reaction in the labia minora both occur rapidly, but the rest of the vagina may take 10 to 15 minutes to return to its usual condition. Similarly, the clitoris re-emerges from its retracted position within a few seconds of orgasm, although complete detumescence usually takes 5 to 10 minutes. Over a similar period, the uterus descends to its usual position in the pelvic cavity. Thus, as in the case of the male resolution phase, the local vasocongestive responses in women are resolved in two stages, the first being rapid and the second much slower. The more general bodily reactions also subside and a film of perspiration which is independent of activity may appear over much of the body.

The strong similarity, as well as some important differences, in the male and female response cycles will be apparent from these summaries. For instance, local vasocongestion produces penile erection and other reactions in the male, as well as vaginal lubrication and swelling in the female. Similarly, the orgastic response consists of muscular contractions in both sexes. On the other hand, the existence of an emission component is uncertain and there is no refractory period in the female orgastic phase, in contrast to the male ejaculation phase.

AGING

The sexual response cycle remains essentially the same throughout life, but the natural aging process produces some changes in the reactions of middle aged and older people. They are still capable of reaching orgasm but their responses tend to be slower and more attenuated than when they were younger (Masters and Johnson, 1966).

Male response cycle

Older men can still get erections but it takes them longer than the few seconds required by younger men (Solnick and Birren, 1977). Once an erection is attained, the older man is able to maintain it for a longer period before he reaches orgasm. However, if he does lose an erection before orgasm, then he is likely to experience greater difficulty in recovering it. Additionally, the usual changes in the scrotal sac, the elevation and enlargement of the testicles and the pre-ejaculatory emission of fluid, may all be reduced or absent during the erection phase in the aging male.

It is in the ejaculation phase that most of the physiological changes occur. The emission component with its accompanying feelings of ejaculatory inevitability may be shortened or not happen at all, so that orgasm is sometimes experienced as a one stage process. During the expulsion component there are fewer muscular contractions and the semen spurts out with less force. The refractory period lengthens, so that many men in their fifties and older cannot obtain another erection within 12 to 24 hours after they have ejaculated. There is a lowering of the subjective demand for orgasm, which occurs less frequently in older men. They may engage in and enjoy intercourse without necessarily ejaculating on every occasion, but when they do reach orgasm this is still a pleasurable experience for them.

Once orgasm has occurred, the resolution phase is less prolonged in older men. Their erections disappear much more rapidly, sometimes within a few seconds, compared to the slower two stage process that is characteristic of younger men.

Female response cycle

The anatomical changes associated with the menopause are reflected in the sexual response cycles of women aged over about fifty years. During the lubrication-swelling phase, it may take 4 to 5 minutes for the vagina to become lubricated compared to 15 to 30 seconds in younger women, and the transudate is also less profuse. The vagina does not lengthen and expand to the same extent or as quickly. Although an orgasmic platform is produced, this is not as full as in the earlier years. The labia minora do not swell so much and the sex skin reaction may be absent or reduced. There may be no enlargement of the uterus in postmenopausal women and its elevation from the pelvic cavity is less marked and longer delayed. However, there do not appear to be any changes in the clitoral responses of older women.

They remain capable of having multiple orgasms throughout life, but there are fewer muscular contractions during each climax. As in men, the female resolution phase is completed much more immediately and rapidly with increasing age.

Thus, although there are physiological changes in the sexual response cycles as part of the natural aging process, older men and women do retain the capacity for pleasurable sexual performance until well into the seventh and eighth decades of life. In some older people this capacity is impaired either by physical illness or by their adverse psychological reactions to the biological changes of the aging process, and these contingencies are considered in the remainder of this chapter and in Chapter 4. However, the natural aging process in itself is not regarded as a sufficient cause of sexual dysfunction.

ILLNESS

Sexual dysfunction does sometimes arise from organic causes such as illness, surgery, or drug effects. Although extremely important when present, these are generally regarded as being less prevalent than the psychological causes discussed in the next two chapters (Kaplan, 1974; Masters and Johnson, 1970). Moreover, even when there is an organic cause, its effects may be influenced by psychological factors. For instance, a temporary or slight impairment of sexual capacity of organic origin, may persist and worsen if the client becomes unduly anxious about his sexual performance. Such psychological reactions to organic causes are discussed in Chapter 4, while the emphasis in the present chapter is on the organic causes themselves. It is beyond the scope of this book to consider the very many causes in any detail, but some indication of their general nature is given here, to be followed in later chapters by discussion of their possible contributions to particular sexual dysfunctions.

In the first place, sexual performance can be impaired by any illness that is debilitating, painful, or incapacitating; including, for instance, the cardiac, renal and arthritic disorders which are considered below, as well as the more transient symptoms of influenza, migraine, sunburn, muscle strain, or a bone fracture. In addition to the general effects on sexual functioning which accompany many such illnesses, there are more specific effects arising from certain morbid conditions involving the genital organs themselves or the neural, endocrine, or vascular mechanisms that subserve sexual behaviour.

Cardiac disorders

Recent reviews of the evidence available on the sexual functioning of patients suffering from cardiac disorders are provided by Friedman (1978), Regestein and Horn (1978), and Wagner (1977), and a particularly important investigation is reported by Hellerstein and Friedman (1970). Their subjects were middle aged men who had been married for long periods and were participating in a physical fitness programme. Among them, was a group of 48 patients who had experienced myocardial infarctions, and of these 18 complained of one or more cardiac symptoms in association with sexual intercourse. The symptoms were usually tachycardia or angina pectoris, but in only 5 patients had these been severe enough to stop an act of intercourse already in progress. The average interval between a myocardial infarction and the resumption of sexual intercourse was 16.4 weeks, and 60% of the patients considered the frequency of this to be lower than before the coronary event, a finding that the investigators attribute to psychological factors rather than the direct influence of cardiac symptoms on the performance of intercourse. Among the psychological factors mentioned in the report are depression, anxiety, diminished sexual interest, fears of relapse or death during sexual intercourse, and its limitation by the wife of the patient concerned.

Continuous electrocardiogram monitoring indicated that the heart rates of the subjects during intercourse were not significantly different from those recorded during their daily work and social activities, and Hellerstein and Friedman estimate that the energy cost of intercourse is similar to those of climbing a flight of stairs or walking briskly. If a patient is able to undertake these everyday activities without difficulty, then he is likely to be able to engage in intercourse with an accustomed partner, and the authors consider the risk of this leading to death through coronary occlusion to be negligible. However, they do suggest, that there is an appreciably greater chance of this occurring during intercourse with an unfamiliar partner, for instance, in an extra-marital affair or after a long period of marital abstinence. Presumably, this enhanced risk is due to the increased stressfulness of attempting intercourse with a fresh partner, so that heart rate and blood pressure become markedly high; and this again points to the importance of the patient's psychological reactions to the cardiac disorder.

In another study, Bloch et al. (1975) followed up a group of patients at an average of 11 months after they had suffered a myocardial infarction. The group consisted of 88 men and 12 women with a mean age of 58 years and a range of 28 to 71. Their reported frequencies of sexual intercourse had decreased from a monthly average of 5.2 before the infarction to 2.7 at the time of follow up 11 months later. This reduction was not related to the ages of the patients or to their degree of physical fitness, and the investigators attribute it mainly to the same kinds of psychological factors as those mentioned by Hellerstein and Friedman.

The upshot of these two studies seems to be that intercourse ceases altogether for periods of about four months after a myocardial infarction, and that subsequently it tends to be resumed at a lower frequency than before. After suitable advice, it is usually quite feasible and safe for postcoronary patients to engage in intercourse with their wives, although cardiac symptoms may be experienced in some cases. The reduction in frequency of intercourse does not appear to be due mainly to the direct effect of any such symptoms during it, but rather to the psychological reactions of the patient and spouse which are considered further in Chapter 4. One must also take into account the possible side effects on sexual functioning of any antihypertensive medication, and we return to this point later in the present chapter.

Renal disorders

The results of an American national survey of the sexual functioning of patients on maintenance haemodialysis and recipients of renal transplants, are reported by Levy (1973). A response rate of 67% was obtained to the postal questionnaire, and this yielded a total sample of 345 men and 174 women.

All the haemodialysis patients of both sexes had experienced a marked decrease in the prevalence and frequency of intercourse following the onset of uraemia, which is characterized by symptoms of headache, vertigo, vomiting, blindness, and later by convulsions and coma. Out of the 287 men on haemodialysis, only 27 had never engaged in intercourse before the onset of uraemia, but 135 had not done so since then. Similarly, among the 142 women, there were 13 who had not had intercourse before becoming uraemic, while 47 had not done so afterwards. Moreover, the numbers of these men and women who engaged in intercourse at least three times a week before uraemia were 38 and 21 respectively, compared to 4 and 8 afterwards. Among the men, 160 (59%) out of 287 considered themselves to have a current 'potency problem' in getting or maintaining an erection or of decreasing sexual drive, compared to only 44 prior to the onset of uraemia, although Levy considers this last figure to be an underestimate. Among the 142 women, there were 90 who usually experienced orgasm during intercourse before they became uraemic, while only 47 did so afterwards.

Turning to the transplant recipients, some reduction in the prevalence and frequency of intercourse was common among the 56 men, and 24 of them reported having a potency problem as defined above. No similar consistent reduction in intercourse had been experienced among the 30 women transplant patients, nor had they had any greater difficulty in reaching orgasm, so that there was no evidence of sexual impairment in this particular group of respondents.

The initiation and continuation of haemodialysis was followed by a deterioration of sexual functioning in 35% of the men and 24% of the women, some improvement being reported by only 9% of men and 6% of women. This general worsening of sexual functioning despite the recovery of physical health during dialysis, is considered by Levy to point to the importance of psychological factors in the aetiology of sexual dysfunction among sufferers from renal disease.

The results of several subsequent investigations (Abram et al., 1975, O'Brien et al., 1975, Salvatierra et al., 1975, Steele et al., 1976, Thurm, 1975) are generally consistent with those of Levy in indicating a high prevalence of sexual impairment in renal patients. For instance, Steele et al. (1976) studied 17 such patients on haemodialysis and their husbands or wives, by means of self-administered questionnaires. The majority of couples said that their frequency of intercourse had declined since dialysis began, and 13 out of the 17 were having intercourse less than once a month although they would have liked it more often. Out of the 9 male patients, there were 7 who had difficulty in getting or

contribute to another alleged complication of diabetes mellitus, this is retrograde ejaculation in which the ejaculate empties into the bladder instead of spurting out from the penis. The prevalence of this and other ejaculatory difficulties in diabetic men has not been determined, but even some of those who become impotent retain the capacity to ejaculate through the flaccid penis (Ellenberg and Weber, 1966; Greene and Kelalis, 1968; Klebanow and MacLeod, 1960). Unfortunately, at present there is no effective way of treating erectile or ejaculatory problems arising from diabetic autonomic neuropathy, they are irreversible even if the disease itself is well controlled. This does not necessarily imply a similar poor prognosis for the treatment of sexual dysfunction arising from other physical or psychological factors in diabetic patients (Mills, 1976; Renshaw, 1978).

The first investigation into the occurrence of sexual dysfunction among diabetic women was reported by Kolodny in 1971. In a group of such women, aged 18 to 42 years, there were 44 (35.2%) who had not reached orgasm in the preceding year despite having engaged in intercourse. This was significantly different from the 6% who had not reached orgasm in a control group of women suffering from illnesses other than diabetes. Moreover, all the non-orgasic control subjects had never reached orgasm, whereas 40 of the 44 non-orgasic diabetic subjects had been orgasic until after the onset of diabetes. From the data presented in this study, it is not possible to identify the pathogenic mechanism leading to orgasic dysfunction in diabetic women but autonomic neuropathy is one possibility.

The only other study of sexual functioning in diabetic women is reported by Ellenberg (1977), whose results are in marked contrast to those of Kolodny (1971). Ellenberg's 100 subjects were aged 20 to 74 years, and 54 of them had clear evidence of diabetic neuropathy, while the remaining 46 did not. Among the 54 patients with neuropathy, there were 44 who reported normal libido and orgasic reaction, the corresponding figure for the 46 patients who did not exhibit signs of neuropathy being 38. Thus, there was no demonstrable difference between the patients with or without neuropathy, and the proportions of sexual dysfunction in each group are probably not discrepant from that for non-diabetic women. Moreover, the incidence of dysfunction among Ellenberg's female subjects is much lower than that reported for male diabetics and the contribution of neuropathy appears to differ between the sexes. No adequate explanations are yet available for these discrepancies between the results of Ellenberg's study and those of other investigations.

Endocrine disorders

Diabetes mellitus is one of the commonest endocrine disorders, but many others are alleged to cause sexual dysfunctions. In broad outline, the mechanism concerned involves the hypothalamus, the pituitary gland, and the gonads or sex glands. The hypothalamus regulates pituitary action by transmitting two chemical factors, a follicle stimulating hormone releasing factor (FSH–RF) and a luteinizing hormone releasing factor (LH–RF). These stimulate the release of two gonadotropins from the pituitary gland, one is the follicle stimulating hormone (FSH), and the second is called the luteinizing hormone (LH) in females and the interstitial cell stimulating hormone (ICSH) in males, because of its different site of action in the two sexes. These gonadotropins stimulate the gonads to produce sex hormones, which are predominantly androgens from the testes in the male and oestrogens and progesterone from the ovaries in the female. Each sex produces smaller amounts of those hormones which predominate in the opposite sex, and both sexes have an additional source of androgens in the adrenal glands.

Disorders affecting the gonads or the pituitary or adrenal glands have been alleged to produce impaired sexual drive and arousal in both sexes and impotence in the male (Escamilla, 1976; Johnson, 1968). Among the causes of hypogonadism are congenital defects like Klinefelter's syndrome in which males have an extra X chromosome, diseases such as hepatic cirrhosis which renders about 70% of male sufferers impotent due to testicular atrophy, and castration as a surgical treatment for cancer of the prostate. In hypopituitarism, the deficiency of gonadotropins may arise from lesions of the pituitary gland. Adrenal dysfunction might consist of excessive secretion in Cushing's syndrome, or of hypofunction or feminizing tumours in the adrenal glands. It should be stressed that the evidence for an association between some of these conditions and sexual dysfunctions is not strong, in some cases only a few clinical reports being available. Moreover, where an association does exist, it is difficult in the present state of knowledge to attribute it to a particular pathogenic mechanism. Often, low levels of sex hormones, particularly androgens, have been implicated, but while the importance of these hormones for sexual development is indisputable, the extent of their influence on adult sexual behaviour is far less clear (Beach, 1967; Beach and Ford, 1965; Luttge, 1971; Spitz et al., 1975).

There is fairly conclusive evidence that the oestrogen and progesterone hormones do not have an important influence on female sexual behaviour, for instance, surgical removal of the ovaries in adult women is not usually accompanied by a reduction in sexual drive. The greater influence of androgens is indicated by the much more frequent loss of drive following removal of the adrenal glands, which are the main sources of these hormones in females, and by the enhancement of drive that often accompanies the therapeutic administration of androgens to women patients. However, a deficiency of oestrogen does contribute to sexual dysfunction in the not uncommon cases of atrophic vaginitis. The withdrawal of oestrogen at the menopause leads to degenerative changes in the vagina that lower its resistance to infection, trauma, and chemical agents. Consequently, these may cause inflammation of the vagina with accompanying pain when intercourse is attempted (Easley, 1974).

The testes are the main sources of androgen hormones in males, but their removal in adulthood commonly has little effect on sexual drive and the capacity for erection is retained by many men who have been castrated (Mack, 1964; Tauber, 1940). Some impotent men do have low levels of androgen in their blood and urine, but to some extent at least, this may by a result rather than a cause of their impotence (Cooper, 1972, 1974a). If the deficiency of androgen is a significant cause, then one would expect greater improvement than is usually obtained from its therapeutic administration to those impotent patients who have low androgen levels. More speculatively, it is possible that such levels are a function of the stress of being impotent and/or the lack of sexual activity that accompanies it, for there is some evidence that androgen levels can be depressed by stress (Kreuz et al., 1972) and raised by sexual intercourse (Fox et al., 1972).

It is possible that an essential minimum of androgen hormones is needed at the receptor sites in the external genitalia of both sexes, and this could be supplied by the adrenal glands in cases where the ovaries or testes have been removed. Above this minimum however, hormonal influences do not appear to be important determinants of the sexual behaviour of human adults and their role in the causation of sexual dysfunction remains uncertain (Brown et al., 1978; Kraemer et al., 1976; Schiavi and White, 1976).

Vascular disorders

The local vasocongestive reactions in the erection and lubrication/swelling phases of the sexual response cycles may be impaired if the blood supply to the genitals is interfered with by disease or injury (Canning et al., 1963; Medical Aspects of Human Sexuality, 1977b).

For instance, impotence can arise from thrombotic occlusion of the terminal arteries to the penis in Leriche's syndrome (Pierini and De Giorgi, 1963), or from damage to the blood vessels and valves of the penis as sequelae to priapism; that is a persistent erection in the absence of sexual stimulation and desire (British Medical Journal, 1965).

SURGERY

Problems of sexual functioning may follow certain surgical or obstetrical interventions either directly, as a result of the organic damage ensuing from the operation, or indirectly from the patient's psychological reactions to its consequences. Consideration of the latter is deferred until Chapter 4, the present discussion being restricted to the direct contribution of postoperative organic damage.

One instance of this is the pain during intercourse that is experienced by some women as a complication of the stitching they received during the obstetrical procedure of episiotomy (Wabrek and Wabrek, 1975). Another is the condition of retrograde ejaculation exhibited by the majority of men who have undergone a prostatectomy, and if this was by the perineal route then it is commonly followed by impotence (Zinsser, 1975). In either case, the problem arises from the operative damage to the neural mechanisms serving erection and ejaculation. Similarly, these mechanisms and responses may be impaired as a result of a lumbar sympathectomy, or of rectal surgery such as an ileostomy or colostomy

(Zinsser, 1975; Burnham *et al.*, 1976). Finally, there is the example of limb amputations that can entail mechanical problems for coital positioning (Cummings, 1975; Mourad and Chiu, 1974).

DRUGS

As in the case of illness, any drug that is generally debilitating or incapacitating, or which specifically affects the neural, endocrine or vascular mechanisms concerned, may contribute to sexual dysfunction. It is beyond the scope of this book to consider such drug side effects in any depth and some comprehensive reviews are already available (Beaumont, 1976; Kaplan, 1974; Mills, 1975; Story, 1974; Taylor Segraves, 1977), therefore only a brief and selective summary is presented here. However, it should be noted that these reviews reveal the scarcity of methodologically adequate studies in the field, so that the evidence available must be regarded as very tentative. In particular, there is very little information indeed on the side effects of drugs on the sexual functioning of women.

Sedatives

Sedative drugs, like alcohol or barbiturates, have a depressing effect on brain functioning, including its influence on sexual responsiveness. This may be temporarily enhanced by moderate amounts of these drugs, but their ingestion in larger quantities is accompanied by a rapid loss of sexual capacity. The empirical evidence concerning these effects in both male and female social drinkers is excellently reviewed by Wilson (1977), who cites *inter alia* two laboratory studies of male college students whose penile tumescence in response to erotic films was physiologically monitored and found to be slightly facilitated by a low dose of alcohol, while higher doses were accompanied by marked suppression of erections (Briddell and Wilson, 1976; Farkas and Rosen, 1976).

A persistent pattern of heavy drinking or alcoholism may sometimes lead to chronic impotence, although the evidence is not very extensive (Wilson, 1977). When it does occur, this may be due to general debilitation, neurological damage or hepatic cirrhosis. Certainly, testicular atrophy and impotence are reported as common sequelae of alcoholic liver disease (Scheig, 1975; Van Thiel, 1976; Van Thiel and Lester, 1977), and abstinence cannot reverse such testicular failure once it has developed. Little is known about the effects of alcohol abuse on female sexual functioning (Wilson, 1977), but it may produce ovarian failure to parallel testicular failure in men, and there may also be atrophic changes in the vagina leading to dyspareunia.

Major tranquillizers

The phenothiazine, thioxanthene, and butyrophenone groups, have been reported to produce decreased sexual drive, erectile dysfunction and ejaculatory difficulties in some patients. These dysfunctions, and particularly the last, appear to be especially common among patients who are taking thioridazine (mellaril) in the phenothiazine group.

Among 57 such patients studied by Kotin *et al.* (1976), there were 60% who complained of some sexual dysfunction, compared to only 25% of 64 similar patients on other major tranquillizers. Difficulties in achieving erection were reported by 44% of the thioridazine patients and by 19% of the others, while maintaining erections was considered to be a problem by 35% of those on thioridazine compared to 11% of those on other major tranquillizers. Most strikingly, none of the patients in the latter group reported any changes in ejaculation, while these were experienced by 28 (49%) of the 57 patients in the thioridazine group. The changes consisted of an absence of ejaculate in 19 cases and a decreased amount of ejaculate in 9 cases, and there is evidence to suggest that retrograde ejaculation is occurring in these patients. This problem appears to be an especially common side effect of thioridazine medication.

Antidepressants

The two major groups of antidepressant drugs, the monoamine oxidase inhibitors and the tricyclics, have each been held to produce erectile problems and delayed or inhibited ejaculation, but there appears to be scarcely any systematic evidence to support this view (Mills, 1975; Story, 1974; Taylor Segraves, 1977).

Antihypertensives

Many of the drugs commonly used to control blood pressure are liable to have adverse side effects on sexual functioning (Carver and Oaks, 1976; Page, 1975).

For instance, guanethidine sulphate (Ismelin) is known to cause erectile and ejaculatory difficulties, including retrograde ejaculation, in over 50% of men on therapeutic dosages. Similar difficulties, as well as loss of drive, are reported in smaller proportions of patients on methyldopa, rauwolfia alkaloids or ganglionic blocking agents.

Narcotics

Addiction to drugs like heroin and morphine tends to decrease sexual drive and to delay or inhibit ejaculation, but erectile problems are less frequent although not unknown (Piemme 1976).

In a study of 57 heroin addicts conducted by Cushman (1972) in New York, it was found that 66% reported reduced drive, 68% a delay in ejaculation time beyond 25 minutes, and 49% some form of erectile problem. These dysfunctions disappeared as the narcotic was withdrawn, and the former addicts showed striking increases in their sexual activity. A similar improvement occurred during a methadone treatment programme for heroin addicts, but methadone is itself a narcotic of a long-acting kind, and its use is often accompanied by retarded ejaculation.

Oral contraceptives

Considerable controversy exists over whether or not oral contraception is accompanied by a reduction of sexual interest among women, as well as over the possible reasons for any such association. In a report by the Royal College of General Practitioners (1974) it is concluded that oral contraceptive users do complain of loss of interest more than non-users, but that this difference may be an artefact of the variation in reporting opportunities between the two groups. One possible reason for any loss of interest in users is a depressive reaction either to the 'pill' itself or to any other factor. The Royal College report concluded that there is no evidence that oral contraceptive users experience severe depression more than non-users, but recent evidence suggests that the issue of the possible depressive effects of oral contraceptives is by no means resolved (Trimmer, 1978). Another possible organic reason for any loss of sexual interest among women using oral contraceptives is the deficiency of vaginal lubrication that these sometimes produce, and which in turn may cause dyspareunia and the avoidance of sex. In addition to these possible organic reasons for loss of interest, this may reflect the individual psychological reaction of the woman concerned to the oral contraception. For instance, while this may increase her interest, if for example it relieves a fear of an unwanted pregnancy, it may also decrease interest, if taking the 'pill' is for example accompanied by guilt, anxiety over side effects, or frustration of a desire to become pregnant. Clearly, this whole issue of the possible association between oral contraception and inadequate sexual interest is extremely complex and at present unresolved.

CONCLUSION

The natural changes of the aging process and the illnesses, surgery, and drugs outlined in this chapter may serve its purpose of indicating the wide range of organic factors that can contribute to sexual dysfunction. This may be a direct contribution, or it may arise indirectly from the individual's psychological reaction to the organic condition as discussed in Chapter 4. The clear implication for clinical practice is that the possible existence and influence of organic factors must be taken into account when one is assessing or treating patients complaining of a sexual dysfunction.

3

Previous Learning Experiences

To reiterate a point made earlier, although organic factors must not be overlooked in the assessment and treatment of sexual dysfunction, it is commonly held that psychological causes are more prevalent. These may be of an historical kind, having occurred in the client's previous learning experiences, or they may be contemporary conditions that are currently impairing sexual functioning. The latter are discussed in the next chapter, while this one is devoted to the contribution of previous learning experiences.

In the literature, very many historical and contemporary factors are alleged to contribute to sexual dysfunction, but the evidence for this is often extremely inadequate. Commonly, it is based upon a small and unrepresentative sample of clinical cases, without any comparable enquiry among suitably selected control subjects. Furthermore, when historical or contemporary factors are identified in the circumstances of sexually dysfunctional clients, these factors are often assumed to have contributed to the dysfunction without eliminating other possible explanations. For example, it may be assumed that marital discord has produced a sexual dysfunction without considering that the reverse might be the case, or that there may be a reciprocal causal relationship in which both the discord and the dysfunction contribute to each other, or that they may have both resulted from a third condition such as psychiatric disorder in one of the partners, or even that the coexistence of the discord and dysfunction is purely coincidental. These important limitations in the available evidence need to be borne in mind constantly throughout this and the following chapter.

LEARNING CONDITIONS

In the present chapter, we shall first consider some learning *conditions* that may contribute to sexual dysfunction, including various traumatic experiences, an excessively restrictive upbringing, and adverse family relationships. This is followed by some speculative discussion about the possible nature of the learning *processes* through which such conditions exert an influence on later sexual development.

Traumatic experiences

The clinical literature contains many reports of sexually traumatic incidents in the histories of dysfunctional clients, either during their childhood years or on some later occasion. As children they may have been caught masturbating and severely punished for this, their nocturnal emissions may have attracted strong parental disapproval, or they may have been sexually assaulted or involved in incestuous acts. For instance, in one study of 96 male and female patients who had received psychoanalytic treatment for sexual dysfunction, it was found that 32% of them had participated in some form of bizarre sexual activity within their own families, when they were aged between five years and adolescence (O'Connor and Stern, 1972).

Another vulnerable point for trauma in some clients is their initial experience of sexual intercourse. Quite commonly this is anticipated with considerable anxiety as well as high expectations of pleasure, and it may occur in conditions of rush and doubtful privacy, perhaps in the back of a car or with the parents of one of the partners present elsewhere in the house. Not surprisingly in such circumstances, a girl may fail to respond sexually or a boy may lose his erection or ejaculate too quickly, and these failures are usually accompanied by strong feelings of disappointment, humiliation and anxiety which sometimes lead to the avoidance or impairment of further attempts at intercourse. In the O'Connor and Stern study, 79% of the psychoanalytic patients had attempted premarital intercourse, but only 55% performed successfully in this. Moreover, at least 35% of all these patients were considered to have had initial sexual experiences of a traumatic nature, such as rape, incest, or sexual failure.

Similar incidents occurring after the initial experiences may also prove damaging to sexual functioning. For instance, 4 of the 17 cases of retarded or absent ejaculation reported by Masters and Johnson (1970) were said to have originated in a single traumatic event, such as a husband returning home unexpectedly to see his wife in bed with her lover just after he had ejaculated into her vagina, or another couple being surprised during intercourse by their children entering the bedroom.

While traumatic experiences such as those described are commonly reported in the histories of clients presenting with sexual dysfunctions, it is important to recognize that these experiences are not invariably followed by such difficulties. There is some evidence to suggest that many people in the general population have had similar experiences, and that they are not necessarily reflected in subsequent sexual performance. For instance, in a representative sample of english young people aged 15 to 19 years, only 48% of the boys and 30% of the girls said they like their first experience of sexual intercourse, and 17% of the boys and 62% of the girls did not reach climax during it (Schofield, 1965). However, when these subjects were followed up seven years later, the majority had continued to have intercourse and only 5% did not enjoy it (Schofield, 1973). In several groups of women drawn from the general population in America, no correlation existed between ratings of disturbance at first intercourse made retrospectively by the subjects and their subsequent sexual behaviour (Fisher, 1973). Similarly, Terman (1938, 1951) found no significant relationship between frequency of shocking premarital sexual encounters and adequacy of orgasm in marriage, and Kanin and Howard (1958) could find few instances in which negative sexual experiences during the honeymoon or early marriage had longer term effects on marital sexual adjustment. Thus, although traumatic experiences may well contribute to sexual dysfunction in some individuals, this is not an inevitable consequence, and it is not clear why some people should be more vulnerable than others in this respect.

Restrictive upbringing

Many factors indicating an excessively strict moral or religious upbringing are commonly reported in the histories of dysfunctional clients, and their sexual impairments are often alleged to have originated in these early experiences. Thus, 30% of O'Connor and Stern's (1972) psychoanalytic patients were judged to have been reared in an atmosphere of excessive sexual prohibition and another 25% grew up in households where the subject of sex was totally ignored. On the basis of their extensive clinical experience, Masters and Johnson (1970) repeatedly indicated severe religious orthodoxy as an important cause of sexual dysfunction in a significant proportion of their patients.

In restrictive homes there tends to be either no discussion of sexual matters, together with censorship of television, radio, and reading material, or else the children are constantly admonished about the sinfulness, immorality and dirtyness of sex. It is often described as having the sole purpose of reproduction rather than being a legitimate source of pleasure. Boys are warned that impure thoughts, masturbation, nocturnal emissions, and petting or intercourse before marriage are all unacceptable as well as carrying the risks of mental or physical illness. Fear of an unmarried pregnancy is instilled into girls, who are vehemently cautioned about the dangers of sexual advances from men and the importance of preserving virginity until marriage. Even then, intercourse is to be regarded as a painful and nasty wifely duty and not something to be enjoyed. In childhood, any manifestation of sexual interest or exploration is viewed as disgusting or immoral, and discovery entails humiliation, disapproval, and punishment. Later, a young person's social activities have to be approved and scrutinized to prevent any sexual involvement arising, and even engaged couples may have virtually no physical contact with each other before marriage.

The alleged outcome of such a restrictive upbringing is a young adult who is grossly lacking accurate sexual knowledge and deeply imbued with negative sexual attitudes. The long association of fear, guilt, and disgust with sexuality may not be easily reversible on marriage, instead it may persist and overgeneralize so that what should be an enjoyable and socially valued sexual relationship is impaired by some form of dysfunction. However, while the clinical literature is persuasive about the occurrence of such adverse effects in some individuals, these are not inevitable consequences of an excessively restrictive upbringing.

There is evidence to suggest that many people do survive such early experiences without apparently suffering any serious impairment of their sexual behaviour in later life. In Fisher's (1973) american samples, a woman's ability to reach orgasm, degree of sexual satisfaction, preferences for particular forms of sexual stimulation, and the liberality of her sexual standards, were all unrelated to the sexual attitudes of the woman's parents as revealed in her answers to questions about;

> how freely they talked about sex,
> how much they approved or disapproved of sexual expression,
> their attitude towards nudity,
> how reluctant they were to display affection,
> how comfortable they were about touching her body,
> their reactions to her first period and first serious date,
> and, the nature of the sex education they provided.

Similarly, in a representative sample of swedish women who were attending an antenatal clinic during a first pregnancy, their capacity for orgasm and degree of sexual satisfaction were unrelated to negative or austere attitudes towards sexual matters by their parents, and to whether or not the woman had obtained sexual information from her own mother (Uddenberg, 1974). Finally, a woman's ability to attain orgasm was not found to relate to her early sex education in Terman's (1938, 1951) work, or to her religious devoutness in the studies by Kinsey *et al.* (1953) and Fisher (1973). Thus, as in the case of traumatic experiences, we are left with the currently unanswerable question of why a restrictive upbringing is followed by sexual dysfunction in some people and not in others.

Adverse family relationships

The nature of the family relationships experienced during childhood and adolescence gives rise to a third group of factors that are reputed to contribute to sexual dysfunction. For instance, Masters and Johnson (1970) cite examples of parents who were so dominating, demanding, and perfectionistic that they destroyed a son's confidence in his own masculinity and sexual capacity, and thus contributed to his impotence. The same problem was associated in some other patients with a history of seductive behaviour by a mother towards her son, in conjunction with an absent or ineffective father. Even into adolescence, these boys tended to share a bed or bedroom with their mothers, who in some cases manipulated their son's genitals. Such experiences may lead to feelings of guilt or fear during later attempts at sexual intercourse, with consequent erectile failure.

In Uddenberg's (1974) study of 101 swedish women from the general population, a negative experience of the father and a lack of acceptance on the part of the mother seemed to be detrimental to sexual adjustment in adulthood. Those women who reported having had a poor relationship with their father, and who characterized him as austere, hasty tempered or uncommunicative, tended to have more orgastic difficulty and to be less sexually satisfied. The subjects' reports on their early relationship with their mother did not relate to later sexual adaptation. However, when the mothers themselves were interviewed about their attitudes towards their daughter as a child, these were found to have been more negative and ambivalent among the mothers of women who complained of low orgastic consistency and less sexual satisfaction. One possible reason for the lack of congruence between the reports of the subjects and those of their mothers, is that the daughter may have been less aware of an ambivalent attitude on the mother's part.

The influence of a girl's early relationship with her father on her later sexual development was identified also in Fisher's (1973) study of american women from the general population. Those women who reported that their father had treated them 'casually', in a permissive rather than a controlling manner, were likely to have low orgastic capacity, whereas this was unrelated to their reports on how they were treated by their mother. The apparent importance of a father's influence on his daughter's sexual development may stem from the fact that he provides the girl with her first significant relationship with a man, and a negative experience in this relationship may generalize to later interactions with other men.

There is a *prima facie* discrepancy between the reports of those women with low orgastic capacity in Uddenberg's study who characterized their father as austere, hasty tempered and uncommunicative, and the reports of similar women in Fisher's samples who described their father as having treated them 'casually' and permissively. The latter writer suggests that this kind of paternal treatment might have been viewed by the daughter as indifference and lack of genuine concern for her welfare, and to the extent that this is true it may reduce the apparent discrepancy.

Other reported features of the early social relationships of sexually dysfunctional clients include the experience of death in the immediate family and of severe discord or separation between the parents. Before reaching the age of 16 years, 18% of O'Connor and Stern's (1972) psychoanalytic patients had experienced the death of a parent, and another 10% that of a sibling, making a total of 28% compared to an estimated 9% in the general population. Among the same group of patients, another 23% had experienced a traumatic separation between their parents through divorce or other circumstances. Fisher (1973) found that his low orgastic women were more likely to have been unable to set up a relationship with their father, because he had died early or was absent from home for long periods, but a similar association was not established in respect of the mothers of these women. Finally, Uddenberg (1974) demonstrated that parental discord was related to low orgastic consistency and less sexual satisfaction in daughters. He also observed that women who had grown up in discordant homes, more often than others reported an unsatisfactory early relationship with their father, and more often had difficulties in establishing stable and satisfactory relationships with men.

There are a number of possible explanations for an association between early experiences of death, discord or traumatic separation in the family and later sexual impairment, but one plausible hypothesis is advanced by Fisher (1973) among others. He observed that women with orgastic difficulties tend to be preoccupied with the loss of people or objects they value, and uncertain about the permanence and reliability of their relationships with significant people in their lives. These characteristics may reflect the disruption and insecurity that the women had experienced in childhood, which might have instilled a very basic fear of losing anyone whom they love and a consequent avoidance of really meaningful emotional attachments. Thus, the degree of intimacy, warmth, trust, and love involved in a sexual relationship of any depth, may be very threatening to some sexually dysfunctional clients, as well as being beyond their capacity for emotional commitment to another person (Levay and Kagle 1977).

LEARNING PROCESSES

The kinds of traumatic experience, restrictive upbringing and adverse family relationships discussed above, provide some *conditions* for learning sexually dysfunctional behaviour, and it remains to consider the *processes* of learning through which such behaviour is acquired in those conditions. To my knowledge, there has not been any direct study of these learning processes in the specific context of sexual dysfunction, but it is a fundamental assumption in the behavioural approach that the same processes are involved in the acquisition of both acceptable and problematic behaviour (Jehu *et al.*, 1972). On this assumption, one can speculate about some of the processes operating in the development of a sexual dysfunction, but their respective contributions remain to be investigated empirically.

The learning conditions described contain many instances of sexuality being associated with aversive events, such as disapproval, punishment, failure, disappointment, and assault. If these events are simultaneously paired with sexual stimuli and responses on a number of occasions, then the process of *classical aversive conditioning* may occur, as a result of which the attractiveness of sex is reduced and instead it becomes a source of anxiety for the person concerned. Theoretically, this process is distinguished from that of *instrumental punishment conditioning*, where the aversive event follows as a consequence of the sexual behaviour, and results in a decrease in its frequency. Additionally, the sexual situation and behaviour leading up to the aversive consequences, become discriminative stimuli or informational cues that signal the likelihood of these consequences occurring. A particular danger of associating aversive events with sexuality is that their effects may extend beyond the particular situations and behaviour to which they were applied originally. For instance, sexual curiosity and exploration may be deemed unacceptable and punished in childhood, but the effects of this may generalize and persist into later marital sexual relationships so that these are impaired by anxiety and other stress reactions, as discussed in the next chapter. In summary, the outcome of classical aversive conditioning and instrumental punishment conditioning, is that a variable range of sexuality declines in frequency and acquires the properties of eliciting anxiety and signalling unpleasant consequences.

In order to reduce these anxiety reactions and to prevent the aversive consequences, an individual learns to avoid sexual stimulation and behaviour. Through *passive avoidance conditioning*, he or she learns not to attend to the stimulation or not to engage in the behaviour by simply taking no action perhaps by abstaining from looking at erotic material or not becoming involved in activities like cuddling, kissing, or petting. By means of *active avoidance conditioning*, a person learns to perform alternative activities so that he or she does not manifest any sexual interest or behaviour. For instance, a young person who has experienced disappointment or failure during early attempts at intercourse, might subsequently pursue other activities so intensively that there is no time left for friendships with the opposite sex.

The avoidance of sexuality by either passive or active means tends to be very persistent, even when there is no longer any risk of it having aversive consequences in the current circumstances. One reason for this is that the avoidance behaviour is *negatively reinforced* by the reduction in anxiety it produces. Thus, the anxiety elicited by the presence of erotic material is lessened when this is ignored, and that evoked by the prospect of a date is removed if this cannot be kept because of other commitments. A particularly unfortunate consequence of the persistent nature of avoidance behaviour, is that it prevents nature of avoidance, is that it prevents exposure to fresh sexual experiences that might have proved pleasant and successful, and thus have corrected the earlier adverse influences.

Another reason for the persistence of avoidance behaviour is that it may be maintained by inappropriate reward or *positive reinforcement*. A young man might be praised by his parents for spending his time in 'useful' activities rather than 'wasting' it with girls, or his self-esteem may be raised if he successfully avoids looking at erotic material. Furthermore, rewards can be inappropriately applied to certain forms of sexual behaviour, as well as to avoidance responses. For instance, an inexperienced man might be encouraged to ejaculate quickly by a prostitute who has other customers waiting, or by a girlfriend who wishes him to finish as soon as possible in case they are caught in the act, but this promotion of rapid ejaculation reduces his opportunity of learning to exercise voluntary control over the orgastic and ejaculatory reflexes, so that he may later present with the problem of premature ejaculation.

Another example of the inappropriate rewarding of certain sexual behaviour arises when clients have had a long history of obtaining the reward of orgasm only by masturbating in one specific and very constrained way, so that they have become incapable of reaching orgasm under any other conditions. McGovern and his co-authors cite the case of a woman who could only reach orgasm by laying on her stomach, pressing her legs together, placing a sheet between her genitals and her hands, and then stimulating herself by cupping her hands over her genital area (McGovern *et al.*, 1975). Another woman could only attain orgasm by masturbating while standing up (Snyder *et al.*, 1975). A male client who had never been able to ejaculate during sexual activity with his wife or any previous partner, was only able to do so if he lay on his back and stimulated his testicles with a piece of cloth, while another man suffering from erectile dysfunction had masturbated since the age of about seven years by inserting his finger under his foreskin and stimulating his glans penis, consequently he had a long history of ejaculating through a flaccid penis and this had been rewarded by the accompanying pleasure.

A contribution to sexual dysfunction may be made by inadequate, as well as inappropriate, positive reinforcement. Desirable sexual behaviour that is not followed by adequate reward tends to decrease in frequency. Thus, a child whose questions about sex are ignored may stop seeking knowledge in this area, and another whose physical expressions of affection are not returned may cease communicating with other people by bodily means. Adequate reward is an essential component of the process of *discrimination learning*. The danger of the effects of aversive events generalizing beyond the situations and behaviour to which they were originally applied, has been noted. To prevent this happening, it is necessary to specify any alternative situations and behaviour that would be acceptable, and to ensure that the performance of this behaviour in these situations is adequately rewarded. Thus, parental disapproval of a child masturbating in public needs to be accompanied by an indication that this is acceptable in private, and its performance in these circumstances will be rewarded by the pleasure the child derives from it. Similarly, it should be made clear to a young person that parental disapproval of intercourse during early adolescence does not apply to marital sexual relationships, which can be looked forward to as a legitimate source of great pleasure for both partners. Thus, the possible chronic impairment of a wide range of sexual activities through their association with aversive events, needs to be counteracted by proper opportunities for discrimination learning, and this involves the specification and reward of desired behaviour in appropriate circumstances.

In addition to the direct learning experiences already described, sexually dysfunctional behaviour may also be acquired through indirect *observational learning* processes, in which the client imitates the behaviour of exemplary models. These could be either real people observed in everyday life, or else perceived in symbolic form through the media of reading material, pictures, films or television programmes, and not only sexual acts, but also the associated attitudes and emotional reactions can be transmitted in this way. It follows that any significant lack of suitable modelling experiences may contribute to a failure to acquire desirable sexual behaviour, as might occur in those restrictive families where sex is never discussed and there is no physical expression of affection between the members. Similarly, if the adolescents in such families are forbidden to attend teenage parties, then they miss opportunities to observe how their peers interact with the opposite sex.

Unsuitable, as well as inadequate, modelling experiences may contribute to sexually dysfunctional behaviour. Parents who refuse to discuss sex and censor all sexual material in the home, who constantly warn about the sinfulness, dirtyness, and dangers to health of sex, and who disapprove of all forms of sexual expression, such as masturbation and nocturnal emissions, may transmit similar behaviour and negative sexual attitudes to their children.

Of course, not all observed behaviour is imitated and one important factor in determining whether or not this does happen is the consequences of the behaviour for the model. In general, if the model is rewarded for the behaviour then the observer is more likely to emulate it, while if the model is punished then imitation is less likely. Thus, a boy who observes his brother being punished for exhibiting sexual curiosity or exploration, is less likely to show similar interests or behaviour himself.

Finally, a contribution to sexually dysfunctional behaviour may be made by *cognitive learning* processes, through which relevant information is attended to, classified, retained, and utilized to guide sexual performance. Obviously, it is not possible for these processes to operate satisfactorily if the necessary information is not available, perhaps because of the censorship of all sexual material and discussion in a restrictive home. Even if the information is available, it may be ignored in order to avoid the anxiety and anticipation of punishment associated with any manifestation of sexual interest.

The next possible point of breakdown in cognitive learning occurs when available information is attended to satisfactorily, but is then inappropriately classified or labelled. For instance, nocturnal emissions might be classified as 'dirty' and masturbation as 'sinful' or 'dangerous', or the label of 'impotence' might be applied to a temporary loss of erection during an early attempt at sexual intercourse in unpropitious circumstances.

After information has been attended to and classified it still may not be retained in the memory for future use, and among the many reasons for this is the 'motivated' forgetting, or repression, of material that is associated with aversive events such as traumatic sexual experiences.

Information that is stored in the memory may later be retrieved and utilized to interpret current experiences and to guide future behaviour, and certain errors in these cognitive processes might contribute to sexual dysfunction. For instance, if a person interprets his own sexual performances in the light of unrealistically high standards or otherwise applies low self-evaluations to them, then anxiety and avoidance reactions may impair future performance. Another possible form of error is to make an incorrect inference from stored information. For example, it might be inferred that sexual activity is inevitably painful or unpleasant because these were the accompaniments of a specific traumatic experience. Lastly, errors may arise because future actions are planned on the basis of certain assumptions or beliefs about the nature of the situation concerned, the behaviour itself, and its probable consequences. To the extent that these assumptions are incorrect, then the plans for action based upon them may be correspondingly inappropriate. Thus, as a result of having experienced disruption or insecurity in early family relationships, a client may believe that no loving relationship is to be relied upon, and therefore avoid any emotional intimacy or commitment.

CONCLUSION

This chapter is not intended to constitute a comprehensive and exhaustive discussion of the alleged historical causes of sexual dysfunction, but rather to indicate the general nature of the learning conditions and processes concerned, and to demonstrate the inadequacy of the evidence at present available. However, it seems likely that the kinds of previous learning experiences described do sometimes interact with various contemporary conditions, as well as with organic factors, to produce some impairment of sexual functioning, and this is discussed in the following chapter.

4

Contemporary Conditions

The contemporary conditions that currently impair sexual functioning may exist in the client's environment or in his own thoughts and feelings, and they can contribute to sexual dysfunction in several ways. In the first place, it is the contemporary conditions that lead to the sexual behaviour being judged inadequate. Although organic factors and previous learning may have contributed to the origin and development of the behaviour, it constitutes a dysfunction only when it is judged to be inadequate in the current situation, according to the kind of criteria discussed in Chapter 5. For instance, either diabetes or a seductive mother might have impaired a man's ability to obtain erections, but he may only complain of this inadequacy when it prevents him from consummating a newly-contracted marriage. Similarly, although organic factors or previous learning experiences may have contributed to sexually dysfunctional behaviour, this is initiated and maintained by the contemporary conditions. Thus, an impotent man is unable to get an erection in a current sexual situation, and the anxiety evoked by this failure will tend to maintain the problem. Moreover, in some cases there appears to have been relatively little contribution from organic factors or previous learning, and the dysfunction seems to have arisen very largely in response to the contemporary conditions. A woman may, for example, have enjoyed a very satisfactory sexual adjustment throughout her earlier life and marriage, until she learns of her husband's affair with another woman, at which point the wife becomes unable to respond or reach climax in the marital sexual relationship.

In addition to the important contribution of contemporary conditions to the definition, initiation and maintenance of sexual dysfunction, these are also emphasized in a behavioural approach because they constitute the focus for any therapeutic intervention. Even when organic factors or learning experiences have in the past contributed to the origin of a dysfunction, these earlier conditions cannot be dealt with in treatment, one can only attempt to modify their adverse effects on the client's current sexual behaviour in relation to the circumstances prevailing at the present time.

PSYCHOLOGICAL STRESSES

Sexually dysfunctional behaviour may be initiated and maintained by contemporary psychological stresses of a sexual or non-sexual kind. According to Lazarus (1966), psychological stress involves exposure to conditions which are frustrating or threatening to an individual or that entail a conflict for him. A condition in which a desired course of action cannot be carried out or brought to a conclusion is deemed to be frustrating, and the inability of an impotent man to engage in intercourse or of an aroused woman to reach climax are examples of this category of stress. The term 'threat', is used to refer to the anticipation of harm, that is any consequence that the individual considers to be undesirable. Thus, sexual intercourse may be threatening to a girl who anticipates that it will be painful for her, or to a boy who fears that he will incur ridicule from his partner for ejaculating too quickly. A conflict situation exists when an individual is faced with two responses or goals that are incompatible because the response necessary to accomplish one goal, prevents the performance of a response that is essential for the attainment of the other goal. For instance, a girl may desire to have intercourse with her boyfriend, but in the current circumstances this would expose her to the risk of an unwanted pregnancy. Similarly, a husband might become sexually aroused during an extra-marital encounter, and yet not want to be unfaithful to his wife.

These definitions imply that stress cannot be identified solely in terms of those circumstances that apparently involve frustration, threat or conflict, because individuals differ in their reactions to similar conditions. What is stressful for one person is not necessarily so for another, therefore both the conditions and the person's reactions need to be taken into account. These reactions may be of an emotional, overt, or cognitive kind. For instance, when sexual activity is stressful to a person this may be indicated by the anxiety he experiences over his sexual performance, by his physical avoidance of sexual encounters, and by his adoption of a spectator role to monitor his own sexual responses. Whether or not an individual exhibits such stress reactions in particular conditions is strongly influenced by previous learning. For instance, intercourse may be stressful to a man who has experienced failure previously, or to a woman who has been brought up to expect it to be nasty and painful. Thus, previous learning experiences and contemporary conditions may interact to produce stress reactions that impair sexual functioning, and these conditions and reactions are considered further below.

Sexual stresses

Sexual anatomy or responses

The clinical literature contains many instances of patients who have exhibited stress reactions to certain components of sexual anatomy or response. Some impotent men are reported to fear the female genitals, or more particularly to dislike their smell or secretions. Similarly, some women patients find it stressful to see, touch, or smell their husband's penis or seminal emissions. Men presenting with retarded or absent ejaculation commonly find this component of the sexual response to be stressful for them, perhaps because of some earlier traumatic experience such as being discovered in the act of masturbation or intercourse and punished for this, or from apprehension about the partner's reaction if she is 'soiled', 'defiled' or impregnated by his semen. A woman who does not reach orgasm may be afraid to do so because she thinks she might be injured, lose her self control, become promiscuous, or have her life changed in a fundamental way as if orgasm is some kind of transcendental experience after which she can never be the same person as before. Finally, there is the example of women suffering from vaginismus to whom the prospect of penile penetration is very stressful, perhaps as a result of its previous association with pain or sexual assault.

Anticipation of harm

A closely related group of stresses involves the anticipation of some kind of harm. This may be of a physical nature; perhaps consisting of an injury, a painful experience or an unwanted pregnancy; in other cases, the harm may be of a psychological kind, such as a lack of satisfaction or threatening degree of intimacy in sexual relationships. One example is the fear exhibited by some impotent men that they will hurt or damage their partner during penetration or intercourse, and this belief is likely to be enhanced if she has similar expectations. As far as the risk of an unwanted pregnancy is concerned, there is some evidence that this can impair sexual responsiveness in women (Landis et al., 1950; Rainwater, 1965; Terman, 1938), and it was mentioned by 11 (24%) out of 46 sexually dysfunctional men studied by Cooper (1969a). Clearly, a persistent lack of satisfaction during intercourse can be a very frustrating stressful experience, for instance, a woman who repeatedly fails to gain pleasure or to reach climax, may begin to feel resentful and angry, and progressively to avoid further sexual encounters. These stress reactions may be especially likely if she believes her partner to be inconsiderate of her needs, and the situation can be still further exacerbated if a wife is unable to communicate her lack of satisfaction and sexual preferences to her husband because she has been brought up to assume that he will always know about his wife's sexual reactions and is fully responsible for them. Lastly, some clients are very threatened by the physical intimacy and emotional involvement with another person that are implicit in a sexual relationship. This may be because they have previously been hurt in close relationships and therefore have come to avoid them and to alienate themselves from other people.

Anticipation of failure

The anticipation of failure and other related worries about sexual performance appear to be among the most significant stresses contributing to sexual dysfunction (Kaplan, 1974; Masters and Johnson, 1970). Perhaps as a result of previous difficulties, a man might anticipate failure in obtaining and maintaining erections or in controlling a tendency to ejaculate too quickly, and a woman may be apprehensive about her ability to respond sexually or to reach orgasm. The partners of such clients may also experience performance stresses, for example the wife of an impotent man might seriously doubt her sexual attractiveness when she cannot arouse him, and the husband of an inorgastic woman become very unsure about his skill as a lover.

Such anticipation of failure by either partner is likely to be especially stressful if it is compounded by certain other related conditions. One of these is the expectation that any failure would lead to ridicule, criticism, anger or rejection by the partner. Another is subjection to performance demands that cannot be met, for example, an impotent man's anticipated failure is bound to be realized and reinforced when he is unable to produce erections to satisfy any strong demands for intercourse being made by his wife. Some individuals impose an excessive performance demand upon themselves in the particular form of an overconcern about pleasing their partner during lovemaking. While a wish to do this is inherent in a satisfactory sexual relationship, it can become excessive to the point where one partner's desires and gratification are completely subordinated to those of the other partner. Typically, a wife may be so concerned to ensure her husband's sexual pleasure that she is reluctant to ask him to prolong foreplay or to stimulate her as she would like, consequently she fails to become aroused or to reach orgasm herself. Often such overconcern arises from the perceived threat of being rejected by the husband if he is insufficiently pleased, and the wife may be especially vulnerable to this form of threat because of the current instability of the marriage or the insecurity she experienced in her childhood relationships.

Moral or religious contraventions

Any form of sexual activity that contravenes a person's moral or religious standards may be stressful for that individual. Those whose standards include a complete prohibition on intercourse before marriage, may well be physically unresponsive if they attempt to engage in this. Unfortunately, in some but by no means all such cases, this abhorrence of pre-marital sex may be overgeneralized to a marital sexual relationship, so that the individual continues to feel very anxious and guilty over lovemaking with his or her spouse. Another example in this category is the situation where a man is unable to have a satisfactory sexual relationship with his wife because he perceives her to be too pure, virtuous, and sacred to be contaminated by his erotic desires or advances. Consequently, the wife may not appear to her husband as a sexually attractive and exciting woman, or his erotic feelings towards her may cause him much anxiety and guilt. Some men in this situation are able to perform sexually with certain other women, such as casual pickups or prostitutes, whom they regard as more degraded and less worthy of respect than their wives. A somewhat similar situation arises in the cases of certain clients who have engaged in erotic activities with a parent in the past, and are subsequently unable to have a satisfactory sexual relationship with a spouse because this symbolically recapitulates the previous 'taboo' relationship. In contrast to the last three examples, there are other individuals whose marital sexual relationships are perfectly adequate, but who become dysfunctional in an extra-marital affair because of the guilt this arouses.

Non-sexual stresses

While this discussion of the kinds of conditions that may impair sexual behaviour is concentrated on sexual stresses, it is important to recognize that non-sexual stresses can have similar effects. The man who is worried about losing his job or any other occupational or financial problem, and the woman who is seriously concerned about a sick relative, may each exhibit stress reactions that adversely affect their sexual functioning.

Stress reactions

Emotional reactions

In the first place, sexual behaviour can be impaired by the negative emotional reactions that tend to accompany all forms of stress, and which include depression, anger, guilt, and especially anxiety. For instance, stresses which entail profound disappointment and lowered self-esteem for an individual may be particularly likely to result in depressive reactions, and the association between these and sexual functioning is referred to in a later section. Similarly, any persistent lack of sexual satisfaction especially, if accompanied by an apparent lack of consideration by a partner, may elicit strong reactions of anger, which are discussed below in the context of partner discord. As far as guilt is concerned, this may arise in relation to any sexual activity that contravenes an individual's moral or religious standards, so that it might, for example, disrupt his sexual responses during pre-marital or extra-marital lovemaking.

The damaging effect of anxiety on sexual arousal is particularly strongly emphasized by Masters and Johnson (1970), who argue that arousal occurs as the natural reaction to sexual stimulation, and that it does not require and cannot be produced by any deliberate effort or act of will. This does not contradict the fact that arousal can be elicited by erotic phantasies which are to some extent under the voluntary control of the individual concerned (Rosen et al., 1975; Rubin and Henson, 1975). The important point being made by Masters and Johnson is that arousal can only occur in response to some effective form of sexual stimulation. They argue further, that sexual arousal is especially vulnerable to disruption by performance anxiety. This is elicited by performance stresses such as the anticipation of failure in lovemaking, and it serves to distract the individual from the ongoing sexual stimulation and thus to prevent arousal occurring, so that a man may present with impotence or a woman with vasocongestive dysfunction. At a physiological level, anxiety and other negative emotional reactions are assumed to interfere with the satisfactory operation of the neural and/or endocrine mechanisms that subserve the erectile and lubrication-swelling responses, but the precise nature of this disruptive process is at present unknown (Bancroft, 1970).

Overt reactions

A second major group of stress reactions consists of those involving various aspects of overt activity. A specific example is the involuntary spasm of the muscles at the entrance to the vagina that occurs in clients suffering from vaginismus, whenever penetration is threatened or attempted. Similarly, the muscular contractions that comprise the orgastic reflex in both sexes are inhibited among some women who have difficulty in reaching orgasm and in men who cannot ejaculate. All these overt reactions constitute avoidance responses since they prevent penetration, orgasm, or ejaculation from occurring, as well as reducing the anxiety associated with them.

A similar avoidance function is served by many other overt reactions to stress. There may be a progressive reduction in the frequency of sexual encounters, sometimes to the extent of complete cessation. To avoid these, clients may excuse themselves on grounds of illness or tiredness, or they may fill all their available time with extra work or other non-sexual activities. Sometimes a quarrel is provoked just before going to bed, or one partner may stay up long after the other has retired. Any residual sexual activities tend to be very constricted so that the most stressful aspects are avoided or minimized. For instance, some couples never see each other in the nude and always make love in the dark, or there may be complete abstinence from genital fondling or other kinds of foreplay.

Quite commonly, the restriction of such relatively specific sexual behaviour extends to other aspects of a couple's relationship. all kinds of bodily contact, including physical expressions of love and affection such as kissing and cuddling, may be discontinued in order to avoid the risk of these escalating into a sexual encounter. Some couples stop communicating with each other about their sexual responses, preferences, and difficulties, because they find any discussion of these topics to be embarrassing and distressing. Unfortunately, this can seriously impair their sexual interaction. For this to be mutually satisfying, it is essential for the partners to let each other know about the kinds of stimulation that are pleasing or irritating for them, and to express enjoyment during pleasurable stimulation so that their partner is reinforced for providing this. They may also need to communicate support to each other, for instance, a wife who is having difficulty in attaining an orgasm, may depend upon reassurance from her husband that he is not getting bored or resentful during the prolonged foreplay she requires to reach climax. A final example of the inappropriate generalization of overt avoidance responses arises among those dysfunctional clients who do not have a spouse or other long term partner. Often such clients will increasingly avoid social contacts with the opposite sex, in case any of these might develop into a sexual relationship in which the client's inadequacy would be revealed. As discussed in the previous chapter, all forms of avoidance behaviour tend to be very persistent because its performance is constantly reinforced by the reduction of anxiety, and sometimes by inappropriate reward as well. A particular disadvantage of this, is that it deprives the client of new learning opportunities, which might otherwise have modified the stressful nature of the conditions that evoke the anxiety and avoidance reactions.

Cognitive reactions

A final group of stress reactions consists of those of a cognitive nature, and it includes the *cognitive monitoring* of sexual performance, or what Masters and Johnson (1970) call 'spectatoring'. For instance, an impotent man who anticipates failure, is prone to observe himself to see if he is getting an erection, how full it is becoming, and whether or not he is losing it. His wife also will tend to monitor his sexual arousal, as well as her own performance to see if this is helping or hindering him. Similarly, a sexually unresponsive woman may watch closely to see if she is lubricating or getting any erotic feelings, and her husband may constantly scrutinize her reactions as well as the efficacy of his own lovemaking. Such monitoring of sexual performance by both partners, puts them in the role of spectators, rather than participants, at their own sexual encounters. They seem to be standing at the foot of the bed watching what is happening, rather than becoming deeply involved in their lovemaking: one client likened spectatoring to having a geography lesson instead of a trip round the world. The point made very strongly by Masters and Johnson is that the detachment of the spectator role, together with the distraction of the monitoring process itself, result in the individuals concerned being cut off from the sexual stimulation that would otherwise evoke sexual arousal as a natural response.

There is some experimental support for the reduction of sexual arousal by cognitive monitoring in the results of a laboratory study conducted by Geer and Fuhr (1976). They had male subjects attend to nonerotic cognitive tasks of varying difficulty which were presented through one ear, while an erotic tape recording was played into the other ear. A very significant inverse relationship was found to exist between the complexity of the tasks and the erectile responses of the subjects. The degree of sexual arousal they exhibited was progressively lower as the tasks increased in difficulty and required more attention. Geer and Fuhr hypothesize that this distracted the subjects from the erotic stimulation or interfered with it, so that they became less aroused. These authors add that without further investigation their findings cannot safely be generalized from auditory to other forms of sexual stimulation, from men to women, or from the laboratory to natural situations, but nevertheless they do constitute some much needed experimental evidence on certain clinical observations that are of considerable importance to the explanation and treatment of sexual dysfunction.

Another kind of cognitive reaction is the avoidance of erotic thoughts and feelings that are stressful to the person concerned, so that his awareness of this disturbing material is to some extent reduced. The actual process of *'cognitive avoidance'* may be under the conscious and voluntary control of the individual, or in varying degrees it may operate involuntarily and without his awareness. In either case, the result is that the client does not perceive the sexual stimulation he is receiving, nor does he experience the pleasurable feelings usually associated with it, consequently his sexual arousal and gratification are impaired. Thus, activities like kissing, caressing, and even the direct stimulation of the clitoris or glans penis, fail to evoke erotic sensations and feelings of sufficient intensity, or alternatively these are switched off as soon as a stressful point is reached in the sexual encounter. In extreme cases, such sensations and feelings are totally lacking, a condition sometimes referred to as 'sexual anaesthesia'. For instance, a client described the sensation of her husband stimulating her clitoris as like having her big toe touched. A similar lack of awareness of genital sensations may underlie some cases of premature ejaculation, in which the man does not perceive the approach of orgasm and therefore is unable to exercise voluntary control over it.

Individual differences

Having looked at stress conditions and reactions in general terms, we are left with the problem of why similar conditions impair sexual functioning in some individuals while leaving others unaffected in this respect. At present, these individual differences cannot be adequately accounted for, but a number of points are worthy of consideration. First, there is some evidence that certain psychological characteristics are associated with a wide range of stress disorders. For example, Rees (1976) reports that some characteristics, including timidity, meekness, trait anxiety, marked sensitivity, and obsessionality, were all commoner among groups of patients suffering from asthma, vasomotor rhinitis, hay fever, urticaria, or peptic ulcer, than in corresponding groups of control subjects. It is important to note that in this and other studies, such characteristics were not associated with any particular stress disorder, and they may be conducive to the development of all disorders of this kind. Therefore, it still remains to explain why a sexual dysfunction occurs in preference to some other alternative.

One possibility is that sexually dysfunctional clients are especially vulnerable to stresses of a sexual nature. Because of previous learning, they may have a low threshold for the evocation of stress reactions during sexual encounters, consequently it is their sexual behaviour that is particularly prone to disruption by anxiety, avoidance, spectatoring, and similar responses.

However, this does not account for the occurrence of sexual dysfunction under stressful conditions of a non-sexual nature, whereas this could be explained by the 'response specificity' hypothesis advanced by Lacey and his co-workers (Lacey, 1950; Lacey et al., 1953; Lacey and Lacey, 1958). According to these investigators, each individual has a characteristic pattern of response, so that if he is subjected to sufficient stress of any kind whatsoever, then he will tend to develop a disorder in a particular bodily system. For instance, this might be asthma in the respiratory system; tachycardia, or hypertension in the cardiovascular system; a peptic ulcer in the gastrointestinal system; or a sexual dysfunction in the genito-urinary system. There is some evidence in the work of Lacey's group, that the particular vulnerability of the system affected in each individual is determined at least in part by genetic factors, but diet and previous disease history may also contribute.

The first possibility of sexually dysfunctional clients being especially susceptible to sexual stresses, and the further possibility of them having a vulnerable genito-urinary system, are not necessarily mutually exclusive and they could occur together. It must be emphasized that at present these possibilities are little more than pure conjecture, and they also still leave open the further question of why clients develop one type of sexual dysfunction rather than another. The conditions and processes responsible for this aspect of individual variation cannot be identified from the information which is currently available.

PARTNER DISCORD

A frequent but not invariable association between sexual dysfunction and marital discord is commonly reported in patient groups. For example, without describing the populations concerned, Kaplan (1974) states that 75% of her patients who presented with marital problems of a non-sexual kind were found to have a sexual complaint, while among those presenting with such complaints some 70% also had non-sexual marital problems. Frank *et al.* (1976) studied 29 couples seeking marital therapy, and 25 couples seeking sex therapy, at Western Psychiatric Institute and Clinic at the University of Pittsburgh, which provides these forms of treatment in separate specialty clinics. No significant differences in the incidence of sexual difficulties was found between the two groups, but such differences in favour of the sex therapy group were found on several self-ratings of the general marital relationship by the couples; for instance, over one half of the sex therapy couples rated their marriage as 'happy' or 'very happy' compared with only one quarter of the couples seeking marital therapy. Finally, in a group of 6 women referred for treatment of secondary orgastic dysfunction, 4 of the women and 4 of their husbands obtained scores indicative of marital discord on the Lock–Wallace Marital Adjustment Test. In contrast, such scores were obtained for only 1 woman and 1 husband in a group of 6 women referred for primary orgastic dysfunction (McGovern *et al.*, 1975). All these findings must be regarded with some caution because they are not necessarily derived from representative patient groups, but they do serve to demonstrate that sexual dysfunction and marital discord are frequently but not inevitably associated, and there is additional support for this in two studies of women from the general populations in America and Sweden respectively, in which no correlation was found between capacity for orgasm and quality of marital relationship (Fisher, 1973; Uddenberg, 1974).

Nevertheless, sexual dysfunction and marital discord are related in some couples, in which case the dysfunction may have caused the discord, or the opposite may have happened, or perhaps most probably there was a reciprocal causal relationship between the two problems. These complex interactions are illustrated in the following discussion, where sexual dysfunction and marital discord are each conceptualized as a particular form of stress, involving conditions of frustration, threat, and conflict, and evoking reactions similar to those described above.

Stress conditions

Deficient reinforcement

Following a seminal paper by Stuart (1969), many behaviourally oriented writers have made the assumption that marital discord arises from some failure of reciprocal positive reinforcement between the spouses. It is suggested that people enter into matrimony when they anticipate that this will be more satisfying than remaining single, and afterwards they expect some exchange of rewarding behaviour with their spouse on a reasonably equitable basis. In various ways, these expectations may not be realized (Azrin *et al.*, 1973). The marriage may simply be insufficiently rewarding compared to the single state, or there may be an inequitable dispensation of rewards between the partners, so that a wife who consistently tries to please her husband becomes disappointed and resentful when he shows no appreciation of her efforts and makes little attempt to give her any pleasure. In some cases, only specific aspects of one spouse's behaviour are rewarded by the other: for instance, some wives complain that their husband is only interested in them for sex. Sometimes a spouse fails to recognize that the partner is providing considerable amounts of reward, an example being the husband who takes his wife for granted and does not notice the trouble she takes to please him. In the course of a marriage there are many changes in the reinforcement value of different kinds of behaviour, initially it may be especially rewarding to a wife if her husband works very hard to earn the money they need to set up house and start a family, later the husband's help with children and the support and companionship he gives his wife may be valued much more highly than his occupational achievements. Such shifts in reinforcement value need to be recognized and accommodated, otherwise earlier reinforcers will continue to be dispensed although they have lost their potency, while newer more appropriate rewards are withheld. Another source of failure to provide desired rewards is inadequate communication between the partners, an example being an inhibited wife's inability to tell her husband what she would like during their lovemaking. The basic assumption that non-reciprocated reinforcement underlies marital discord is still largely untested, but there is some preliminary support in a study by Birchler *et al.* (1975) who found that distressed couples, relative to non-distressed couples, reported significantly fewer pleasing behaviours between spouses, and significantly more displeasing behaviours.

In this approach, it is further suggested that spouses tend to react to failures of reciprocal reinforcement in ways that compound rather than ameliorate the discord between them. Initially, they may attempt to make the partner's behaviour more rewarding by positive means such as polite requests and encouragement, but if these fail then there is a tendency to resort to aversive methods like nagging, criticism, ridicule, and threats. The use of such *coercion* is reinforced if it is successful in producing the desired changes in the partner's behaviour, consequently it may be employed more frequently in future (Patterson and Hops, 1972). Moreover, the use of aversive control by one spouse tends to be reciprocated by the other: for example, some observations of family interactions reported by Patterson and Reid (1970) yielded a median correlation of 0.65 between the proportion of aversive interaction 'given' and 'received'. Often this leads to an escalation of the confrontation, for if coercive attempts are met with counterattack rather than compliance, then there is a tendency to intensify the aversive exchanges on both sides, until eventually one of the partners capitulates. In this way, very high amplitude coercion is reinforced and shaped up, while the positive reinforcement it was intended to produce is in fact diminished rather than increased. A second kind of reaction to non-reciprocated reinforcement is *withdrawal* from the marriage relationship either emotionally or physically. All attraction and affection towards the unrewarding spouse may disappear, or the partner may turn for reinforcement to an extramarital affair, to friends, to drink, or to a return to the single state. In any event, the pattern of mutual reward between the couple is worsened rather than enhanced by such withdrawal reactions.

There are a number of aspects of marital interaction in which some breakdown of reinforcement may occur (Azrin *et al.*, 1973). One partner may not contribute to lovemaking in ways that would please the other. A husband may not share in the upbringing of any children of the marriage, or even support his wife in this task. Some mutually satisfactory division of household responsibilities may be lacking, or the contribution of one spouse in this area may not be properly appreciated by the other. The arrangements made by a couple for the allocation and control of their financial resources can be inadequately rewarding for either or both partners. One of them, may be to some extent deprived of reinforcement by the occupational commitments of the other, for instance, when this involves frequent or prolonged absence from home. Because of such absences or for other reasons, the enjoyment of social activities may be impaired because they are not shared by both spouses: for example, the distressed couples studied by Birchler *et al.* (1975) reported significantly fewer spouse accompanied activities and significantly more nonspouse accompanied behaviour, in comparison with the nondistressed couples. The same group of researchers (Vincent *et al.*, 1975) have conducted a laboratory study in which distressed couples emitted a significantly greater proportion of negative problem solving statements and a significantly smaller proportion of positive problem solving statements, than nondistressed couples. The negative statements included complaints, criticisms, denials of responsibility, excuses, put downs, interruptions, and disagreements, while positive statements were those indicating a solution to the problem, acceptance of responsibility and compromises. This investigation provides some limited support for the association of unrewarding communication processes with marital discord, in this case involving a lack of constructive problem solving, but also often extending into other aspects of communication such as empathy between partners and the conveyance of acceptance, affection, and approval by physical and verbal means. Finally, the degree of independence exercised by each partner can involve some impairment of mutual reinforcement between them: for instance, a spouse may not be given sufficient freedom and the necessary resources to enable him or her to pursue activities and make decisions independently of the other. Conversely, a husband or wife may be so lacking in reasonable autonomy that their partner's independence is unduly restricted.

Rejection of partner

Whether or not they are conceptualized in terms of non-reciprocated reinforcement, there are certain patterns of marital discord that seem to be quite commonly associated with sexual dysfunction. One of these is the rejection of a partner who is perceived as unattractive or disliked, and whose sexual approaches therefore tend to be insufficiently stimulating and annoying rather than arousing. For instance, according to Masters and Johnson (1970), one of the most frequent causes of female orgastic dysfunction is lack of attraction to a partner who fails to meet the woman's expectations in respect of qualities such as masculinity, intelligence, interesting companionship, achievement and physical appearance. Ultimately, the rejection of a partner may amount to a total lack of commitment to the marriage, perhaps accompanied by a desire to end it, and we shall see below that this threat is a very prevalent source of anxiety among sexually dysfunctional couples.

Dominance–submission conflicts

A second relevant pattern of discord involves (dominance-submission conflicts between the spouses (Harbin and Gamble, 1977). Perhaps as a result of childhood experiences and feelings of inadequacy, some individuals need constant reassurance about their superiority and control of situations, and this can lead to the depreciation and subordination of others. Thus, some spouses may be in competition with each other to dominate the marriage, so that friction and hostility arises between them. Sometimes, the desire to dominate may impair sexual functioning in a specific way: for example, in the case of a wife who cannot respond or reach orgasm because this would represent submission to her husband, or that of a man who ejaculates prematurely to avoid compliance with a wife who initiates and demands intercourse. It should be noted that the domination of one partner by the other does not inevitably entail competition and conflict, for some individuals actually prefer a very dominant partner and may not be able to respond sexually unless someone else is in control of the encounter, while conversely, there are other individuals who can only function satisfactorily with someone who is very unassertive and compliant.

Sexually dysfunctional partner

Lastly, when one partner is suffering from some form of sexual dysfunction, this may contribute to discord between the spouses, sometimes with additional adverse effects on the sexual capacity of either or both of them. Quite commonly it seems, a problem of impotence or of retarded or absent ejaculation is attributed by a wife to the husband's rejection of her. She may believe that he finds her unattractive, that her lovemaking is inadequate, and that he does not love her, consequently she often tries to obtain reassurance by making sexual demands upon him which only serve to exacerbate his difficulty. Likewise, the husbands of wives who are unable to become aroused or to reach orgasm, may interpret this as rejection and try to force their wives to respond. Feelings of rejection are common also among the partners of men who are afraid to let themselves go in lovemaking in case they ejaculate prematurely, and we have already noted the tendency of these wives to experience resentment and anger because their husband is perceived as gratifying himself while disregarding his wife's sexual satisfaction.

To conclude this discussion on the stressful nature of marital discord, it seems clear that conditions such as deficient reinforcement, partner rejection, dominance–submission conflicts, and the existence of sexual dysfunction in a spouse, may all involve frustration, threat and conflict, and are likely to evoke stress reactions in some of the individuals exposed to them. The general nature of these reactions is discussed above, and only those aspects that are especially relevant to marital discord are considered in the next section.

Stress reactions

Rejection anxiety

Any threat of rejection by a partner appears to be a potent source of anxiety in many sexually dysfunctional clients. Not only does this reaction entail the generally disruptive effects of anxiety on sexual arousal discussed above, but in particular the anticipation of sexual failure and other performance related stresses, are likely to be compounded if they are expected to be met with rejection rather than understanding by the partner. If clients are apprehensive about being humiliated, criticized or deserted for any inadequacy in their lovemaking, then this is likely to distract them from the ongoing sexual stimulation so that it fails to evoke arousal. Moreover, clients who fear rejection, may be so concerned to ensure their partner's sexual pleasure, that they completely subordinate their own satisfaction. For instance, a wife may be unwilling to ask her husband to provide the kind of stimulation she needs to become aroused and reach orgasm, in case he should resent this request and perhaps leave her for another woman who is less demanding and more responsive.

Anger

In addition to anxiety, the emotional reaction of anger can also disrupt sexual behaviour. We have seen that clients may become angry if their spouse does not reward them adequately, is disliked, competes with them for dominance, or is sexually dysfunctional. In all these circumstances it is difficult for clients to respond sexually with a partner towards whom they are experiencing considerable feelings of anger. As in the case of anxiety, the precise physiological mechanisms involved in the disruption of sexual arousal by anger, are currently unknown.

Aggression

The same patterns of marital discord that elicit the emotional reaction of anger, sometimes instigate overt reactions of an aggressive kind. However, anger and aggression are not inextricably linked (Bandura, 1973). Whether anger is accompanied by aggression or another alternative such as avoidance or constructive problem-solving, probably depends on the responses the client had learned for coping with provocation and their relative effectiveness in the contemporary conditions. Conversely, aggressive acts are not necessarily accompanied by anger, they can be performed 'in cold blood'.

If the term 'aggression' is taken to include any form of behaviour that may result in physical or psychological injury to a person, then it may consist not only of verbal abuse and physical assaults, but also of more subtle expressions of hostility in the context of a couple's sexual relationship (Kaplan, 1974). When lovemaking is anticipated, it may be prevented or spoiled by one of the partners provoking a quarrel or starting a discussion on some topic that evokes anxiety in the spouse. Sexual approaches may be made only at times when intercourse is impracticable or not desired by the other partner, alternatively a hostile recipient may respond consistently with apathy, complaints of fatigue or illness, or outright refusal. Some individuals persist in presenting themselves in a physical unattractive manner, or in behaving in annoying ways, so that it is difficult for their partner to respond sexually to them: for instance, a wife may not become aroused if her husband is unwashed, smells of alcohol, or uses foul language. During sexual encounters, one partner may withhold pleasurable and effective stimulation from the other, and dysfunctions such as impotence and premature or retarded ejaculation can serve to frustrate a spouse's satisfaction.

These, and many other forms of aggression may be evoked by stressful marital interactions of an aversive nature. They can also be instigated by the prospect of incentives such as obtaining desired rewards from a spouse or of success in a competition for domination between the partners. If such reinforcing consequences do follow aggressive behaviour, then it will tend to be maintained and perhaps increased in frequency and intensity: a specific examples of this being the reinforcement and shaping up of any coercive methods of obtaining rewards which have proved successful.

PSYCHOLOGICAL REACTIONS TO ORGANIC FACTORS

The organic changes involved in the aging process, physical illnesses, surgery and drug effects, constitute further possible sources of psychological stress. Their direct contribution to sexual dysfunction is considered in Chapter 2, where it is noted that they might also contribute indirectly through the individual's psychological reaction to them. Often these direct and indirect influences interact with each other, so that a minimal or transitional impairment of organic origin becomes more severe and persistent when it evokes reactions such as performance anxiety, avoidance and spectatoring. Consequently, similar organic changes are associated with a wide variety of sexual functioning, which reflects the extent and nature of the stress reactions elicited in different individuals.

Aging

Among the organic changes occurring in the sexual response cycle of the older male are a slowing down of erection, a decline in the forcefulness and frequency of ejaculation, and a lengthening of the refractory period. These, and other such changes, do not necessarily entail any cessation or disruption of pleasurable sexual performance (Martin, 1977). For instance, in some longitudinal studies of large groups from the general population conducted at Duke University, it was found that at age 68 years, some 70% of men still regularly enjoyed sexual activity, while 25% still did so even when they were 78 years old (Pfeiffer, 1974, 1975). There is some corroboration of these proportions in the work of Kinsey *et al.* (1948) who reported that about 80% of men aged 60 years, and 20% of those aged 80, were still capable of sexual intercourse. However, if a man regards the natural organic changes of the aging process as signifying the onset of impotence or the end of his sexual life, then these stresses can evoke performance anxiety, depression, spectatoring, and avoidance reactions, which in turn may result in the incapacity he fears. To some extent, the potential stressfulness of the natural changes is fostered by the cultural stereotype of the older man as being sexually impaired, so that any possible indication of this immediately elicits considerable worry and loss of confidence in the individual concerned.

There is a similar stereotype of the post-menopausal female, who is expected to be devoid of sexual interest and incapable of pleasurable sexual performance, otherwise she may be regarded as unnatural or immoral. In consequence, some older women experience considerable anxiety, guilt, and depression over their continuing sexual desires, and they may come to avoid all sexual activity in their later years. In fact, the slower and less profuse lubrication, diminished swelling of the genitalia, and fewer muscular contractions during orgasm, that are characteristic of the post-menopausal woman, do not prevent her from becoming aroused or reaching climax, and given adequate opportunity she can continue to enjoy regular sexual activity (Van Keep and Gregory, 1977). For example, Christenson and Gagnon (1965) have reported that 70% of married women aged 60 were still engaging in sexual intercourse. When this is discontinued by the older woman, it is often because she has lost her husband: in the Duke studies, only 39% of the women subjects had intact marriages, compared to 82% of the men (Pfeiffer, 1975). However, perhaps for the reasons discussed in the previous paragraph, a husband may be unwilling to engage in regular sexual activity even if he is still present: thus, it was usually the husband rather than the wife who was responsible for any cessation of sexual activity that occurred in the intact marriages described by Pfeiffer (1975).

During the menopause, women undergo certain physical and psychological changes that sometimes make them anxious, depressed, and aggressive, with possible adverse effects on their sexual functioning. In particular, they may

Table 2. Nature of sexual problems in the physically disabled (Stewart, 1975)

Problem	Number and % of cases in which exhibited	
Problems of sexual potency and capacity		
Impotence/partial impotence (in men)	19	
Lack of clitoral/vaginal sensation (in women)	9	
Low libidinal urge, lack of sexual desire	17	
Generalized weakness, reducing desire/pleasure/capacity	7	
	52	(24.1%)
Problems of physical comfort		
Stiffness of joints/muscles makes sexual postures/motions difficult and/or painful	21	
Constant pain reduces desire/pleasure	24	
Tremor/spasm during intercourse, etc.	3	
Severe vertigo during intercourse	2	
Appliances/dressings make intercourse, etc. difficult or uncomfortable	1	
	51	(21.7%)
Problems of physical safety		
Severe breathlessness during physical excitement	21	
Heart palpitations during sexual excitement	10	
Brittleness of bones affecting sexual postures/motions	1	
Grand mal convulsions accompany intercourse	3	
	35	(15.3%)
Problems of paralysis		
Voluntary adoption of sexual postures/motions impossible	12	(7.9%)
Problems of affect		
Unfounded fears as to safety reduce intercourse and/or other sexual activity	9	
Unfounded fears as to hereditary considerations reduce intercourse and/or pleasure	2	
Extreme self-dissatisfaction through comparative sexual incapacity	5	
Self-view as repellent/rejected	12	
	28	(13.8%)
Problems of sexual relationships		
Decline in marital relationship attributed to sexual difficulties of respondent	10	
Severe bodily deformity reduces 'attractiveness'	14	
General avoidance of and difficulty in relationships reduces opportunity for sexual relationship	13	
	37	(17.2%)

become especially concerned about their declining attractiveness, which can exacerbate their vulnerability to rejection anxiety. Consequently, this is very likely to be evoked if the husband becomes impotent or avoids sexual encounters, and perhaps even when he exhibits the natural changes of the aging process in his sexual responses. Any such natural or dysfunctional limitations in a husband's sexual performance, may be worsened if his wife exerts pressure for intercourse as a form of reassurance about his attraction and loyalty to her, and perhaps also in an attempt to ensure his pleasure so that he will not leave her for a younger woman. The upshot of this discussion is that the aging process does not necessarily produce sexual dysfunction in either men or women, and when this does occur in the healthy old person it may be due to psychological factors such as performance or rejection anxiety.

Illness and surgery

The organic changes involved in a physical illness are sometimes entirely responsible for any associated sexual dysfunction, but in many cases this is the result of an interaction between these changes and the individual's psychological reactions to them. Some much needed light is thrown on the sexual functioning of the physically disabled by a recent study in an English city (Stewart, 1975). The subjects were 212 disabled people drawn from a survey of the general population, and representing a wide range of disorder in varying degrees of severity. They were aged 20 to 64 years, and 23% of them were unmarried compared to 16% of the same age group in the total population of England and Wales. In the study, sexual problems were defined as obstacles to the satisfaction of sexual need, and the nature and prevalence of those encountered in the subjects are shown in Table 2 below. At least one, and often more, of these problems were currently exhibited by 111 (54%) of the subjects, and an additional 28 (18%) had suffered similar difficulties at some time since their disablement but these had either been overcome or they had ceased to be regarded as important by the individual concerned. Thus, a total of 72% of the subjects had experienced a sexual problem at some time. There is no comparable information available about the prevalence of such problems among people who are not disabled, but Stewart estimates 20% to 40%, in which case his disabled group is substantially more impaired. Among the 149 subjects who had experienced sexual problems, these were attributed exclusively, or almost exclusively, to organic factors in 66 (44.5%) subjects, to organic and psychological factors in 54 (35.5%) and entirely, or almost entirely to psychological factors in 22 (15%), while the origin could not be determined in the remaining 7 (5%) subjects.

Anticipation of harm

There are many psychological reactions to illness and surgery that can impair sexual behaviour. Some patients will find this stressful because they anticipate that it will harm them in some way. For instance, those who have had a life-threatening illness, such as a myocardial infarction, may fear the occurrence of a relapse or sudden death during intercourse. Postsurgical patients who have had operations such as an ostomy, renal transplant, or prostatectomy, may be apprehensive that these will be damaged if they engage in sexual activity. For some, this will have been associated with pain, perhaps in the form of angina pectoris or arising from an arthritic joint or a local genital disorder, consequently sex is regarded with some trepidation in case the discomfort is repeated. Finally, such anxiety reactions to the prospect of harm of some kind may be elicited not only in the patients themselves but also in their partners, who may therefore impose varying degrees of abstinence or restriction upon the sexual relationship.

Anticipation of failure

A second source of stress associated with illness and surgery is the anticipation of sexual failure. Patients may believe that these experiences will have totally destroyed their sexual capacity, and this conviction may be strengthened by the cultural stereotype of the 'sexless invalid'. In many societies, sexuality is equated with youth, physical attractiveness and good health, while the chronically ill or handicapped are considered to be asexual, lacking both interest and ability in sexual performance. In fact, only very rarely does illness or surgery have such a totally destructive effect, it is much more usual for any direct impairment to be of a temporary or partial nature, although this may become more permanent or comprehensive if it is compounded by performance anxiety. Thus, for reasons such as bodily weakness or lack of confidence, a patient's initial attempts to resume sexual relations may not be successful, and if this leads to the anticipation of continued failure then the temporary incapacity may be prolonged. Similarly, as a direct result of his illness or surgery, a man may suffer from retrograde ejaculation while otherwise retaining his sexual capacity and pleasure, but these may also be adversely affected if he becomes unduly concerned about his apparent failure to produce an ejaculate.

Depressive reactions

Illness or surgery can also be accompanied by depressive reactions that adversely effect sexual behaviour, and there are a variety of reasons why such reactions might arise. Sometimes they may be a direct physical corollary of the illness, as in the case of depressive symptoms produced by the effect of uraemic toxins on the brains of patients suffering from renal disorders. Other patients may become depressed because of the chronic pain they are experiencing, perhaps from an arthritic disorder. Then there are the stresses of having a life-threatening illness, of adjusting to changes in the form and functioning of one's body, and of being very dependent of other people, as well as the enforced restriction of recreational and occupational activities and the lowering of social status and self-esteem that are sometimes associated with invalidism.

Impairment of self-concept

This leads on to the commonly damaging effects of illness or surgery on patients' self-concepts, and the implications of this for their sexual functioning. One aspect of the self-concept is the image a person has of his or her own body, and this may be very adversely affected by changes such as limb amputations, an ostomy or mastectomy, scarring from burns or surgery, foul genital infections, and loss of control over bowel, bladder, or locomotor functions.

Such changes also have implications for a second aspect of the self-concept, that of gender identity, for they may reduce the confidence of patients in their masculinity or femininity. A particular example of this is the threat to female identity experienced by some women as a result of a mastectomy or hysterectomy operation. In addition to body image changes, a patient's gender identity may also be challenged by any doubts about sexual adequacy or sexual attractiveness, as well as by any restrictions imposed by illness upon the performance of the normative gender roles; for instance, the expectation that a man will go out to work and earn to maintain himself and his family.

Finally, the self-esteem aspect of the self-concept may be markedly lowered by the changes in body image and gender identity already described, as well as by other factors such as increased dependency on others. It seems likely, in conclusion, that any damage caused by illness or surgery to these several aspects of the self-concept will undermine the confidence of patients in their sexual capacity, with consequent adverse implications for their sexual relationships, and this view is generally supported by the available empirical evidence (e.g. Fitting *et al.*, 1978; Frank *et al.*, 1978; Meikle, 1977; Polivy, 1977; Ray, 1977).

Rejection anxiety

Closely related to a damaged self-concept is the rejection anxiety experienced by some patients, as a result of the same conditions that threaten their body image, gender identity, and self-esteem. Thus, a young man may fear that any advances he might make to a girl are likely to be rejected because she finds his physical limitations or deformities so unattractive or repulsive. Similarly, a disabled married woman may fear that she will lose her husband's love and that their marriage may break up.

Partner discord

Sometimes, of course, there is a realistic basis for rejection anxiety; a potential or existing partner may find the disabled person to be unattractive because of his or her physical appearance, depressed mood or restricted ability to reciprocate positive reinforcement in any aspect of the couple's interaction. For instance, a patient's sexual inadequacy may deprive the partner of satisfaction in this aspect of the marriage, or a disablement might preclude a mutually acceptable sharing of childrearing, domestic, or occupational responsibilities, so that extra burdens fall upon the well partner. This may entail some reduction in family income, and perhaps disputes over the control of financial resources and expenditure. A couple's social activities and holidays are likely to suffer curtailment, so that their relationship becomes less rewarding in this respect. The handicapped person may be very dependent on the partner, and this can escalate into being overdemanding of help and attention with consequent restriction of the partner's autonomy and freedom. These can also be restricted for the disabled person by the gross overprotection exercised by some well partners, a particular example of this, cited earlier, is their unwillingness to resume sexual activity in case this might be harmful. Such overprotection has the additional unfortunate consequences of limiting the contribution a disabled person can make to the marriage, as well as reducing opportunities for pleasure and lowering self-esteem. For these, and many other possible reasons, there may be a particular risk of serious discord arising among couples in which there is a disabled partner, with possible adverse effects on their sexual relationships. However, this rather negative discussion should not be read as implying that serious discord is inevitable or even frequent in such marriages, they may well be perfectly stable and very rewarding to both partners. Indeed, the impact of illness could be largely determined by the quality of the marital relationship before its onset, so that good marriages are sustained and perhaps strengthened, while others may worsen and perhaps break up.

Avoidance reactions

The many stresses involved in chronic illness can also evoke avoidance reactions, so that a single disabled person may not make any attempt to establish sexual, or even social, relationships with members of the opposite sex, and a regime of abstinence from all sexual activity may be instituted and maintained by either or both partners in a marriage. In this context, it is worth noting that even minimal or very temporary impediments to sexual functioning arising from illness, are sometimes welcomed as personally and socially acceptable excuses for the permanent avoidance of sexual activity when this is stressful for some reason other than the illness.

Drugs

Sometimes the medication prescribed for a physical or psychological illness is wholly or partly responsible for an associated sexual dysfunction. This may be a direct effect of the drugs as discussed in Chapter 2, but there may be an additional contribution from the individual's psychological reactions to them. Thus, a temporary or partial impairment during the administration of tranquillizing, antidepressant, or antihypertensive medication, may be prolonged and exacerbated if it elicits performance anxiety and other stress reactions.

Probably by far the commonest example of the non-medical use of drugs contributing to a sexual dysfunction is the inability of the male to obtain an erection after drinking alcohol. If such failure causes him to become anxious about his performance in future, then this may impair his next attempt at intercourse, until this process results in the escalation of a temporary difficulty into a condition of chronic impotence. This kind of experience was reported by 35 out of the 213 men referred to Masters and Johnson (1970) with a complaint of secondary impotence. Sexual dysfunction can also be caused or aggravated by the marital discord that often accompanies alcohol abuse. This problem can have very deleterious effects on a family's socioeconomic circumstances, and it may lead to the rejection of the drinker by the other spouse, as well as to considerable friction between them; understandably, their sexual relationship may suffer as a result.

PSYCHIATRIC SYNDROMES

There appears to be a fairly commonly held view that any neurotic or psychotic condition is likely to lead to some disruption of sexual behaviour. For instance, the replies to questionnaires completed by 18 psychiatrists and 122 psychiatric inpatients indicated that more than four-fifths of the psychiatrists and 39% of the patients believed that most psychiatric disorders might interfere with sexual functioning, while more than two-thirds of the psychiatrists and a quarter of the patients thought that recovery from these disorders might be retarded by sexual activity (Pinderhughes et al., 1972). In these circumstances, it would not be surprising if some such patients were unnecessarily apprehensive about resuming sexual relations with their partners, so that the psychiatric disorder constitutes a stress condition producing reactions that may disrupt sexual behaviour in these cases.

However, such disruption is not an inevitable corollary of a psychiatric disorder. For instance, there is evidence from at least one controlled study to show that groups of psychotic and neurotic women may differ little from normal women in their sexual behaviour (Winokur et al., 1959). In this study, the various groups of such women did not differ significantly in respect of frequency of orgasm, enjoyment of coitus and incidence of dyspareunia, but a significantly higher proportion of the psychotics compared to the neurotics and controls had intercourse less than once a week.

Conversely, only a proportion of clients presenting with a sexual dysfunction are found to have an associated psychiatric disorder. This was an infrequent occurrence in a group of 20 couples treated by Masters and Johnson, and psychiatrically assessed by Maurice and Guze (1970). Similarly, among dysfunctional males, only 21 (5%) out of 486 were found to be psychiatrically disordered by Geboes et al. (1975a), and only 6 (11%) out of 53 were judged by Cooper (1968a) to be suffering from clinical neurosis. Finally, Munjack and Staples (1976) found a group of 44 women who were seeking treatment for orgastic dysfunction, to be identical to a normal comparison group in their psychological characteristics, and to be less neurotic than a group of psychiatric out-patients, except that the normal subjects were less depressed than the other two groups.

Furthermore, in several studies of women from the general population, no consistent relationship has been found between psychological disturbance and orgastic capacity (Fisher, 1973; Raboch and Bartak, 1968, b; Uddenberg, 1974). However, in one of these studies (Raboch and Bartak, 1968a) a particular group of inorgastic women was significantly more neurotic than a group of controls with good orgastic capacity. All the subjects were gynaecological patients, and they were allocated to one of three groups. The first consisting of 316 patients with good orgastic capacity constituted a control group, a second group of 279 women were inorgastic but did not experience intercourse as painful or distasteful, while this was the experience of another group of 69 inorgastic women who also had feelings of discomfort after intercourse. It was this last group which exhibited significantly more neurotic symptoms than the control subjects.

On this evidence, it seems reasonable to conclude that while a psychiatric disorder and a sexual dysfunction do co-exist in some individuals, there is not an inevitable association between the two types of problem. It remains to consider if they are especially strongly associated among patients exhibiting certain psychiatric syndromes that are commonly alleged to involve some impairment of sexual functioning.

Anxiety disorders

The disruptive effect of negative emotions such as anxiety and depression on sexual arousal is noted earlier, but somewhat surprisingly, there does not appear to be any adequate evidence for an association between anxiety neurosis and sexual dysfunction.

Indeed, among a group of 31 men and women who were chronic sufferers from this form of neurosis, there were few who had experienced any decrease in sexual activity, the majority found it gratifying, and some reported that it ameliorated their anxiety (Winokur and Holeman, 1963).

Depressive disorders

Perhaps even more unexpected is the paucity of systematic evidence on the frequently alleged association between depression and sexual dysfunction. The clinical literature contains many references to the impairment of sexual interest and performance in depressed patients, but empirical support for this is hard to find.

An exception is the study by Cassidy et al. (1957) of 34 men and 66 women who were diagnosed as suffering from manic-depressive psychosis, and compared with 50 medically sick control subjects. Sexual function was reported to have decreased in 63% of the manic-depressives and in 39% of the controls. Within the manic-depressive group, 83% of the males, and 53% of the females, had experienced a decrease in libido.

In those cases where depression and sexual dysfunction do co-exist, the individual concerned could have become depressed as a reaction to the dysfunction, or this may be symptomatic of the affective disorder.

Hysterical disorders

There is more evidence for an association between hysterical neurosis and sexual dysfunction, although they are not invariably linked (Winokur and Leonard, 1963). In a study by Purtell *et al.* (1951), 50 women with a diagnosis of hysteria were compared to groups of healthy or medically ill control subjects. Sexual problems of various kinds were reported by 98% of the hysterics and 52% of the medically ill controls. These problems included sexual indifference in 86% of the hysterics and 29% of the healthy controls, an absence of sexual pleasure in 73% of the hysterics compared to 15% of the healthy controls, and dyspareunia in 63% of the hysterics but in only 7% of healthy controls.

Another group of 14 women with a previous diagnosis of hysteria were studied by Winokur and Leonard (1963) who compared their findings with those of Kinsey *et al.* (1953) in respect of the general population. The sexual lives of the hysterics were not unusual during the premarital and early marital stages, but thereafter there was a marked deterioration manifested in unusual decreases in frequency of intercourse and incidence of orgasm. Additionally, there were complaints of dyspareunia from 11 (76%) of the hysterics, an incidence that can be compared to those of 19% for patients suffering from anxiety neurosis (Winokur and Holeman, 1963), and of 7% and 15% for normal women as reported by Purtell *et al.* (1951) and Winokur *et al.* (1959) respectively.

Why hysterics appear to be relatively more prone to difficulties in their sexual lives, and in particular why these seem to deteriorate after the early stages of marriage, are unanswerable questions at the present time (Winokur and Leonard, 1963). One possibility is that sexuality becomes increasingly stressful to them as the marriage progresses, perhaps because it involves a more threatening degree of intimacy with the partner (Levay and Kagle, 1977). Another, is that their neurotic behaviour causes increasing marital discord (Bergner, 1977), which is reflected in the impairment of sexual functioning. The entirely speculative nature of these and other possible explanations must be emphasized in the light of the current lack of evidence.

DEFICIENT OR FALSE INFORMATION

In Chapter 3, we see that previous learning conditions such as traumatic experiences, a restrictive upbringing or adverse family relationships, may deprive individuals of sufficient knowledge about sexuality or transmit false information to them on this topic. Moreover, even if adequate knowledge does become available, it may be so stressful to some individuals that they engage in the avoidance reactions of ignoring, distorting, forgetting, or failing to discuss the material with their partner. However they arise, it seems clear that ignorance and misconceptions can contribute to sexual dysfunction. Many common sources for these are discussed in Chapter 8 in the context of the provision of information during interviews, and at the present stage they are merely exemplified by certain cultural myths about sexual functioning that have been described and rebutted by Masters and Johnson (1966).

One of these myths is the notion of two different types of female orgasm, one being produced by direct stimulation of the clitoris and the other by the movement of the penis in the vagina. The implication that the latter type is normal and superior, may lead to excessive importance being attached to a wife achieving orgasm exclusively by means of her husband's penile thrusting, when some direct stimulation of the clitoris would be more effective for her. Similarly, some couples may strive constantly to attain the simultaneous orgasm that they consider to be the normal and expected culmination of every act of sexual intercourse, consequently this may be disrupted by performance anxiety and spectatoring. These reactions may be evoked also by unrealistic beliefs about sexual capacity; for instance, that men are able to obtain erections and engage in intercourse at all times, with any partner and in any circumstances. A final example is the misconception which is still not uncommon among men complaining of sexual dysfunction, that their penis is unusually small and that this is adversely affecting their ability to satisfy their partner, as well as signifying a lack of virility (Toussieng, 1977). In fact, of course, Masters and Johnson (1966) have shown that there is little individual variation in penile size during erections, and in any case this is quite unrelated to female satisfaction and male virility.

DEFICIENT OR INAPPROPRIATE STIMULATION

Some clients may be dysfunctional because they lack adequate and appropriate stimulation to achieve satisfactory arousal and orgasm. Thus, a couple's foreplay may be insufficiently prolonged and sensitive to the wife's individual preferences for her to become aroused, or she may be inorgastic because she does not receive the direct clitoral stimulation she needs to reach climax. Such gaps in lovemaking may arise from sheer ignorance, for example, about the importance of foreplay or clitoral stimulation to the woman concerned, or activities such as these may be so stressful that they evoke reactions that prevent their performance. These might include the physical avoidance of the activities and a reluctance to communicate a desire for them to the partner, as well as their deliberate withholding as an act of aggression in certain cases of marital discord.

One category of clients who are particularly subject to deficient stimulation are the physically handicapped. In the next chapter, we see that they and their partners often require specific advice about alternative positions for intercourse, a variety of non-coital practices, and the use of prostheses such as vibrators.

The possibility of older males constituting a similar vulnerable category is raised in an interesting paper by Edwards and Husted (1976). They suggest that the aging process may involve a slow, progressive loss of tactile sensitivity, so that older men become more dependent on other sensory and imaginary sources of sexual stimulation. As a preliminary investigation of this hypothesis, the authors ascertained the vibratory thresholds of 20 male volunteers aged 19 to 58 years, and found a significant positive correlation of 0.49 between penile sensitivity and age. Furthermore, penile sensitivity was negatively correlated with the frequency of sexual intercourse recorded by the subjects over a four week period, and this correlation persisted even with age partialled out, although Edwards and Husted are careful to point out that a causal relationship cannot be inferred. They also discuss the desirability of assessing the tactile sensitivity of sexually dysfunctional men and the speculative possibility of enhancing this by chemical means, as well as reporting that an attempt to conduct a similar investigation with a group of women was unsuccessful because vibration of the clitoris proved too erotic to yield reliable data.

A proportion of people are dependent on various unconventional activities, phantasies, or partners for satisfactory sexual functioning, so that this is impaired if these particular forms of stimulation are lacking during lovemaking. Some examples would include a male transvestite's preference for wearing female clothing during intercourse, the use of sadomasochistic phantasies in order to enhance arousal and reach climax, and the need for a partner of the same sex among those who are predominantly homosexually oriented. As far as the last condition is concerned, Masters and Johnson (1966) ascribed an aetiological role to homosexuality in the case of one woman who was not orgastic with her husband, in two others suffering from vaginismus, as well as in the cases of 6 out of 32 men presenting with primary impotence and 21 out of 213 with secondary impotence. These complaints of impotence referred of course to impairments of erection during lovemaking with female partners, and the men concerned may well have had no such difficulty with males, although an unknown proportion of individuals with homosexual preferences do experience some impairment of their sexual functioning with members of their own sex.

Table 3. Causation of sexual dysfunction

Organic Factors
1. Illness
2. Surgery
3. Drugs

Previous Learning Experiences
4. Traumatic experiences
5. Restrictive upbringing
6. Adverse family relationships

Contemporary Conditions
7. Psychological stresses
8. Partner discord
9. Psychological reactions to organic factors
10. Psychiatric syndromes
11. Deficient or false information
12. Deficient or inappropriate stimulation

CONCLUSION

A behavioural approach to the causation of sexual dysfunction is presented in Chapters 2, 3 and 4, and summarized in Table 3. It is conceptualized as resulting from the interaction of a variety of organic factors, previous learning experiences and contemporary conditions.

Certain illnesses or drugs can impair sexual functioning directly, and this may also result from the individual's psychological reactions to such organic factors as well as to the natural changes of the aging process.

Previous experiences of a traumatic, restrictive or interpersonal nature, may constitute learning conditions that adversely affect a person's later sexual responses in certain contemporary conditions.

These include the various kinds of stress that are summarized in Table 4, as well as certain psychiatric disorders and deficiences of information or stimulation. The impaired sexual behaviour is initiated and maintained by such current conditions, and they constitute important influences on its definition as dysfunctional.

In subsequent chapters, the implications of this aetiological approach for the assessment and treatment of sexual dysfunction are examined.

Table 4. Stress and sexual dysfunction

Stress Conditions

1. Sexual stresses

    (a) anatomy/responses
    (b) anticipation of harm
    (c) anticipation of failure
    (d) moral/religious contraventions

2. Non-sexual stresses
3. Partner discord
4. Organic factors

Stress Reactions

1. Emotional

    (a) anxiety
    (b) depression
    (c) guilt
    (d) anger

2. Overt

    (a) avoidance
    (b) aggression

3. Cognitive

    (a) avoidance
    (b) monitoring

Part 2

The Dysfunctions

5

Definition and Classification

The present chapter is devoted to the general issues of defining and classifying sexual dysfunctions, while the following two chapters contain discussion of the nature and causes of particular dysfunctions in males and females respectively.

DEFINITION

Sexual failure of varying severity is probably experienced by most people at some time in their lives. Many young men ejaculate very quickly during their early sexual encounters. The inability to obtain or sustain an erection is a frequent accompaniment of tiredness or drinking. Women may engage in intercourse and even enjoy it although they do not reach orgasm on some or all occasions. A married couple may have sex much less often than their neighbours, or an elderly couple less often than when they were younger. A marriage may not have been consummated after many years because the wife's vaginal muscles contract to prevent penetration whenever she is approached sexually by the husband she loves.

At what point do such failures amount to a sexual dysfunction, and how is this to be defined when there are no absolute standards of sexual competence and satisfaction? One approach is to regard it as sexual behaviour that is judged to be inadequate by the client or other people. No one is expected to be completely competent and satisfied on all occasions, therefore a less than perfect performance is not sufficient in itself to constitute a dysfunction. Additionally, there must be some subjective judgement of inadequacy, and this may be influenced by a variety of factors which have not been systematically investigated but are likely to include: the nature of the sexual behaviour, the context in which it occurs, its consequences, the extent to which it deviates from normative standards, and certain personal characteristics of the client and other judges.

Nature of the behaviour

This emphasis on the subjective nature of judgements of inadequacy does not imply that the actual behaviour is unimportant, only that it is not sufficient in itself to define sexual dysfunction. The main forms of behaviour that may be judged to be dysfunctional are introduced in Chapter 1, and described further in Chapters 6 and 7. They include various impairments of erection or ejaculation in men, of vasocongestion or orgasm in women, and of interest and pleasure in both sexes. Some of the criteria that are likely to be applied in judging the adequacy or otherwise of these components of sexual behaviour are discussed in the following sections.

Context of the behaviour

Few people would expect themselves or others to be sexually competent and satisfied in response to every form of stimulation, with any partner, at any time, and in any setting. Therefore the context of the sexual behaviour provides a number of criteria for judging its adequacy.

A wide range of visual, manual, oral, and genital activities, as well as erotic phantasies, can be sexually stimulating, and there is considerable individual variation in response to these. Most commonly, it is some difficulty in responding adequately to sexual intercourse that leads to a complaint of dysfunction, although similar difficulties may also be experienced in response to other activities such as masturbation.

Sexual response is likely to be judged inadequate if it is insufficient in relation to stimulation which the client or others expect to be more effective. For instance, consistent failure to reach orgasm after an appropriate period of pleasurable engagement in foreplay and intercourse might be regarded as inadequate, whereas such failure during more hurried or less enjoyable experiences would not be so regarded. Similarly, a man who is homosexually oriented might be more concerned over his failure to respond to sexual stimulation from another man, than if this occurred during a heterosexual encounter.

This leads to partner suitability as a factor influencing judgements of inadequacy. These are perhaps less likely to be made if the sexual difficulty is restricted to encounters with a partner who is considered to be unsuitable by the person making the judgement. Thus, a wife might not consider herself to be sexually dysfunctional because she cannot reach climax with a husband whom she dislikes and resents, while retaining the capacity to do so with some other more attractive and loved partner. In contrast, another client may not consider himself dysfunctional because he has difficulty in obtaining an erection during an extra-marital encounter which evokes considerable guilt and anxiety, when no such impairment is experienced in his relationships with his wife.

Several temporal variables are likely to be relevant in judging the adequacy or otherwise of a person's sexual functioning. Some of these relate to the sexual responses *per se*; for instance, if a man cannot maintain an erection at least until he reaches climax himself, then this would certainly be considered dysfunctional in many cases. Similarly, if a man ejaculates before, or at the point of, intromission, then again this is likely to be regarded as an inadequate way of responding. In deciding whether or not a client is suffering from retarded or absent ejaculation, one would take into account the duration of his exposure to sexual stimulation without reaching climax. The expected duration of the refractory period would need to be considered in judging a man's failure to achieve a second erection and ejaculation within a short interval of time.

Another relevant time factor is the persistence of the impaired sexual behaviour. Sometimes this is adversely affected during menstruation, pregnancy or the post-partum period, and transitory failure is a common experience that occurs for very many reasons including the consumption of alcohol, fatigue, and life stresses of various kinds. Such temporary or intermittent fluctuations do not usually lead to a complaint of sexual dysfunction.

Last among these temporal variables is the frequency of the behaviour being judged. Thus, in a later section on orgastic dysfunction we note some evidence that most women reach climax during only a proportion of their experiences of sexual intercourse, and that this proportion increases from about 63% in the first year of marriage to about 85% in the twentieth year (Kinsey *et al.*, 1953). Such evidence may suggest that even quite frequent failure to reach climax might not be regarded as a sign of significant sexual dysfunction, especially during the early period of a marriage. We see in another later section on inadequate sexual interest that this problem is a fairly common complaint among clients seeking treatment for sexual dysfunction, but there is also some evidence to suggest that a low frequency of intercourse is not in itself usually considered to constitute sexual inadequacy among people in the general population. For example, in one English sample of such couples aged 16 to 45 years, the actual rate varied from at least once daily (1%) to less than two or three times a month (8%), with a median of twice a week. However, most of the couples considered their own frequency to be average whatever their actual rate. Even among those whose frequency was less than two or three times a month there were 39% who considered this to be about average (Gorer, 1971).

Next, certain conditions in the setting where the sexual behaviour occurs may influence judgements of inadequacy. For example, some difficulty in responding when there is a risk of being interrupted or overheard by another person, could well militate against such a judgement. This might also be less likely if the individual concerned considered the setting to be too brightly lit or lacking in a romantic ambience. Similarly, a girl's failure to respond sexually in the uncomfortable conditions of a cramped small car on a cold night would probably not be regarded too seriously.

Consequences of the behaviour

The occurrence of various adverse consequences that often accompany impaired sexual behaviour is likely to increase the probability of it being defined as a dysfunction. If the behaviour is physically painful for the individual concerned there is a high probability of it being judged inadequate, and this is also likely to happen when strong feelings of disappointment, humiliation, anxiety, guilt, depression, or anger, are evoked by a sexual difficulty. A related criterion for inadequacy is the extent of any damage to the person's self-concept.

For example, a man's self-esteem may be lowered by feelings of humiliation and inferiority arising from his inability to obtain or maintain an erection, and his sense of gender identity may be impaired by this failure to meet the sexual aspects of the masculine role. If such an incapacity becomes known publicly it may markedly lower a man's social status, especially in groups whose members attach a high value to virility. Indeed, it is a fear of such demeaning exposure to their friends that precipitates many single clients into seeking treatment.

Many other requests for treatment arise from the concern, frustration, and disturbance being experienced by the partner of the main client. It is quite usual for a partner to share in the kind of distressing feelings and damage to the self-concept that are described in the previous paragraph, especially if the sexual problem is attributed to some deficiency in his or her attractiveness or lovemaking skills. In consequence, the partner may interpret the problem as signifying rejection, and perhaps as threatening desertion, by the client.

In view of such reactions by both partners to some difficulty in their sexual relationship, it is readily understandable that considerable discord may arise in their general relationship, and this is another factor that often seems to contribute to a judgement of sexual inadequacy and a request for treatment. In particular, the feelings of rejection, resentment and anger that are commonly evoked in the partner of a sexually dysfunctional client are very likely to cause friction between them, and this topic is discussed at greater length in Chapter 4.

Deviance of the behaviour

Sexual behaviour that deviates from normative standards of various kinds is liable to be considered inadequate. Thus, impaired behaviour that is a symptom of any of the organic disorders discussed in Chapter 2, would be regarded as a deviation from the health standard that demands an absence of pathology. Any sexual difficulty, such as vaginismus or erectile dysfunction, that prevents the consummation of a marriage, would contravene legal norms and constitute grounds for a decree of nullity in England and many other countries. Similarly, according to the norms of many religions, the performance of sexual intercourse is an important purpose of marriage and an obligation on both partners. Consequently, an inability to engage in intercourse is a transgression of these norms and often an impediment to entering marriage as well as a reason for its dissolution. A definition and complaint of sexual dysfunction may also ensue when the impaired behaviour is relatively infrequent according to statistical norms. Two examples of these are the frequencies of orgasm and of intercourse in marriage that are cited above, and another is the incidence of failure to reach climax among married women that is discussed in a later section on orgastic dysfunction. Unfortunately, little information is available about the occurrence of various forms of sexual behaviour in general populations, and its value is often limited by biases in sampling and data collection.

This leads to the important influence of social norms for sexual behaviour on judgements of inadequacy. For instance, married couples are usually expected to engage in sexual intercourse and a persistent inability to do so is very likely to be considered dysfunctional. Moreover, there is evidence indicating that this expectation of successful intercourse is now widely held to apply within premarital relationships (Libby, 1977; Reiss, 1977; Zuckerman, 1976), and the establishment of this norm may increase the prevalence of feelings of inadequacy among those for whom premarital sex is unacceptable or difficult on personal, moral, or religious grounds.

Not only are successful sexual relationships prescribed within marriage, and increasingly before marriage, but it is possible that the so-called 'sexual revolution' has raised the expected standards of skill and gratification in these encounters. I do not know of any systematic evidence for recent change in this respect, but the popular literature and clinical impression would certainly suggest that men are expected to be able to 'give' a woman an orgasm, and she is expected to be able to achieve climax on one or more occasions during an encounter. Individuals who fall short of such standards in some degree, are liable to feel sexually inadequate and may seek therapeutic help. For instance, Ginsberg *et al.* (1972), in a paper entitled *TheNew Impotence*, claim that complaints of impotence are more frequent than they used to be, although they do not present any supporting evidence for this statement. They go on to suggest that this increased incidence may reflect a change from an earlier view that sex is primarily a source of pleasure for the male, to a current expectation of orgastic release for the female which she actively seeks for herself. Some vulnerable men are unable to cope with this enhanced demand for performance, or with the loss of the complete control that they formerly exercised over sexual activity, and complaints of impotence may result.

Characteristics of the client

Personal characteristics such as the age and sex of the client may influence judgements of inadequacy. Thus, in Chapter 2 it is noted that certain natural changes occur in the sexual response cycles of men and women as they become older. For instance, men do not obtain erections as rapidly as they did earlier in their lives, and they do not feel a subjective need to reach climax as frequently as before. Providing such changes are recognized as part of the natural aging process, they are not likely to be considered as signs of inadequacy in an older man, whereas similar changes in someone younger might be thought to indicate a dysfunction.

We note above that the Victorian ideas (Taylor, 1959) of women being less interested and less gratified in sexual activity than men are probably becoming less prevalent, but they are still held by some individuals, who may therefore be more ready to define inadequate interest or pleasure as dysfunctions in men than in women.

An additional factor that could increase the probability of a dysfunction being defined in males compared to females, is that the impaired behaviour is more likely to preclude participation in intercourse by a man. For example, this is impossible for him if he cannot obtain an erection or if he ejaculates before intromission is accomplished. In contrast, a woman who does not lubricate adequately can engage in and enjoy intercourse with the assistance of an artificial lubricant, and one who cannot reach orgasm is at least able to participate in intercourse and it may still be a pleasurable experience for her.

Characteristics of the judge

A wide range of people, including clients themselves, are involved in the evaluation of sexual adequacy and the judge's own personal characteristics can affect their decisions. One relevant characteristic is the role of the judge in relation to the client, for this may affect the priority given to different criteria. Clients judging themselves may emphasize certain adverse consequences of an impairment, such as insufficient pleasure, distress, pain or lowered self-esteem. A spouse may emphasize the client's dependence on unconventional stimulation for the satisfactory performance of coitus, or the deleterious effect of an impairment on the marriage. Relatives or friends may attach importance to a couple's failure to conceive a child. Physicians are likely to concentrate on impairments that are symptoms of organic pathology. Lawyers and clergymen may be especially concerned with the non-consummation of a marriage. Therapists involved in the treatment of sexual dysfunction should make broadly based judgements of adequacy, and their greater familiarity with the wide range of individual variation in sexual response and the available statistical norms may inform their assessments of particular clients.

It is possible that younger people are more prone to consider any less than perfect sexual behaviour to amount to a dysfunction. Their elders may tend to have greater experience and understanding of the variable nature of the sexual response, and the level of sexual performance may not feature so prominently in their evaluation of a person's overall adjustment to life.

Conclusion

The upshot of this discussion is that the definition of sexual dysfunction is a complex process, involving not only the actual behaviour concerned but also subjective evaluations of inadequacy made according to a variety of criteria by a range of judges. The behaviour itself may consist of some impairment of interest, arousal, orgasm, ejaculation, or pleasure, and it most usually leads to judgement of inadequacy if the act of coitus is affected. This judgement is more likely if the impairment occurs persistently, despite satisfactory stimulation, with a suitable partner and in an appropriate setting. Other important contributory factors include any adverse consequences of the impairment and the extent of its deviation from normative standards of various kinds. It seems probable that judgements of inadequacy are influenced by certain personal characteristics of the client and of other judges, although this has not yet been demonstrated.

CLASSIFICATION

There are a number of reasons for attempting to classify sexual dysfunctions. It is an essential first step in the study of any kind of behaviour, for it reduces the complexity of a bewildering range of responses by arranging them into some meaningful and more manageable system of categories. The necessary definition of the behaviour to be included in each category also permits its subsequent measurement and facilitates communication between professionals working in the field. Moreover, such classificatory schemes have heuristic value for they highlight topics needing further study, and assist in the acquisition of new information.

The classification proposed in this book and presented in Table 5 is predicated on two assumptions. One of these is that various aspects of sexual behaviour can be separately impaired; including interest, arousal, intromission, orgasm, ejaculation, and pleasure. The second assumption is that most of these aspects can be disrupted in different ways, yielding several categories of dysfunction in males and females respectively. Both these assumptions stay close to the observational data described in Chapters 2, 6, and 7, rather than being derived from any theoretical approach to sexual dysfunction.

Table 5. Categories of sexual dysfunction

Aspect	Male	Female
Interest	Inadequate sexual interest	Inadequate sexual interest
Arousal or intromission	Erectile dysfunction	Vasocongestive dysfunction
		Vaginismus
Orgasm or ejaculation	Premature ejaculation	
	Retarded or absent ejaculation	Orgastic dysfunction
	Retrograde ejaculation	
Pleasure	Inadequate sexual pleasure	Inadequate sexual pleasure
	Dyspareunia	Dyspareunia

It should be noted that this classification categorizes problems not people, so that more than one problem may co-exist in the same individual, and to say that someone has a particular problem or problems does not necessarily imply anything more about that person. Thus, a woman may suffer from both a vasocongestive and an orgastic dysfunction, and to say that she has either or both these problems does not imply that she is a 'frigid' person who is incapable of emotional warmth in her relationships with others.

A corollary of this last point is that categorizing a problem does not entirely determine its treatment. We see in Chapter 12, that similar problems are treated in different ways, because the clients who exhibit these problems are very varied in terms of their personal characteristics and life situations. Nevertheless, the heuristic value of a classification is noted above, and one example of this is the stimulation and facilitation of the development and evaluation of a range of methods for treating certain categories of dysfunction. For instance, the establishment of inadequate interest and inadequate pleasure as distinct categories, immediately reveals the paucity of methods for their treatment and the undemonstrated effectiveness of these procedures.

The classification in Table 5 is based solely upon the definition of the problems in each category, and contains no inferences about the causes of these problems. this is typical of initial classifications in the early stages of study in a particular field, but problems must be defined before their causes can be investigated, and once they are defined then the need to explain them becomes more obvious. In this way classificatory schemes can serve the heuristic function of stimulating and facilitating the study of the causes of different sexual dysfunctions.

In common with other current classifications, the proposed scheme has two major limitations that need to be remedied. One of these is a complete lack of data on the reliability of the system. The extent to which different therapists would agree on the assignment of a client's problems to certain categories is not known. The second limitation concerns the incompleteness of the definitions of the problems in each category. Much fuller information is needed both about the dimensions of the actual behaviour, in terms of its amplitude, duration, frequency, latency, and threshold, and about the factors entering into the subjective judgements of its inadequacy. This point is amply illustrated in the next two chapters.

6

Male Dysfunctions

In this chapter, the male sexual dysfunctions are described and their causes are discussed. The problems covered are inadequate sexual interest, erectile dysfunction, premature ejaculation, retarded or absent ejaculation, retrograde ejaculation, inadequate sexual pleasure, and dyspareunia.

INADEQUATE SEXUAL INTEREST

A client's level of sexual interest may be considered to be inadequate by himself or by his partner. This problem has been referred to by Kaplan (1977b) as 'hypoactive sexual desire' or 'low libido', and by Lief (1977a) as 'inhibited sexual desire'. Their papers constitute significant early communications about a problem that has only just begun to be studied systematically, although it is a relatively common complaint among clients seeking treatment for sexual dysfunction.

For instance, among 486 men presenting at a Belgian clinic (Geboes et al., 1975a), there were 51 (10%) who mentioned loss of libido as their main complaint, although this problem also occurred in conjunction with an erectile or ejaculatory dysfunction in other patients. Those for whom it was the main complaint ranged in age from 25 to 57 years, with an average of 40 years. In another sample of 115 patients presenting at the Marriage Council of Philadelphia (Lief, 1977a), there were 32 (27.8%) who were given a primary diagnosis of inhibited sexual desire. This was the highest percentage in any diagnostic group, and represented 37% of the female patients and 18.7% of the males.

At present, little is known about any differences between males and females in respect of inadequate sexual interest, therefore most of the following discussion is applicable to both sexes.

Description

In the absence of any absolute or prescriptive standards of sexual interest, this can only be defined as inadequate on the basis of the subjective judgements of those concerned. Most people probably experience periods of disinterest in sex, perhaps when they are ill, fatigued, or preoccupied with other more immediately pressing matters, and such temporary fluctuations are not usually considered to constitute a sexual problem for which treatment might be sought. Moreover, there are marriages in which a sexual relationship does not play a significant role, and where its relative or complete absence is not a source of distress for either partner (Martin, 1977). In other cases however, a low level of sexual interest is very disturbing to the individual concerned or to his or her partner, and it may lead to complaints of indifference towards sex, of lack of desire, or of disparity between the partners in this respect, for which treatment is requested.

Such problems of inadequate sexual interest may or may not be accompanied by other forms of sexual dysfunction. Some men and women will rarely, if ever, experience any desire for sexual activity or initiate it themselves, but they are able to function adequately and pleasurably when they do find themselves in a sexual encounter, usually at the instigation of a partner. In other clients, inadequate interest may be associated, for example, with an inability to become aroused, to reach climax, or to experience pleasurable feelings during sexual activity.

Inadequate sexual interest may be global or situational, in that some clients do not experience desire under any circumstances, while others do so only in specific conditions. For example, a wife might have no desire for sex with a husband whom she dislikes or resents, but her sexual interest may remain unimpaired in relation to other potential partners. Similarly, a man might be uninterested in a conventional sexual relationship with his wife, but still experience strong desires for some form of unconventional sexual stimulation, such as that provided during homosexual, paedophiliac, or sado-masochistic activities.

Among the consequences of inadequate sexual interest are certain common reactions by the individual concerned and by his or her partner (Kaplan, 1977b). Sometimes the former individual simply acquiesces to the partner's sexual advances, and responds to them either with tolerant indifference, or, as we have seen, in some cases with arousal and pleasure. Other individuals will strongly avoid sexual encounters, towards which they have markedly aversive reactions of anxiety, disgust or anger. At present, there is no systematic evidence on any possible sex differences in these reactions, but Kaplan suggests that men may be more prone to avoid sex, because of their fear of performance failure when they are uninterested; while women may tend towards passive acquiescence, perhaps because they enjoy the affectional and sensual components of an encounter, if not its erotic aspects, as well as because of a possible fear of losing the partner if they do not yield to his demands. Turning to the reactions of the partners of inadequately interested clients, these range from a sympathetic, and concerned understanding of the problem, through to feelings of rejection, frustration, hurt, and anger; such negative reactions perhaps being especially likely when the lack of interest is construed as an adverse reflection on the attractiveness or virility of the partner, or when his or her sexual approaches are consistently refused.

In some clients, the inadequate sexual interest appears to be primary, in that they have never experienced much desire or engaged in any fairly common activities such as childhood sex play, masturbation, phantasizing, perusing erotic material, petting, and pre-marital intercourse. Other clients seem to have experienced and exhibited an adequate degree of sexual interest until some specific point in their lives, at which their interest declined to an unacceptable level. The onset of a secondary problem of this kind might have coincided with any of a wide variety of circumstances, many of which are mentioned in the next section; for example, getting engaged or married to a previously interesting partner, becoming pregnant or giving birth to a child, or suffering a depressive reaction for some reason.

Causation

Very many of the factors discussed in Part 1 may contribute to inadequate sexual interest. In the first place, this might arise as a direct physical effect of certain organic factors, or indirectly through the client's psychological reactions to them. Thus, any general systemic illness that is debilitating, disabling, or distressing, such as a renal disorder, might be accompanied by loss of sexual interest, or more specifically this may arise from an endocrine condition such as Cushing's syndrome. Similarly, we have seen that low interest is sometimes associated with the administration of certain forms of psychotropic or antihypertensive medication, and that it has been reported as a side effect of oral contraceptives. Among the surgical interventions that may be followed by inadequate sexual interest are hysterectomy and mastectomy in women, prostatectomy in men, and ostomy operations in both sexes. Certain non-pathological organic conditions such as pregnancy (Lief, 1977b) or normal aging may also be accompanied by a loss of sexual interest in some individuals. Finally, it is conceivable that there are individual differences of a constitutional nature in levels of sexual interest, and that this might account for the apparently lifelong lack of desire and activity exhibited by some clients. However, it is impossible to separate the influence of any such innate factors from the contribution of learning experiences, and the existence of constitutional differences in sexual interest is at present entirely speculative.

A second group of causes of inadequate sexual interest involves psychological stresses of a sexual or non-sexual nature, as described in Chapter 4. For instance, a client who anticipates that sexual activity will prove unpleasant, harmful or unsuccessful, may well avoid these threats by losing interest in sex, and this avoidance reaction may occur at both an overt and cognitive level. Similarly, a client's preoccupation with a serious occupational or domestic problem may prelude or reduce his or her interest in sex.

Partner discord is perhaps one of the commonest reasons for a loss of interest in sex. It is very understandable that this may occur if the sexual partner becomes sexually unattractive for some reason, or when there is considerable resentment, anger or hostility between the partners. In such circumstances, the inadequate interest may be restricted to the spouse, and sexual desire may remain unaffected as far as masturbatory activities and extra-marital affairs are concerned.

Depression is another commonly cited cause of inadequate sexual interest, although the paucity of systematic evidence is noted in Chapter 4. According to Lief (1977c), depression may be more damaging to sexual desire than to sexual performance, impairment of the latter often being secondary to inhibited desire. A number of possible explanations for any association between depression and diminished desire are discussed by Spencer and Raft (1977). They suggest that depressive states commonly involve some diminution of the capacities for pleasure, intimacy, motor activity, initiative, assertiveness, risktaking, and humour, all of which are essential aspects of sexual interest and experience. In particular, a depressed client may lose his capacities to engage in, and to enjoy, sexual phantasizing, which plays a vital role in sexual stimulation. Furthermore, some depressed clients may lose interest in sex as a means of depriving and punishing themselves, because they feel undeserving and guilty. Somewhat paradoxically, this may result in the accentuation of these feelings, because the clients may then blame themselves for denying sexual satisfaction to their spouse and for not being a good wife or husband. At a physiological level, it is possible though not yet established, that diminished sexual interest may be due to certain changes in amine levels in the hypothalamus which occur in depressed patients.

Another kind of psychological problem that may be accompanied by a loss of interest in sex are the intimacy dysfunctions (Levay and Kagle, 1977) described in Chapter 11, in which clients have difficulty in functioning sexually under conditions of involvement and commitment with a regular partner, although they may be able to do so quite adequately during relatively impersonal or transient sexual encounters. As the latter give way to an increasingly close and stable relationship during courtship, engagement, and marriage, there may be progressive loss of interest in sex on the part of the primarily affected partner towards the other.

Next, inadequate sexual interest may arise in conditions of deficient or inappropriate stimulation. Those individuals who require unconventional forms of stimulation for satisfactory sexual functioning, may well lack interest in sexual relationships that do not provide these conditions; thus, a predominantly homosexually oriented person may present with inadequate sexual interest within a heterosexual partnership. Another instance of ineffective stimulation that may contribute to loss of interest is the progressive boredom with sex that develops in some marriages, and Goldberg (1977) suggests a number of possible reasons for this. The intense excitement of forbidden and relatively hard to get premarital sexual encounters may not attach to legitimate and readily available sexual opportunities over a lengthy period. During such a time, sexual relationships may also tend to become routinized and lacking in variety. Role conflict may develop between being a steady and reliable spouse, a responsible and dedicated parent, and an ardent and exciting lover, so that a couple may overwhelmingly relate to each other in their roles as spouses and parents, to the detriment of their roles as lovers.

In conclusion, it should be noted that if sexual activity is reduced for any reason whatsoever, then there will be some loss of the rewards contingent upon that activity. If the reinforcement schedule becomes too thin, then the individual's interest and engagement in sexual activity may not be maintained and extinction might occur. Thus, the reinforced practice of sexual responses is likely to be a vital factor in sustaining adequate interest in their performance.

INADEQUATE AROUSAL OR INTROMISSION

Erectile dysfunction

Description

Erectile dysfunction or impotence involves some impairment of the erection phase of the male sexual response cycle, so that vasocongestion of the penis does not proceed normally. It might be defined as a persistent inability to obtain a sufficiently firm erection, or to maintain this during intromission and intercourse. Clearly, such a definition leaves much room for subjective judgements of inadequacy. Some experience of erectile failure is probably universal among men, and when this is to be regarded as persistent enough to merit seeking treatment is a matter for judgement by those concerned. Similarly, some men can only obtain partial erections, and whether these are considered to be in-sufficiently firm may well be strongly influenced by the man's capacity to achieve intromission. Finally, there is the question of how long the partners expect the man's erection to be maintained during intercourse, and this is certainly likely to be judged too short a period if the erection is lost before the man reaches his own climax.

The definition of erectile dysfunction used and the subjective judgements involved will undoubtedly affect any estimate of its incidence, and reliable figures are virtually non-existent at the present time. Perhaps the best estimate available is still that reported thirty years ago by Kinsey and his associates (Kinsey *et al.*, 1948). Among a group of 4108 males, aged 10 to over 80 years, they were 66 who were considered to be more or less totally, and to all appearances, permanently impotent. According to this definition, the incidence rates for impotence were 1.3% by age 35 years, 6.7% by age 50, 18.4% by age 60, 27% by age 70, and 55% by age 75 years.

An impairment of erectile capacity may or may not be accompanied by other forms of sexual dysfunction. Thus, an impotent client may still experience strong sexual desires although he is unable to get an erection, or his level of sexual interest may also be considered to be inadequate. Likewise, such a client may or may not be able to ejaculate through his flaccid or semi-erect penis.

There are individual differences in the timing of erectile failure, some clients cannot obtain an erection at any time during a sexual encounter, while others can obtain an erection initially but lose it subsequently, perhaps at the point of intromission or during intercourse.

These differences in the timing of erectile failure point up the importance of the surrounding circumstances in determining its occurrence. Presumably certain causal influences operate to precipitate a failure in certain circumstances, and this will not occur when these circumstances are not present. Thus most impotent clients are able to obtain and maintain erections on some occasions; for instance, during sleep, on waking, while masturbating, when an attempt at intercourse is impossible; or with a particular partner, whether this be a wife, a mistress, or a prostitute. It is rare for a client to be unable to obtain an erection under any circumstances.

For most men, erectile dysfunction is an extremely frustrating, embarrassing, and humiliating problem to which they commonly react with anxiety, depression, and the avoidance of sexual encounters. Their confidence, self-esteem and gender identity are all likely to be impaired. As far as the wives of impotent men are concerned, sometimes they are very understanding, sympathetic, and supportive, but sooner or later they may come to share many of the negative reactions experienced by their husbands. In particular, a wife may feel that she is no longer loved and attractive, which may lead her to seek reassurance by increasing her sexual demands upon her partner (Clifford, 1977).

Some clients have never been able to obtain and maintain an erection during intercourse with a partner, although they may be able to do so during masturbation or at other times. This pattern is customarily referred to as primary erectile dysfunction, while the secondary form includes those clients whose erectile capacity with a partner was at one time adequate, but who became impaired at some later stage. Primary erectile dysfunction is much rarer than the secondary type; for instance, only 32 out of the 243 impotent clients treated by Masters and Johnson (1970) were categorized as primary in nature.

Several writers have also classified erectile dysfunction according to whether its onset was of an acute or insidious nature, and we see later that this distinction may have aetiological, therapeutic, and prognostic significance. Cooper (1968b) has described a group of 8 cases of acute onset in which the initial erectile failure had occurred in response to a discrete physical or psychological precipitant, such as the honeymoon for 3 sexually ignorant and previously chaste clients, or attempts at intercourse in unsuitable circumstances by 5 previously experienced and competent clients. The average age at referral in this acute onset group was 25.3 years (range 19–30 years), all the clients had sought treatment at their own instigation, and all retained an adequate level of sexual interest and a capacity for arousal in response to erotic stimulation and masturbation. In contrast, in a group of 23 clients whose impotence was of insidious onset, there had been a gradual but progressive falling off of erectile capacity usually over a period of years. The average age of referral in this group was 35 years (range 23–49 years), they had sought treatment only under pressure from their wives in most cases, and they exhibited a marked decline in sexual interest and responsiveness.

In another study, Johnson (1968) describes an acute onset group comprising 17 clients whose impotence dated from their initial attempts at sexual intercourse, and a further 29 clients who had performed normally for a period but then experienced erectile failure in relation to specific events such as engagement, marriage, an affective disorder, or an organic condition in themselves or their wives. An insidious onset group described by the same writer consisted of 9 clients whose impotence had developed over a period of months or years and did not appear to relate to any specific experience. Three of these clients were considered to have always exhibited inadequate sexual interest, 4 had previously shown high levels of interest but had lost these on marriage to sexually inhibited wives, 2 were unable to maintain stable relationships with their partners, and 1 did not receive the unconventional sexual stimulation that he required from his wife in order to be able to function satisfactorily.

Lastly, Ansari (1975) has allocated a series of 65 impotent men to three groups. The first of these consisted of 21 acute onset cases; their erectile dysfunction having been triggered off by psychological or physical trauma such as a first attempt at intercourse, engagement, marriage, vasectomy, surgery on a lumber disc, and bereavement. A second group of 23 cases had an insidious onset of impotence linked with long term psychological or physical trauma, including low sexual response, tubal ligation, the menopause and infidelity among the clients' wives; premature ejaculation in the clients themselves; and marital conflict between the partners. The third group of 21 cases had an insidious onset of impotence without any discernible associated psychological or physical factors, and these clients showed a consistently low interest in sex compared to the other two groups. There was also a significant difference in average age between the acute onset group (29 years) and the two insidious onset groups (46 and 45 years).

Causation

A very wide range of the causal factors reviewed in Part 1 may contribute to erectile dysfunction. It may arise directly from organic events such as illness, surgery, or drug effects, as well as from the client's psychological reactions to these events or to the changes in sexual response that accompany aging.

We have seen that these changes, such as a less rapid erection and a lowered frequency of ejaculation, do not in themselves entail any impairment of erectile capacity, but that this may occur if the changes become sources of stress to an older man, so that reactions such as anxiety or depression are elicited and disrupt his sexual arousal.

In order to avoid repetition of material already discussed in Chapters 2 and 4, a number of illnesses, surgical interventions, and drugs that are most commonly implicated in the causation of erectile dysfunction are summarized in Table 6. This is not a comprehensive list, and it must be reiterated that most of the items are not inevitably accompanied by impotence or any other form of sexual dysfunction. Furthermore, in only a proportion of impotent men is there any evidence of the operation of a relevant organic factor. The size of this proportion varies in different studies and probably reflects the settings where they were conducted and the referral and selection procedures in force. For instance, Masters and Johnson (1970) found a relevant physical condition in only 7 out of 213 secondarily impotent men, while in a Belgian series reported by Geboes *et al.* (1975a) out of 151 men suffering from disturbances of erection this was attributed to organic causes in 86 cases.

Table 6. Organic factors contributing to erectile dysfunction

---

Systemic Illness
1. Renal failure

Local Genital Disorders
2. Peyronie's disease
3. Hypospadias
4. Epispadias

Neurological Disorders
5. Spinal cord lesions

Endocrine Disorders
6. Diabetes mellitus
7. Hypogonadism
8. Hepatic cirrhosis
9. Cushing's syndrome

Vascular Disorders
10. Leriche's syndrome
11. Iliac artery occlusion
12. Priapism

Surgical Interventions
13. Perineal prostatectomy
14. Sympathectomy
15. Cystectomy
16. Ostomy

Drugs
17. Sedatives
18. Major tranquillizers
19. Antihypertensives
20. Narcotics

Several types of previous learning experience that have been implicated in the causation of erectile dysfunction are discussed in Chapter 3. These include seductive behaviour by a mother towards her son, dominating and perfectionist parents, and traumatic initial attempts at intercourse (Ansari, 1975; Cooper, 1968b; Johnson, 1968; Masters and Johnson, 1970). It is noted in that chapter that although such experiences are reported in the histories of some impotent clients, there is evidence also to show that they are not invariably followed by this or any other sexual dysfunction.

Many of the sexual and non-sexual stresses discussed in Chapter 4 are alleged to contribute to erectile dysfunction. For instance, an impotent man may have a specific phobia of the female genitalia, or of some particular aspect of them such as their appearance, smell, or secretions. Others may anticipate some harm from intromission or intercourse, perhaps in the form of a fear of hurting, injuring, or impregnating the partner.

The anticipation of failure is commonly regarded as a particularly frequent contributor to erectile dysfunction, in that a significant proportion of impotent clients report experiencing strong concern during lovemaking over their abilities to obtain or maintain erections or to control ejaculation. There may be some support for this point in the finding by Masters and Johnson (1970) that among their 213 secondarily impotent clients there were 63 who had long histories of ejaculating prematurely. Certainly any threat of failure is likely to be compounded if the client expects its occurrence to be followed by negative reactions from his partner, such as ridicule, criticism, or anger, or if she responds with increased demands for sexual performance which he is unable to meet.

A man's erectile capacity may also be impaired in sexual encounters that involve some transgression of his moral or religious standards. This may occur in very transient or superficial relationships, in an extra-marital affair, or when very restrictive standards are overgeneralized to the marital sexual relationship. It may also occur if a man places his wife on too high a pedestal so that she is not perceived as a sexual being; or if previous sexual experiences of a 'taboo' nature, such as incestuous relationship, are symbolically recapitulated in the marriage relationship, so that the man reacts to his wife as if she were a forbidden partner. Finally, erectile dysfunction may arise when a client is undergoing some form of non-sexual stress, perhaps of an occupational, financial or domestic nature; and the professional preoccupations and overwork leading to so-called 'Barrister's impotence' is one example of this category of stress.

While any of the stress reactions discussed in Chapter 4 may well contribute to erectile dysfunction, it is probable that especially important aetiological roles are played by anxiety reactions, by spectatoring, and by cognitive avoidance. As far as the last two stress reactions are concerned, we have seen that the close monitoring of erectile responses may so distract and detach a man from the ongoing sexual stimulation that this is ineffective in evoking these responses. Similarly, the reaction of cognitive avoidance may prevent a man from perceiving or experiencing pleasurable sexual stimulation, so that again he fails to become aroused.

The distracting and disruptive effects of anxiety during lovemaking are commonly held to be particularly crucial in the aetiology of impotence (e.g. Masters and Johnson, 1970), and there is some support for this contention in the studies by Ansari (1975) and Cooper (1968b) that are cited above. Ansari considers that 14 out of his 21 acute onset cases became impotent as a result of anxiety experienced in a specific sexual situation, and that this initial failure was followed by considerable anxiety and loss of confidence which led to further failure in subsequent attempts at intercourse. Similarly, Cooper reports that all the patients in his acute onset group had experienced anxiety either in anticipation of their first attempt at intercourse, or in response to a later failure of performance in unsuitable circumstances. Moreover, subsequent attempts to redress this failure were accompanied by considerable exacerbation of the anxiety reaction which served to maintain the erectile dysfunction. In Cooper's insidious onset group anxiety was also prominent, but he believes this to be a consequence rather than a cause of the initial erectile failure, and to have arisen as a result of negative reactions from the man's wife to his impotence. Thus, it is suggested that the patients in this group did not seem to be overconcerned about their physical failure to achieve erection, until they were confronted with their inadequacy by a frustrated and angry wife, who also pressured them into seeking treatment.

This leads on to consideration of partner discord as a cause of erectile dysfunction. We have just seen that a wife who reacts to her husband's impotence with criticism and anger may well exacerbate his difficulties. This may also occur if she perceives his lack of arousal as a sign of his rejection or lack of love for her, so that she seeks reassurance by making sexual demands that he is quite unable to meet. In either of these circumstances, the husband is likely to become extremely anxious, especially about his sexual performance, and the disruptive effect of this upon his erectile response has already been noted.

More broadly, if the general relationship between the partners is discordant for any of the reasons discussed in Chapter 4, then the reactions of anxiety, anger, and aggression that this evokes may sometimes initiate or exacerbate a problem of erectile dysfunction in the husband. If he feels angry towards his wife, then he may be unable to respond sexually to her. Indeed, in some cases, the dysfunction may serve as a means of withholding gratification from a wife towards whom the husband feels hostile. Similarly, a wife may express hostility towards her husband by appearing or behaving in unattractive ways so that he fails to become sexually aroused.

Finally, erectile dysfunction may occur in conditions of deficient or inappropriate stimulation. This might be deficient because a couple's sexual practices are insufficiently erotic; particularly when they need to be especially effective, perhaps because of a physical handicap or a possible reduction in tactile sensitivity due to aging, as discussed in Chapter 4. The stimulation provided might also be ineffective because the client's level of sexual interest is inadequate, for any of the reasons reviewed earlier in this chapter; including certain organic conditions, avoidance reactions, partner discord, depression, an intimacy dysfunction, boredom, or lack of reinforced practice. In that section it is noted that an inadequate interest in sex appeared to have been life-long in some clients, and that this could conceivably be due to constitutional factors, although the speculative nature of this possibility is emphasized. In this context, it is worth noting that Cooper (1968b) describes the majority of his insidious onset group of impotent patients as having shown evidence of a low 'sex drive' throughout their lives, and that Ansari (1975) makes a similar observation in respect of his group of patients whose impotence had an insidious onset without any discernible precipitating cause.

Another reason for some men being unable to achieve erection in particular sexual situations is that these do not provide certain forms of unconventional stimulation that these clients need to become aroused. This might consist, for example of utilizing fetishistic articles, cross-dressing, or having a partner of the same sex. Thus, Masters and Johnson (1970) report a predominantly homosexual orientation in 6 out of 32 primarily impotent men, and in 21 out of 213 secondarily impotent men; in each case, the complaint of impotence related to the man's heterosexual partnership.

INADEQUATE ORGASM OR EJACULATION

Premature ejaculation

Description

It is noted in Chapter 2 that orgasm and ejaculation are reflex responses over which most men can exercise some degree of voluntary control, up to the point of ejaculatory inevitability which coincides with the emission stage when the semen is collected from the internal sexual organs and deposited at the entrance to the urethra. Premature ejaculation is perhaps most usefully defined as a lack of adequate voluntary control over the orgastic and/or ejaculatory reflexes. In most clients both of these reflexes will be involved, but it is possible for premature orgasm to occur without the expulsion of an ejaculate in men suffering from retrograde ejaculation, or for premature ejaculation to occur through a flaccid penis without any accompanying sensation of orgasm in men suffering from erectile dysfunction.

As there are no absolute standards for the degree of voluntary control to be expected over the orgastic and ejaculatory reflexes, it can only be defined as inadequate on the basis of subjective judgements by the man and his partner. Among the factors that are likely to influence these judgements are the persistence of inadequate control, the timing of orgasm and ejaculation, and the degree of dissatisfaction experienced by the couple.

It is probable that most men experience occasional or transient episodes of premature ejaculation, perhaps when they are particularly highly aroused or during their early experiences of intercourse, and this is not commonly regarded as a problem for which treatment might be sought unless it becomes more persistent.

The timing of ejaculation is also likely to be an important consideration in reaching this decision. It may occur before, during or shortly after intromission. Some men will ejaculate as soon as the partner undressing or at the commencement of foreplay. For other men, premature ejaculation occurs whenever they attempt to enter the partner, while still others are able to survive some period of vaginal containment before ejaculating. How limited this period needs to be in order to merit the label of premature ejaculation depends on the views of the couple concerned. Most people like intercourse to take place rapidly on certain occasions, and some have a consistent preference for this, so that it does not necessarily have to be more prolonged providing that each partner is satisfied with a shorter encounter. However, rapid ejaculation is likely to be considered a problem if either partner is repeatedly left in a state of dissatisfaction.

For many men, rapid ejaculation is a disappointing, humiliating, and disturbing experience. Their own pleasure is truncated, and they may feel guilty and responsible for depriving their wives of sufficient gratification during arousal and orgasm. In contrast, some other men are not dissatisfied when they ejaculate quickly because they are relatively uninterested in prolonging their own pleasure or in promoting that of their partners, and make little attempt to exercise voluntary control. Others do try to delay ejaculation, but are quite satisfied if they are able to do so for any period that they consider to fall within the limits of normality. In this context, it is worth noting that 75%of american males are reported to ejaculate within two minutes of intromission (Kinsey *et al.*, 1948), although the proportion that consider this to be satisfactory is not known and may possibly have decreased with the growing emphasis on female sexual satisfaction since the study was conducted.

There is no doubt that a couple's expectations concerning the sexual capacity and pleasure of the female partner are important in determining their degree of dissatisfaction with rapid ejaculation by the male. If they consider intercourse to be primarily a source of pleasure for the man, then rapid ejaculation may not be regarded as much of a problem. This may have been a common view in Victorian times when respectable women were not expected to enjoy sex, and it is interesting that Johnson (1968) cites sources in the contemporary medical literature (Lallemand, 1847; Marston, 1871) describing nocturnal emissions, diurnal emissions, and the discharge of semen without orgasm as the main forms of complaint about ejaculation, rather than its prematurity. More recently, there is some evidence (Kerckhoff, 1974; Kinsey *et al.*, 1948; Masters and Johnson, 1970, Rainwater, 1960) to suggest that people in the lower socio-economic classes in America are less likely than those in the higher classes to complain of premature ejaculation, and this difference is attributed to the greater tendency of the former to regard sexual satisfaction as predominantly a male prerogative and to give priority to this over the satisfaction of the female partner. Again, it is possible that this class difference is lessening as the recognition of female sexual capacity and right to gratification becomes more widespread. These expectations are certainly conducive to a couple's identification of premature ejaculation as a problem meriting treatment; for instance, in a series reported by Cooper (1968b) the complaint had usually arisen out of the female partner's frustration at her inability to reach orgasm because of the man's prematurity. This is also likely to be of much more concern to him in so far as he assumes responsibility for his partner's lack of gratification and feels guilty and anxious about his inability to provide this for her.

In view of the varying and subjective nature of the definitions of premature ejaculation, it is understandable that no reliable data exists on its incidence in the general population. However, it is usually regarded as an extremely frequent problem, possibly the commonest of all the male sexual dysfunctions, and perhaps almost universal among men at the commencement of their sexual careers. Some indication of this high prevalence may be gained from the fact that in a series of 448 dysfunctional men treated by Masters and Johnson (1970) there were 186 who suffered from premature ejaculation.

Turning to the circumstances surrounding premature ejaculation, this may occur during masturbation and/or sexual encounters, but its restriction to the latter is probably more usual and is certainly more likely to lead to treatment being sought. During such encounters, the occurrence of ejaculation will reflect the conditions prevailing at particular points in time, including the intensity of the sexual stimulation, the level of the man's arousal, and the amount of pelvic movement by both partners.

The consequences of premature ejaculation for the man concerned will often include feelings of disappointment, humiliation, depression, guilt and anxiety, arising both from his own frustration and his inability to satisfy his partner. In an attempt to exercise more effective control it is quite common for men to resort to various techniques, usually designed to reduce the intensity of sexual stimulation or to distract the man's attention from it, so that he does not become aroused so quickly, Thus, a man may bite his tongue or pinch himself; engage in anti-erotic thoughts; use a condom, topical anaesthetic, or tranquillizing drug; and quite often arrange that his wife will not stimulate him tactually during foreplay, in an attempt to arouse her sufficiently and to have a short period of intercourse, before he becomes too aroused and ejaculates himself. For reasons that are discussed below, such tactics are usually ineffective in ameliorating premature ejaculation and are more likely to exacerbate the problem.

To have a prematurely ejaculating partner is a frustrating and disappointing experience for many women. Initially they may be very understanding, sympathetic, and encouraging, and this is sometimes followed by an improvement in the man's control as he gains sexual experience with an accustomed and reassuring partner. If the problem persists however, then her reactions are likely to become more negative. She may misconstrue the man's attempts to exercise control by not letting himself go in their lovemaking as a sign of his lack of interest or rejection of her. She may become resentful and angry at his apparent preoccupation with his own pleasure and his seeming disregard for her satisfaction, so that she feels used by her partner. Such adverse reactions often compound and extend his sexual difficulties; for instance, he may become even more anxious about his sexual performance and monitor it even more assiduously, which may lead to an exacerbation of his premature ejaculation, to an avoidance of sex manifesting itself as inadequate interest, or to the onset of an erectile dysfunction. This whole pattern of reaction to premature ejaculation sometimes results in the increasing withdrawal of both partners from their relationship; and perhaps to engagement in extra-marital affairs by the wife in an attempt to obtain the sexual gratification she lacks, as well as reassurance concerning her attractiveness and femininity (Masters and Johnson, 1970).

Several writers have described different patterns of onset for premature ejaculation, which may well be of some aetiological and therapeutic significance as discussed below. Schapiro (1943) divided a series of 1130 cases into two main groups. Type A consisted largely of older patients, whose premature ejaculation commenced after a period of adequate control, and who also suffered from erectile dysfunction. Type B comprised a younger age group, who had experienced premature ejaculation since their first attempt at intercourse, but whose sexual interest and erectile capacity were unimpaired. Similarly, among 18 patients described by Johnson (1968) there were 15 early onset cases, whose premature ejaculation had existed since their first attempts at intercourse, while the remaining 3 late onset cases claimed that their premature ejaculation developed after a period of normal sexual functioning, although the author considers that it might have existed earlier.

Cooper (1969b) studied 30 patients complaining of premature ejaculation, and was able to identify three fairly discrete groups which he designated 'Types 1, 2, and 3'. The Type 1 group consisted of 10 men who had experienced premature ejaculation constantly since adolescence, but whose sexual interest and erectile capacities were unimpaired. These patients are very similar to those in Schapiro's Type B group, but there is no equivalent in his classification to Cooper's Type 2 group. This consisted of 7 patients with an acute onset of premature ejaculation, usually when they were already suffering from an erectile dysfunction. The 13 patients in Cooper's Type 3 group are very similar to those in Schapiro's Type A, in that their premature ejaculation occurred after a period of normal functioning and in association with an insidious and progressive decline in sexual interest and erectile capacity.

Masters and Johnson (1970) report that their prematurely ejaculating patients consistently had a history of early attempts at intercourse which were for some reason of a hurried nature; perhaps with a prostitute who encouraged a speedy performance, or in conditions of uncertain privacy when there was a fear of being caught *in flagrante delicto*. These authors attribute the onset of premature ejaculation to such early experiences, but there is no quantitative evidence available either on the proportion of premature ejaculators who report this kind of experience, or on the proportion of those undergoing them who subsequently suffer from inadequate control. Neither is it clear why certain men develop this problem, out of the very large number who must have experienced rushed attempts at intercourse.

Causation

Premature ejaculation is probably very rarely caused by an organic condition, although this possibility should be considered when inadequate control occurs after a period of normal functioning in this respect. Some of these cases may be attributable to neurological disorders, such as a spinal cord tumour or multiple sclerosis, but no systematic evidence is currently available on this point.

In constrast to organic factors, a man's previous learning experiences may be particularly important in the aetiology of premature ejaculation. This is because voluntary control of the orgastic and ejaculatory reflexes is assumed to be acquired by learning, and the success or otherwise of this process will depend on the conditions to which the man is exposed. For example, to the extent that premature ejaculation is a product of rushed early experiences of intercourse, as claimed by Masters and Johnson (1970), then this might be accounted for in terms of the consequent lack of learning opportunities to practise voluntary control, or to the reinforcement of rapid ejaculation so that the man makes little attempt to exercise such control.

Kaplan (1974) offers an interesting hypothesis to explain the non-acquisition or subsequent breakdown of voluntary control over orgasm and ejaculation. She postulates that adequate sensory feedback is necessary for the development and exercise of control over all reflex responses; for instance, in order to be able to control his urinary functions a child must learn to recognize the sensations that signal a full bladder. Similarly, in order to control his orgastic and ejaculatory reflexes a man must learn to recognize the erotic sensations that signal the build up of arousal and the imminence of climax. There are a number of ways in which such recognition might fail to develop or operate; for example, rushed early sexual experiences might deprive a man of some opportunities to learn to recognize these sensations and to exercise voluntary control. Additionally, such control might be impeded or disrupted by distracting anxiety or cognitive avoidance reactions to various stresses so that the man does not perceive his mounting arousal, and these possibilities are considered further below. Thus, like bladder incontinence in children (Jehu et al., 1977), premature ejaculation may arise both as a developmental disorder in which adequate control is not acquired, and as a stress disorder in which it breaks down in conditions of threat. It should be emphasized that these two possible aetiologies are not mutually exclusive, and that they are speculative at the present time.

Any of the stress conditions discussed in Chapter 4 might contribute to premature ejaculation. For example, a man who has ejaculated rapidly on one or more previous occasions, may anticipate a similar failure during his next attempt at intercourse, and this threat is likely to be compounded if he also expects its realization to be accompanied by ridicule, criticism or anger from his partner. This kind of stress among many others, may well evoke stress reactions that disrupt voluntary control of the orgastic and ejaculatory reflexes.

Anxiety, arising from any source, is commonly held to be one such stress reaction, although precisely how it contributes to premature ejaculation is not at present known. One possible explanation proposed by Kaplan (1974) is that the anxiety reactions distract a man from clearly perceiving the build up of erotic sensations towards orgasm and ejaculation so that these are triggered off automatically and without him being able to exercise adequate voluntary control.

Cognitive avoidance is another type of stress reaction that may contribute to premature ejaculation. For instance, it is noted above that many men suffering from this problem will try to delay ejaculation by engaging in anti-erotic thoughts; and Kaplan (1974) claims that many premature ejaculators report an absence of erotic sensation, sometimes amounting to 'genital anaesthesia', as they become intensely aroused and approach climax. Again, it is not clear precisely how such cognitive avoidance reactions contribute to premature ejaculation, but it is possible that like anxiety they also impair the man's recognition of his mounting arousal and his voluntary control over orgasm and ejaculation.

Finally, certain overt stress reactions of an avoidance or escape nature may contribute to premature ejaculation. Thus, the man who ejaculates before, during or shortly after intromission, may thereby avoid or escape from certain aspects of sexual encounters that are for some reason threatening to him. Similarly, the use of delaying tactics such as biting the tongue or pinching some part of the body, may constitute attempts to actively avoid the threat of ejaculating too rapidly or some other stressful feature of the sexual encounter. As mentioned earlier, such tactics are unlikely to be successful and may actually exacerbate the problem. At best, they will delay arousal, but once this reaches a critical level then orgasm and ejaculation will be triggered off automatically as long as the man has not acquired or cannot exercise adequate voluntary control. Indeed, the attempted delaying tactics may actually worsen this control, again perhaps because they distract the man from his erotic sensations and thus reduce his recognition of their escalation towards climax (Kaplan, 1974).

The stresses associated with partner discord may also contribute to premature ejaculation. The discord that sometimes arises from this sexual problem, and which may serve to maintain and exacerbate it, is noted above; but whether the discord stems from this or other sources, it may well be an important causal influence in some cases of premature ejaculation, and consideration needs to be given to any possible explanations for this.

One is that the man may feel threatened by humiliation, criticism or anger from his partner, and the anxiety this evokes might contribute to the problem of premature ejaculation as discussed above. Similarly, if a man has feelings of anger or hostility towards his partner, then these negative emotional reactions might also impair his voluntary control over orgasm and ejaculation, perhaps because these feelings also distract him from his rising erotic sensations.

Next, some cases of premature ejaculation may constitute overt expressions of aggression or hostility between the partners. Thus, a man's rapid ejaculation may serve to frustrate, deprive, and hurt his female partner; or alternatively, Kaplan (1974) cites Sager as suggesting that the man does not want to give up the pleasure of ejaculating quickly and is rebelling against the perceived domination by his partner when she seeks some delay. A woman's expressions of hostility towards her male partner may also serve to instigate or maintain a problem of premature ejaculation. Thus, she might cause him frustration and distress by precipitating his climax before he would like it to happen, perhaps by engaging in vigorous pelvic movements to disrupt his control or by prompting him to finish quickly.

Levine (1975) makes the additional important point that such actions by female partners may arise not only as expressions of hostility, but also as means of avoiding or escaping from sexual situations that are for some reason stressful to the women concerned. The more rapidly the man ejaculates, the sooner the threatening situation is terminated for his partner. In this sense, Levine regards premature ejaculation as not always an exclusively male sexual dysfunction, but sometimes as being a masked female sexual dysfunction which requires a speedy conclusion to intercourse.

Retarded or absent ejaculation

Description

This problem might be defined as a persistent delay or failure in the occurrence of orgasm and ejaculation despite the presence of an adequate erection. The client is able to obtain and maintain erections, without difficulty, but intense stimulation may be continued for unusually lengthy periods before he achieves climax, or he may not do so at all. Clearly, there is room for subjective judgement in deciding when the delay becomes unacceptable, but periods of thirty minutes to an hour or more would probably cause concern to many couples. Similarly, the persistence of the difficulty needs to be taken into account, for intermittent retardation or absence of climax is not uncommon when intercourse is attempted very frequently over a short time or during the refractory period, as well as among older men who often only desire and reach a climax on a certain proportion of their sexual encounters.

It is important to note that both orgasm and ejaculation are retarded or absent in the problem we are discussing, for this needs to be distinguished from another that is sometimes called 'dry run orgasm' in which the man has an orgasm but does not ejaculate. The later problem may reflect the retrograde ejaculation of the seminal fluid into the bladder, as discussed in a later section.

A particular manifestation of retarded or absent ejaculation is the condition referred to by Kaplan (1974) as 'partial ejaculatory incompetence'. This involves a partial impairment of both orgasm and ejaculation. The emission component of the latter is unaffected and the point of ejaculatory inevitability is experienced, but the expulsion component consists of a seepage rather than a spurting of semen, and it is not accompanied by the usual muscular contractions and pleasurable sensations of orgasm. Kaplan suggests that transient occurrences of this phenomenon are not uncommon when men are fatigued, in conflict situations, or in the process of learning to exercise adequate voluntary control during treatment for premature ejaculation, but she cites a personal communication from William Masters saying that its more chronic occurrence is extremely rare.

There is no evidence available on the incidence of all forms of retarded or absent ejaculation in general populations, but it is relatively rare among men who seek treatment for sexual dysfunction. For instance, in two series of such patients, the incidence figures for retarded or absent ejaculation were 17 (3.8%) out of 448 (Masters and Johnson, 1970), and 3 (3.9%) out of 76 (Johnson, 1968). Both Kaplan (1974) and O'Connor (1976) express the opinion that this problem is commoner than these rates suggest, and there is some support for their view in a report by Geboes *et al.* (1975b) that 72 (15%) out of 486 sexually dysfunctional men seen in a Belgian clinic had never experienced climax during masturbation or intercourse.

Among those clients who do seek treatment for retarded or absent ejaculation it is rare for this to be a global problem so that the man never reaches climax under any circumstances. More usually, he does experience nocturnal emissions and is at least able to climax during masturbation, although this may need to be carried out in a very specific manner. In some cases successful masturbation is only possible when the man is alone, in others the partner can be present. She may also be able to bring him to climax by manual and/or oral forms of stimulation.

Some clients are unable to achieve orgasm and ejaculation during intercourse with a particular partner or in certain circumstances, although they can do so with another partner or in different circumstances. One interesting example of this differential responsiveness is provided in a study of 170 convicted male rapists conducted by Groth and Burgess (1977). They found that 58 of these men were sexually dysfunctional during the act of rape, and that 26 of them had been unable to ejaculate, although none reported similar difficulties in their non-assaultive sexual relationships. More commonly, a man may not be able to climax during intercourse with his partner when they fear that one of their children may enter the bedroom or that they will be overheard by a parent who is nearby. There are also those men who cannot reach climax unless certain unconventional forms of sexual stimulation are available, perhaps of fetishistic or sado-masochistic nature. It should be emphasized that such differential responsiveness is not always present, some clients do experience a delay or failure in reaching orgasm and ejaculation in all acts of intercourse regardless of the particular partner and circumstances.

A problem of retarded or absent ejaculation is likely to cause distress for both partners. The man will often feel inadequate and humiliated, and he may fake a climax in an attempt to deceive his partner. His incapacity is likely to be particularly disturbing if it prevents the couple from fulfilling a desire to conceive a child by means of intercourse, and this does seem to be an important factor in leading many men to seek treatment. If a problem of retarded or absent ejaculation is not resolved, then erectile dysfunction may develop, perhaps because of the anxiety and other stress reactions evoked by the original difficulty. It might be thought that a woman would welcome the opportunities for prolonged pleasure and multiple orgasms presented by her partner's delay or failure in reaching climax, but this is certainly not the most usual female reaction to this problem. More probably she will misconstrue it as a sign that the man does not find her sexually attractive or that he is rejecting her, and she may regard herself as an inadequate lover who is unable to bring him to climax.

Some men have always suffered from retarded or absent ejaculation throughout their relevant sexual experience. Others have developed the problem after a period of normal functioning in this respect, in which case the onset was usually but not always precipitated by some specific traumatic incident of the kind discussed below. Thus, Masters and Johnson (1970) report that out of 16 men suffering from retarded or absent ejaculation, and who were or had been married, there were 12 who had never been able to ejaculate intravaginally with their wives, although 2 of these men had done so with another woman or a homosexual partner respectively. The remaining 4 men had been able to ejaculate normally before and during their marriages (of 6 to 21 years duration), until they became unable to do so intravaginally with their wives following some traumatic incident, although 1 of these 4 men remained fully capable with extramarital partners.

Causation

Retarded or absent ejaculation is probably rarely due to organic factors, although this possibility should certainly be suspected when the problem occurs after a period of normal functioning and during masturbation as well as intercourse. The kind of organic factors that are most likely to be relevant are reviewed in Chapter 2, and some of these that have been implicated are summarized in Table 7. It should be noted that the references to these factors in the literature do not always distinguish retarded or absent ejaculation from retrograde ejaculation, and it is sometimes not clear which of these problems is alleged to accompany the organic factor being identified.

Table 7. Organic factors contributing to retarded or absent ejaculation

Systemic Illness
1. Renal failure

Local Genital Disorders
2. Gonorrhea

Neurological Disorders
3. Spinal cord lesions
4. Parkinson's disease

Surgical Interventions
5. Lumbar sympathectomy
6. Spinal fusion surgery
7. Aortic aneurysm surgery

Drugs
8. Antihypertensives
9. Narcotics

Certain previous learning experiences appear to make a significant contribution to some cases of retarded or absent ejaculation. For instance, we note in Chapter 3, that some clients report a long history of masturbating in a very specific manner, and subsequently of only being able to achieve climax in this particular way. Another example occurs in the cases of those clients whose restrictive upbringing has so imbued them with the dangers of getting girls pregnant that their fear of doing so has overgeneralized into the marriage relationship. Lastly, there are those clients whose retarded or absent ejaculation appears to be related to some specific traumatic incident, either early in life or in adulthood. Thus, as boys they may have been caught masturbating and severely punished for this, or their nocturnal emissions might have attracted strong disapproval or punishment. Similar trauma in adulthood might consist of being interrupted during intercourse, having a condom burst when conception is strongly opposed, or being exposed to a wife's miscarriage so that the husband is reluctant to risk impregnating her again. However, not all clients suffering from retarded or absent ejaculation report such previous learning experiences, and many males in the general population must undergo them without developing this problem or any other sexual dysfunction.

Many of the stresses discussed in Chapter 4 might contribute to retarded or absent ejaculation. Perhaps as a result of a very restrictive upbringing in matters such as masturbation and nocturnal emissions, a man may overgeneralize his adverse reactions to the 'sinfulness' of ejaculation into his sexual relationships with his wife. Similarly, this response and that of orgasm may have acquired threatening properties for him because they have been associated with some traumatic episode, such as those mentioned in the previous paragraph. He might also be apprehensive about reaching orgasm because of a possible loss of control during it, or find ejaculation threatening because of his concern about the possible genetic transmission of some undesirable characteristic to his offspring. A man may feel that his semen will 'soil', 'defile', or 'contaminate' a partner, or anticipate that she will perceive an ejaculation in this way and react adversely to it. Some clients are afraid of impregnating a partner, when either she or the client do not want this to happen. Lastly once a man has experienced undue delay or failure in reaching climax, then any anticipated difficulty in doing so in future may well become an additional source of stress to him.

Any of these or other stresses may elicit certain reactions that contribute to a problem of retarded or absent ejaculation, although exactly how this occurs is not known at the present time. One possibility proposed by Kaplan (1974) is that the problem may represent an involuntary inhibition of the orgastic and ejaculatory reflexes. Clearly, this overt stress reaction can serve as a means of avoiding the release of these reflexes, which is for some reason threatening to the individual concerned.

There are several ways in which partner discord might contribute to a retarded or absent ejaculation. If a man no longer finds his partner sexually attractive, then he may not become sufficiently aroused for orgasm and ejaculation to be triggered off. This may also occur if his full arousal is disrupted by feelings of anxiety or anger evoked by his partner. In some cases, retarded or absent ejaculation appears to constitute a refusal on the man's part to submit to his partner's domination and control. For instance, she might be demanding to become pregnant, and his inability to ejaculate may serve as an act of rebellion against this perceived attempt to achieve his submission to her wishes. It may also arise from the client's opposition or ambivalence towards fully committing himself to a relationship with a partner, when intravaginal ejaculation is perceived as entailing such a commitment. A further possibility is that retarded or absent ejaculation may be an expression of hostility towards the female partner, and a means of frustrating her wishes and satisfaction; for instance, by denying her the pregnancy she wants or the satisfaction of feeling sure that her husband finds her sexually attractive and loves her. If such doubts do arise, whether or not they have a basis in reality, then we see above that the female partner may seek reassurance by stepping up her demands and attempts to bring the man to climax, which may extend his original problem into one of erectile dysfunction or a manifest inadequate interest in sex.

Finally, a number of instances of a possible contribution from deficient or inappropriate stimulation to problems of retarded or absent ejaculation have already been mentioned. It is assumed that although a man may be able to obtain and maintain an erection, he does not become sufficiently aroused and excited for orgasm and ejaculation to be triggered off. This might occur in the absence of certain very specific conditions that are required by some men if they are to succeed in masturbating to climax. Alternatively, this may not be achieved in a sexual encounter with a partner who is insufficiently attractive or when some necessary form of unconventional stimulation is lacking.

Retrograde ejaculation

Description

Essentially, retrograde ejaculation is the involuntary discharge of semen into the bladder rather than through the urethra, so that the client still has erections and orgasms but there is no visible ejaculate. This is collected from the internal sex organs and deposited at the entrance to the urethra in the usual way, but the normal reflex closure of the internal sphincter at the neck of the bladder does not occur. Consequently, the semen flows backwards into the bladder instead of being propelled forwards by the muscular contractions of orgasm. One indication of this problem is the cloudiness of urine passed after masturbation or intercourse, and it can be diagnosed from the presence of sperm in the urine at these times.

The problem of retrograde ejaculation needs to be distinguished from the voluntary suppression of ejaculation that some men are able to achieve. It is reported that this practice, termed '*coitus reservatus*', has been used as a method of contraception for many centuries, and that yogis who believe that semen improves the intellect are able to voluntarily direct its flow into the bladder where it can be absorbed for this purpose (Johnson, 1968). More recently, Robbins and Jensen (1978) have presented evidence indicating that some men are able to have multiple orgasms within a short interval and only to ejaculate on the last of these.

Retrograde ejaculation often causes considerable concern because of a couple's fear that they are unable to conceive a child. In fact, they can be reassured that it is quite possible to recover live spermatozoa from the man's urine after masturbation or intercourse and to inseminate his partner with these. It is important also for a man to know that the problem of retrograde ejaculation involves only an absence of a visible ejaculate and not any impairment of erection or orgasm. Otherwise, any unnessary concern about loss of these responses may evoke stress reactions that produce secondary complications of the original problem, such as inadequate interest in sex or an erectile dysfunction. In saying this it must be recognized that the organic factors that have resulted in retrograde ejaculation may in some cases also produce an impairment of erectile capacity, but this is not a necessary or inevitable accompaniment of the ejaculatory difficulty.

Causation

The causation of retrograde ejaculation is probably almost entirely organic in nature. It may consist of any illness, surgical intervention or drug, that disrupts sympathetic control of the internal bladder sphincter, or that prevents complete closure of the bladder neck, and some such factors that are most commonly implicated in the aetiology of this problem are summarized in Table 8.

Table 8. Organic factors contributing to retrograde ejaculation

Neurological Disorders
1. Spinal cord lesions
2. Pelvic fractures (with injury to bladder neck or sacral nerves)

Endocrine Disorders
3. Diabetes mellitus

Surgical Interventions
4. Prostatectomy
5. Lumbar sympathectomy
6. Colectomy
7. Retroperitoneal lymph node dissection
8. Bladder neck surgery
9. Aortic aneuryism surgery

Drugs
10. Major tranquillizers
11. Antihypertensives

INADEQUATE SEXUAL PLEASURE
OR PAINFUL INTERCOURSE

Inadequate sexual pleasure

Description

Clients sometimes complain that they 'feel nothing' during intercourse, or that it is insufficiently pleasurable or satisfying for them. There is very little knowledge available about this category of dysfunction, although it probably includes several different problems which remain to be distinguished from each other. In particular, little is known about any differences between the sexes in this respect, consequently the following discussion refers to both male and female clients.

A male client whose main complaint is of inadequate pleasure, has no difficulty with his erections and is able to achieve orgasm and ejaculation in a normal manner, but these physical responses are not accompanied by subjective feelings of pleasure and satisfaction at an adequate level of intensity. Likewise such feelings are lacking in a similar female client, although her vaginal lubrication and swelling are normal and the muscular contractions of orgasm do occur.

In some cases, erotic feelings are lacking to all forms of sexual stimulation, while in others this absence of response is restricted to stimulation of the genitals. This may extend to an actual anaesthesia in this area, whereby even tactile sensations are not experienced by the client. Such genital anaesthesia is sometimes confined to sexual stimulation, or it may be more general so that the client cannot, for example, feel a physician's examining fingers or the pressure of a speculum.

At this end of the continuum few individuals will have much difficulty in deciding that they have a problem for which treatment should be sought; but this judgement is less straight forward when the erotic feelings are attenuated rather than absent, especially if the person's expectations of sexual pleasure are unclear or unrealistically high. For instance, a woman may have little idea of the kind of pleasure that is usually associated with orgasm, and might expect it to be an ecstatic experience of a mystical nature. This may lead her to report to a therapist that she feels involuntary vaginal contractions and a subsequent sense of calmness and satisfaction, but is not able to have an orgasm. It may be that the physical sensations are not being appropriately labelled, or that they are not as pleasurable as the client thinks they should be (*Medical Aspects of Human Sexuality*, 1975). Certainly, a woman can experience a climax but still find it disappointing, and Offit (1977) has described several circumstances in which this might happen. Some women resemble prematurely ejaculating males in that they climax after brief stimulation, in an attentuated manner, and with little if any accompanying pleasure. This may be similarly lacking with 'incomplete' or abbreviated orgasms comprising only a few contractions that stop before total release is obtained. Most extreme are those cases where a climax is reached and contractions are experienced but with a total lack of erotic pleasure.

The amount of pleasure experienced may vary quite widely in different circumstances. It is quite usual for the pleasureable feelings to fluctuate across occasions, perhaps due to variations in the stimulation received, the recency and frequency of intercourse, and the attractiveness of the partner (Clifford, 1978; Singer and Singer, 1978). For example, although Masters and Johnson (1966) emphasize that all female orgasms are essentially the same, in that they all consist of rythmic contractions of the vaginal, pelvic, and uterine muscles, these writers are equally clear that orgasms vary in intensity and duration both between individuals and in the same individual at different times, and that both the physical and psychological quality of the stimulation being provided are among the factors that influence a woman's experience of orgasm. When this normal range of variation in erotic pleasure is exceeded, then it may be inadequate during masturbation or only during intercourse, and in the latter case with only one partner or with many.

A client suffering from this form of dysfunction might still enjoy the emotional warmth and intimacy of lovemaking although no erotic feelings are experienced. However, this deficiency may also be a source of considerable frustration and distress for the client, as well being threatening and humiliating to the other spouse. In these circumstances, it is understandable that the original problem may sometimes become complicated by the development of erectile dysfunction in males, the impairment of vasocongestion or orgastic dysfunction in females, or inadequate sexual interest inclients of either sex.

All that can be said on the topics of onset and duration is that two male cases are reported by Dormont (1975) in which a complete lack of pleasure during ejaculation began in late adolescence in the context of masturbatory activity, and persisted at least until the ages 31 and 53 years respectively, despite considerable marital and extra-marital sexual experience in each case.

Causation

Such information as there is, indicates that inadequate pleasure is most usually of psychological origin, and the only organic factor that is mentioned as a possible cause is poor tone in the vaginal and pubococcygeal muscles. As a result, these may be very relaxed and relatively insensitive stimulation.

No particular stresses are identified as contributing to problems of inadequate pleasure, although many of those discussed in Chapter 4 might function in this way. This may be especially true if they evoke reactions of cognitive avoidance towards certain forms of sexual stimulation or response that are for some reason threatening to an individual. Awareness of these may be reduced or eliminated, so that the sexual stimulation is not perceived and the erotic feelings that are normally associated with it are not experienced.

Hysterical disorders are sometimes implicated as causes of certain cases of inadequate pleasure. When this involves genital anaesthesia it might be considered a 'conversion symptom', comparable to other hysterical anaesthesias, sensory losses or paralyses (Kaplan, 1974; Weisberg, 1977). Furthermore, it is noted in Chapter 4, that in a study conducted by Purtell *et al.* (1951), some 73% of women with a diagnosis of hysteria reported an absence of sexual pleasure, compared to 15% of healthy control subjects. Some hysterical individuals are described as having what Levay and Kagle (1977) call a 'pleasure dysfunction', that is they have difficulty in identifying, experiencing, or enjoying pleasurable sensations, including those normally associated with sexual activities. These difficulties are not restricted to clients with a diagnosis of hysteria; they may also appear in others, including some of those considered to be suffering from an obsessive–compulsive disorder.

Lastly, inadequate pleasure may be experienced in sexual relationships that have become boring, routinized, and lacking in variety, or in the absence of some preferred form of unconventional sexual stimulation.

Dyspareunia

Description

Dyspareunia is defined as painful intercourse, and the discomfort may be experienced only during erection, insertion, thrusting or ejaculation, or throughout more than one of these processes. The client most commonly refers the pain to his prepuce, glans penis, penile shaft, testicles, groin, public area, rectum, thighs or lower back, although other locations are sometimes involved. He may or may not also experience pain during certain non-coital forms of sexual activity, such as masturbation and manual or oral stimulation by a partner.

The anticipation of pain is clearly stressful to most men, and it may well evoke reactions, such as anxiety and avoidance, that lead to other sexual difficulties. For instance, a problem of inadequate interest, erectile dysfunction, or retarded or absent ejaculation, might serve the function of avoiding those components of the sexual activity that are expected to be painful. Moreover, these components may continue to be sources of stress even when there is no longer any organic basis for pain, for if this has been associated with these aspects of sexual activity in the client's previous learning experiences then they may have acquired the properties of a conditioned aversive stimulus for the individual concerned.

Causation

The aetiology of dyspareunia in males is predominantly of an organic nature, although not exclusively so for psychological factors are involved in some cases (e.g. Sharpe and Meyer, 1973). A comprehensive review of the relevant organic causes is provided by Wear (1976), and the following outline is based upon his excellent discussion.

He mentions a number of conditions of the female genitalia that sometimes cause male dyspareunia. The most common of these is inadequate vaginal lubrication; but congenital anomalies; episiotomies accompanied by attempts to 'tighten up' a gaping introitus; and the distortion, scarring, or shortening of the vagina by surgery or radiation, are each responsible in some cases. A related group of causes are those involving an inflammatory allergic reaction to contraceptive solvents, rubber condoms or diaphragms, hygienic preparations, artificial lubricants, or even the acidity of the normal vaginal secretions.

Certain conditions of the external male genitalia may also cause dyspareunia. When this occurs on erection, then some form of curvature of the penis is especially likely to be responsible; for instance, hypospadias, chordee, Peyronie's disease, penile trauma, and phimosis. Additionally, pain may arise from many inflammatory conditions and infections affecting the external genitalia, such as balanitis, urethritis, and orchitis.

Pathological conditions of the internal male sex organs are associated with pain on ejaculation, rather than during erection, insertion, or thrusting. Such ejaculatory dyspareunia is almost always caused by acute prostatitis and/or seminal vesiculitis.

Finally, certain general illnesses may be accompanied by pain during intercourse. For instance, back pain during thrusting might be experienced by an arthritic patient, or angina pectoris could occur in a cardiac patient.

This concludes discussion of the nature and causation of the male sexual dysfunctions, and in the next chapter we consider those that occur in female clients.

7

Female Dysfunctions

The problems of inadequate sexual interest and inadequate sexual pleasure in women are considered in the previous chapter. This leaves vasocongestive dysfunction, vaginismus, orgastic dysfunction, and dyspareunia to be discussed, and their descriptions and causes are reviewed in the present chapter.

INADEQUATE AROUSAL
OR INTROMISSION

Vasocongestive dysfunction

Description

This type of problem involves some impairment of the lubrication-swelling or vasocongestive phase in the female response cycle, so that vaginal lubrication, the ballooning of the inner two-thirds of the vagina, the formation of an orgasmic platform, and the other physiological changes characteristic of this phase, do not occur normally. Thus, vasocongestive dysfunction in the female is analogous to erectile dysfunction in the male.

It was Kaplan (1974) who very usefully drew attention to the impairment of arousal as a distinct problem in women, separate from orgastic dysfunction, just as erectile problems have long been differentiated from ejaculatory problems in males. Thus, many women suffering from an orgastic dysfunction do become extremely aroused although they cannot reach climax. Conversely, a smaller proportion of clients with some impairment of arousal are able to achieve orgasm. However, this separation of arousal and orgastic problems does not mean that they cannot co-exist in the same client, for most women who have difficulty in becoming aroused are also unable to reach orgasm.

Kaplan refers to problems of arousal in women as 'general sexual dysfunction' (Kaplan, 1974) or 'female sexual unresponsiveness' (Kaplan, 1975). The rather general nature of these terms may reflect her definition of them as including a lack of erotic feelings as well as an absence of lubrication-swelling responses. The term 'vasocongestive dysfunction' is preferred in this book, and it is used more specifically to refer to an impairment of these physiological changes; the lack of erotic feelings being considered a separate problem of inadequate pleasure and discussed in the previous chapter. This further separation of syndromes seems to be desirable because they may or may not be associated in the same client. Some women neither exhibit the lubrication-swelling responses nor do they experience erotic feelings. Other clients lack these physiological responses although they do become psychologically excited. Conversely, there are others in whom lubrication-swelling occurs normally, but without the usual accompanying feelings of sexual pleasure.

There is very little information available about the incidence of impaired arousal among women, perhaps because of the recency of its distinction from orgastic dysfunction and the lack of agreement over its definition and scope. Levine and Yost (1976) studied a series of 59 black women, aged 30–39 years, who were attending a gynaecological clinic for non-sexual complaints. Ten (17%) of these women reported that they were unable to achieve orgasm with a partner by any means, of whom 7 had 'excitement-phase dysfunctions' and 3 'orgasm-phase dysfunctions'. Of the 7 exhibiting the former type of problem, this was of secondary onset following a period of normal functioning in 6 cases, while the remaining woman had always lacked both lubrication and excitement. Bancroft and Coles (1976) report that in a consecutive series of 102 women seen in a sexual problems clinic, there were 63 whose principal sexual dysfunction was 'general unresponsiveness', while another 18 were diagnosed as suffering from orgastic dysfunction. It is not clear how many in the generally unresponsive group were also unable to reach orgasm, but it is interesting that such relatively high proportions of dysfunctional women should be considered to have distinct problems of arousal both in this study and in that of Levine and Yost.

These problems may be experienced in all sexual activities and encounters or only in some of them. For instance, a woman might become aroused during masturbation but not while engaged in foreplay or intercourse. Furthermore, the latter restriction may apply with all partners or only with some particular man, perhaps her husband towards whom she has negative feelings.

Kaplan (1974) suggests that the consequences of impaired arousal for the women concerned are much more varied than those attaching to erectile dysfunction in men. The latter are almost always emotionally disastrous, and while this is also true for many women, there are some who, at least initially, seem to be more accepting of their lack of responsiveness. They will often engage in intercourse to ensure their partner's pleasure, and in some cases because they enjoy its non-erotic aspects themselves. Later however, many of these women are likely to become resentful and angry as their frustration and disappointment continues in sharp contrast to the gratification being experienced by the male partner. In these circumstances it is understandable that a woman may develop a strong lack of interest or antipathy towards sex and avoid it whenever possible.

The consequences of impaired arousal for the partners of the women concerned are also varied. Some do not expect any more positive sexual response from a woman, while others find it deeply distressing either because of the lack of gratification being experienced by the female partner, or because they perceive this as an adverse reflection on their own sexual attractiveness and competence.

As indicated in the Levine and Yost (1976) study cited above, an impairment of arousal may be primary in the sense that the client has never been able to become adequately aroused with a partner, or it may be secondary in that it commences after a period of normal functioning in this respect. Not uncommonly, this period occurs mainly during dating and courtship, with the dysfunction commencing fairly shortly after marriage. Secondary losses of the capacity for arousal are usually quite persistent before they are considered to amount to a problem for which treatment is sought, some temporary impairment of arousal commonly being accepted at times of particular stress or partner discord.

Causation

The only organic factors that have so far been shown to make a specific contribution to vasocongestive dysfunction are those that are known to reduce vaginal lubrication. Perhaps the most prevalent of these is an oestrogen deficiency arising from the menopause, from premature ovarian failure, or from a lesion anywhere in the hypothalamic-pituitary-ovarian axis. Neurological disorders and diabetes mellitus that disrupt the neural control of the vasocongestive reflexes are additional causes of reduced vaginal lubrication. More generally, it seems at least possible that some of the organic factors that have been shown to contribute to the problems of inadequate interest and orgastic dysfunction might also adversely effect arousal, but this has not yet been demonstrated and is at present entirely speculative.

Any of the stresses discussed in Chapter 4 might contribute to a vasocongestive dysfunction, but none of these have yet been shown to be especially closely associated with this problem. Similarly, none of the stress reactions discussed in that chapter is known to be specifically responsible for the impairment of arousal, but this may well result from the disruptive effects of negative emotional reactions, such as anxiety and anger, as well as those of cognitive monitoring and avoidance. As far as the last type of stress reaction is concerned, it may contribute to vasocongestive dysfunction by reducing or eliminating the client's awareness of erotic sensations and feelings, as discussed in the earlier section on inadequate pleasure. The precise functional relationships between these erotic experiences and the lubrication-swelling responses are not known, but it is likely that the former do serve to promote the latter. To the extent that this is true, then any cognitive avoidance of erotic sensations and feelings will tend to impair vasocongestion.

It follows that if a woman feels angry or hostile towards her partner, or if she fears that he will reject or desert her, then these negative emotional reactions to the stress of partner discord may well disrupt her lubrication-swelling responses. These can also be adversely affected if allowing him to arouse her is perceived as yielding to his domination and control, or as providing him with a source of gratification that the woman would prefer to withhold. Lastly, she may well not respond to him with arousal if she no longer finds him an attractive partner, so that he is not an effective source of sexual stimulation for her.

This leads to the contribution of deficient or inappropriate stimulation to problems of vasocongestion. Clearly, these are likely to arise in the absence of sexual stimulation of sufficient intensity and of a kind that is effective for the woman concerned. For instance, she may well not become adequately aroused if foreplay is too brief or not attuned to her preferences, or if she requires some form of unconventional stimulation that is lacking. Thus, a woman with homosexual preferences might respond quite adequately to a female partner, although the lubrication-swelling responses are absent during sexual encounters with her husband.

Vaginismus

Description

This type of dysfunction can be defined as a spastic contraction of the muscles at the outer third of the vagina and the perineum, which occurs as an involuntary reflex response to a threat of vaginal penetration. Consequently, intromission is either completely prevented or only possible with great difficulty and pain. Sometimes the local muscular spasm is accompanied by similar contraction of the adductor muscles in the thighs so that they cannot be separated, and by assumption of a particular posture involving an arched spine and backward extension of the head. In addition to muscular spasms, many clients suffering from vaginismus also experience considerable fear of penetration; and either or both of these aspects of the problem may result in the non-consummation of a marriage, sometimes over a period of many years. However, such clients are often quite able to become aroused and to reach orgasm by means of other forms of sexual stimulation that do not involve or threaten vaginal penetration.

No information is available on the incidence of vaginismus in general populations, and there is little more on its incidence among those seeking treatment for sexual dysfunction. In the series of 342 such women treated by Masters and Johnson (1970) there were 29 (9%) suffering from vaginismus, and the equivalent figure in the Bancroft and Coles (1976) study cited above is 12 (11%) out of 102 clients.

Occasionally, vaginismus is limited to penile insertion, but much more usually it extends to penetration by any object; including, for example, the self-insertion of a tampon, and a physician's attempt to introduce an examining finger into the vagina.

The husbands of women suffering from vaginismus are often said to be too considerate towards them, and to be weak, gentle, timid, passive, and anxious individuals, who collude with their wife in preserving her dysfunction because both of them are afraid of the aggressive element in sexual activity, or more particularly of the wife being hurt or damaged during it (Ellison, 1972; Friedman, 1962). However, to my knowledge, no comparable information is available on the prevalence of similar characteristics and collusion in marriages where the woman either suffers from another form of sexual dysfunction or is free from problems of this kind. Until such comparable information becomes available it is difficult to assess the significance of the allegations concerning the partners of women suffering from vaginismus.

The consequences of vaginismus for the woman concerned include anxiety and pain if intromission is attempted, as well as feelings of humiliation, disappointment and inadequacy arising from her inability to engage in intercourse. She may also fear that this could lead to desertion by her partner, and a particular source of distress for many clients is their failure to conceive a child. In all these circumstances, it is understandable that sexual encounters become so disturbing to some women that they avoid them whenever possible.

The male partner of a woman suffering from vaginismus is likely also to experience frustration and disappointment, and sometimes to perceive the problem as signifying rejection of him as a lover. Perhaps as a result of these psychological reactions and a long history of denied or failed attempts at intromission, the male partner may develop a sexual dysfunction himself. We see below that there is some evidence for an association between vaginismus and erectile dysfunction, but the nature of any causal relationship between these problems is not yet determined.

Like other sexual dysfunctions, vaginismus may be primary, in that the threat of penetration has always evoked muscular contraction, or it may be a secondary problem that developed after some period of time during which penetration could be accepted without difficulty.

Causation

A later section on female dyspareunia includes information about the many organic factors that can cause pain during intromission and intercourse, and the presence of any of these factors may also result in the occurrence of vaginismus whenever painful penetration is threatened.

Perhaps more commonly, such painful or otherwise distressing accompaniments of penetration have occurred in the client's previous learning experiences and although these aversive conditions are no longer extant she continues to respond to the threat of penetration with muscular contraction and anxiety. In addition to the problem of dyspareunia *per se*, several other types of traumatic events are often reported to have been experienced by patients suffering from vaginismus. These include certain unpleasant experiences in childhood involving such procedures as the administration of an enema, the passing of a catheter, or a vaginal examination, as well as sexual assaults and distressing initial attempts at intercourse. At present, no information is available on the prevalence of such experiences among women suffering from vaginismus compared to those complaining of other sexual dysfunctions, or to those who are without problems of this kind.

Another type of previous learning experience that is often implicated in the aetiology of vaginismus is an excessively restrictive upbringing. For example,

Masters and Johnson (1970) report that 12 of their 29 patients with this problem had family backgrounds in which sexuality was considered to be dirty, sinful, and contrary to very orthodox religious beliefs. However, in an English clinic, Duddle (1977) compared 32 patients seeking treatment for vaginismus with 50 control subjects attending for contraceptive advice only. No significant differences were found between the two groups in respect of the strength of their religious beliefs or in the methods of sex education to which they were exposed. Moreover, those suffering from vaginismus were actually more sexually experienced and responsive before marriage than the controls.

Whether or not as a result of previous learning experiences any attempt at penetration is stressful for the client with vaginismus. It may be threatening because she anticipates that it will hurt or injure her, or that it will prove to be yet another disastrous and distressing failure. There may be a fear of contracting venereal disease, of an unwanted pregnancy, or of contravening some moral or religious objection to sexual activity that the client no longer upholds but which has overgeneralized into her marriage from a restrictive upbringing. A woman may also find penetration threatening because it has long been associated with the frustration of having a dysfunctional partner who is unable to collaborate in making intercourse a satisfying experience for her. As mentioned above, some clients suffering from vaginismus do have a dysfunctional partner; for instance, this was so in 7 of the 32 couples reported by Duddle (1977), and several of the husbands of the women with this problem seen by Masters and Johnson (1970) exhibited either erectile dysfunction or premature ejaculation. The extent to which such male dysfunctions are a cause of vaginismus, or a result of it as discussed above, is not yet clear.

The muscular contractions of vaginismus, together with any accompanying anxiety, can each be conceptualized as involuntary reactions to certain stresses associated with penetration, such as those just described. The contractions can be regarded as overt stress reactions, occurring either as unconditioned responses to an actual painful condition, or as conditioned responses to some aspect of penetration that has been previously associated with discomfort or distress. In either case, the spasm serves as a means of avoiding the threat of penetration, just as a blink serves to protect the eye from a foreign object. Similarly, any accompanying anxiety reactions can be regarded as unconditioned fear responses to an existing problem of dyspareunia, or as conditioned fear responses to some feature of penetration that has been previously associated with certain traumatic events for the client.

Turning to deficient or false information as possible causes of vaginismus, Ellison (1972) suggests that a very large proportion of women suffering from this problem are ignorant and misinformed about sexual matters, and that this is a major source of their fear of penetration. For instance, the most widely held misapprehension among Ellison's patients was that the hymen is a tough barrier that completely obstructs the entrance to the vagina, so that it has to be broken with much accompanying pain and bleeding. However, the prevalence of ignorance and misunderstanding among such patients must be considered in relation to Duddle's finding referred to above, that there were no significant differences in methods of sex education between them and normal control subjects (Duddle, 1977). Although it is possible of course, that those who subsequently developed vaginismus avoided acquiring knowledge from equivalent educational opportunities because this was too disturbing for them.

Lastly, some cases of vaginismus may arise in conditions of inappropriate sexual stimulation. Thus, Masters and Johnson (1970) report that among their 29 patients, there were 2 with a homosexual orientation who were dysfunctional in heterosexual encounters.

INADEQUATE ORGASM

Orgastic dysfunction

Description

This type of dysfunction consists of an involuntary impairment of the orgasm phase in the female response cycle, so that difficulty or failure is experienced in releasing the reflex contractions of the vaginal and pelvic musculature. Thus, the problem is analogous to that of retarded or absent ejaculation in the male.

A client's sexual difficulties may be limited specifically to some impairment of orgastic capacity or this may be accompanied by other forms of dysfunction. For instance, while many inorgastic women retain a high level of sexual interest, this is inadequate in some other such clients. It may be that they lose interest because of their continuing frustration and disappointment at not reaching climax, but it is possible also that inadequate interest contributes to the orgastic dysfunction in some cases.

Similarly, the lubrication-swelling responses will occur normally in many women who are nevertheless unable to reach climax, while there are other such clients who also suffer from a vasocongestive dysfunction. This impairment of arousal may well prevent the client from achieving orgasm, or the stress reactions that such failure evokes could disrupt the lubrication-swelling responses.

Lastly, some women do not reach climax but still obtain a great deal of pleasure from their sexual activities, while others complain of inadequate pleasure in addition to their orgastic dysfunction. It is easy to see that a constant failure to reach climax might well be followed by some loss of pleasure in sexual activities, and that an absence of erotic feelings could also contribute to an impairment of orgasm. What is not quite so obvious, particularly in view of the current emphasis on the desirability of female orgasm, is that some women are able to derive enjoyment and satisfaction from their sexual relationships despite the fact that they do not achieve climax. For instance, although Wallin and Clark (1963) found a strong positive correlation between frequency of orgasm and enjoyment of coitus, some 17% of the women in their sample enjoyed intercourse very much although they experienced orgasm infrequently or not at all. Similarly, 73% of a group of women studied by Butler (1976) reported that it was not necessary for them to have an orgasm in order to enjoy sexual relations, and 39% said that they could obtain a sense of relief of sexual tension without attaining orgasm.

This leads to the issue of when some difficulty or failure in reaching orgasm is to be regarded as amounting to an orgastic dysfunction for which treatment might be sought. The number of women who achieve climax during every sexual experience is relatively small, and in the absence of any absolute or prescribed standards of performance in this respect, reliance must be placed on subjective judgements of inadequacy by those concerned. Among the criteria that are likely to be involved in these judgements are the persistence and frequency of orgastic failure, and circumstances in which it occurs, and the degree of dissatisfaction that is entailed.

In judging the persistence and frequency of failure it is relevant to consider the statistical information that is available on the attainment of orgasm during intercourse by married women drawn from the general population of the United States, and this is summarized in Table 9. It should be noted that this information is subject to biases in sampling and data collection, and that the results from different studies are not exactly comparable because the categories of attainment used are not identical. Nevertheless, this material does offer some background for judgements of orgastic inadequacy, as well as some indication its incidence in the general population. For example, in the investigation reported by Kinsey *et al.* (1953), the proportions of women who had never reached orgasm during marital coitus declined from 25% in the first year of marriage to 11% in the twentieth year, and the single corresponding figures given in three other studies were 8% (Terman, 1951), 5% (Fisher, 1973), and 8% (Butler, 1976). Additionally, Kinsey *et al.* (1953) calculate that marital coitus leads to female orgasm in around 63% of occasions during the first year of marriage, compared to 85% during the twentieth year.

Turning to the circumstances in which orgastic failure occurs, one important aspect of these is likely to be the nature of the sexual stimulation that is being experienced at the time. Some women seek treatment because they are unable to reach orgasm in response to any form of stimulation, while others complain that they cannot do so during intercourse. The latter group usually feel that penile thrusting is the only 'right' and 'normal' way to achieve climax, and that additional manual stimulation should not be necessary even if it is effective. The male partner often shares this view, and he may interpret the woman's failure to climax during intercourse as a sign of her rejection of him or of his incompetent love-making. In the last resort, the choice of conditions under which a woman would like to be able to reach orgasm is a matter for herself and her partner, but they are likely to make a more informed and realistic decision in the light of some important points advanced by Kaplan (1974).

In the first place she describes the wide range of stimulation that is effective in eliciting orgasm in women, and suggests that in this respect they may be distributed along a normal bell-shaped curve. At the lower extreme are those women who are unable to achieve climax in response to any form of stimulation.

Table 9. Attainment of orgasm by married women during intercourse

Source	Attainment of orgasm during intercourse	Proportion of subjects (%)
Terman, L. (1951)	Always or almost always	44
	Never	8
Kinsey, A.C. *et al.* (1953)	On 90 to 100 per cent of occasions	39–47
	Never	11–25
Wallin, P. (1960)	Always	23
	Usually	49
	Never or sometimes	28
Fisher, S. (1973)	Always or almost always	38
	Never	5
Hunt, M. (1974)	On 90 to 100 per cent of occasions	53
	Never or almost never	15
Butler, C.A. (1976)	Always	12
	More than 50 per cent of occasions but not always	51
	Less than 50 per cent of occasions	24
	Never	8

Next are those women who can only reach orgasm by masturbation. In the middle are those who require their partner to provide direct clitoral stimulation by manual, oral, or mechanical means, if they are to attain orgasm. Then comes the group of women who can reach a climax during penile thrusting alone. Finally, at the higher end of the curve, are those who respond with an orgasm to forms of non-genital stimulation such as breast caresses or erotic phantasies.

The second point made by Kaplan (1974) is that this normal distribution of orgastic responsiveness to a range of stimulation may in part reflect the normal variation of thresholds for the female orgastic reflex, although various pathological factors will also contribute to individual differences in orgastic capacity. In this respect, it is suggested that the orgastic reflex is like any other reflex, and Kaplan (1975) cites the example of the patelar reflex that may require anything from a light tap to sharp bang on the tendon in order to elicit a knee jerk, while still remaining within normal limits; however, this reflex can also be inhibited by 'pathological' factors such as a high level of anxiety in the patient. The speculative nature or this explanation for the observed differences in orgastic responsiveness is emphasized, together with our current inability to distinguish normal variation in thresholds from their pathological alteration (Kaplan, 1974).

Implicit in Kaplan's propositions is the assumption that direct stimulation of the clitoris by manual or other means is a more effective trigger for orgasm in many women that its indirect stimulation during intercourse. Some empirical support for this assumption is cited in the section on genital assignments in Chapter 9, where it is noted that traction on the clitoral hood and pressure from the pubic bone provide only indirect stimulation of the clitoris during penile thrusting.

The nature of the current sexual stimulation is by no means the only aspect of the circumstances in which orgastic failure occurs that is likely to enter into judgements of inadequacy; for instance, among other relevant features are some that are associated with the male partner in an encounter. Some women are unable to achieve climax with any man, while others can do so with a partner who possesses certain attributes. For example, there are women who can only reach orgasm in secret and risky extra-marital affairs, while others are unable to do so in those circumstances although they have no difficulty with a husband who is far less attractive to them than a lover. Perhaps, either the excitement of an affair, or the security of a marital relationship, is the more important influence on the orgastic responses of the women in each group, although several alternative explanations are also quite feasible. Another fairly common example of selective orgastic responsiveness is the situation where a woman has been able to reach orgasm quite satisfactorily throughout her marriage, but then becomes unable to do so when there is some deterioration in the general relationship between the spouses for any of a wide variety of reasons.

The degree of dissatisfaction that orgastic failure entails for the woman and her partner will very probably be an important factor in their judgements of inadequacy and the need for treatment. We note above that some women are able to derive enjoyment and satisfaction from their sexual relationships although these do not culminate in orgasm, but for many other women this impairment is a considerable source of distress. They feel frustrated, disappointed, and concerned at their lack of orgasm. Instead of being relaxed and satisfied by a pleasurable release from tension they are liable to be left in a state of irritability or fatigue. The unresolved pelvic vasocongestion sometimes leads to pain being experienced during or after intercourse. Damage may occur to the woman's self-concept, for she may think that there must be something very wrong with her if she cannot have an orgasm and consequently feel ashamed of herself. In order to hide her inadequacy she may fake orgasm with a partner, and this is especially likely to happen if she fears that he will react adversely to her failure to reach climax, perhaps by becoming resentful or angry, by rejecting her, or by blaming himself. In all these circumstances its understandable that inorgastic women will often lose interest in sex, and do everything they can to avoid or shorten their sexual encounters.

While some men are uncaring about a female partner's inability to reach climax, there are many others for whom this is also a source of great distress. They feel considerable concern and sympathy for the woman, and may blame their own incompetent lovemaking for her problem. It is also sometimes misinterpreted as an adverse reflection on the man's attractiveness to his female partner, and this view is likely to be bolstered if she loses interest in sex and avoids it whenever possible. Frequently, the male partner becomes frustrated, resentful, and angry, and when the woman is experiencing similar feelings, it is readily understandable that confrontations will occur and escalate, so that considerable discord may develop between them.

Causation

If intercourse is painful for a woman, due to any of the reasons discussed in the next section on dyspareunia, then this may well impair her capacity to reach orgasm. Otherwise, few organic factors have been implicated as direct causes of orgastic dysfunction, the most obvious of these being renal disorders and diabetes mellitus, the respective contributions of which are considered in Chapter 2.

The following Chapter 3, includes a discussion of a range of previous learning experiences of an adverse kind that are commonly reported in the histories of women suffering from orgastic dysfunction, but it is noted, that this problem does not inevitably follow such experiences which are also undergone by many women who do not subsequently develop any form of sexual dysfunction (Fisher, 1973; Terman, 1938, 1951; Uddenberg, 1974). This does not mean that a traumatic experience, a restrictive upbringing, or adverse family relationships are not important causal factors in particular cases of orgastic difficulty, but the only such experience for which there is evidence of a significant association with this kind of difficulty is a poor daughter/father relationship, or one that is disrupted by the father's early death or prolonged absence from home (Fisher, 1973; Uddenberg, 1974).

Any of the stresses discussed in Chapter 4 could evoke reactions that disrupt the orgastic reflex. In particular, a woman might find it threatening to abandon herself to the experience of orgasm because this might involve a loss of control over herself or a change in her personality. She may fear that she will scream or lose consciousness, or even urinate or defecate, and perhaps also that she will appear ugly or unattractive to her partner during orgasm. A client may believe that once having achieved climax she will no longer be the same person, and could perhaps become promiscuous or sexually insatiable. Another group of relevant stresses are those of a performance nature, so that the woman is anxious that she will not be able to reach orgasm, and this fear is likely to be especially acute if she is under pressure from her partner to succeed, or if she anticipates that failure to do so will be followed by his criticism or hostility. A related form of stress arises when a woman is so overconcerned about ensuring her partner's pleasure that she completely subordinates her own sexual preferences and satisfaction, consequently, she may for example, be most reluctant to ask him for the kind of stimulation she needs in order to reach climax. Women who are worried that their partner may reject or leave them are often particularly vulnerable to this last source of stress.

The involuntary inhibition of muscular contractions in orgastic dysfunction can be regarded as an overt reaction to stresses such as those discussed in the previous paragraph. Clearly, it serves to avoid the attainment of climax which is for some reason threatening to the woman concerned. It is possible that other stress reactions such as anxiety and spectatoring could also disrupt the orgastic reflex, but precisely how this might happen is not known at the present time, except in so far as these reactions impair arousal so that it does not build up sufficiently for orgasm to occur, as discussed in the earlier sections on vasocongestive dysfunction and inadequate pleasure.

Although no correlation was found between capacity for orgasm and quality of marital relationship in groups of women drawn from the general populations of the United States and Sweden (Fisher, 1973; Uddenberg, 1974), there is no doubt that orgastic dysfunction and partner discord are associated in some couples. This may be more likely when orgasm is impaired after a period of normal functioning in this respect; for instance, in the study by McGovern et al. (1975) mentioned in Chapter 4, marital discord was found to be more prevalent in couples where the woman was suffering from secondary orgastic dysfunction, than in those where her dysfunction was of a primary nature.

To the extent that partner discord is a cause, rather than a result, of orgastic dysfunction, then there are a number of ways in which this could occur. If a couple is engaged in a conflict over who is to control their relationship, then the woman might perceive reaching orgasm as an act of submission to her partner. If he is not sufficiently attractive to her or if she feels anger towards him, then her sexual arousal may be impaired so that it does not build up to orgasm. The inability to achieve this might also serve as an expression of hostility towards a disliked or hated partner, especially if he perceives the woman's failure as an adverse reflection on his own masculinity and virility. A woman might also hold back from orgasm because she sees it as implying a greater commitment to a relationship with her partner than she is prepared to make, or as increasing her dependence on him for sexual gratification so that she becomes more vulnerable to any threat of his rejection or desertion. Finally among these examples, is the situation where an existing orgastic dysfunction is worsened or maintained by a partner's pressure on the woman to achieve orgasm, or by her anticipation of a critical or hostile reaction from him if she fails to do so.

Finally, a woman may have difficulty or fail in reaching orgasm because the sexual stimulation she receives is deficient or inappropriate. For instance, foreplay or intercourse may not be sufficiently prolonged or sensitive to her preferences for her to be able to attain a level of arousal at which orgasm could occur. The importance of direct clitoral stimulation as a trigger for orgasm in many, but not all, women is discussed above, and if sufficient and appropriate stimulation of this kind is not provided then orgasm may well fail to occur.

Among the many possible reasons for such a deficiency of suitable stimulation is ignorance on the part of the woman concerned or her partner, of its importance in triggering orgasm and of how it is most effectively and pleasurably provided to meet her preferences. Other reasons include a reluctance by the woman to communicate these preferences to her partner, an avoidance of the stimulation required because it is stressful to either or both of them, or its withholding by the male partner as an expression of hostility towards the woman.

INADEQUATE SEXUAL PLEASURE OR PAINFUL INTERCOURSE

The problem of inadequate pleasure in women is considered in the previous chapter, leaving dyspareunia to be discussed in this section.

Dyspareunia

Description

During intromission or intercourse, and after it has ended, women may experience pain at the entrance to the vagina, the clitoris, the vaginal barrel, or the internal pelvic organs.

Dyspareunia may be associated with any other sexual dysfunction in the same client. It is readily understandable that painful intercourse might lead to inadequate interest or pleasure in sex, to a disruption of the vasocongestive or orgastic responses, or to vaginismus; and we see below that these other dysfunctions may also contribute to dyspareunia.

Causation

The very many organic causes of female dyspareunia are reviewed by Masters and Johnson (1970), Musaph and Haspels (1977), and Wabrek and Wabrek (1975), and the following outline is largely based on these sources. This refers mainly to the relevant local genital disorders, but it is important to recall that discomfort during intercourse can also arise in certain systemic diseases; for instance, from inflamed joints in arthritis, or from angina in cardiac disorders.

The commonest causes of pain at the entrance to the vagina are hymenal problems, tender scars, inelastic tissues, certain conditions affecting Bartholin's glands, and vaginismus which is discussed in an earlier section. The hymen may be imperforate, microperforate, rigid, or scarred, making intercourse impossible or painful (Greer, 1975). Tender scar tissue may form at the hymen or elsewhere in the genital area, sometimes as a result of trauma or sexual assault, but more usually following the obstetrical procedure of episiotomy. In postmenopausal women, the tissues of the labia and vagina sometimes become relatively inelastic due to the withdrawal of oestrogen. More rarely, introital pain may arise from an enlargement of Bartholin's gland in the labia minora, perhaps due to an infection or cyst.

Painful inflammation or irritation of the clitoris can arise from an accumulation of smegna under the hood, and from lesions or scar tissue on the shaft (Fordney–Settlage, 1975). Another cause of discomfort is too vigorous manual stimulation of the clitoris during masturbation or lovemaking.

Pain in the vaginal barrel is usually experienced in the form of burning, itching, or aching sensations, and it is likely to occur both during and after intercourse. Perhaps the most prevalent source of such discomfort is insufficient lubrication, due to any of the factors discussed in the earlier section on vasocongestive dysfunction. A related source of vaginal pain is atrophic vaginitis, arising either from oestrogen deficiency in postmenopausal women, or from radiation in those who have had radium treatment for cancer, both of which lead to a thinning of the lining of the vagina so that its resistance to infection, trauma, and chemical agents is lowered. Whether or not atrophic vaginitis is present, a woman may experience irritation and inflammation in the vaginal passage as a result of a variety of infections, or of allergic sensitivity reactions to certain chemical agents in contraceptive substances or devices, in hygienic preparations, or in clothing fabrics or detergents.

Pelvic pain occurs with deep penile thrusting (as if the penis is hitting something inside), or it may commence shortly after intercourse has ended. Many types of pathology affecting the internal pelvic organs are sometimes responsible, including infections, cysts, tumours, fibroids, and endometrial tissue growths. The vagina may be foreshortened or scarred after hysterectomy; or the broad ligaments that support the uterus may be lacerated, usually accompanied by retroversion and enlargement of this organ. Lastly, pelvic pain may arise from intense vasocongestion resulting from prolonged sexual stimulation and not relieved by orgasm (*Medical Aspects of Human Sexuality*, 1978).

It will be apparent from the foregoing outline that female dyspareunia is often a direct effect of organic pathology, but this does not exclude a contribution from psychological factors in some cases. For instance, any of the stress conditions discussed in Chapter 4 may evoke certain stress reactions that contribute to painful intercourse. Among the more obvious examples of these are the anxiety or anger reactions that disrupt vaginal lubrication, and the overt reaction represented by the muscular spasm in patients suffering from vaginismus. One particular stress that may elicit such reactions is the anticipation of pain during intercourse because such discomfort has been experienced in the past, although the organic pathology that caused it at that time is no longer present.

It is possible though not yer demonstrated that such stress reactions might help to explain the prevalence of complaints of dyspareunia among women with a diagnosis of hysteria. Their relatively high exposure to sexual stresses and to partner discord is indicated in Chapter 4, where it noted also that in one study 79% of these patients complained of pain during intercourse (Winokur and Holeman, 1963), while in another the equivalent figure was 63% of hysterics compared to 7% of healthy controls (Purtell *et al.*, 1951).

This concludes discussion of the male and female sexual dysfunctions, and we turn in the next part of the book to consideration of their treatment.

Part 3

An Overview of Treatment

8

Therapeutic Interviews

The purpose of this part of the book is to describe a range of components that can be drawn up to constitute treatment programmes for sexual dysfunction. These components are selected and implemented to suit individual clients, as discussed in the next part on assessment and the planning of treatment. In the present part the various components are covered at a purely descriptive level, almost all evaluation of their efficacy being deferred until Part 5.

In broad terms, the available components can be categorized into some general therapeutic contributions provided in interviews between the therapists and the clients; certain sexual assignments undertaken by couples when alone in their own homes; some relatively specific behavioural procedures; and various forms of physical treatment used as ancillaries to those other components. The last three categories are considered in subsequent chapters, while therapeutic interviews are discussed in this chapter.

The more general therapeutic contributions provided in a series of interviews between the therapists and clients, include the provision of information, the modification of attitudes, and the management of the sexual assignments. This does not imply that information transmission and attitude change are restricted to the interview situation, they also occur during the sexual assignments and specific treatment procedures, but they are important components of any treatment programme and almost invariably play a large part in the interviews.

PROVISION OF INFORMATION

One function of therapeutic interviews is to provide clients with the information they need to rectify any deficiencies or inaccuracies in their knowledge of sexual matters that may contribute to their dysfunction or impede its successful treatment.

Aging

Aging clients may require information about the natural organic changes to be expected in their sexual response cycles and the implications of these for their sexual capacity and enjoyment. Thus, men may need to appreciate that it is quite natural for their erections to occur less rapidly and for them to ejaculate less frequently, but that such changes do not signify the onset of impotence or the cessation of pleasurable sexual performance for the remainder of their lives. Similarly, older women may need to be informed that slower and less profuse lubrication, together with fewer muscular contractions during orgasm, are natural changes with aging, and that the menopause does not destroy all sexual interest and capacity. Accurate information on matters such as these may well help to prevent or alleviate any adverse psychological reactions to the natural organic changes of the aging process.

Illness, surgery, or drugs

Similar prophylactic and therapeutic advantages are likely to accrue from the provision of information about the implications for sexual functioning of an illness, surgical intervention, or drug. For instance, where appropriate, postcoronary patients and their spouses should be quite specifically advised that is feasible and safe to resume intercourse, otherwise the prospect of this may be very stressful for them and they may unnecessarily restrict their sexual activities, sometimes to the extent of complete abstinence. Patients suffering from a neurological disorder and their partners may be helped very considerably if it is explained to them that a sexual dysfunction is attributable to the organic condition rather than any lack of virility or loss of love, and it may be especially important to convey this when the illness is of a less visible kind like diabetes mellitus. Such couples also need to know that neurological damage does not inevitably entail some loss of sexual capacity, but that when this does occur it is usually partial rather than complete. Thus, a man with a spinal cord injury may still be able to respond to tactile stimulation of his genitals, or the other forms of sexual stimulation, if not to both. Likewise, his residual responses may include brief or partial erections, ejaculation through a flaccid penis, or the successful and pleasurable performance of intercourse despite the occurrence of retrograde ejaculation. This last problem and its associated residual capacity, is also commonly reported after prostatectomy operations, and it is one example of a dysfunction that needs to be explained to couples as being direct result of the surgical intervention, and as involving only partial rather than complete loss of sexual capacity. Similarly, if this is temporarily impaired as a result of drinking alcohol or of taking tranquillizing, antidepressant or antihypertensive medication, then both partners should be helped to appreciate the correct cause of the sexual difficulty and that it will be resolved once the drug is discontinued. Such information may serve to avoid or mitigate any adverse psychological reactions to an organic condition, which otherwise might extend or prolong a limited or transient impairment of sexual functioning.

In addition to understanding the effects and limitations arising from any relevant organic condition, clients and their spouses may also require information about how their residual potential for sexual functioning can be realized to the fullest possible extent. This will include advice about preparing for sexual activity. Thus, postcoronary patients should not attempt intercourse with a full stomach, others with spinal cord injuries should empty their bladder and bowel just before intercourse so that involuntary voiding does not occur during it, and those with catheters will need to remove these or to fold them over the penis during intromission. It may be desirable to place pillows or cushions so that they provide protection, reduce discomfort, facilitate movement and maintain balance, for patients such as limb amputees or those suffering from an arthritic disorder. Secondly, it may be necessary to discuss the use of alternative positions for intercourse. An arthritic woman who cannot abduct and externally rotate her hips is unable to have intercourse with her partner laying on top of her and between her legs, but it may be quite feasible if he is astride her almost closed legs or in certain other positions. Similarly, a side by side or female superior position is indicated for couples in which the man has had a myocardial infarction, and for whom the traditional male superior position is usually inadvisable. This is because it requires the man to support his own weight on his arms, and the sustained isometric muscle contraction this involves is known to increase peripheral vascular resistance and to raise aortic blood pressure, which enhances the risk of cardiac symptoms occurring. Next, couples may profit from the provision of information that leads to the modification of their aspirations concerning intercourse; for instance, that it can be a very pleasurable experience even if it is not performed strenuously or does not culminate in ejaculation or orgasm. The same point applies to a couple's use of non-coital forms or sexual activity to supplement or replace penile–vaginal intercourse when this is difficult or impossible. In the context of their total relationship, both partners may derive enormous satisfaction from practices such as holding and touching each other, petting, mutual masturbation, oral sex, and the use of prosthetic aids like a vibrator or artificial penis. Some discussion of these techniques may well help such couples to explore and utilize them effectively.

Sexual anatomy and responses

We turn now from the provision of information concerning the nature and management of the effects of aging, illness, surgery, and drugs on sexual functioning, to that required by all clients. In the first place, this includes sufficient and accurate knowledge about the genital anatomy and responses of their own and the opposite sex. Thus, a man may need to be informed that penises differ little in size when erect, of the location of his wife's clitoris, or of the reality of the muscular spasm if she suffers from vaginismus. The fact that sexual responses are natural reactions to sexual stimulation often needs emphasizing, so that clients realize that responses such as erections or lubrication cannot be produced by any deliberate act of will on the part of the husband or wife concerned. Certain misconceptions about the female orgasm may need to be dispelled; for instance, that any differences in the subjective experience of orgasm in response to various kinds of stimulation do not signify that there is more than one kind of orgasm at a physiological level. Furthermore, the wife is not going to be injured if she reaches orgasm and this will not entail complete loss of control over her own functioning, nor is it liable to make her promiscuous or to otherwise alter her personality or life style in any fundamental way.

Finally, many couples are helped by the provision of information about the very wide variation in sexual behaviour and the absence of any absolute norms. Among the many possible examples is the information that men are not always able to become aroused under any conditions, and that all women cannot reach orgasm by penile thrusting alone. There is wide variation between couples in the frequencies of intercourse they find acceptable, and this does not culminate in simultaneous orgasm on every occasion. It is not at all unusual for couples to engage in mutual masturbation, oral–genital contacts, and a variety of coital positions, nor is it uncommon for people to dream or fantasize occasionally about forms of sexual behaviour, perhaps of an adulterous, incestuous, or homosexual nature, that they would not be prepared to put into practice.

Anticipation of harm

The provision of relevant information may serve to reduce any anticipation of harm from sexual activities; for instance, any false expectations that these might cause the relapse or death of a postcoronary patient, or that a postoperative state might be damaged, or that pain and discomfort might be experienced. Similarly, it may be wise to ensure that clients suffering from a psychiatric disorder do not believe this to have been caused by their sexual activities, or that the resumption of these might aggravate or prolong the condition. Some dysfunctional men may need accurate information from an authoritative source to convince them that penetration will not hurt or injure their female partner. Finally, if a couple are concerned about the possibility of an unwanted pregnancy, then it is important for them to receive proper contraceptive advice, including accurate information about the effectiveness of the various methods available to them.

Anticipation of failure

Information is very often given to clients in order to counteract some unrealistic anticipation of sexual failure. For a variety of reasons, including aging, illness, drug effects and previous difficulty, a man may be wrongly convinced that he is bound to fail to get an erection, or a woman that she will never be able to reach orgasm, and each may be helped by knowledge of the naturalness of these responses unless they are disrupted by stress reactions such as anxiety or spectatoring. Likewise this information may relieve a wife's unfounded belief that her husband's inability to obtain an erection is a reflection of her declining attractiveness, or a man's incorrect assumption that his insufficiently skilled lovemaking is to blame for his wife's difficulty in reaching orgasm. It can also be very beneficial for the partner of a dysfunctional client to express understanding and acceptance of the sexual problem, in order to counteract any unrealistic expectations that it will elicit adverse reactions from the partner such as ridicule, criticism, anger, or rejection.

Moral or religious beliefs

While it is not the function of a therapist to deliberately attempt to impose his own values on clients, he may quite properly provide them with certain kinds of information to reduce the stressfulness of sexual behaviour which contravenes their moral or religious beliefs. One instance is the correction of any misinterpretation of religious dogma that unnecessarily restricts a client's sexual activities or enjoyment. An example of this is the case of a Roman Catholic woman suffering from vaginismus, who thought it wrong for herself and her husband to engage in foreplay in case this resulted in either of them committing the sin of reaching orgasm outside the act of intercourse. This case also demonstrated the advantages of arranging for an authoritative religious adviser to assist in resolving difficulties of this kind.

Secondly, it may be beneficial for clients to appreciate that some impairment of sexual behaviour is not surprising if this is attempted in circumstances that contravene their own standards of conduct, and that any such failure does not necessarily signify that they will also be dysfunctional under different conditions that are morally acceptable to them. Thus, a girl who has been brought up to believe that pre-marital intercourse is wrong, may well fail to lubricate or reach orgasm if it is attempted, but she will not necessarily experience any similar difficulty in a subsequent marital relationship. Likewise, a man who believes that adultery is wrong may not be able to get an erection in an extra-marital affair, while experiencing no such problem with his wife. In either of these examples, of course, the impairment might generalize to morally acceptable situations if the original failure is compounded by stress reactions such as performance anxiety or cognitive monitoring, and the risk of this occurring may be much reduced if the individual concerned is properly informed along the lines suggested.

Non-sexual stresses or partner discord

There may be a similar advantage in helping clients to understand that their sexual functioning can be adversely affected by various non-sexual stresses or by marital discord, but that providing these conditions are relieved, and the original impairment is not compounded by stress reactions like performance anxiety, then a temporary problem need not escalate into a permanent dysfunction. Thus, once an occupational or financial problem is resolved there may be a spontaneous recovery of sexual interest and capacity, or an improvement in the general relationship between spouses may be accompanied by the return of the wife's ability to reach orgasm during lovemaking with her husband.

Stress reactions

In addition to acquiring information about any stress conditions that may be contributing to their difficulties, most couples also need to learn something about their stress reactions and the disruptive effect of these on their sexual functioning.

The reactions of performance anxiety and spectatoring are often readily recognized by clients, and it can be beneficial for them to appreciate how these can distract and detach them from their lovemaking so that the natural response of sexual arousal does not occur. Another instance of how relevant information about stress reactions can be helpful arises when there is a decline in the frequency of a couple's sexual activities and in all physical expressions of affection between them. Such changes are commonly misinterpreted as signifying the cessation of love in the marriage, and it can be very reassuring for clients to recognize them as specific ways of avoiding situations that have become stressful because of the sexual difficulties being experienced.

Deficient or inappropriate stimulation

Lastly, when couples are not exchanging sufficient and appropriate sexual stimulation due to some gaps in their knowledge, then these may be filled by the provision of relevant information. For instance, a husband may learn of his wife's need for more prolonged foreplay that is attuned to her sexual preferences, in order to enable her to become more highly aroused and to reach orgasm. Similarly, a wife may need help to understand that her husband is only able to obtain an erection under very specific conditions, such as when he is wearing certain articles of female clothing during lovemaking. Some basic knowledge about this kind of unconventional sexual behaviour both by her husband as an individual and among other males, is a necessary precondition for any meaningful discussion between the partners about how the behaviour is to be accommodated or modified in their sexual relationship. Very many other examples of the kind of information that may improve the effectiveness of sexual stimulation are cited throughout the remainder of this chapter, as well as earlier in this section with particular reference to the physically disabled.

Methods of providing information

Information on any of the topics mentioned above can be imparted in number of ways. In addition to giving didactic instruction, the therapists may objectively restate what the clients say about their difficulties and reactions. This 'reflective teaching' or 'mirroring', as Masters and Johnson (1970) call it, can help couples to recognize and understand their own functioning. An impotent man may realize how strongly he anticipates erectile failure, or an inorgastic woman may come to appreciate how her sexual sensations and feelings are switched off as she approaches climax.

A variety of audio-visual aids are commonly used to supplement verbal instruction from the therapists; for example, the female genital anatomy may be demonstrated by means of illustrations or models, and there are films and videotapes available for teaching about sexual responses and techniques. Couples may also be asked to read certain material which the therapists have selected as being especially relevant and suitable for these particular clients, and it is sometimes suggested that they read this aloud to each other. This practice may facilitate communication between them about sexual matters and have a disinhibiting effect, in addition to conveying the information concerned.

Some therapists utilize a conjoint medical examination by a physician as a means of instructing couples about their sexual anatomy and physiology. This may be done routinely with all clients (Croft, 1975; Murray, 1976; Skynner, 1976a), or only when it is especially indicated; as in cases of vaginismus where a physical demonstration of the reality of the muscular spasm is likely to be beneficial for both partners (Masters and Johnson, 1970). Where appropriate, other informants may be recruited by the therapists; for instance, an authoritative religious adviser to correct any misinterpretations of dogma that are impeding sexual functioning. Another example, is the use of peer informants, such as physically handicapped people who discuss their own sexual problems and solutions with clients facing similar difficulties.

In addition to transmitting information from the therapists and other informants to the clients, the interviews may also facilitate an exchange of information between the clients themselves. Perhaps because of their inhibitions, they have often never really talked to each other about topics such as their likes and dislikes in sexual activity or their feelings about its impairment, or they may have discontinued all discussion of them as an avoidance reaction. Thus, talking with the therapists about such matters may have the important spin-off of sanctioning, facilitating, and enhancing communication between the partners themselves, in other words there may be a catalytic effect. Consequently, a wife might be enabled to demonstrate her own genital anatomy to her husband and to show him where and how she likes to be stimulated. Similarly, the wife of an impotent man can reassure him that any sexual failure will not be ridiculed or criticized, and he can explain to her that he is avoiding sexual encounters and all physical expressions of affection not through any loss of love or attraction towards her but because he is so apprehensive about his own sexual performance. This leads to the important general point mentioned earlier, that the provision of information is not restricted to the therapeutic interview component of the approach being described, clients also gain a great deal of knowledge when they engage in the sexual assignments and specific treatment procedures that are discussed later in this chapter.

MODIFICATION OF ATTITUDES

This second function of therapeutic interviews is quite closely related to the provision of information, for attitudes are commonly defined as a combination of feelings and beliefs that predispose a person to respond in a positive or negative manner to the object of the attitude, and the belief component reflects the adequacy and accuracy of his knowledge about that object.

Such attitudes require modification when they are impairing sexual functioning or impeding its therapeutic improvement. For instance, some clients expect sex to be unpleasant or regard it as dirty, degrading, immoral, or sinful, while particular activities, such as those of an oral–genital kind, may be thought to be indicative of abnormality or perversion. Other adverse attitudes include an achievement orientation towards sex so that the individual is grossly overconcerned with reaching a certain result or standard of performance, rather than simply relaxing and enjoying sex as a natural function that requires no special effort. This kind of orientation is associated in some clients with idealistic attitudes towards sexual relationships, so that they aspire to quite unrealistic levels of performance and gratification.

In addition to such deleterious attitudes towards sexual behaviour *per se*, this can also be adversely affected by attitudes of dislike, rejection, or hostility between the partners, as well as by their attitudes towards the sexual problem and its treatment. Quite commonly, clients have little confidence in their own ability to cope with the sexual problem, and they are 'demoralized' in the sense of being disheartened, bewildered, confused, and disordered (Frank, 1973). Their attitudes towards treatment may also be disadvantageous, in that they have scant faith in the likelihood of it helping them effectively.

It is clear that any of these attitudes towards sexuality, the partner, the client's own problem, or to his treatment, will involve not only certain beliefs but also some accompanying feelings such as anxiety, depression, guilt, or anger.

Therapeutic relationship

In order to modify such adverse attitudes, and to facilitate the whole treatment programme, it is necessary to establish certain general conditions in the course of the early interviews with clients. One of these conditions, the therapeutic relationship, is considered to be an important source of beneficial change in almost all approaches to treatment, including behaviour therapy (Frank, 1973; Truax and Carkhuff, 1967; Wilson and Evans, 1976; Wilson and Evans, 1977).

The results of a considerable body of research are generally, but not unequivocally, supportive of the conclusion that the quality of the relationship and the outcome of treatment are both strongly influenced by the levels of empathy, warmth, and genuineness exhibited by the therapist and perceived by the client (Bergin and Suinn, 1975; Gurman, 1977; Mitchell *et al.*, 1977; Truax and Carkhuff, 1967; Truax and Mitchell, 1971).

In this context the term *empathy* is defined as the 'ability to perceive and communicate accurately and with sensitivity both the feelings and experiences of another person and their meaning and significance . . . we step into the other person's shoes and view the world from his emotional and perceptual vantage point . . . . This allows us to contribute to the expansion and clarification of the other person's own awareness of his experiences and feelings' (Truax and Mitchell, 1971, p. 317). The term '*warmth*' is used to refer to several features of effective therapeutic relationships. The therapist is receptive and spontaneous when communicating with the client, and 'acceptance' is conveyed to him through the therapist's non-judgemental and non-dominating manner. Moreover, an unconditional positive regard for the client is expressed, together with a deep concern for his welfare. These features provide an atmosphere that is non-threatening, safe and trusting, as well as promoting self respect in the client. Finally, the therapist's *'genuineness'* means that he is a real and authentic person with clients, rather than adopting any pretence or hiding behind the facade of his professional or other roles. This provides the basis for an honest and open therapeutic relationship.

When this relationship is characterized by high levels of empathy, warmth, and genuineness, it is likely to be accompanied by a reduction in the client's demoralization, as well as an improvement in communication between him and the therapist, whose therapeutic influence is also enhanced. As far as *reduction in demoralization* is concerned, the client becomes convinced that his welfare is of real concern to the therapist who is committed to pursuing it, and this discovery in itself can boost morale and overcome feelings of isolation and alienation (Frank, 1973). In consequence, the client's motivation and capacity for coping with his problems are likely to be improved. Good *communication* is facilitated because the therapist is increasingly trusted by the client who is correspondingly more willing to risk disclosing his problems and feelings. The therapist's *influence* on the client is likely to be enhanced because their relationship of mutual trust, respect and attraction tends to reduce the client's defensiveness, increase his openmindedness, and generally make him more accessible to treatment with greater potential for beneficial changes in attitudes and behaviour.

Causal explanation

A second general condition for effective treatment is some understanding between the therapist and the client about the causation of the problem concerned. The provision of *any* plausible explanation for difficulties that previously seemed inexplicable and strange may be very reassuring to clients (Frank, 1973; Sloane *et al.*, 1977), but some factors have been identified that tend to make such explanations especially helpful (Jones *et al.*, 1971, Valins and Nisbett, 1971). One of these factors is the attribution of the client's complaints to *normal* rather than pathological causes (Ross *et al.*, 1969), an example being the explanation of slower erections and fewer ejaculations in terms of the natural aging process rather than the onset of impotence. Another such factor is the attribution of problems to causes of a *temporary* rather than a permanent nature, thus it may be helpful for a client to know that a traumatic failure to get an erection was due to the amount of alcohol he had consumed at the time rather than a chronic physical or psychological disorder. In particular, an explanation in terms of transient causes may enhance the client's confidence in the possibility of improvement, which bodes well for the outcome of treatment as we see in the next paragraph. Lastly, it may be helpful if problems are seen as arising from *external* causes rather than being the personal responsibility of the individual concerned (Phares, 1973). Thus, it may be less distressing for a man to be able to attribute his impotence to diabetes or a spinal injury, rather than a lack of masculinity or virility. Similarly, a wife may be relieved to appreciate that she has lost all interest in sex as a reaction to the stress of serious illness in the family and not because she no longer loves her husband.

Prognostic expectancy

A third general condition for positive change in clients is that they have some expectation of receiving effective help. Most forms of treatment, including behaviour therapy, are in part successful because they enhance the client's hope of relief from his problem, and the significant influence of this expectation on the outcome of treatment has long been recognized in the literature on placebo effects and prognostic expectancies (Fish, 1973; Frank, 1973; Goldstein, 1962; Shapiro, 1971; Wilkins, 1973). For example, Friedman (1963) asked psychiatric patients before their initial interview to complete a symptom check list describing how they felt at that time, and then to complete the list again saying how they expected to feel after having six months' treatment of their own choice. The difference between these two scores gave a measure of expected improvement. After the initial interview they again filled in the check list, and the difference between this score and that on the first administration was taken as a measure of symptom reduction. A significant positive correlation was found between the measures of expected improvement and symptom reduction. A second possible example of the relationship between patient prognostic expectancies and therapeutic outcome is provided by Frank *et al.* (1959). They randomly assigned neurotic patients to one of three types of treatment: group therapy for one and a half hours a week; individual therapy for one hour a week; or individual 'minimal contact' therapy for half an hour every two weeks. After six months' treatment, there was a significant reduction of symptoms in all three groups, but no significant differences between groups in this respect. Furthermore, those patients who had dropped out of treatment within a month improved as much as those who completed six months' treatment. Thus, symptom relief was unrelated to the type or duration of therapy and seemed to occur quite promptly. The investigators sought therefore, an explanatory factor which was common to all the patients, and suggested that this might be the expectation of help aroused in their initial contact with a therapist.

Such an expectation is probably derived from several factors in the therapeutic situation, including the therapist's ability to offer an explanation for the client's problem, as discussed above. For example, Wolberg (1967) writes that 'Assignment of the illness to its responsible determinants tends to alleviate fear of the unknown. It matters little whether the identified source is factual or not. So long as the patient believes it, his catastrophic sense of helplessness is palliated. The healer may diagnose the condition as due to infestation with evil spirits, or regression to an anachronistic psychosexual level of development, or operations of unconscious conflict, or to a disrupted biochemical balance within the body. If the patient accepts the diagnosis, his very focusing on a presumed source of mischief opens up new possibilities of action. . . .Rituals to exorcise offended spirits or to destroy them; free associations to liberate unconscious foci of conflict; medicaments to reinstate the biochemical balances; conditioning to restore the individual to healthy habit patterns; whatever the theory of aetiology, pertinent measures are executed to resolve the problem source . . . '(p.27). Another factor that enhances the expectation of being helped is the client's confidence or faith in the therapist. This stems from a therapeutic relationship of the kind discussed above, and from the apparent or real expertness and status of the therapist which have been shown to influence the client's respect for him (Goldstein, 1971; Strong and Schmidt, 1970). Finally, the expectation of benefit from a programme of treatment is likely to be influenced by the extent of the client's confidence in the procedures to be used, therefore they are implemented it is important to discuss their rationale and efficacy very thoroughly with clients.

So far we have considered the general therapeutic conditions of an effective relationship, an acceptable causal explanation and an adequate expectation of help. Typically, these conditions are necessary or facilitative rather than sufficient for successful treatment. They constitute a foundation for this, but the deployment of more specific procedures aimed at particular therapeutic targets is also required in most cases. As far as the modification of adverse attitudes towards sexual behaviour is concerned, among the specific procedures that might be used in interview situations are sanctioning, self-disclosure, role playing, and cognitive or rational restructuring.

Sanctioning

A therapist who is liked, respected, and trusted constitutes an authoritative source of sanction for positive sexual attitudes. He can give a client the permission and reassurance he needs to regard his sexuality as something to be enjoyed and valued, rather than as unpleasant, dirty, degrading, abnormal, or perverted.

Similarly, the therapist can use his influence to modify performance oriented or idealistic attitudes towards sex; for instance, an elderly man can be reassured that intercourse is still an appropriate and pleasurable activity for him and his wife even if he does not ejaculate on every occasion, or the self-imposed pressures on a couple to reach simultaneous or multiple orgasms can be relieved by the authoritative sanctioning of more realistic levels of performance.

While it is not part of a therapist's role to attempt to change a client's moral or religious convictions concerning various forms of sexual behaviour, it is not uncommon for clients who have themselves abandoned these beliefs still to be unable to rid themselves of the guilt and inhibitions associated with them. In these circumstances, such clients may be helped by the therapist's permission to practise and enjoy the activities concerned. In other cases, clients may need the therapist's support to adhere to their convictions in the face of contrary pressures from other people. Thus, someone who believes that premarital intercourse is wrong, may be helped by the therapist's reassurance that there is no reason to engage in it unless he or she wishes to do so.

Self disclosure

As a means of conveying sanction and promoting positive attitudes in clients, it is sometimes appropriate and helpful for the therapist to disclose his own sexual attitudes and practices (Jourard, 1964). To some extent this is inevitable during their discussions, but it can also be employed more deliberately and explicitly. This may be an effective technique for changing attitudes providing that it is used sensitively and within the context of a relationship of mutual liking, respect and trust, otherwise the client may simply reject the therapist and his views.

Roleplaying

Roleplaying is another technique that may be used to change attitudes in interview situations (Corsini, 1966). The client is asked to take the role of another person and to present the attitudes of that person in an involved manner. For instance, a client who regards sex as degrading or unpleasant, could play the role of someone who values and enjoys his sexuality, and the arguments that person might use to support his position would be expressed by the client to the therapist. In this way the client may increase his understanding of an alternative viewpoint to his own, and perhaps persuade himself of its validity. There is in fact, considerable evidence from laboratory studies and rather less from clinical settings, that participant roleplaying does produce greater attitude change than passive exposure to the same arguments (Goldstein and Simonson, 1971).

The findings also suggest a number of factors that are likely to enhance attitude change through roleplaying. One of these is the client's *public commitment* to the alternative attitudes through his involved expression of them to the therapist. Cohen (1964) accounts for the effect of this factor in terms of dissonance theory (see below) and argues that: 'If a person is led to express outwardly an attitude which is discrepant from his actual private attitude, a state of dissonance results. Since the behaviour is fixed, dissonance in such a setting can be reduced by changing one's attitude so that it becomes consistent with the behaviour one has engaged in publicly. There is no dissonance remaining because private attitude and public expression are now consistent with each other.' (pp.82–3). A second factor that appears to enhance the effectiveness of roleplaying is the degree of *improvisation* it involves for the client. On this point, Hovland *et al.* 1953) comment that when a person has to improvise he thinks up 'exactly the kinds of arguments, illustrations, and motivating appeals that he regards as most convincing . . . (he) . . . is induced to 'hand-tailor' the content so as to take account of the unique motives and predispositions of one particular person—namely himself.' (p.237) An additional reason advanced by Janis and Gilmore (1965) is that '. . . when a person accepts the task of improvising arguments in favour or a point of view at variance with his own personal convictions, he becomes temporarily motivated to think up all of the positive arguments he can, and at the same time suppress thoughts about the negative arguments which are supposedly irrelevant to the assigned task. This "biased scanning" increases the salience of the positive arguments and therefore increases the chances of acceptance of the new attitude position.' (pp. 17–18) These quotations are examples of the views expressed in the unresolved theoretical debate about the most appropriate explanation for attitude change through roleplaying, but from a clinical standpoint there are strong indications for the pragmatic usefulness of the technique.

Cognitive restructuring

The same can be said about the method of cognitive or rational restructuring, stemming from Albert Ellis's rational-emotive therapy, but currently being increasingly integrated with behaviour therapy by Ellis himself as well as other writers (Beck, 1970; Bergin, 1970; Ellis, 1962, 1969, 1973, 1975; Goldfried et al., 1974; Lazarus, 1971; Mahoney, 1974; Meichenbaum, 1972, 1974; Nawas, 1970; Ullman, 1970). The basic premise underlying this method is that a person's assumptions, expectations or beliefs about a situation have a significant influence on his emotional or behavioural responses to that situation. If these 'things people say to themselves', their 'internal sentences', or their 'self-verbalizations' about a situation, are of an irrational or illogical nature then they are likely to be conducive to feelings and actions that are inappropriate responses to the situation itself, although they may be quite appropriate to the person's subjective interpretation or labelling of that situation. Thus, if a client believes incorrectly that any attempt to engage in intercourse is bound to result in failure or prove an unpleasant experience, then he may well respond with anxiety and avoidance behaviour that are inappropriate reactions to the act of intercourse per se. To evoke such reactions it is not necessary for the irrational beliefs to be explicitly and deliberately expressed, they may be more in the nature of an implicit and automatic labelling process, and there is some empirical evidence to support the assertion that they can have a significant influence on a person's emotions and overt behaviour (Goldfried and Sobocinski, 1975; May and Johnson, 1973 Rimm and Litvak, 1969; Russell and Brandsma, 1974; Velten, 1968). It is important to note that this assertion does not imply that emotional reactions are always mediated by a person's beliefs about a situation, in some cases they may be more appropriately conceptualized and treated as relatively direct conditoned responses to the situation itself.

However, where a client's beliefs do appear to be relevant to his difficulties, then the implication for treatment is that 'If people . . . become emotionally disturbed because they unthinkingly accept certain illogical premises or irrational ideas, then there is good reason to believe that they can be somehow persuaded or taught to think more logically and rationally and thereby to undermine their own disturbances' (Ellis, 1962, p. 191). Towards this end, Goldfried et al. (1974) have formulated a set of therapeutic guidelines for systematic rational restructuring, and these are outlined in the following discussion. Their first step is to present the rationale for the method to the client, in the form of an easily comprehensible explanation along the lines described in the previous paragraph and with an emphasis on the general principles involved rather than the client's own problems. Next, and again before analysing these particular problems, Goldfried *et al.* suggest that some commonly held irrational assumptions should be reviewed with the client to determine the extent to which he concurs with them and to help him recognize their untenability. The irrational ideas discussed are selected for their possible relevance to the client concerned, and two examples are the idea that one should be thoroughly competent, adequate, and achieving in all possible respects if one is to consider oneself worthwhile (Ellis, 1962, p. 63), and the idea that it is awful and catastrophic when things are not the way one would very much like them to be (Ellis, 1962, p. 69). Rather than the therapist attempting to persuade or coerce the client into rejecting such extreme ideas, there is evidence to suggest that encouraging him to present his own arguments against them is likely to be more effective (Brehm, 1966; Brehm and Cohen, 1962; Davison, 1973).

Hopefully, these introductory steps will have led the client to agree in principle that a person's beliefs can influence his emotions and behaviour, and that some beliefs are of an irrational kind. From this point onwards, the treatment shifts to focus on the client's own problems. These are reviewed with him, in order to identify the circumstances in which they occur, and the rationality or otherwise of the thoughts and underlying beliefs evoked by them. The client may be misinterpreting the situation in a quite inaccurate or unrealistic way. For instance, an elderly man may misinterpret a slowing down of the erectile process as a sign of impotence; a person who is disabled may assume this to mean that his sexual life is finished; or permanent sexual incapacity may be expected after the experience of a temporary failure due to alcohol, stress at work, or the unpropitious circumstances in which the encounter took place. Additionally, a client may draw unwarranted conclusions from the occurrence of the problem, so that its significance is distorted and it is not placed in proper perspective. One example is the client who does not achieve the standard of sexual performance he sets for himself, and therefore concludes that he is a totally worthless person. This kind of implication may reflect his acceptance of the commonly held belief mentioned above, that one should be thoroughly competent, adequate, and achieving in all respects if one is to consider oneself worthwhile (Ellis, 1962). Some other instances of unwarranted conclusions include the beliefs that the existence of a sexual problem necessarily implies that one will be rejected by one's partner, and that the performance of all or some kinds of sexual activity means that one is a thoroughly degraded, wicked, or perverted person.

It is unlikely that even very rigorous discussion of such irrational assumptions, expectations and beliefs will be sufficient in itself to achieve their modification. Additionally, clients need to be taught to do something different in those situations that cause them to become disturbed. First, the client should stop and consider what he is thinking about the situation that makes it disturbing for him, so that a previously automatic thought pattern is now subject to rational scrutiny. Second, he should try to replace any irrational thoughts with others representing a more accurate, realistic, and balanced view of the situation, while noting the reduction in disturbance that accompanies this reappraisal. With practice, such rational restructuring becomes a less deliberate and more automatic process.

The training of clients in rational restructuring may be facilitated by various procedural aids, including the imaginal presentation and behavioural rehearsal of the disturbing situations during the therapeutic interviews, as well as *in vivo* assignments for the client to carry out in his natural environment. The first procedure has much in common with the use of systematic desensitization (see below) as a self-control procedure, in that a hierarchy of problematic situations is formulated with client, who progresses through these in imagination using certain coping skills to reduce any adverse emotional reactions. Thus, the client is asked to imagine the situation that is least disturbing to him, and to try to discover and speak aloud any irrational ideas that may be contributing to the feeling he is experiencing. He then attempts to rationally restructure these ideas, sometimes with prompting by the therapist. In this way, the client progresses through the hierarchy of situations that are difficult for him, the irrational ideas evoked by each of them being scrutinized and modified in turn. The procedure of behaviour rehearsal follows essentially the same lines, the only major difference being that the problematic situations are enacted in the form of overt behaviour during the therapeutic sessions, rather than simply being imagined by the client. This makes behaviour rehearsal a less suitable procedure in some instances, for when the problematic situations are of a specifically sexual kind, it may be undesirable or unethical to contravene their customary private nature by asking the clients to simulate them in the presence of the therapist. Finally, in order to promote the generalization of rational restructuring from interview situations to the natural environment, the clients are encouraged to use the technique whenever they become disturbed in the course of their everyday lives, and in the case of problems of sexual impairment this instruction may be combined with the prescription of sexual assignments as discussed in the next section.

Dissonance theory

So far in this section, it has been suggested that the modification of attitudes requires the basic conditions of a good therapeutic relationship, a causal explanation of the client's problem, and an expectation of effective help on his part, in the context of which more specific attitude change procedures are used including sanctioning, self-disclosure, roleplaying, and cognitive restructuring. The mechanism of attitude change involved in all these procedures is often said to be the reduction of inconsistency between one attitude and another or between attitudes and overt behaviour, and the task of the therapist is to provoke such inconsistency so that the client changes his attitudes and/or his overt behaviour in order to achieve greater consistency. The extensive literature on dissonance theory contains evidence that people do strive for such consistency, and any dissonance is aversive to them so that they try to reduce it by making the necessary changes in their attitudes or behaviour (Brehm and

Cohen, 1962; Chapanis and Chapanis, 1964; Festinger, 1957; Zimbardo, 1969).

Basically, the therapeutic strategies available for the promotion of dissonance and its consequent attitudinal changes, are of a cognitive, affective, or behavioural kind (Bandura, 1969). The *cognitive* approach consists of attempts to demonstrate inconsistencies among the client's beliefs or to confront him with discrepancies between these and the reality of a situation, and procedure of cognitive restructuring obviously relies heavily on this particular strategy.

In contrast, the *affective* strategy is strongly represented in those methods that concentrate on changing a client's emotional reactions to certain situations. For instance, the procedure of systematic desensitization (see below) is aimed specifically at the reduction of anxiety, but there is evidence to suggest that the achievement of this goal is also accompanied by congruous attitudinal changes (Bandura, Blanchard, and Ritter, 1969). Thus, desensitizing a client to some aspect of sexual behaviour that elicits anxiety, may serve not only to reduce this unpleasant feeling, but also to change his belief that the behaviour is harmful or wrong, and to promote a more favourable attitude that may predispose him to perform the behaviour concerned.

Finally, attitude change may be achieved by getting the client to engage in certain behaviour without incurring any unpleasant consequences, thus providing him with objective evidence that his negative attitudes towards this behaviour are unrealistic and inconsistent. Among the many treatment methods that may involve this *behavioural* approach to attitude change are the sexual assignments of a sensate focus or pleasuring nature which are described below. Essentially, a couple are encouraged to engage in limited forms of sexual activity in gently graded steps, so that they perform the behaviour without experiencing anxiety or other adverse consequences and probably with some degree of enjoyment. In consequence of such experiences, their attitudes towards sexuality are likely to become more positive.

The upshot of this discussion is that any change in a person's beliefs, feelings or actions is likely to entail some corresponding attitudinal change in order to maintain consistency. Moreover, such changes in attitude may be produced not only in the course of therapeutic interviews, but also by means of sexual assignments or specific behavioural procedures. It does not follow that a person's attitudes towards a certain situation are necessarily reflected in his overt behaviour in that situation (Fishbein, 1967; Wicker, 1969). The lattter is determined not only by the person's attitudes, but also by his motivation, knowledge and skills, as well as the opportunities available to him to engage in the behaviour and the norms governing its performance. Thus, a client might hold attitudes towards sex that are generally favourable, but these may not be reflected in adequate and enjoyable sexual activities for any of several reasons; a temporary disinterest, perhaps due to depression, a physical illness or a non-sexual stress; some lack of information or skill which results in inadequate sexual technique; the absence of a suitable partner; or the operation of personal or social norms of sexual conduct which preclude its performance in the current situation. Thus, an adequate programme for the treatment of sexual dysfunction is usually a broadly based intervention encompassing much more than attitude change alone.

MANAGEMENT OF SEXUAL
ASSIGNMENTS

A variety of sexual assignments for couples to carry out when they are alone together are described in the next chapter, and the present section constitutes a brief introduction to the therapeutic management of these assignments in interviews. In the first place, these are used to prescribe the assignments to be undertaken before the next interview. This involves explaining the underlying rationale and negotiating the nature of the assignment with the clients. In particular, they will often need to be reassured that undertaking them as part of a treatment programme may seem somewhat contrived and mechanistic rather than a spontaneous and romantic expression of their love for each other, but that the learning of any skill is initially a very deliberate process which only later results in a smooth, automatic performance. This is just as true for interpersonal skills as it is for those of learning to write, paint, play a musical instrument, or drive a car, and it may help clients if they think to their own experiences of learning skills such as these compared to their current performances of them. A strong commitment to the spontaneity of sexual activities may lead to difficulties in initiating sexual assignments for some couples, and in such cases Maddock (1975) proposes that the therapists assume initial responsibility for rigidly time-structuring and monitoring the implementation of the assignments, after which the couple themselves gradually take over responsibility for negotiating their own schedules for assignments and other sexual activities.

The progress of couples in attempting a sexual assignment is monitored in subsequent interviews. These cover not only their physical activities and reactions in considerable detail, but also what they were feeling and thinking at the time. For instance, while many couples find pleasuring assignments to be extremely pleasurable; there are others who report that they were unable to undertake them because of insufficient time or opportunity; that they found them to be very contrived and strange; that they became tense and anxious during an assignment; or were unable to concentrate on it because their thoughts wandered to irrelevant matters, perhaps of an occupational or domestic nature. Such negative reactions provide the therapists with extremely valuable clues to the nature of the couple's difficulties, and they offer a basis for the discussion and resolution of these. Indeed, Masters and Johnson (1970) stress that they expect and want couples to make 'mistakes' in conducting the assignments so that they can learn from the explanations provided by the therapists.

The necessary steps to circumvent or resolve any such obstacles to therapeutic progress are also implemented or planned in the interviews. This may involve any appropriate combination of providing information and modifying attitudes along the lines described above; the prescription of further sexual assignments, either repetitions in the same or amended form of those already attempted, or others of a different kind; and the use of one or more of the specific behavioural procedures, or physical treatments, that are discussed below. Each of these therapeutic tasks of prescribing and monitoring sexual assignments and of resolving any obstacles revealed by them, is discussed and illustrated at greater length in the next chapter which is devoted to these assignments.

9

Sexual Assignments

The functions of these assignments can be summarized as the reduction of stress reactions to sexual behaviour, the promotion of effective sexual stimulation and responses, and the revelation of impediments to adequate sexual functioning. We see below, that the assignments are structured in non-threatening ways so that stress reactions such as performance anxiety, avoidance behaviour and cognitive monitoring are likely to be reduced.

In contrast, the assignments tend to promote more effective stimulation and responses, by enabling couples to commence or resume their participation in sexual activities; to experience positive emotional reactions to these activities; to develop positive attitudes of acceptance and liking towards a variety of sexual practices; and to facilitate communication between the partners about their sexual reactions and preferences so that they become more stimulating and attuned to each other.

Lastly, as indicated above, a couple's experiences in attempting the assignments may reveal hitherto unrecognized impediments to their sexual functioning. This new information enables the therapists to modify or extend the tentative formulation of the problem they made during the initial assessment and to conduct treatment accordingly. It is perhaps one of the particular advantages of using sexual assignments that they do require clients to actually participate in the kind of sexual encounter that is presenting problems for them. The more traditional alternative of simply discussing their previous experience of such encounters is subject to serious limitations and distortions, and these may only become apparent to the therapists and the clients when the latter actually attempt to engage in the activities concerned so that any obstacles are immediately and starkly revealed. Several types of obstacle or 'resistance' are discussed by Munjack and Oziel (1978), including the client's inadequate understanding of the assignment, his lack of the skills required to implement it, an absence of motivation or positive prognostic expectancy, the evocation of anxiety or guilt, and the existence of positive reinforcement or secondary gains for dysfunctional behaviour. As indicated above, these and other obstacles may be overcome by means of any of the components of treatment discussed in this part of the book, and the paper by Munjack and Oziel contains some specific suggestions for resolving the obstacles they describe.

For descriptive purposes, the sexual assignments are grouped below according to whether they involve general pleasuring, genital stimulation, or sexual intercourse. The coverage is not completely comprehensive or very detailed, but the more important assignments are discussed in sufficient depth for their major procedural features and therapeutic uses to become apparent.

GENERAL PLEASURING

This type of assignment was developed by Masters and Johnson (1970) who referred to them as 'sensate focus' exercises, and used them at the commencement of the treatment of all clients suffering from any form of sexual dysfunction. In behaviour therapy programmes, they are employed more selectively and flexibly to suit individual clients, but are still valuable in a large proportion of cases. The couple is asked to abstain from intercourse as well as all attempts to bring the partner to orgasm by any other means. This interdiction is welcomed by most clients, either because it legitimizes their existing sexual abstinence, or because it excuses them from further stressful attempts at sexual performance. While abstaining from intercourse and other explicitly sexual activities, the couple will take it in turns to explore the sensual pleasures of touching and caressing each other's bodies with tenderness and affection. Initially the breast and genital areas should be excluded, but otherwise couples are left to discover for themselves where and how they each like to be touched, without more explicit direction from the therapists. It is suggested that couples experiment with the use of a moisturizing lotion during the pleasuring sessions. Basically, this solves any problem of rough or dry hands; but Masters and Johnson (1970) say that it can also help to overcome inhibitions about touching the partner's genitals, the application of the lotion constituting a more acceptable reason for doing so; and that it can reduce any adverse reactions to bodily fluids such as semen or vaginal lubrication. These writers report a less favourable therapeutic outcome among clients who find the use of lotions to be unacceptable, but further evidence is needed on this point.

It is important for clients to ensure their privacy during pleasuring sessions so that they are free from fear of interruption, and they are encouraged to undertake them in a psychological climate of closeness and warmth, rather than when they are feeling tired, tense or at odds with each other. This does not mean that couples must necessarily just wait for such circumstances to occur spontaneously, they can arrange to participate in mutually congenial activities that are likely to result in an appropriate atmosphere for pleasuring. Taking a bath or shower together is sometimes suggested as a relaxing and intimate shared experience that can lead naturally into pleasuring, but a joint outing or simply eating or watching television together can serve just as well, and Annon (1974) has organized such activities into a structured programme of dating sessions to provide a suitable context for pleasuring and other sexual assignments. The essential point is that couples should not meet in bed as relative strangers for their pleasuring sessions, and that these are not timetable chronologically whatever the feelings of the partners may be at the time.

With most couples it is suggested that they commence pleasuring in the nude so that they are not distracted from it by having to undress. However, some clients are not at all accustomed to being naked together and would find it extremely embarrassing. In such cases, it may be necessary to start treatment at an even earlier stage in order to assist the clients to feel at ease in each other's presence while completely undressed. They might, for instance, be given assignments involving progressive partial undressing, or of being nude together under conditions of gradually increasing lumination. Some clients may be helped to cope with their anxiety reactions to nudity by a programme of relaxation training or imaginal desensitization (see below).

Masters and Johnson (1970) advocate that the therapists take responsibility for nominating the partner who is to lead off by pleasuring the other, so that the couple are relieved of the burden of this decision, and Kaplan (1975) emphasizes its crucial nature in some cases. For instance, she cites the example of a wife who is extremely anxious and inhibited about imposing any demand for her own gratification upon her husband; consequently, it may be easier for her to accept pleasuring, if she has previously provided this for him. Couples are advised to pleasure each other for as long as this is enjoyable to them both, but never to the point of fatigue or boredom, and they may change roles as 'giver' or 'receiver' whenever they wish during a session. One function of the role of giver is to discover and implement various ways of touching and caressing that give pleasure to the receiver. However, this task is also an enjoyable experience for the giver, whose second and equally important function is to explore and appreciate the sensations and feelings evoked by touching and caressing the receiver. (Thus, the terms 'giver' and 'receiver' are relative rather than absolute). The task of the receiver is to identify where and how it is pleasant or unpleasant to be touched, and to communicate this information to the giver as a guide to further pleasuring. Otherwise, the receiver concentrates entirely on the tactile stimulation he or she is receiving, without being distracted by irrelevant thoughts, perhaps of an occupational or domestic nature; or by worries about the giver's reactions to the pleasuring, such as whether he or she is finding it tedious or boring; or by cognitive monitoring for signs of sexual arousal, like an erection or vaginal lubrication. The couple should understand that arousal is not necessarily to be expected during these general pleasuring sessions, and whether or not it occurs is not of primary importance.

This follows from the rationale for pleasuring assignments, which is explained to couples before they undertake them. One reason for these assignments is the reduction of stress reactions to sexual situations. Quite often couples have been avoiding any physical expression of affection as well as sexual foreplay, in case these should lead on to yet another stressful attempt to perform intercourse. This threat is removed by the therapeutic contract to abstain from such attempts, and the associated avoidance reactions are correspondingly alleviated. Similarly, the agreed abstinence is likely to reduce performance anxiety and spectatoring. The risk of failure is minimized since there is no particular level of performance to be attained, and the responses that would have been necessary to achieve any such level need no longer be monitored. Thus, there is a shift in the couple's attention away from an achievement orientation focused on the attainment of particular responses such as an erection or orgasm, and towards the enjoyment of the sensations and feelings they are experiencing at any point in time during their mutual pleasuring.

A second reason for undertaking these pleasuring assignments is the promotion of effective sexual stimulation and responses. An extremely important component of these is sensitive tactile stimulation, and the assignments provide opportunity for couples to develop and deploy the necessary skills in this respect. They also enable clients to discover the kind of touching that is pleasant and arousing for them, and to communicate this to their partner, so that they become more attuned to each other's reactions and preferences. As couples progress along these lines in the relatively stress free conditions of the pleasuring assignments, they are likely to experience feelings of warmth, closeness, tenderness, affection, and sensual pleasure, as well as positive changes in attitude so that a variety of sexual activities become more acceptable, attractive and valued.

Such positive feelings and attitudinal changes are perhaps the commonest reactions to general bodily pleasuring, and couples are usually pleased that they have been able to resume a physical relationship and to find that they can give pleasure to each other by touching, without necessarily having to achieve particular responses such as an erection or orgasm. Their emotional reactions tend to be of a sensual rather than sexual nature, but sometimes the latter do occur with such intensity that the couple break the ban on intercourse and orgasm. This 'mistake' can be a good sign of growing sexual responsiveness and confidence, or it may indicate some obstacle to progress that requires therapeutic attention. For instance, an insecure wife may be unable to withhold intercourse from her husband in case he should reject or desert her; or one partner might be sabotaging the assignments because of the hostility felt towards the other, so that they cannot collaborate together in the programme.

These two examples illustrate that various stress reactions are sometimes evoked by pleasuring assignments despite all therapeutic efforts to make them as non-threatening as possible. Another such reaction is the performance anxiety that is experienced by clients who believe that they are insensitive, unskilled and unsuccessful in their attempts to pleasure their partner, or who expect to become highly aroused and to achieve particular sexual responses during the assignments. A further source of anxiety for some clients is the degree of intimacy and involvement with another person that is entailed in pleasuring. Others experience strong feelings of guilt because they have participated in the pleasuring activities, or have responded to these with arousal and pleasure. Anger may be evoked by having to pleasure a partner who is disliked or rejected, and this emotional reaction is sometimes accompanied by physical expressions of hostility such as touching the partner in rough or irritating ways so that satisfactory pleasuring is precluded. Another stress reaction of an overt kind is the physical avoidance of the assignments so that not uncommonly couples will report that they have not had the time or opportunity to carry them out, or that they found them so ticklish that they could not continue. Likewise, cognitive avoidance may occur, perhaps in the form of a total lack of sensation or feeling in response to the pleasuring, so that couples tend to report that they found it tedious, boring or rather silly. Alternatively, cognitive avoidance may be exhibited in an inability to concentrate on the assignment, the client being easily distracted by irrelevant thoughts or by the associated reaction of congnitive monitoring. The latter may consist of the continued observation by a client of his own sexual responses, or of a preoccupation with the partner's reactions lest she is experiencing fatigue, boredom, or resentment during their mutual pleasuring.

As discussed above, when any such obstacles to therapeutic progress are revealed by the pleasuring assignments and reported in the interviews, then the necessary steps are taken to circumvent or resolve them by providing additional information, modifying attitudes, utilizing specific behavioural or physical treatment procedures, or prescribing further assignments. If some particular aspect of these is stressful for a client, then it is sometimes possible to circumvent this while proceeding with the remainder of the programme; for example, if full exposure in the nude is difficult initially, then this can be deferred while pleasuring proceeds in reduced light or with partial clothing. In other cases, an assignment may be repeated after some further explanation, support and encouragement from the therapists. Thus, it may be necessary to re-emphasize to an impotent man that erections are not to be expected or monitored during general bodily pleasuring, and that he should focus entirely on the immediate sensations and feelings this evokes. Similarly, a wife who is prone to rejection anxiety may need to be reassured that abstinence from intercourse and being pleasured by her husband are crucial but temporary aspects of treatment, which are acceptable to him and will not result in her being rejected or deserted.

GENITAL STIMULATION

Genital pleasuring

Once couples are able to respond positively to general bodily pleasuring, then this can be extended to include the breast and genital areas. The rationale and principles for such genital pleasuring are essentially the same as those for general pleasuring, and it is important to stress that this is gradually extended to incorporate genital pleasuring rather than being superseded by it. The agreement to abstain from intercourse remains in force, and clients are instructed to touch the partner's genitals in a tender and teasing manner with the aim of enhancing sensual and sexual feelings, while avoiding the vigorous, rhythmic, demanding kind of stimulation that is aimed directly at bringing the partner to orgasm. The couple is advised to start with general pleasuring in the ways they have learned to enjoy, and then to gradually incorporate genital pleasuring by moving back and forth between caressing the genitals and the rest of the body, with each partner communicating his or her preferences concerning genital touching to the other.

Before couples undertake this assignment, they are provided with adequate information about the structure and function of the genital organs, as a basis for effective mutual stimulation. For instance, a man may need to learn the location of his wife's clitoris, and that many women prefer to be stimulated in that area and the labia minora, rather than more deeply inside the vagina. However, adequate vaginal lubrication (or a substitute, such as a sterile jelly) needs to be spread to the clitoris if its stimulation is not to be irritating or painful. Moreover, the glans of the clitoris is hypersensitive and discomfort can be caused if it is directly stimulated at an early stage of lovemaking, consequently a wife may prefer to be stimulated less directly via the clitoral shaft or the mons area generally. It is, of course, axiomatic that such information concerning preferences in general be supplemented and if necessary corrected by the information about individual preferences that is communicated between the partners concerned.

The reduced stress reactions and more effective stimulation during genital pleasuring often enable clients to become sexually aroused, whereas this was impossible when they were pressuring themselves to achieve an erection, to experience erotic feelings, to reach orgasm or to perform intercourse. Sometimes the degree of arousal is so intense that a couple go on to intercourse or the orgasm by other means, and this may be either a beneficial or an adverse occurrence as discussed above. Similarly, the stress reactions to general pleasuring can also be evoked by genital pleasuring, especially by the more explicitly sexual features and connotations of the latter. Thus, anxiety and avoidance reactions may be elicited by the appearance, smell or secretions of the partner's genital organs; fondling these, or having one's own genitals fondled, may entail considerable guilt or revulsion; or a man might exhibit performance anxiety, and cognitive avoidance of his mounting erotic feelings, in case these result in premature ejaculation. If any such obstacles to satisfactory sexual functioning are revealed by the genital pleasuring assignments, then appropriate steps are taken to resolve these impediments by means of the therapeutic strategies discussed above in the context of general pleasuring.

Attitudes towards masturbation

In addition to genital pleasuring, several other assignments involving either self-stimulation of the genitals or their stimulation by a partner are used in the treatment of a variety of sexual dysfunctions. Before such assignments are undertaken, it is necessary not only to explain the therapeutic rationale for doing so, but also in many cases to provide clients with accurate information about masturbation and to modify their negative attitudes towards it. For instance, some clients will need to be reassured authoritatively that there is no evidence of physical harm or mental illness being caused by masturbation (Comfort, 1967; Hare, 1962), and that it is not by any means a rare form of sexual behaviour even among married people. Thus, in the now rather dated Kinsey studies (Kinsey et al., 1948, 1953) there were 92% of men and 58% of women who admitted having masturbated to orgasm at some time in their lives, and more recent investigations suggest incidence rates approaching 100% for men and 85% for women (Dearborn, 1967; Miller and Lief, 1976). The Kinsey figures for masturbation among married subjects in their late twenties and early thirties were about 40% for men and about 30% for women, while in a recent study or 38 similarly aged couples drawn from the Danish general population the corresponding figures were 60.5% and 26.8% (Hessellund, 1976).

This study also indicates the prevalence of negative attitudes towards masturbation. It was viewed as wrong, unnatural, repellent, and morbid by 26.1% of the husbands who still practised it, compared to 20.0% of those who no longer did so, while the corresponding figures for the wives were 35.7% and 16.7% respectively. The more negative attitudes among those who still masturbated is attributed by the investigator to the feelings of guilt this evoked, and similar reactions have been reported by other writers. For instance, in a sample of university students, Greenberg and Archambault (1973) found that guilt feelings in connection with masturbation occurred in 40% of men and 48% of women. Similarly, a group of boys and girls aged 13 to 19 years were surveyed by Sorensen (1973) who reported that among those currently masturbating only 19% claimed never to have felt guilty about this. The prevalence of such negative attitudes and emotional reactions to masturbation, indicates the importance of dealing with them when prescribing and monitoring any sexual assignment that involves genital stimulation.

Reduction of stress reactions

In common with all sexual assignments, those involving genital stimulation may serve to reduce stress reactions and to promote effective stimulation and responses. There are some clinical reports of genital stimulation being used explicitly to reduce particular stress reactions. Thus, the anxiety and muscular spasm induced by the prospect of penetration in a client suffering from vaginismus, was treated in this way by Wilson (1973). The young woman concerned was able to become aroused and to reach orgasm during mutual masturbation with her boyfriend. She was instructed to imagine increasing finger insertion into her vagina, at progressively earlier stages of their masturbation sequence. When she could imagine this without experiencing anxiety, then her partner actually inserted his finger into her vagina, initially just before she reached orgasm and subsequently at earlier points in her arousal process. This resulted in the client preferring to reach orgasm with her boyfriend's finger inserted, and it was followed by the commencement of intercourse without penile penetration evoking a vaginal spasm or any feelings of anxiety in the client. It is postulated that these stress reactions had been reduced by her arousal and orgasm during masturbation, and some possible theoretical explanations for this are considered in the discussion of desensitization later.

A similar approach has been used by Zilbergeld (1975) to reduce stress reactions in dysfunctional men who did not have sexual partners. While masturbating themselves, these clients imagined the situations that caused them

144

difficulty, such as losing an erection or ejaculating prematurely, and if any anxiety was experienced then they stopped masturbating and instead focused on a relaxing image. In this way, the clients progressed through a hierarchy of stressful sexual situations until they could imagine them all without anxiety, and the author considers that this helped them to cope with similar problems in real life situations.

Orgastic dysfunction

Genital stimulation can also be used in the treatment of women who have never reached orgasm by any means. The initial therapeutic goal with many such totally inorgastic clients is to help them to achieve their first climax. This resolves any doubts they may have about their capacity to do so, and begins to alleviate any fears of being harmed, losing self control or suffering any other adverse effect as a consequence of orgasm. The first experience of climaxing also provides the client with information about the nature of the stimulation and reactions that preceded it, which she can then communicate to her partner for incorporation in their lovemaking.

Given the initial goal of a first orgasm, there are several reasons for thinking that this is most likely to be achieved by the woman stimulating her own genitals. Kinsey *et al.* (1953) found that more women could reach orgasm through masturbation than by any other means, including sexual intercourse. Indeed, among the women in their sample, 62% had masturbated at sometime in their lives, and 58% had reached climax in this way. The remaining 4% consisted mainly of women who had made very few attempts to masturbate, and nearly all those who had experimented seriously soon learned to reach orgasm. Moreover, there is other evidence from the laboratory research by Masters and Johnson (1966), that masturbation produces orgasms which are more intense, both subjectively and physiologically, than those resulting from intercourse or manual stimulation by the partner. A further point is made by Bardwick (1971), who suggests that an intense orgasm increases the vascularity of the vagina, labia, and clitoris, which in turn enhances the woman's capacity for reaching orgasm in future.

The apparent superiority of masturbation as a means of achieving climax may arise from the intensity of the stimulation it provides as well as the accompanying freedom from certain possible sources of stress. Although sexual intercourse is a highly gratifying psychological experience, at a mechanical level it is not a particularly effective way of providing the clitoral stimulation that seems to be important in triggering off the orgastic reflex in women. During intercourse such stimulation occurs only indirectly, through traction on the clitoral hood from penile thrusting, and from pressure on the clitoral area by the pubic bone, whereas genital manipulation of the clitoris during masturbation constitutes a more direct and intense form of stimulation. Furthermore, when a woman stimulates herself in private she is not subject to certain possible stresses, such as the observation and monitoring of her performance by her husband; any time pressures his presence may impose upon the duration of the self-stimulation and the speed of her response to it; or the relinquishment of responsibility for stimulation to him when the wife fears that she may be overwhelmed and lose her self-control if this is too intense. However, although a husband may not be directly involved in the early masturbatory assignments being undertaken by his inorgastic wife, it is important for him to understand the rationale for them, so that she is reassured by his acceptance and support.

Lo Piccolo and Lobitz (1972a) have proposed a nine-step series of masturbatory assignments for totally inorgastic women. The general outline or their programme can be summarized as follows, but they stress that it requires modification to suit individual clients (Lobitz *et al.*, 1976):

Step 1: In order to increase her self-awareness the client is asked to examine her nude body and appreciate its attractive features. A hand mirror is to be used to examine her genitals and she is to identify the various parts of these with the aid of diagrams. Many clients express amazement at the extent of their self-discovery during this step.

Step 2: The client is asked to explore her genitals tactually as well as visually, and to prevent performance anxiety she is not given any expectation of arousal at this point. Instead, the aim of the first two steps is to reduce the stressfulness of seeing and touching the genitals and to accustom the client to the idea of masturbation. Strong anxiety and avoidance reactions to this assignment are not uncommon, but can usually be overcome with support from the husband and therapists.

Step 3: Tactile and visual exploration of the genitals is to be continued with the object of locating sensitive areas that are pleasurable to touch.

Step 4: These sensitive areas are now to be manually stimulated, and the female therapist discusses ways of doing this, including the use of a lubricant to heighten pleasure and prevent discomfort.

Step 5: If the client has not reached climax during the previous step, she is asked to increase the intensity and duration of the genital stimulation. It is important for her to realize that she may have to continue stimulation for a prolonged period, of perhaps 30 minutes to an hour, to give herself sufficient opportunity of reaching orgasm. Many women are inclined to abandon their attempts much too soon, and they need to be encouraged to continue until they reach orgasm or become tired or sore. Sometimes feelings of tension and discomfort are experienced during this process, and it may help to discontinue stimulation for a very brief period, but the client should try to push through any such feelings rather than giving up the attempt. During this assignment, clients are encouraged to use erotic phantasies, literature and pictures, in order to heighten arousal and to distract themselves from any performance anxiety or spectatoring.

Step 6: If step 5 does not result in orgasm, the client is asked to repeat it using a vibrator (see below) to stimulate herself. In cases of clients who fear loss of self-control during orgasm, it may be helpful if they roleplay their conception of the orgastic response in an exaggerated manner. The simulation of anticipated reactions such as involuntary screaming or gross muscular movements, may alleviate their stressfulness and sometimes results in the occurrence of a real orgasm during the roleplay.

Step 7: Once a woman has reached orgasm on her own, she is asked to stimulate herself while her husband is watching. The object of this step is to reduce the stressfulness to the woman of exhibiting arousal and orgasm in the presence of her husband, and to provide him with information about the kind of stimulation that his wife prefers.

Step 8: This consists of the husband stimulating his wife in the way she has demonstrated to him in the previous step. It is important that he follow her guidance concerning her preferences and that he continue to stimulate her for a sufficiently lengthy period without interruption. Otherwise she will have insufficient opportunity to become aroused and reach orgasm, or this process will be disrupted and her arousal level will drop.

Step 9: Once the woman reaches orgasm during step 8, then the couple are asked to engage in intercourse while the husband concurrently stimulates his wife's genitals, either manually or with a vibrator.

Modified versions of the Lo Piccolo and Lobitz programme have been published in the form of self-help manuals by Barbach (1975) and Heiman *et al.* (1976). The use of these manuals has not yet been evaluated, but some evidence on the efficacy of the programme with inorgastic women when delivered by a therapist is reviewed in Chapter 16.

At the present stage it only remains to add that the programme has also been employed in the treatment of some women who are unable to reach orgasm during intercourse, although they can do so by masturbating in one specific and very restricted way. An example of this is the case cited in Chapter 3 of the woman who could only attain orgasm by masturbating when standing up. She was treated successfully by placing a ban on masturbating in this way, while teaching her to respond to a wider range of sexual stimulation by implementing the Lo Piccolo and Lobitz programme in a laying down position (Snyder *et al.*, 1975).

Retarded or absent ejaculation

A male sexual dysfunction for which genital stimulation has an important therapeutic role is that of retarded ejaculation. Like inorgastic women, men suffering from this condition may never have been able to reach orgasm by any means, or more commonly they may not be able to do so during intercourse while retaining their capacity in other circumstances, most usually, when masturbating in privacy. The fundamental principle in treating the latter kind of case is to gradually shape the client's ejaculatory response towards the goal of ejaculating in his partner's vagina during sexual intercourse (Kaplan, 1975). This principle is implemented in a series of assignments which constitute successive approximations to the ultimate goal, and at each step the client's sexual arousal is used to block any anxiety aroused by the prospect of ejaculating. To heighten his arousal and to distract himself from any such anxiety reactions or spectatoring, he is advised to utilize phantasized, written or pictorial material of an erotic kind.

Clearly, each client requires an individually tailored programme, but this might begin with:

1. his existing capacity to masturbate to orgasm when he is alone in the house, and then proceed through the following further steps,
2. masturbating to orgasm with his wife in the next room,
3. going to the bathroom to masturbate after having had intercourse without ejaculating,
4. remaining with his wife to masturbate after intercourse,
5. the wife manually stimulating her husband to orgasm after intercourse,
6. repetition of 5, with ejaculation being produced progressively nearer to the vagina,
7. the wife stimulating her husband almost to ejaculation, at which point he enters her vagina and a combination of manual and vaginal stimulation is continued until he ejaculates inside her wife,
8. at this stage, Kaplan (1975) advocates the use of what she calls 'the male bridge manoeuvre', which consists of the same combination of vaginal and manual stimulation, but with the man signalling to his partner when he is approaching ejaculation, so that she discontinues her manual stimulation and he reaches orgasm by penile thrusting alone,
9. finally, it is often possible to fade out the manual element in the combined stimulation if the couple wish to do so.

At any point in such programmes, it may be helpful for some clients to utilize a vibrator (see below) in order to intensify the genital stimulation, and such an aid may by especially valuable, although not always essential, in the treatment of male clients who have never had an orgasm by any means (Geboes *et al.*, 1975b; Schellen, 1968).

Premature ejaculation

Turning now to premature ejaculation, two methods of genital stimulation that are very commonly used in the treatment of this dysfunction are the 'stop–start' and 'squeeze' techniques. The former was introduced by Semans (1956), and it has been further developed by Kaplan (1974, 1975) whose procedure is described below. The squeeze technique is a variation of stop–start, that was first developed by Masters and Johnson (1970) in their pioneer clinical work and since used very extensively. At a pragmatic level, both methods appear to be quite effective in helping clients to acquire voluntary control over the ejaculatory reflex, but how this result is achieved is still unclear.

The stop–start technique consists of the wife manually stimulating her husband's erect penis until he feels near to orgasm, at which point he signals to her and she stops stimulating him. Within a few seconds his urge to ejaculate will subside, and the wife resumes genital stimulation until the husband once again signals to her to stop. This procedure is repeated about four times during a session and on the last occasion the man goes on to ejaculate. After about two such successful sessions, the procedure is repeated using a lubricant on the penis to enhance sensitivity and arousal, and this is followed by the performance of intercourse in the stop–start format as described in the next section.

The husband is asked to follow certain instructions whenever he and his wife are using the stop–start technique. So that he can learn to recognize the approach of orgasm, he should focus attention on his genital sensations and not allow himself to be distracted from these in any way. Apart from signalling to his wife when she is to stop stimulation, the husband should not try to control or hold back from orgasm, otherwise he may cognitively avoid his genital sensations rather than increasing his awareness of them. Finally, in order to be able to concentrate on these sensations, the husband has to ignore his wife's sexual gratification while they are actually using the stop–start method, and to help him to do this, the couple are encouraged to agree how the husband can give his wife an orgasm at other times.

The squeeze method is essentially similar to stop–start, except that instead of simply stopping stimulation at the husband's signal, the wife squeezes his penis just below the glans for 3 or 4 seconds, as a result of which his urge to ejaculate disappears and he may lose part of his erection. Masters and Johnson (1970) say that the wife should grip the penis with her thumb on the frenulum and two fingers on the opposite surface of the penis, one on each side of the coronal ridge. The pressure should be quite hard, and the wife may need to be reassured that this will not hurt or injure her husband. According to these authors, the squeeze technique is not effective when used by the man himself during masturbation, since any improvement in ejaculatory control will not generalize to sexual encounters with a partner. However, Lo Piccolo and Lobitz (1972b) report that they have prescribed the squeeze technique during masturbation, to build up confidence in ejaculatory control before resumption of sexual relations with a partner, or where the wife finds the technique repugnant, and that good transfer of ejaculatory control has been achieved in these cases.

Erectile dysfunction

The stop–start and squeeze techniques can also be used in the treatment of impotence (Kaplan, 1974; 1975; Masters and Johnson, 1970). Where a client fears that a lost erection cannot be recovered, the couple may be advised to produce such losses deliberately by means of stopping genital stimulation or squeezing the penis, and then to continue with stimulation so that an erection is usually regained.

Another possible component for the treatment of impotent men, particularly those without a partner, is a programme of self-stimulatory assignments devised by Annon (1974). He advises such clients who report little or no arousal, to explore and identify any effective sources of sexual stimulation in written, pictorial, or phantasy form, and to use these during masturbation in order to evoke erotic feelings and erectile responses. If the client has been accustomed to ejaculating through a flaccid or only partially erect penis, then he is asked to defer orgasm until he attains a progressively fuller erection, so that the link between an absence of erection and orgasm is replaced by one between a full erection and orgasm. It is suggested also that the client masturbate with his non-dominant rather than his dominant hand, which is said to convey the feeling of the penis being larger than before and to produce somewhat different penile sensations. Once the client can reliably obtain full erections by masturbation using any form of erotic stimulation, then he is advised to incorporate phantasies of himself with a full erection and engaging in sexual activities with a partner, and particularly to phantasize himself having intercourse with a full erection when he reaches orgasm during masturbation. Annon claims that the association of these phantasies with self-stimulation and orgasm, facilitates the generalization of erections from masturbation to shared sexual activities.

SEXUAL INTERCOURSE

Impaired arousal in women

A third group of sexual assignments involve some form of penile–vaginal intercourse. One of these was introduced by Masters and Johnson (1970) as part of their treatment for orgastic dysfunction and it is referred to by Kaplan (1974, 1975) as 'non-demand coitus'. After the couple have become aroused by general and genital pleasuring, the woman adopts the female superior position and inserts her partner's penis into her vagina. Initially, she simply contains the penis while experiencing the sensations and feelings this evokes. These may be enhanced by the woman contracting her vaginal muscles on the penis, and subsequently, as her arousal mounts, by her moving slowly up and down on the penis and experimenting with other different movements. She is told to think of the penis as hers to play with, and to concentrate on her own sensations and pleasure without worrying about her partner's gratification at this stage. If he becomes too aroused, then movement can be stopped for a while, and he can either remain inside his partner or withdraw until his excitement subsides. Such withdrawal and re-insertion is often a teasing and arousing experience for the woman, and her arousal may also be maintained by clitoral stimulation while penile movement is suspended. The assignment continues for so long as the woman wishes or more rarely until she reaches orgasm. At this point, the man is either given an orgasm intravaginally by thrusting, or extravaginally by manual or oral stimulation.

Thus, the essence of this assignment is the absence of demands on the woman to achieve any particular level of performance or to subordinate her own preferences and pleasure to those of her husband. In contrast, the assignment provides opportunity for her to explore and appreciate the vaginal sensations and erotic feelings evoked by her husband's penis; in this way it constitutes an extension of genital pleasuring, with the husband using his penis rather than his hands to touch and caress his wife, who enjoys the immediate pleasure this gives without deliberately striving for orgasm. It may be that she will nevertheless reach climax, in which case the couple can proceed to have intercourse as they wish. If this does not happen, then a further programme of treatment for orgastic dysfunction may be followed.

Orgastic dysfunction

As part of such a programme, couples may engage in what Kaplan (1975) calls the 'bridge manoeuvre'. This assignment may help women whose sexual arousal is satisfactory during intercourse, and who can attain orgasm by direct clitoral stimulation but not by penile thrusting alone. If the couple would like this to produce orgasm, then it can be combined with manual stimulation of the clitoris until the woman is near to climax, at which point the clitoral stimulation is stopped and the woman thrusts vigorously on the penis in order to trigger off her orgasm. The cessation of manual stimulation may be followed by a lowering of the wife's level of arousal, and the bridge manoeuvre may have to be repeated several times before she attains orgasm. During this process, the husband might reach climax first, in which case the couple can undertake the assignment again when they next have intercourse. The manual stimulation of the wife's clitoris can be provided by herself or the husband, but it is sometimes preferable for wives to stimulate themselves so that they can maximize their pleasurable feelings and not have to worry about the task being tedious, tiring or annoying for the husband. If desired the stimulation of the clitoris can be done with a vibrator (see below) rather than manually, and once a woman can reliably reach orgasm by penile thrusting alone then its combination with more direct clitoral stimulation can be progressively faded out if this is what the couple would like to happen.

Erectile dysfunction

Turning now to male dysfunctions, a type of non-demand coitus is often included in treatment programmes for impotence. When the client is reliably obtaining erections by general and genital pleasuring, the erect penis is then inserted in the vagina where it is contained with only limited movement of a non-demanding kind. After a brief period, the penis is withdrawn and the assignment is repeated on several occasions during a session, at the conclusion of which the partners may give each other an extravaginal orgasm by manual or oral means if they so wish. The primary purpose of such repeated insertion and containment without any deliberate attempt to achieve intravaginal orgasms is to reduce the stress reactions to these aspects of intercourse which are commonly experienced by men who complain of erectile dysfunction, but the assignment also provides opportunity for them to enjoy the sensations and feelings arising from the penis being in the vagina. The same aims may be pursued by two variations of non-demand coitus, the 'quiet vagina' and 'stuffing' techniques (Annon, 1974; Hartman and Fithian, 1974). The former consists of the couple laying in each other's arms with the penis inserted in the vagina and only minimal movement for a period of about 20 to 30 minutes. As the name implies, the stuffing technique requires either partner to 'stuff' the flaccid or partially erect penis into the vagina, after which the man just relaxes and enjoys the sensations and feelings, with only slow controlled movements and no deliberate attempt to produce an erection or orgasm.

Ejaculatory dysfunctions

As far as ejaculatory dysfunctions are concerned, the use of the male bridge manoeuvre in cases of retarded or absent ejaculation is mentioned above, and the treatment of premature ejaculation commonly includes an extension of the stop–start or squeeze techniques into penile–vaginal intercourse. After stop–start has been employed extravaginally, it is repeated intravaginally. With the woman in the superior position and the penis inserted, the man places his hands on her hips and controls her up and down movements until he approaches ejaculation, at which point he stops her until the urge to ejaculate recedes and coital movement is then resumed. This process is repeated on about four occasions, on the last of which the man goes on to ejaculate. The squeeze technique is extended into intercourse in an essentially similar manner, the only difference being that as the man approaches orgasm he withdraws his penis and the woman applies the squeeze extravaginally.

Having described a range of sexual assignments involving general pleasuring, genital stimulation, or sexual intercourse, we turn in the next chapter to a review of some relatively specific behavioural procedures and of certain forms of ancillary physical treatment.

10

Specific Behavioural Procedures and Ancillary Physical Treatment

A third major category of possible components for treatment programmes consists of a range of relatively specific behavioural procedures. Like the sexual assignments, they are designed to reduce stress reactions, to promote effective stimulation and responses, and to reveal any obstacles to satisfactory sexual functioning. This last function is implicit in all the specific procedures discussed below, but otherwise many of these tend to have a relative emphasis on either the reduction of stress or the promotion of more adequate behaviour. Thus, relaxation, desensitization, flooding, and vaginal dilatation, can be conceptualized as predominantly stress reducing; while classical conditioning, biofeedback procedures, phantasy training, and certain hypnotic techniques are concentrated more on the acquisition, performance, and maintenance of satisfactory sexual responses. It is important to recognize that this difference in emphasis is relative rather than absolute. The procedures are described only in sufficient detail for their general nature and purposes to become apparent, and the references cited will need to be consulted for fuller information on the clinical implementation and theoretical explanation of each procedure. Consideration of their efficacy in the treatment of various sexual dysfunctions is largely deferred until Part 5.

RELAXATION TRAINING

It is not unusual for clients to report that their attempts to undertake sexual assignments or similar activities were prevented or impaired by high levels of tension and anxiety. If these stress reactions are persistent, then it may be desirable to help the client to reduce them by means of a programme of muscular relaxation training. The basic rationale for this is that muscle tension is in some way related to anxiety, and if an individual can learn to relax his muscles then this is commonly accompanied by some alleviation of the associated anxiety reactions so that a feeling of calmness prevails (Bernstein and Borkovec, 1973; Jacobson, 1938, 1964; Wolpe, 1958).

Most behaviour therapists teach clients to relax by means of training procedures derived from the pioneer work of Jacobson (1938). He found that by systematically tensing and relaxing various muscle groups and learning to discriminate the associated sensations, it is possible to markedly reduce muscle tension and to feel deeply relaxed. His very long system of training was much shortened by Wolpe (1958), and it is his version of Jacobson's 'progressive relaxation training' that forms the basis for current practice. This is admirably presented in an excellent manual by Bernstein and Borkovec (1973) which should be consulted for an adequate understanding of relaxation training procedures.

In very broad outline, these writers recommend that, after explaining the rationale to a client, the therapist should take him through a sequence of 16 muscle groups:

1. Dominant hand and forearm
2. Dominant biceps
3. Nondominant hand and forearm
4. Nondominant biceps
5. Forehead
6. Upper cheeks and nose
7. Lower cheeks and jaws
8. Neck and throat
9. Chest, shoulders, and upper back
10. Abdominal or stomach region
11. Dominant thigh
12. Dominant calf
13. Dominant foot
14. Nondominant thigh
15. Nondominant calf
16. Nondominant foot

In respect of each of these groups, the client's attention is first focused on the muscles concerned. The therapist then explains and demonstrates how these are to be tensed up; for instance, those of the hand and lower arm are tensed by making a tight fist, and those of the stomach by making this hard. On the word 'now' or some other prearranged signal, the client tenses the particular muscle group, and maintains the tension for about 5 to 7 seconds while the therapist directs his attention to the feelings of tension being experienced. At a further signal, such as the word 'relax', from the therapist, the client releases the tension and his attention is focused on the feelings of relaxation by appropriate comments from the therapist over a period of about 30 to 40 seconds. This tension–release cycle is repeated a second time for each muscle group, and the client then practises relaxation in the therapeutic sessions and at home on his own. When deep relaxation can be obtained in the original 16 groups, these are combined into 7 and then into 4 groups. The client is taught next to relax after simply recalling the feelings of tension in each of these groups without actually producing tension in them. The final step is for the client to learn to count himself down into a state of deep relaxation in time with his rate of breathing.

Bernstein and Borkovec estimate that this programme might take about 10 sessions, and it may be extended by further training in 'differential' and/or 'conditioned relaxation'. The purpose of the former is to enable a client to maintain a generally low level of tension while engaged in some activity. Commonly, the muscles involved in any particular activity are kept at an unnecessarily high level of tension, and this is also present in those muscles that are not relevant to the activity concerned. Thus, the client is trained to retain only a sufficient degree of tension in the relevant muscles for efficient performance, while otherwise relaxing and reducing stress. Clearly, this could be a useful skill for clients who experience tension during the performance of sexual assignments or similar activities. They may also be helped to cope with these stressful situations by training in conditioned relaxation, so that they become able to lose tension in response to a self-produced cue word, such as 'calm' or 'relaxed'.

Once a client has been taught the necessary relaxation skills, he is able to use these himself to reduce any tension and anxiety that may be experienced in sexual situations. This is a considerable advantage, for practical and ethical considerations usually preclude the provision of more direct treatment by a therapist in such circumstances.

DESENSITIZATION

Modern interest in this second method of reducing negative emotional reactions to stress, stems from the experimental and clinical work of Joseph Wolpe which culminated in his now classic text *Psychotherapy by Reciprocal Inhibition* (Wolpe, 1958). This work started with the induction and resolution of so-called 'experimental neuroses' in cats. When these animals were electrically shocked while confined in a small cage, they developed strong and persistent anxiety reactions to the cage itself and to the laboratory where the experiment was conducted. Although the cats were never shocked again, these anxiety reactions were not significantly reduced either by the mere passage of time, or by exposure to the cage situation.

Wolpe observed also that the animals refused to eat in the cage or in the laboratory, even when they were hungry. However, when he moved them through a series of rooms that were progressively more unlike the laboratory, they eventually reached a room where eating did occur. Wolpe explained these observations by postulating that the anxiety responses were stronger than the feeding responses in the laboratory, so that eating was inhibited, whereas in rooms which were sufficiently dissimilar to the laboratory, the anxiety responses were weaker and could be inhibited by the stronger feeding responses.

He then attempted to use this assumed 'reciprocal inhibition' between anxiety and feeding to eliminate the anxiety reactions to the cage. The cats were fed in the room where eating occurred until no signs of anxiety were observed. They were then moved to another room which was a little more like the laboratory and again fed until there were no signs of anxiety. This procedure was repeated through a series of rooms of increasing similarity to the laboratory. Eventually, the animals could eat in the laboratory and in the cage itself, apparently without anxiety. This absence of anxiety reaction to the cage persisted even when the animals were no longer fed there, so that it appeared to have been eliminated, rather than only temporarily suppressed by the feeding responses.

Wolpe was interested in the possible application of these findings to the therapeutic reduction of human anxiety reactions, and to this end he developed his procedure in two ways. First, he found some responses in addition to eating which were alternatives to anxiety and more appropriate for general therapeutic use. These included relaxation, and sexual arousal for use in the treatment of impotence and frigidity. Wolpe second development was to establish that asking a patient to imagine the anxiety-evoking situations was often as effective therapeutically as exposing him to them in reality. This facilitated the desensitization of anxiety reactions to a wide range of events which are difficult to treat in reality; for instance, a sexual assignment which is either so stressful to a client that he is totally unable to undertake even an approximation to it, or where he lacks a partner with whom he could attempt it. Thus desensitization treatment procedures have come to consist essentially of, first, selecting a response which is an alternative to anxiety, and if necessary training the patient to perform it satisfactorily. The second step is to identify the events which evoke anxiety and to rank them from the least to the most disturbing, in one or more hierarchies. Desensitization itself starts with the elicitation of the alternate response to anxiety: for example, a state of relaxation and calmness might be induced in the patient. The least disturbing event is then presented to him, and when this no longer evokes anxiety the procedure is repeated for the next most disturbing event in the hierarchy, and this continues until the patient has been desensitized to every event requiring treatment.

It was as an alternative response to anxiety that Wolpe became interested in Jacobson's progressive relaxation training. This is discussed above, and it only remains to note that it is not the only way of inducing relaxation during desensitization sessions. Another possible psychological technique is hypnosis (Wolpe, 1969; Wolpe et al., 1973), and certain drugs have also been used. The most notable of these is methohexitone sodium (Brietal, Brevital), a quick acting barbiturate which is injected intravenously to maintain relaxation while desensitization is in progress (Brady, 1966, 1967, 1971; Friedman, 1966, 1968; Friedman and Lipsedge, 1971; Kraft and Al-Issa, 1968; Mawson, 1970). In addition to relaxation, the response of sexual arousal is mentioned above as being among those identified and developed by Wolpe as alternatives to anxiety, and this is considered further below in the context of *in vivo* desensitization.

In order to ensure that a client's anxiety reactions are mild enough to be inhibited by the alternative response, he is exposed to the stressful conditions in a gradual manner by proceeding through one or more hierarchies of items representing the least to the most disturbing of these conditions. These anxiety hierarchies are constructed by the client and therapist in collaboration, and the following is an example from an early paper by Lazarus (1963) on the treatment of frigidity (the most disturbing items being at the head of the list):

' 1. Having intercourse in the nude sitting on husband's lap.
2. Changing positions during intercourse.
3. Having coitus in the nude in a dining room or living room.
4. Having intercourse in the nude on top of a bed.
5. Having intercourse in the nude under the bed covers.
6. Manual stimulation of the clitoris.
7. Husband's fingers being inserted into the vagina during precoital love play.
8. Caressing husband's genitals.
9. Oral stimulations of the breasts.
10. Naked breasts being caressed.
11. Breasts being caressed while fully clothed.
12. Embracing while semi-clothed, being aware of husband's erection and his desire for sex.
13. Contact of tongues while kissing.
14. Having buttocks and thighs caressed.
15. Shoulders and back being caressed.
16. Husband caresses hair and face.
17. Husband kisses neck and ears.
18. Sitting on husband's lap, both fully dressed.
19. Being kissed on lips.
20. Being kissed on cheeks and forehead.
21. Dancing with and embracing husband while both fully clothed.'(p.276)

It is crucial to the success of desensitization that the items comprising the hierarchies should adequately represent the stress conditions that evoke anxiety in individual clients. For instance, intercourse might evoke anxiety, because the appearance, smell, or secretions of the partner's genitals are aversive, or because pain, harm, or failure is anticipated. Each of these various stress conditions could yield a different hierarchy, although they are all related to the act of intercourse. Thus, if the appearance of the partner's genitals is a source of anxiety, then the hierarchy might progress from exposure to representations of these in diagrammatic, pictorial, or model form, through brief, partial, and/or distant exposures to the actual organ, and finally to more prolonged, complete, and proximate visual contact. In contrast, if pain on penetration is anticipated, then a hierarchy might consist of items commencing with single and multiple finger insertion by the woman herself and then by her husband, and progressing to penile insertion under the control or each partner, with increasingly vigorous movement, and in various coital positions. It follows that desensitizing a client to a hierarchy that is inappropriate is likely to prove ineffective, and considerable clinical skill and judgement are often needed to identify and select the crucial conditions to be covered in particular cases.

To facilitate imagery in systematic desensitization (see on next page), the individual items in a hierarchy should be highly specific, concrete and realistic situations, in which the client has actually experienced anxiety or where he would expect to do so if exposed to them. These items should also constitute a reasonably representative sample of the whole range of relevant situations that evoke varying degrees of anxiety. This enables the items to be ordered in gradual steps from the least to the most disturbing, with approximately equal intervals of difficulty between them. Once a hierarchy is constructed along these lines, it may be presented to the client in the systematic, *in vivo* or self-control versions of desensitization.

Systematic desensitization

The term 'systematic desensitization' usually refers to a version in which the client imagines the hierarchy items and muscular relaxation is used as the alternative response to anxiety. Thus, before deciding to use this procedure, the therapist must ensure that the client is able to imagine the scenes vividly; to respond to these images with anxiety; and to relax satisfactorily, either after prior training or under the influence of hypnosis or a drug. Most clients are able to meet these requirements, in which case the process of desensitization itself can be commenced.

There are many technical variations in the way this is done (Paul, 1969a; Marks, 1975) but Wolpe now advocates the following procedure (Wolpe, 1969; Wolpe *et al.*, 1973). The client is deeply relaxed, and then asked to imagine the lowest item in a hierarchy. When he has done so he signals by raising his finger, and the image is maintained until he gives a further signal to indicate that he is experiencing anxiety, or for a period of about 5 seconds, whichever is sooner, at which point the therapist instructs him to stop imagining and once more to relax himself. He is then asked to report how much anxiety was experienced during the imaginal presentation, and this is often done in numerical form on a 'subjective anxiety scale' of zero for absolute calm up to 100 for the worst anxiety the client has ever experienced. After about 20 seconds or more of relaxation, this process is repeated with the image being maintained for 20 to 30 seconds on this occasion, and it is further repeated until zero anxiety is reported. The next highest item is then dealt with in a similar manner until the client is desensitized to the whole hierarchy. As each item can be imagined without anxiety, whenever practicable the client actually exposes himself to the equivalent situation in real life, for there is evidence to suggest that this expedites, tests and generalizes his therapeutic progress (Agras, 1967; Sherman, 1972). When the anxiety reactions are not eliminated to an item either in imagination or in real life, then some relatively radical change in the treatment programme may be indicated, or it may simply be necessary to revise the hierarchy perhaps by inserting some less stressful intermediate items.

This systematic desensitization procedure is fairly standard, and one technical variation that may be especially useful in the treatment of sexual dysfunction, is for the spouse of the client to be involved in certain aspects of it such as the construction of hierarchies and the presentation of items from these during desensitization. Madsen and Ullman (1967) suggest that this will enhance the spouse's commitment to the treatment programme; assuage any worries that he or she may have about what it involves; promote understanding of the client's difficulties and how the spouse can best contribute to their resolution; and facilitate the transfer of therapeutic gains to real life situations. Another possible procedural variation is to present hierarchy items in graphic rather than imaginal form, by means of videotapes, films or slides of sexual activities. Obler (1973) used this as a supplementary technique when his subjects had difficulty in imagining a particular item, or whole hierarchies can be constructed from a pool of videotapes and presented via this media (Caird and Wincze, 1974; Wincze and Caird, 1976).

In vivo desensitization

The essence of the '*in vivo*' version of desensitization is that the client proceeds through the hierarchy of anxiety eliciting conditions in real life rather than in imagination. Various alternative responses to anxiety may be employed; for instance, a client might use relaxation to counteract any tension and anxiety he experiences during sexual assignments or similar activities; but in these particular situations it is especially appropriate to capitalize on his sexual arousal for this purpose. Thus, Wolpe (1969) advocates that the couple are advised to proceed gradually through a series of successive approximations to intercourse, without expecting or pressing for this to occur, so that any anxiety is mild enough to be inhibited by sexual arousal, the pleasure of which also serves to reinforce their sexual activities. The strong similarity between this precedure and a structured programme of sexual assignments, such as general and genital pleasuring followed by non-demand coitus, will be readily apparent, and the latter can quite feasibly be conceptualized in terms of *in vivo* desensitization.

Self-control desensitization

The self-control version of desensitization is based on the hypothesis that it is best regarded as a training in coping with anxiety reactions, so that the client is able to reduce these himself by applying the skills he has learned (Goldfried, 1971, 1973; Meichenbaum, 1973, 1974). This emphasis entails certain procedural modifications in systematic desensitization treatment, commencing with the exposition of a rationale to the client that stresses the use of relaxation as a coping skill in disturbing situations. Similarly, during relaxation training and hierarchy construction, the importance of tension as a cue for the client to relax himself is emphasized. It follows that when he experiences tension and anxiety reactions to hierarchy items during desensitization sessions, he is instructed to relax these away himself rather than having the presentation terminated as in the standard procedure. Finally, the client is specifically trained and encouraged to use his relaxation skills to cope with stress in real-life situations.

The general effectiveness of desensitization procedures in reducing in-appropriate anxiety reactions is well substantiated (Bergin and Suinn, 1975;

Marks, 1975; Paul, 1969a, b) and their specific contribution to the treatment of sexual dysfunction is considered in later chapters. However, the crucial ingredients and theoretical mechanisms responsible for the efficacy of the procedures are still far from clear, and they remain the topics of much experimental investigation and theoretical debate (Bergin and Suinn, 1975; Borkovec, 1973; Davison Wilson, 1972, 1973; Goldfried, 1971; Hoon et al., 1977a; Kazdin and Wilcoxon, 1976; Leitenberg et al., 1969; Marks, 1975; Mathews, 1971; Valins and Ray, 1967; Van Egeren, 1970, 1971; Van Egeren et al., 1971; Wilkins, 1971, 1972; Wilson and Davison, 1971; Wolpe, 1958; Wolpe et al., 1973).

FLOODING

Whereas desensitization involves only gradual and brief exposures to stressful situations with explicit use of an alternative response to alleviate any anxiety reactions that are evoked, the method of 'flooding' consists of more rapid and prolonged exposures to such situations without the deliberate use of an alternative response. The rationale for the method follows from the discussion of avoidance conditioning in Chapter 3, where it is noted that some individuals learn to avoid sexual situations, or to escape from them, in order to reduce the anxiety they evoke and to prevent their anticipated aversive consequences. This avoidance behaviour tends to be very persistent even when there is no longer any risk of such consequences, in part because it is negatively reinforced by an accompanying reduction in anxiety, but also in some cases because it is positively reinforced by certain rewards. As a result, the individual never enters or remains in such sexual situations and is deprived of all opportunity to learn that they are really quite pleasant and harmless rather than being aversive or damaging. The aim of flooding is to correct this deficiency by exposing the client to the stressful situation for a prolonged period while preventing avoidance and escape responses. As these responses and the associated anxiety reactions are not reinforced during the period of exposure, they will eventually be extinguished by the flooding procedure.

The stressful situation can be presented in imaginal, graphic, or real form, and there is evidence to suggest that the client must remain exposed to it until a significant reduction in anxiety occurs (Gauthier and Marshall, 1977). These and other procedural matters are reviewed by Marks (1975), who notes the current lack of a firm empirical basis for any adequate guidelines to the conduct of flooding treatment, and indicates that there appears to be some support for the greater effectiveness of in vivo exposures for durations of about two hours. His review, and others by Bergin and Suinn (1975) and Morganstern (1973), also demonstrate the inadequacy of the available evidence on the efficacy of flooding, as well as the continuing nature of the theoretical debate concerning its therapeutic mechanisms.

As far as sexual dysfunction in particular is concerned, to my knowledge the only published report on the specific use of a flooding type procedure is a paper by Hogan (1975) who discusses the implosive treatment of frigidity. This form of treatment was first described by Thomas Stampfl in the early nineteen sixties (Levis, 1974; Marks, 1972; Morganstern, 1973, 1974; Stampfl, 1967; Stampfl and Levis, 1967), and the major difference between implosion and flooding lies in the use of psychodynamically derived themes in the former procedure. This practice is based on the assumptions that most avoidance responses stem from childhood trauma, and that there are common areas of conflict which concern most individuals. These conflicts relate to the psychosexual stages postulated by Freud, and they include oral, anal, oedipal, and aggressive themes. It is towards these that implosive therapy is directed, and scenes based upon them are presented in a highly dramatic and extreme form to the client who is required to phantasize his participation in them with great vividness and emotional intensity. Hogan's (1975) paper does not include any systematic evidence on the outcome of implosive therapy in cases of frigidity, but its general effectiveness, crucial ingredients and theoretical mechanisms are reviewed by Morganstern (1973) and Marks (1975).

Although Hogan's paper appears to be the only explicit reference to the use of a flooding type procedure in the treatment of sexual dysfunction, there are several other techniques used in such treatment that might reasonably be conceptualized in that way. For instance, couples who are not accustomed to being in the nude together and who find this embarrassing or disturbing, may be advised to spend prolonged periods with each other while undressed so that any anxiety or avoidance reactions this evokes are thereby reduced. Similarly, the prolonged periods of masturbation undertaken by many women clients who have never achieved orgasm could serve as flooding experience, and this may also be implicit in the exaggerated roleplays of orgasm performed by some such clients. Finally, prolonged exposure to erotic films and literature is sometimes used to reduce the anxiety and inhibitions that clients are experiencing in relation to the sexual topics depicted in the material shown to them.

VAGINAL DILATATION

Features of *in vivo* desensitization and flooding can be seen also in the vaginal dilatation procedures which gynaecologists have used for many years to treat women suffering from vaginismus. More recently, these procedures have been incorporated as one component in comprehensive programmes for the treatment of this condition (Kaplan, 1974; Masters and Johnson, 1970).

As far as the dilatation component specifically is concerned, after explaining and demonstrating the reality of the muscular spasm to both partners, Masters and Johnson provide a set of vaginal dilators in graded sizes for the couple to use in their own home. Initially, the husband inserts the smallest dilator with manual guidance from his wife, until she is able to accept this with less of a spasm. This procedure is then repeated with the progressively larger dilators, and the wife's manual guidance is gradually replaced by verbal directions to her husband. When she can accommodate one of the larger dilators, she is encouraged to retain it in her vagina for several hours during sleep. The dilators may be made of glass or rubber, and a lubricant is usually applied to them to facilitate easy and painless insertion.

Kaplan has found that these artificial objects are not acceptable to many patients, and therefore recommends that the fingers of both spouses are used for dilatation purposes. The wife first inserts the tip of her own finger into the entrance of the vagina, to be followed by the whole finger and then two fingers. In some cases she is advised to insert a tampon without removing the covering, and to retain it for several hours. When penetration by two fingers, can be accepted without discomfort, then the steps up to this point are recapitulated with the husband progressively inserting and moving his fingers under his wife's manual guidance.

While the use of their own fingers rather than artificial dilators is preferred by some patients, there are others who find the latter more acceptable; perhaps because their use seems to be a more clinical procedure with stronger connotations of therapeutic prescription and sanction. Similarly, while Masters and Johnson advocate the initiation of the procedure by the husband, Kaplan suggests that it may be less stressful for the wife to undertake this herself. At present, there is no evidence which strongly favours the use of dilators or fingers, or the commencement of their use by either the wife or the husband, and decisions on both these procedural points can be negotiated with the individual couples concerned.

We turn now from the procedures of relaxation, desensitization, flooding, and vaginal dilatation that have a relative emphasis on stress reduction, to those that are predominantly directed towards the acquisition, performance and maintenance of satisfactory sexual responses. The latter procedures include classical conditioning, biofeedback, phantasy training and certain hypnotic techniques.

CLASSICAL CONDITIONING

To my knowledge, there is only one published report on the use of classical conditioning, in the treatment of sexual dysfunction (Asirdas and Beech, 1975), although it has also been employed to promote sexual responses to more usual stimuli among clients complaining of various forms of unconventional sexual behaviour, such as paedophilia or homosexuality (Freeman and Meyer, 1975; Herman et al., 1974; McConaghy, 1975).

Asirdas and Beech investigated classical conditioning as a possible means of enhancing interest among dysfunctional clients who were bored or indifferent towards sexual activity. Their male subjects could become aroused in response to slides depicting erotic scenes, and these were presented as unconditioned stimuli for durations of up to 180 seconds, or less if a full erection was obtained before then. These subjects also selected (from a set of 100) 10 'artistic' slides of nude women, which together with sexual phantasies about the client's partner, were to serve as conditioned stimuli. Before conditioning, these artistic slides and the accompanying phantasies did not produce arousal and erections in the men concerned. The conditioning procedure consisted of following an unconditioned stimulus with exposure to a conditioned stimulus for a period of 30 to 50 seconds. This procedure was implemented 10 times during each session, and three sessions a week were conducted over a period of three weeks, making 90 trials in all.

As the investigators were unsure about the equivalence of visual erotic material for men and women, they utilized the sexual excitement produced by a vibrator as the unconditioned stimulus for their female subjects; with a romantic tape recording of an erotic encounter, together with sexual phantasies involving the client's partner, as conditioned stimuli. With these modifications, the conditioning procedure used with the male subjects was carried out by the females in their own homes.

Asirdas and Beech stress the exploratory nature of their study, and conclude very tentatively that the conditioning procedure was followed by positive changes in the subjects' sexual attitudes and activities in relation to their partners. However, these investigators did not include any direct physiological measures of arousal in their assessment of outcome; and Langevin and Martin (1975), who did this by means of penis plethysmography in two conditioning experiments with male volunteer subjects, concluded that their results raised doubts about whether erections can be classically conditioned, at least at mild levels of arousal. They add that some clinical studies have indicated the greater possibility of this occurring at higher levels of arousal approaching orgasm, but that this requires further experimental investigation.

BIOFEEDBACK

Another approach that is at a very exploratory stage in the treatment of sexual dysfunction involves the use of biofeedback procedures to provide the individual with immediate information about his own bodily processes, so that he can exercise greater control over them. The general nature, efficacy and theoretical explanation of these techniques are reviewed by Blanchard and Young (1974) and Yates (1975), and the experimental investigation into their influence on erectile and female vasocongestive responses in normal subjects has begun (Hoon et al., 1977b, Rosen, 1976, 1977). However, little information is currently available about the possible clinical applications of biofeedback in the treatment of sexual dysfunction.

In one report, Csillag (1976) has described its use to enhance erectile responses in six patients suffering from psychogenic impotence. Penile erection was measured plethysmographically and informational feedback was given to the subjects both visually on a polygraphic recording and by means of an auditory tone that varied in pitch with the changing diameter of the penis. The experiment consisted of two sessions daily for eight days, and in each session the subjects were exposed to four conditions:

1. *Phantasy without feedback*
   the subject was asked to phantasize a sexually arousing situation whilst relaxing.

2. *Phantasy with feedback*
   the subject was asked to phantasize a sexually arousing situation, to try to achieve an erection and to use the visual and auditory feedback.
3. *Stimulus without feedback*
   subjects were instructed to relax whilst viewing erotic slides.
4. *Stimulus with feedback*
   subjects were instructed to try to achieve an erection whilst viewing the same slides and utilizing the visual and auditory feedback.

Unfortunately, the report does not distinguish clearly the respective effects of the 'with' and 'without' feedback conditions, within each session, but all 6 patients were able to increase progressively their erectile responses over the eight days of the experiment, and in 5 cases this improvement was generalized to their sexual performance with a partner. In contrast, six volunteer control subjects showed more variable increases in penile diameter during the early days of the experiment but these were not sustained, perhaps because of habituation or loss of interest in the study.

More intensive investigation of the clinical potential of biofeedback in the treatment of sexual dysfunction is clearly needed; and it must be stressed that the crucial ingredients among the many components of these procedures still remain to be identified, as discussed in the reviews cited above.

PHANTASY TRAINING

The importance of sexual phantasies as sources of arousal is noted in Chapter 2, but some dysfunctional clients have only very limited capacity for such phantasizing. In order to enhance this source of erotic stimulation for these clients, Flowers and Booraem (1975) have developed a 13 step programme of phantasy training:

Step 1. The client repeatedly looks at a non-sexual painting with his eyes open and then closes them and describes it in great detail.

He is assigned to do this with pictures and colourful objects in his natural environment, to keep a daily record of these attempts, and reward himself for them.

Step 2. Parts of graphic and interesting, but non-sexual, literary material are read aloud with feeling to the therapist, and the client then closes his eyes to visualize the passage with himself in the major role.

Between sessions, the client practises this task with self-reinforcement (this is also included in all subsequent assignments).

Step 3. Passages from two different non-sexual works are read aloud to the therapist, and the client then closes his eyes and integrates them into a single phantasy which is recounted to the therapist and tape-recorded for feedback to the client.

The task is repeated as an homework assignment, with the client's phantasies being recorded or written for subsequent discussion with the therapist.

Step 4. A repetition of step 2, except that sexual material that evokes only low levels of anxiety is introduced.

Step 5. A repetition of step 3, using low anxiety level sexual material.

Step 6. The client records instances of sexual attraction towards people or situations, and ranks these according to the intensity of the attraction experienced.

He also creates a low anxiety level sexual phantasy about the event after it is over.

Step 7. A repetition of step 6, except that the client creates the phantasy at the same time as he experiences the sexual attraction.

Step 8. The same as steps 3 and 5, except that both passages include medium anxiety level sexual material.

Step 9. The client creates medium anxiety level sexual phantasies based on the experiences recorded in step 6, and without the aid of literary material.

Step 10. Records are again kept of sexual attraction, and low anxiety level sexual phantasies are created during the experience, with medium level phantasies following after it has ended.

Step 11. As for steps 3, 5, and 8, except that both passages to be integrated should include high anxiety level sexual material.

Step 12. High anxiety level sexual phantasies are created based on experiences of attraction, but without the aid of literary material.

Step 13. The same as step 10, except that medium to high anxiety level sexual phantasies are produced to current experiences of attraction.

The authors report general improvements in the sexual interest and behaviour of clients who have undergone this training, but its particular contribution is not distinguished from those of other components in the comprehensive treatment programmes, and any changes in ability to phantasize are not specifically assessed.

HYPNOSIS

There are several possible uses for hypnotic techniques in the treatment of sexual dysfunction. Most traditionally perhaps, they have been employed in the investigation, recall and abreaction of traumatic sexual experiences (Alexander, 1974; Cheek, 1976; Deabler, 1976; Fabbri, 1976; Levit, 1971; Smith, 1975). Secondly; hypnosis is sometimes used to facilitate the stress reducing procedures of relaxation, desensitization, flooding and vaginal dilatation (Astrup, 1974; Fabbri, 1976; Fuchs, 1975; Fuchs *et al.*, 1973). The present discussion will focus on the use of hypnotic suggestion to promote sexual responses either during the trance state or after it is terminated.

The use of the former technique as part of the treatment of a woman who had never experienced orgasm is described by Cheek (1976). While she was in a trance, the therapist asked her the following question:

Q. 'Would it be all right for you to really feel what a climax can be like for you and your husband if I go out of the room to examine some patients?'
A. (finger signal) 'Yes'.
Q. 'Other normal women who have never been made to feel guilty about their sexual feelings have told me that when they have felt a warmth of love between themselves and their husband that they have had orgasms being kissed on their lips, caressed around their breasts and kissed on their neck. They have had orgasms just as they feel his penis entering their vagina, again as they move their hips from side to side bringing his penis in contact with the very sensitive nerves on each side of the vagina inside. They say they have felt a build up to a climax as they rapidly contract and relax their vaginal muscles around the whole length of the firm penis 10 or 12 times and that this can be repeated. Each climax becomes stronger because a woman is able to have an orgasm repeatedly without having to wait the way man has to wait. The strongest of all can be when you feel him swelling inside you at the moment he is reaching climax. You can even come again just by contracting your muscles around him inside after he has ejaculated. Please orient your memory now back to some time that could have been perfect for you and your husband had you known then what you are learning today and as it would have been if you had never had any fears or guilt feelings given you by your mother. Let your body feel all the sensations from the top of your head down to your heels. I am going out to examine some patients and I will not need this room. First, go over, the experience having just your fingers telling you how much you are feeling, then as you keep going over it you will start to feel it physically at a conscious level. When your inner mind knows that you can select what kind of climax you can have and how many you want to have, when you know that you are really satisfied your right arm will begin to lift up as though you had those balloons attached to it. When that occurs please let yourself come out of hypnosis and open the door so I know you are through.'(p.25)

Posthypnotic suggestions to promote the performance of adequate and pleasurable sexual behaviour have been utilized by Alexander (1974) among others. For instance, an impotent man who exhibited considerable performance anxiety, was asked under hypnosis

'to imagine lovemaking in a ski lodge in the evening – a cozy room, a fire. The patient was given the following suggestion: "Just enjoy her – don't perform. Touch, kiss, and if anything happens, let it happen." He was told to take his assets for granted – he did not have a thing to prove. Suggestions were given for self-confidence, drive, preparation, the enjoyment of the drive and concentration on what he is doing . . .' (p.37).

The wide range of hypnotic techniques available are described in several general texts (e.g. Crasilneck and Hall, 1975; Hartland, 1966; Weitzenhoffer,

1957; Wolberg, 1948), and these also include some brief mention of the application of the techniques in the treatment of sexual dysfunction, although with little evaluation of their efficacy beyond individual case reports.

ANCILLARY PHYSICAL TREATMENT

The progress and outcome of a programme of interviews, assignments and behavioural procedures is sometimes facilitated and enhanced by certain forms of ancillary physical treatment, including exercises for the vaginal muscles, the administration of hormones or drugs, and various prosthetic or mechanical aids.

Vaginal muscle excercises

Kegel (1952) has postulated an association between poor tone in the pubococcygeus and other vaginal muscles, and a lack of sexual sensation in that area together with limited capacity for arousal and orgasm. Accordingly, he developed methods of helping women who complain of such problems to locate the relevant muscles and to exercise them so that they become stronger, hopefully with accompanying improvement in sexual responsiveness (Deutsch 1973).

A programme of vaginal muscle training based upon Kegel's work is well described by Annon (1974):

> *Step 1.* In order to locate the pubococcygeus muscle the woman is asked to sit on the toilet with her legs spread well apart and to attempt to start and stop the flow of urine. In this position only the pubococcygenus muscle can control this function.
>
> *Step 2.* Having identified the muscle, the aim is to repeatedly stop the flow after passing about a teaspoonful of urine, although this usually takes some practice to achieve.
>
> The woman is asked to perform this exercise while urinating, and to similarly tighten and relax the muscle for 1 or 2 second periods on other occasions. The exercise should be repeated 10 times in a row, at least 6 times a day, for the first week.
>
> *Step 3.* During the following week, the exercise is discontinued while urinating, but increased to 20 repetitions in a row on each of 6 daily sessions, a total time of about 8 minutes a day.
>
> *Step 4.* At the same time a new 'twitching' exercise is commenced. This comprises contracting and releasing the pubococcygeus muscle as rapidly as possible, and it approximates to the muscular contractions of orgasm. About 10 such twitches are performed successively, on at least 6 occasions a day.
>
> During this exercise, the woman is asked to imagine whatever erotic phantasies she finds stimulating, so that the vaginal contractions and sensations begin to be associated with sexual arousal.
>
> *Step 5.* In the third week, the number of repetitions of each exercise is

progressively increased; the number of successive contractions to approximately 300 a day, taking a total time of 20 minutes; and of twitches to approximately 100 a day.

This fairly strenuous utilization of the muscles may produce some temporary soreness, which can be dispelled by a suspension or reduction of exercises.

There seems little to be gained from increasing the number of repetitions any further, but clients may continue to use the exercises for as long as they wish. To date, there has been no systematic evaluation of such vaginal muscle training programmes, but some clinicians do report improvements in vaginal sensation, arousal and orgastic capacity (Annon, 1974; Hartman and Fithian, 1974; Kegel, 1952; Kline–Graber and Graber, 1978).

Hormone or drug therapy

Most contemporary reviewers of the relevant literature conclude that the administration of androgens is generally of little value to impotent males, including even those whose urinary testosterone level is low (Cooper, 1972, 1974a; Johnson, 1968, 1975; Schiavi and White 1976). There are however some clinical reports of benefit being derived, particularly among older clients (Cooper, 1974a; Fellman et al., 1975; Maddison, 1974) and in certain cases of gonadal failure (Beumont et al., 1972), but the specific or placebo nature of any such effects have not been distinguished. In most of the studies to date, the administration of the hormones has been employed as a relatively isolated procedure, and it is possible, although not yet demonstrated, that their effectiveness might be enhanced if they were included as only one component in a more comprehensive treatment programme. Any temporary priming of sexual responsiveness by the androgens might then be exploited to dispel psychological impediments like performance anxiety, rather than being obscured and negated by such difficulties.

Attempts have also been made to treat erectile dysfunction with certain combinations of androgens and substances reputed to have aphrodisiacal qualities. One such preparation, Afrodex, consists of methyl testosterone, nux vomica extract and yohimbine. Initially, it seemed to hold considerable therapeutic promise, but subsequent statistical re-analysis of the most important evidence for its efficacy has shown this to be disappointing (Roberts and Sloboda, 1974). Furthermore, Cooper et al. (1973) have been unable to replicate the apparent early success of Afrodex with a similar preparation, Portensan Forte, consisting of methyl testosterone, yohimbine, pemoline, and strychnine.

Contemporary reviews of the literature on hormone therapy with female clients generally conclude that the administration of oestrogens appears to have little influence on sexual functioning, except when they are prescribed to relieve atrophic vaginitis causing dyspareunia (Dmowski et al., 1974; Easley, 1974; Greenblatt et al., 1972). In contrast, the administration of androgens does seem to enhance sexual interest and arousal in many women, possibly because it increases the sensitivity of the genitalia and particularly the clitoris. There is however, a risk of virilization as a side effect in some vulnerable women.

Certain drugs can be valuable in facilitating sexual activities among clients suffering from a physical illness. For instance, nitroglycerine taken just before intercourse may prevent angina pectoris in cardiac patients, and a beta-adrenergic blocking agent such as propranolol may help to reduce their blood pressure and heart rate during coitus (Fox, 1970; Schneider, 1974). Similarly, arthritic patients may be advised to take their customary analgesic or anti-inflammatory medication about half an hour before intercourse so that this coincides with the drug's maximum pain-relieving effect, but they should also be warned that increasing the dose above a certain level may reduce their interest and pleasure in sexual activity (Hamilton 1975a).

Prosthetic or mechanical aids

One aid used to assist men suffering from erectile dysfunction is the Blakoe Suspensory Energizer Ring (manufactured by Blakoe Ltd. 229 Putney Bridge Road, Putney, London SW15, England). It is made in more than 20 sizes to provide a good fit for each individual client, and comprises an ebonite rectangular 'ring' which opens on a swivel for placement high up under the scrotum and around the root of the flaccid penis, so that when the ring is closed it surrounds the freely hanging penis and scrotum. The device contains five small metal electro-galvanic plates on opposite inner surfaces, which set up a mild steady electric current when the plates make contact with the moist acid-containing skin of the genitalia (no batteries or recharging are required). Clients are advised to wear the appliance during intercourse or masturbation, and as much as possible at other times.

Cooper (1974b) has conducted a double blind crossover trial of the Blakoe energizer against a similar placebo ring which did not contain any electrodes, and the major findings are that both rings were associated with significant improvement in erectile capacity, and that no significant difference was found between the Blakoe and placebo rings in this respect. Thus, it appears that the efficacy of such appliances may derive mainly from their common mechanical and/or placebo properties, rather than any specific electrical effect.

Another possible source of assistance for the impotent male is some form of penile splint, either worn externally or as a surgical implant (Grabstald and Goodwin, 1973). The modern external versions are usually made of plastic, and are used to carry the flaccid or partially erect penis into the vagina so that an act of intercourse can be performed. This may have the advantages of enabling the man to gratify his partner; and perhaps of relieving any anxiety he may feel about intromission or intercourse, so that it may subsequently become possible for him to dispense with the splint. Some clients however, and perhaps particularly those whose impotence is associated with an irreversible organic condition, will need to rely on a splint permanently in which case a surgical implant may be indicated.

A relatively simple kind of implant consists of a silicone rod which permits the penis to hang pendulously and to be erected by hand to achieve intromission (Apfelberg *et al.*, 1976; Lash, 1968; Loeffler and Iverson, 1976; Loeffler and Sayegh, 1960; Pearman, 1967; Tudoriu 1977a, b). Perhaps the best current indication of the efficacy of this type of implant is contained in the report by Apfelberg *et al.* cited above; 23 out of 25 patients achieved satisfactory intercourse without problems or complications. Certain functional and cosmetic advantages are claimed for another more sophisticated inflatable hydraulic type of implant developed by Scott *et al.* (1973). Two silicone rubber cylinders are inserted into the corpus cavernosa in the penis, and then connected by tubing to a reservoir in the provesical space. The radiopaque fluid in this reservoir can be pumped into the cylinders by a means of a bulb actuator situated in the scrotum, so that the penis becomes erect. It can subsequently be returned to the flaccid state by means of a release valve in the pump. Once the apparatus is implanted surgically, the client then operates the bulb himself in order to inflate or deflate his penis. To my knowledge, the only available information on the efficacy of this device is contained in some illustrative case reports (Divita and Olsson, 1975; Scott *et al.*, 1973; Stewart and Gerson, 1976).

Disabled clients and others who are totally impotent are perhaps the most likely users of some form of artificial penis. The real penis is usually inserted into the prosthesis, which is held in place by means of straps. These aids are available with built in vibrators to increase the intensity of stimulation, as well as with artificial testicles that can be filled with a warm fluid to be ejaculated as a substitute for semen. Like the penile splint, an artificial penis can enable an impotent man to give satisfaction to his wife, perhaps with beneficial repercussions on his own self-esteem and the relationship between them, but I do not know of any controlled trials of the efficacy of this kind of aid.

Perhaps the most comonly used sexual aids are the various electro-vibrators which are manufactured in many different forms and materials. Often they are penis shaped or built into an artificial penis; but they are also available as an integral part of a simulated vagina for male use, or supplied with accessory fitments designed to stimulate the glans penis. All of them provide very intense stimulation, and may therefore facilitate and enhance arousal and orgasm among both men and women in whom these responses are impaired. If this is due to the anxiety evoked by responses such as female orgasm of male ejaculation, then the provision of these experiences by a vibrator may so relieve the client's concern that the aid subsequently becomes unnecessary. Additionally considerable satisfaction may be derived from a vibrator by clients of either sex who lack a sexual partner; as well as by the wives of men suffering from erectile dysfunction or premature ejaculation, especially if the aid is utilized by the couple as part of their lovemaking activities, even if these cannot extend to full intercourse.

The aids reviewed in this section by no means exhaust those available; for instance, others include weighted hollow balls which oscillate when worn intravaginally and reputedly strengthen the surrounding muscles in this way, and there are various forms of clitoral stimulator to be worn over the root of the penis during intercourse. These, and many of the aids mentioned above, are currently lacking any systematic evaluation. However, this is worth pursuing, as certain devices may well play a useful role in more comprehensive programmes of treatment or management for some dysfunctional clients, always providing that they and their partners find the aid acceptable and are able to use it without revulsion or guilt.

GENERAL CONCLUSION

The wide range of procedures that may be drawn upon to constitute comprehensive treatment programmes for sexually dysfunctional clients are listed in Table 10, and categorized into therapeutic interviews, sexual assignments, specific behavioural procedures, and ancillary physical treatment.

The functions of such interviews include the provision of information, the modification of attitudes and the management of sexual assignments. Information is provided to rectify any deficiencies or inaccuracies in sexual knowledge that may be impairing sexual functioning or impeding its therapeutic improvement. Similarly, when such impairment or impediment is due to adverse attitudes, then some attempt to modify these may be made in the interview situation. A therapeutic relationship is established, a causal explanation for the

Table 10. Possible components of
treatment for sexual dysfunction

Therapeutic Interviews
1. Provision of information
2. Modification of attitudes
3. Management of sexual assignments

Sexual Assignments
4. General pleasuring
5. Genital stimulation
6. Sexual intercourse

Specific Behavioural Procedures
7. Relaxation training
8. Desensitization
9. Flooding
10. Vaginal dilatation
11. Classical conditioning
12. Biofeedback
13. Phantasy training
14. Hypnosis

Ancillary Physical Treatment
15. Vaginal muscle exercises
16. Hormone or drug therapy
17. Prosthetic or mechanical aids

problem is agreed, and an expectation of effective help is promoted. These general conditions are usually necessary or facilitative rather than sufficient for attitude change, and more specific procedures such as sanctioning, self-disclosure, roleplaying or cognitive restructuring are also used in most cases. Both the provision of information and the modification of attitudes are not restricted to the therapeutic interviews, they can also occur during the sexual assignments and specific behavioural procedures. The third function of interviews, the management of sexual assignments, involves their prescription and monitoring, together with the initiation of steps to circumvent or resolve any difficulties revealed by their implementation.

This revelation of barriers to therapeutic progress is one function of the sexual assignments, and they also serve to reduce stress reactions evoked by sexual activities, as well as to promote more effective sexual stimulation and responses between the partners. The assignments are broadly categorized according to whether they predominantly involve general pleasuring, genital stimulation, or sexual intercourse.

The relatively specific behavioural procedures serve the same functions as the sexual assignments. Any of these procedures may reveal areas of difficulty in sexual functioning, but some of them also have a relative emphasis on stress reduction, while others have such an emphasis on the promotion of more adequate sexual behaviour. Among the predominately stress reducing procedures are relaxation training, desensitization, flooding, and vaginal dilatation; while the more promotional procedures include classical conditioning, biofeedback, phantasy training, and hypnotic suggestion.

Finally, certain forms of ancillary physical treatment, such as vaginal muscle exercises, hormone or drug therapy, and prosthetic or mechanical aids, are sometimes used to facilitate and enhance more comprehensive programmes of interviews, assignments, and behavioural procedures.

It is emphasized that such programmes are individually planned and implemented to suit particular clients, in the light of the nature of their problems, the resources available for treatment and the goals of therapy. The assessment of these matters together with the planning and monitoring of treatment are considered in the next chapter, while the utilization and evaluation of various procedures in the treatment of particular dysfunctions are discussed in Part 5.

Part 4

Assessment and Planning Treatment

11

Assessment of Problems and Resources

Before the treatment of sexual dysfunction is attempted it is necessary to identify and specify the client's problems and the contemporary conditions that influence them, to ascertain the resources available for treatment, to select and specify its goals, and to plan a suitable programme. In this and the following two chapters, we consider the kind of information needed at each of these stages and the methods used to obtain it.

ASSESSMENT OF PROBLEM(S)

Description of problem(s)

Information is gathered about all aspects of sexual functioning that are judged to be inadequate by either partner or some other relevant person, such as the referral agent or therapist, and these judgements will reflect the kind of factors discussed in Chapter 5. The information obtained will cover the nature, frequency, timing, and surrounding circumstances of the problem at the current time, as well as its duration, onset and course up to that point. Each of these topics is exemplified in the following paragraphs.

Nature of dysfunction

A clear account of the nature of the current problem is obtained in considerable detail. For instance, in the case of a woman who complains that she is 'frigid', it would be necessary to ascertain exactly what is meant by this term. She might be referring to a lack of interest in sex, to some impairment of arousal, or to a difficulty in reaching orgasm, or perhaps to a combination of these deficiencies. Further, if there is an impairment of arousal, this may or may not include an absence of the physiological components of vaginal lubrication and swelling, in addition to the inability to experience erotic sensations.

This leads to the important general point that an adequate account of a client's problem comprehends its emotional and cognitive aspects as well as its overt behavioural manifestations; not only what the client is doing or not doing, but also what he or she is feeling and thinking. Thus, a 'frigid' woman might be suffering considerable performance anxiety in relation to her inability to reach orgasm, or she might believe that to do so would entail total loss of self-control, and these would constitute important elements in her total problem.

Thus, the initial task is to obtain a specific and comprehensive description of the nature of the problem in clear operational terms. Such an account serves to reduce the vagueness and ambiguity which commonly characterize the original presentations of complaints by clients, and to enhance the precision and reliability of the whole assessment process.

Frequency and timing

Further information is gathered about the frequency and timing of the current problem. Clearly, it is important to discover whether it occurs during every sexual encounter or only on certain occasions, and for some types of problem the issue of timing is quite central. Thus, a complaint of premature ejaculation may mean that this is happening as soon as the client becomes aroused or after some longer interval of time. Similarly, complaints of orgastic dysfunction or retarded or absent ejaculation must be related to the duration of the stimulation the client has received without being able to reach climax.

Surrounding circumstances

The last aspect of the current situation about which information is gathered, concerns the surrounding circumstances of the problem; it may, for instance, occur only in the presence of a partner who exhibits certain characteristics, such as being dominant or demanding, or in certain physical settings, perhaps where privacy or comfort is lacking. Such circumstances are discussed at greater length in a later section devoted to contemporary influences on problems.

Duration

Turning now from the contemporary nature, frequency, timing and surrounding circumstances of the problem, information is gathered also about its duration, onset, and course.

As far as the duration is concerned, a client's problem may be 'primary', in the sense that it has always existed, or 'secondary' in that at some time he or she was able to function adequately in that particular respect; for example, a woman may never have been able to reach orgasm, or this impairment may have followed a variable period of time during which she was free from any such difficulty.

Onset

In the case of secondary problems, it is clearly important to determine the circumstances of their onset, including the age of the client at the time, whether the problem developed suddenly or gradually, any possible precipitating factors and the reactions it evoked in the individuals concerned. Thus, it would be helpful to know that a man aged fifty became impotent quite suddenly after he failed to get an erection when he had been drinking, and that he had reacted to this failure with considerable anxiety about his sexual capacity, while his wife became extremely demanding in an attempt to reassure herself that he still found her attractive.

Course

Finally, the course of the problem since its onset may have remained fairly constant or it may have fluctuated, in which case information is needed about any factors accompanying these variations. Such factors may yield clues to the determinants of the problem; thus, a woman's orgastic capacity may have fluctuated with the current state of her general marital relationship, which might indicate the possible contribution of partner discord to the sexual dysfunction. Similarly, some clues to possible causal influences may be derived from information about any fluctuations in the course of the problem which have accompanied any previous attempts to resolve it either by the couple themselves or through earlier therapeutic interventions. For example, the fact that a woman's orgastic capacity was enhanced whenever the couple engaged in particularly lengthy periods of foreplay might suggest some deficiency of stimulation as contributing to her current difficulty in reaching climax. Likewise, the persistence of a sexual dysfunction after a relevant organic condition has yielded to medication may indicate the influence on the dysfunction of the client's psychological reactions to his illness.

Contemporary influences on problem(s)

It will be apparent that a description of the problem along the lines suggested above already begins to provide some indication of the contemporary conditions that influence its occurrence, and these are further explored more thoroughly and comprehensively in the broad categories of situational antecedents, organismic variables and situational consequences. This inquiry will reflect the material discussed in Chapters 2 and 4, therefore to reduce repetition only a few illustrative examples of each category are given in the following discussion.

Two preliminary points should be noted about the information gathered in each category. First, this is obtained in sufficient detail for each contemporary influence to be defined in very specific and clear operational terms, so that the precision and reliability of the whole assessment process is thereby enhanced.

Secondly, although the information concerns the contemporary influences on the problem it is very likely to be derived in part from an historical examination of the client's previous learning experiences of the kind discussed in Chapter 3, for these can provide important clues to the contemporary influences. Thus, a traumatic experience in the past might suggest that a client could be anticipating some harm in a sexual encounter at the present time, but this possibility would need to be thoroughly checked for we have seen that such an adverse outcome is not an inevitable consequence of previous sexual trauma. Similarly, a grossly restrictive upbringing might indicate the existence of current negative attitudes towards sex or a lack of accurate knowledge in this area, and a serious disruption in a client's early relationships with his parents may point to the possibility of current difficulty in establishing and maintaining an intimate, trusting relationship with a sexual partner. Thus, such previous experiences can constitute useful sources of hypotheses about possible contemporary influences on the problem.

Additionally, these experiences can be used to check similar hypotheses derived from an assessment of the current situation. For instance, if a wife's loss of sexual responsiveness appears to reflect her husband's current unfaithfulness, then it may be useful to check if she reacted similarly to any previous incidents of adultery on his part. We turn now to consideration of each of the three categories of contemporary influences on the problem which were mentioned above.

Situational antecedents

This first category includes those environmental conditions that immediately precede the sexually dysfunctional behaviour, and which serve to promote its occurrence. In behavioural terms these conditions constitute the external eliciting and discriminative stimuli for the problematic responses.

Such situational antecedents might include certain features of the sexual encounter itself, the partner with whom it is undertaken, its timing and setting, and any concomitant stresses of a non-sexual kind. For instance, among the many features of an encounter that may impair a client's sexual responses, are the sight of the partner's genital organs or contact with their emissions, any attempt at penile insertion, a lack of contraceptive provision, performance demands by the partner, and deficient or inappropriate sexual stimulation. Sexual performance may also prove inadequate when it is attempted with an unattractive or discordant partner, or in the context of a premarital or extramarital relationship. The timing and setting of the encounter may be important; thus, if it is very hurried then certain clients will not be able to respond adequately, and some will be inhibited in settings where privacy is not assured, where they are physically uncomfortable, or where a sufficiently romantic ambience is lacking. Finally, sexually dysfunctional behaviour may occur when clients are exposed to some form of non-sexual stress, such as a risk of losing a job, or an illness in the family.

Organismic variables

Sexually dysfunctional behaviour is influenced not only by external environmental conditions, but also by organismic or person variables that function within the individual and serve to mediate how he responds to external influences. Such organismic variables include the individual's thought processes, emotional feelings, and organic states. We have seen, for example, that if a client thinks a sexual encounter will prove harmful, unpleasant, or unsuccessful, then his performance may well be impaired, and that this may also occur if the encounter arouses feelings of anxiety, anger, or guilt, or if it is attempted when certain organic conditions are operative. At the simplest level, these might consist of the client being cold, tired, or uncomfortable during the encounter, but they may also involve the states of menstruation, pregnancy, or the post-partum, as well as the natural changes of the aging process and the illnesses, drugs, and surgical inventions discussed in Chapter 2.

It will be evident that information must be gathered about any such relevant organismic variables when the therapist is assessing the contemporary influences on a client's dysfunctional behaviour.

Situational consequences

This third category of influences to be explored consists of those environmental consequences of the problem which serve to maintain, and perhaps exacerbate, its occurrence. Particularly important instances of such consequences concern the reactions of the partner to the dysfunctional behaviours. If this leads to criticism, ridicule, anger, or rejection, then it is likely to persist and possibly worsen. This is also the probable outcome if a client's failure is followed by increasing performance demands from a partner who feels frustrated or unloved. Moreover, if a client feels hostile towards his or her partner, then the distress caused to the partner by the client's inadequacy, may actually be rewarding to the client, and thus serve to maintain the dysfunctional behaviour.

ASSESSMENT OF RESOURCES

A second major area for assessment concerns those potentialities and limitations in the available resources that may facilitate or hinder treatment, and these can be considered in three broad categories according to whether they relate to the client's environmental situation, to the client personally, or to the professional therapist and the services at his disposal.

Situational resources

Clearly important in this category are the potentialities and limitations inherent in a client's sexual partnership. Is the quality of the general relationship between the partners likely to facilitate or hinder the treatment of their sexual problem? What are the implications for treatment if the client lacks a regular sexual partner? Similarly, what if both partners are sexually dysfunctional? In addition to such vital issues concerning a client's partnership as a therapeutic resource, one must also consider many other aspects of his or her situation, including certain socioeconomic features that are exemplified later in the following discussion.

General relationship between the partners

The frequent, but not inevitable, association of sexual dysfunction and partner discord was noted in Chapter 4, and when these problems do co-exist in the same couple, one is faced with the choice of offering treatment which is directly focused upon the relief of the dysfunction, or marital therapy aiming at an improvement in the general relationship between the partners. The former type of treatment would be composed of components drawn from those outlined in Part 3, while the nature of marital therapy would reflect the theoretical orientation of the therapist (see reviews by Beck, 1975; Berman and Lief, 1975; Gambrill, 1977; Glisson, 1976; Greer and D'Zurrila, 1976; Gurman and Rice, 1975; Hops, 1976; Jacobson and Martin, 1976; Paquin, 1977; Patterson *et al.*, 1976; Skynner, 1976b; and Thomas, 1976).

Conceivably, programmes of direct treatment for sexual dysfunction or of marital therapy could be carried out as alternatives to each other, or consecutively in either order, or concurrently; and each type of therapy might be conducted by the same or different therapists. In the present state of knowledge there are no well founded guidelines as to which of these several possible courses is likely to prove most beneficial to an individual couple, although some general indications are considered below. What does seem to be important is that the focus of a particular programme on the dysfunction or the general relationship should be clearly recognized and adhered to by the couple and the therapists concerned. This does not preclude the possibility of changing from one form of therapy to the other if this appears to be desirable at any point. For instance, it is often difficult to ascertain during the preliminary assessment, that the degree of discord between the partners is such that they cannot cooperate in the direct treatment of their sexual dysfunction, but this may soon become apparent when they attempt to implement the prescribed sexual assignments, in which case a change to a marital therapy focus might be recommended and negotiated with the couple.

The fact that a particular therapeutic programme is focused upon the sexual dysfunction or upon the general relationship, does not mean that its effects will necessarily be restricted to the problem being treated. Not uncommonly, one has a strong clinical impression that the direct treatment of sexual dysfunction is accompanied by more widespread beneficial repercussions on a couple's general relationship. Through their participation and mutual cooperation in the programme, they may seem to be emotionally closer to each other, to be much more affectionate and trusting, and to be communicating more openly and effectively. If the treatment is successful in relieving the dysfunction, this may markedly reduce any resentment or hostility that has spilled over from it into the general relationship. Sometimes difficulties in this relationship are discovered by the couple in the course of their treatment for sexual dysfunction, and they may then attempt to rectify these difficulties either by their own efforts or in a subsequent programme of marital therapy.

There is some more systematic support for such clinical impression in a study by Brown (1976) of couples who received direct treatment for sexual dysfunction. Among the 53 couples who completed treatment, 86% reported at termination that their general relationship had changed for the better, and 4% that it had changed for the worse. The comparable proportions for all 72 couples who entered treatment, including those who terminated before completion, were 63% and 27%. A three month follow-up was instituted and among the 64 couples who could be included, they were 73% who rated their general relationship as having changed for the better since termination of treatment, and 4% who rated it as having changed for the worse; while 74% then considered their general relationship to be very much as they would want, compared to 8% for whom this was not the case.

Complementary systematic evidence on the possible beneficial effects of marital therapy on sexual dysfunction does not appear to be available, although again there is some clinical support for such repercussions from treatment focused upon the general relationship (e.g. Gill and Temperley, 1974).

A basic point to be considered in assessing the general relationship between partners, is the capacity and willingness of each of them to participate and cooperate in a programme for the direct treatment of sexual dysfunction. Masters and Johnson (1970) insist that these must be conjoint programmes, and the following are among the reasons they advance for the necessary involvement of both partners. If one of them is left out of the treatment, then he or she may not understand how to facilitate it, and may even unwittingly hinder its implementation and effectiveness. For example, a wife might become overdemanding in a misguided effort to encourage her impotent husband's returning—but still fragile—erectile capacity; or a husband might mistakenly proceed too quickly to full active intercourse when his previously unresponsive wife is just beginning to allow herself to experience some sexual sensations and feelings.

Such unhelpful forms of behaviour may sometimes occur as expressions of hostility by a partner towards a client, and it is not possible for the therapist to try to reduce these because of the partner's absence from the treatment situation; indeed, this exclusion may actually exacerbate the partner's feelings of resentment and anger.

Certainly, the absence of one partner will not serve to promote an improvement in communication between them, which is often a necessary element of therapeutic progress, and it may actually worsen whatever communication remains.

To conclude these arguments in favour of conjoint therapy, we may note our earlier discussions in Chapters 4 and 9, on the importance of the partner's reactions for the instigation and maintenance of a client's sexually dysfunctional behaviour, and on the essential nature of the willing participation and cooperation of the partner for the performance of many of the sexual assignments that are commonly prescribed. It follows that the quality of the general relationship between the partners is an important influence on the willingness of each of them to be involved in treatment, which in turn is likely to be an important influence on the outcome of such treatment.

This emphasis on the desirability of conjoint therapy, does not preclude the possibility of conducting individual assessment interviews, or of prescribing assignments to be carried out by one of the partners alone, both of these practices being quite usual; but it does mean that both partners are involved in the overall programme whenever this is at all possible. Circumstances do arise, of course, when this is not possible even though a client does have a regular partner; he or she may, for example, be effectively precluded from attending treatment sessions due to unusual work commitments. In such cases, the therapist can try to help the client to transmit to the partner, some understanding of the dysfunction, of the treatment programme, and of the part the partner can play in it. It is also possible to deploy any of the procedures outlined in Part 3, that do not require the active participation of a sexual partner. While far too little attention has been given to ways of helping clients whose partners are unable or unwilling to participate in treatment, it probably has to be recognized that this situation is likely to remain less satisfactory than conjoint therapy for most clients.

A couple's ability to meet the standard basic requirement of joint involvement in therapy, is not sufficient in itself to ensure their effective mutual cooperation in a programme. This may be totally negated or disrupted if a severe degree of discord exists between the partners. If either of them is so uncommitted to the marriage that he or she is disinterested in improving their sexual relationship, or if so much hostility exists between them that they cannot cooperate together in the programme, then this is most unlikely to be successful. More probably the sexual assignments will not be undertaken, or they will be sabotaged in some way. For example, a husband may neglect to follow the guidance he has received about his wife's sexual preferences and thus prevent her from becoming aroused or reaching climax, or a wife may continue to be critical or sexually demanding in the face of her husband's inability to obtain or retain an erection.

Because of the high probability of difficulties such as these arising, Sager (1974) suggests certain prerequisites for the direct treatment of sexual dysfunction which include the couple's ability to put aside any hostility during the treatment period, their willingness to accept each other as sexual partners, and a genuine desire to work together towards the enhancement of their mutual sexual satisfaction. Many couples with some degree of discord may still be able to meet these requirements, and their disinterest or disharmony are such that they can be resolved or circumvented in a programme of direct treatment for sexual dysfunction. In more severe cases of discord, where the requirements cannot be met, then it is often more appropriate to offer marital therapy with the aim of improving their general relationship, perhaps to be followed by the direct treatment of sexual dysfunction if this problem remains when the discord has been reduced.

There is some empirical support for an association between partner discord and lack of success from the direct treatment of sexual dysfunction in a study of 36 dysfunctional couples conducted by Mathews *et al.* (1976), who report a significant tendency for less change in sexual functioning to occur when the initial general relationship was poor.

Availability of a regular partner

Because of the importance attached to the involvement of two willing and cooperative partners in the direct treatment of sexual dysfunction, it is clearly necessary to ascertain the availability of a regular partner and the implications for treatment of a deficiency in this respect.

Many therapists will only accept clients who do have partners, but this is to deny treatment to many dysfunctional individuals at least until they are able to establish a relationship with a partner who is willing to participate and cooperate in a treatment programme. Unfortunately, the establishment of such a relationship is in itself a problem for many individual clients, for they have often experienced difficulty and distress in earlier sexual encounters which has caused them to avoid even social contacts with members of the opposite sex in case these should lead on to sexual situations where their inadequacy will be exposed. Thus, a vicious circle develops in which these clients cannot obtain treatment for sexual dysfunction because they do not have a regular partner, and they cannot obtain such a partner because of their sexual dysfunction. Therefore, despite the very real difficulties, it does seem important to try to find ways of helping dysfunctional clients who do not have a regular partner.

One such way, developed by Masters and Johnson (1970), is to treat male clients in the context of a temporary relationship with a surrogate partner provided by the therapists. This facility was not offered to female clients, because when Masters and Johnson started their programme in 1958, they felt that their two week period of treatment was not long enough for a dysfunctional woman to establish the kind of personal relationship with a partner that she would need to succeed in therapy. In the light of changing cultural attitudes towards female sexuality since that time, Belliveau and Richter suggested in 1970 that Masters and Johnson might then have been prepared to provide male surrogates, if suitable men who would not primarily seek their own sexual gratification could be found, which Masters and Johnson were said to doubt. However, quite recently, Masters has expressed adherence to their original decision not to use male surrogates (Masters *et al.*, 1977). He seems to base this view on the fact that they have never been asked to supply one, although the demand characteristics of their particular therapeutic situation may well have influenced their experience in this respect.

The female surrogate was conceived as a third member of the therapy team with the two co-therapists, and her role was to act as a substitute for a regular partner. After establishing an easy and comfortable social relationship, the client and surrogate would proceed through a programme of sexual assignments in consultation with the therapists, in the same manner as regular partners. The aim was to implement this programme within the context of a warm and responsive, but not a romantic or dependent, relationship between the client and his surrogate partner.

Masters and Johnson did not contemplate using prostitutes for this task, which they conceived as requiring much more than a purely physical sexual performance, otherwise the sexual experience would probably not be therapeutically effective and might well be damaging. Instead, volunteers were used as surrogates, and they were very carefully screened for this role, some 60% being rejected. The 13 women who were accepted and who participated, were aged 24 to 43 years, and all of them were educated at least to High School level, many being university graduates. None were married when they acted as surrogates, but all but 2 of them had been married previously. They were all sexually experienced and not sexually dysfunctional. Their motives for volunteering appeared to include interest in sexual problems, compassion for those suffering from them, and desires for social contacts and sexual relief. These surrogates were given some systematic training in human sexuality, and more specifically on the causes and treatment of sexual dysfunction.

The male clients treated with surrogate partners achieved similar therapeutic outcomes to those treated with regular partners. Out of the 41 men treated with surrogates, 32 were functioning successfully at termination of treatment, and on follow up six years later, 24 of these 32 were married and only 1 had relapsed into his dysfunction.

Despite this degree of success, Masters and Johnson subsequently decided that they had to discontinue using surrogates, partly because they had been threatened with litigation by the husband of one of them (Le Roy, 1971), but also because some surrogates began to consider themselves as therapists (Masters et al., 1977). For a variety of legal, professional, ethical and practical reasons, the original example set by Masters and Johnson has been followed by few therapists (Apfelbaum, 1977; Wolfe, 1978). The present writer has no experience of using surrogate partners, and in Britain they are known to be employed only at the Institute for Sex Education and Research in Birmingham (Cole, 1975). In the United States, a survey of the use of surrogate partners by health professionals was conducted by Malamuth et al. (1976), but the 111 respondents were not necessarily representative of their professions. Only 28% of this group had actually referred a client to a surrogate and all of these would do so again, but 87% said that they would so refer if this were clearly legal.

Jacobs et al. (1975) have reported on some interviews they conducted with 2 female and 1 male surrogate in California. These informants estimated that 95% of surrogate practise in the United States was conducted in that state, and they themselves belonged to a local organization for surrogates with a membership of about 25. The purposes of this organization were to maintain professional standards for surrogates, and to afford them legal protection. It screened the suitability of applicants for surrogate practice, provided some systematic training which included several weekend workshops, and arranged supervised practice under the guidance of a professional therapist. The practices of the 3 surrogate informants are described in the paper, and among the more formal of these are the acceptance of clients only on written referral from a mental health professional, and the requirement of a legal release signed by the client indicating voluntary participation in surrogate therapy, as well as a written consent from the spouse if the client is married.

Instead of professional therapists providing surrogates for dysfunctional clients who lack regular partners. It is sometimes appropriate to try to enhance the capacities of the clients themselves to find their own partners. Some individual clients have deficits in the heterosocial skills required to establish and maintain a relationship with a potential sexual partner, and they may be helped by a programme of training focused upon the development of such skills. These include, for example, a number of verbal and non-verbal components that Barlow *et al.* (1977) have identified as being necessary for male clients if they are to be successful in initiating relationships with women. The man's voice needs to have certain qualities of loudness, pitch, inflection, and dramatic effect; he will be able to initiate conversation, to follow up on female vocalizations, to ensure the continued flow of conversation, and to verbalize interest in the female's activities or appearance; and during their interactions he should exhibit appropriate facial expressions, make eye contact with the female, and laugh at suitable times and in suitable manner. The procedures available to train socially inadequate clients in skills such as these are reviewed by Curran (1977), Gambrill (1977), Heimberg *et al.* (1977), Hersen and Eisler (1976), and Liberman *et al.* (1975).

However, not all dysfunctional clients who lack a partner are socially inadequate, and even those for whom such deficits have been remedied by social skills training may still not implement their newly acquired capacity to establish and maintain a relationship with a potential sexual partner. In both circumstances, the clients have the necessary skills but do not implement these to relate to a potential partner; in other words they have a performance rather than a skill deficit. One very common reason for this is a fear that any social contact with the opposite sex may entail a sexual encounter in which the client's dysfunction will be exposed. Furthermore, even if individual clients are able and willing to relate to potential partners, they may be frustrated in this respect by a variety of factors that restrict the opportunities open to them; for instance, barriers of age, disability, geographical isolation, or cultural expectations.

In any of the circumstances described in the previous paragraph, it is usually wise to attempt to build up sexual confidence and competence in individual clients by deploying any of the procedures outlined in Part 3 that are at least partially feasible in the absence of a partner. These include the provision of information, modification of attitudes, self-stimulation assignments, relaxation, desensitization, flooding, vaginal dilatation, classical conditioning, biofeedback, phantasy training, hypnosis, and ancillary physical treatment.

At present, almost all the available evidence on the feasibility and efficacy of these procedures with individual clients concerns the group treatment of inorgastic women, and this is discussed in Chapter 16. However, clinical experience does suggest that very real limitations are likely to be encountered at some stage in treatment, unless the client is able to enter into a relationship with a sexual partner. Without this direct experience, it is difficult for the therapist to assess the client's progress or to help him resolve any obstacles that might arise in his sexual functioning with a partner, and the client is likely to remain unsure of his sexual competence until this is tested with a partner. Nevertheles, despite these very real limitations, it does seem desirable to develop and implement any procedures that are feasible with individual clients, as the only alternative to denying them any treatment for their sexual dysfunctions.

Finally, in the cases of socially inadequate clients, there are currently no firm guidelines on the relative desirability of providing social skills training prior to, or concurrently with, the treatment of sexual dysfunction; or on whether the two forms of treatment are better administered by the same or different therapists; but again it is probably important for the focus of each to be clearly distinguished by the therapists and clients concerned.

Sexual dysfunction in both partners

It is not at all uncommon to find that some degree of sexual dysfunction exists not only in the main complainant but also in his or her partner (Langmyhr, 1977). This was so in 43.7% of the couples treated by Masters and Johnson, and in the study by Mathews *et al.* (1976) mentioned earlier; there were 18 couples in which the wife was the main complainant, and in this group 3 of the husbands had experienced erectile failure in circumstances where this was an inappropriate reaction, and 8 of them had some degree of premature ejaculation; in another group of 18 couples in which the husband was the main complainant, all of the wives had difficulty in reaching orgasm and 13 of them experienced some lack of sexual interest or arousal.

Clearly, such combinations of dysfunction in both partners have important implications for the therapeutic resources they are able to provide for each other, and these will need to be taken into account when planning treatment. The variety of possible combinations, as well as many other individual differences between couples, precludes the prescription of any ideal method of treating dysfunctions in both partners. They might be treated concurrently, or consecutively in either order, but whatever is proposed will need to be negotiated with both partners so that each understands and accepts the goals and priorities of the programme.

Socioeconomic resources

In addition to assessing the nature of a client's sexual partnership as an important therapeutic resource, one must also gather and consider information about many other aspects of a couple's life situation that may facilitate or hinder treatment for sexual dysfunction. For instance, are they living in accommodation that affords sufficient privacy for them to carry out the sexual assignments? Do their work commitments permit them to spend sufficient time together to undertake these assignments in a suitably relaxed and intimate atmosphere, as well as regularly to attend treatment sessions with the therapists? Are the couple experiencing so many other pressing social or financial problems that their sexual difficulties are likely to assume a much lower priority in the demands upon their attention as treatment proceeds? These are a few illustrations of the many practical factors that may have a crucial influence on the process and outcome of therapy, and it is vitally important not to neglect such apparently mundane matters when assessing the situational resources for treatment.

Personal resources

The second major area in the assessment of resources concerns the personal potentialities of clients for treatment, consideration being given both to their assets and their deficits in this respect. To avoid repetition in the following discussion, it is concentrated on the personal resources of the main complainant, but those of the partner need to be similarly assessed.

Motivation

Important among the resources of each partner is their degree of motivation, for this is likely to influence their cooperation, persistence, and response in treatment.

In part, motivation can be assessed from the couple's actual behaviour; for example, the regularity of their appointment keeping, their assiduity in carrying out prescribed sexual assignments, and their verbal expressions of a desire for change and an expectation of effective help in treatment.

However, the surrounding circumstances are also useful sources of information. Each may be experiencing a certain degree of distress as a result of the dysfunction, and the main complainant may have sought help on his own initiative or because he received strong pressure or encouragement from his partner. A successful outcome in treatment may be likely to be very rewarding to the complainant both in terms of the relief of his distress and of benefits such as pleasurable sexual experiences, an improved general relationship with his partner, the ability to have children, and enhanced self-esteem. On the other hand, the possibility of a successful outcome might entail certain threats and disadvantages for some complainants. For instance, an improvement in a wife's sexual responsiveness might imply capitulation to her husband in the only area of their relationship where she has previously been able to assert herself against his dominance and control. Similarly, an improvement in a husband's premature ejaculation may entail the cessation of this means of frustrating a wife towards whom he feels hostile and whom he wants to punish, and the relief of retarded or absent ejaculation may mean that he is no longer able to deny her the child she so badly wants. Success in the treatment of sexual dysfunction might also raise new problems for some complainants. It might reveal difficulties in the general relationship between the partners that have previously been masked by the dysfunction. It could expose socially inadequate complainants to the self-imposes expectation that they must now succeed in finding a partner, the previous excuse of sexual dysfunction no longer being valid; or a wife who does not want children might become exposed to the expectations of her husband and relatives that she will now start a family. All these surrounding circumstances, together with complainant's behaviour, may provide clues to his degree of motivation for treatment.

Organizational capacity

Goldfried (1976) makes the valuable point that a client's capacity to organize his own time and commitments is an important resource affecting the process and outcome of those treatment programmes that require the implementation of any kind of homework assignment. These would include the sexual assignments discussed in Chapter 9, and a client who does have difficulty in organizing suitable occasions for their performance, or who constantly procrastinates, is at a considerable disadvantage.

In some cases this difficulty reflects an avoidance of the tasks because they are threatening, in others it is due more to personal disorganization, but in either event it calls for attention in the treatment programme if this is to proceed satisfactorily. The reduction of avoidance reactions is discussed in Part 3, and among the procedures that might be employed to improve personal organization are the structuring of assignments in formal contracts between the client and the therapist, self-monitoring and recording of their performance by the client, and close supervision together with appropriate reinforcement by the therapist.

Educational and socio-economic levels

Perhaps because of the referral and screening systems in operation, the patients seen by Masters and Johnson (1970) were drawn from the middle class or above, and 72.7% of them were college or university graduates. This raises the question for many people of whether the direct treatment of sexual dysfunction is feasible with patients drawn from other socio-economic and educational levels. Subsequent experience with a wide range of patients seen in ordinary clinical facilities in many countries, including the Health Service in Britain, does suggest that this form of treatment is quite viable with patients from lower socio-economic and educational levels and that there is no reason to regard these as necessary contraindications, although the socio-economic resources for treatment will need to be assessed as discussed in an earlier section.

Religious and moral beliefs

We noted earlier that dysfunctional clients are sometimes misinterpreting religious dogma concerning sexual behaviour, or are unable to rid themselves of the guilt and inhibitions associated with moral or religious beliefs which they have long abandoned, and that the correction of such inaccurate information or the modification of such negative attitudes are often important therapeutic tasks of varying difficulty.

However, this still leaves those clients who are correctly interpreting the sexual standards of their religion or moral code, and who retain a genuine belief in their validity. In these circumstances, it would be improper for a therapist to try to persuade them otherwise, but the beliefs might impose significant limitations on the process and outcome of treatment for dysfunction. For instance, an inorgastic woman who believes that self-stimulation is sinful, may well present special problems if assignments involving this are to be excluded from her treatment programme. Similarly, a couple who believe the so-called 'safe period' to be the only acceptable method of contraception, but who are also unsure of its efficacy, may fear and avoid intercourse if they do not want to have a child. It is sometimes possible to pursue treatment without the client having to contravene such genuine beliefs, but occasionally these may prove insurmountable barriers to therapeutic progress.

Organic conditions

As discussed in Chapters 2 and 4, a person's sexual functioning may be directly impaired by the aging process, illness, drugs, or surgery, but in most such cases there is some residual capacity and this is often further impaired by adverse psychological reactions to such physical limitations. Thus, it seems highly desirable and feasible to provide treatment opportunities for dysfunctional clients who exhibit some relevant organic condition; with the aims of reducing any adverse psychological reactions that are exacerbating the problem, and of realizing any residual capacity for sexual functioning and satisfaction possessed by themselves and their partners.

Psychiatric syndromes

There does not appear to be any systematic evidence on the process and outcome of the direct treatment of sexual dysfunction when this co-exists with a psychiatric syndrome. Masters and Johnson (1970) did not accept psychotic patients, but they were prepared to admit to their programme many patients who were undergoing psychotherapy for a psychoneurosis. Unfortunately, little further relevant information is given about this particular group of patients, and the outcome of their treatment cannot be distinguished from those of other patients in the study.

Kaplan (1974) does not accept patients who are acutely schizophrenic, paranoid, or depressed, or those with a history of these conditions whose sexual symptoms serve as a defence against them. She reasons that such patients would be unable to cooperate in the direct treatment of sexual dysfunction, and might actually react adversely, so that it is better to arrange for them to receive appropriate treatment for their psychotic disorder. On the other hand, Kaplan does accept patients who are neurotic, mildly depressed, or exhibiting some paranoid tendencies, and those who have a history of schizophrenic or severe depressive episodes but are currently in remission. Such acceptance is always providing that the sexual dysfunction is not serving a defensive function, and that the patient seems amenable to direct treatment for sexual dysfunction and shows little risk of reacting adversely to it. Kaplan does not systematically report her results with such patients, but she mentions their varying outcomes, including some successes, and notes the lack of clear prognostic criteria at the present time. Until these are better established, it seems reasonable to consider clients with a psychiatric diagnosis for admission to programmes of treatment for sexual dysfunction, in the light of their probable ability to cooperate and benefit without any adverse effects on their concomitant disorders.

Two particular problems that are likely to present special difficulties in such programmes, have recently been discussed by Levay and Kagle (1977), who refer to them as 'pleasure dysfunctions' and 'intimacy dysfunctions' respectively. The former consist of difficulties in identifying, experiencing and enjoying pleasurable sensations. Sometimes this is a very generalized problem in which the client appears to deny any pleasure or joy to himself over wide areas of his life, usually including the sexual sphere, but in other cases the problem may be restricted to the latter area. In either event, he does not derive any pleasure from his sexual activities. For instance, general pleasuring by the partner may be accompanied by a total absence of pleasurable sensations, and the therapeutic instruction to be 'selfish' when receiving pleasuring may even evoke discomfort and anxiety. Similarly, the kind of genital stimulation that is very enjoyable for most people, may be quite ineffective with a client suffering this inability to experience pleasure. According to Levay and Kagle, such clients sometimes respond well to the direct treatment of sexual dysfunction because the therapeutic prescription of enjoyment in the sexual assignments relieves them from having to take personal responsibility for any pleasure they may experience. However, more severe cases of pleasure dysfunction, are said often to relapse during or after such direct treatment, because it has not been of sufficient duration for the client to acquire a new self-concept as a sexual being who is entitled to sexual pleasure. Levay and Kagle epitomize the pleasure dysfunctions by saying that clients suffering from them are impaired from having sex *for themselves*.

Similarly, these writers epitomize the intimacy dysfunctions by saying that the clients affected have difficulty in having sex *with another person*. Sometimes they can function quite adequately during impersonal or fleeting sexual encounters, but not under conditions of involvement and commitment with a regular partner. In the latter, more meaningful type of relationship, their ability to experience and enjoy any feelings of closeness to the partner is seriously impaired, so that they seem to be emotionally isolated and inaccessible. During treatment, they can sometimes respond well to individually focused assignments, but not in those that require mutual interaction between the partners, and they are prone to relapse when the external therapeutic pressure for sexual activity and involvement with the partner is terminated. Levay and Kagle recommend that clients suffering from an intimacy dysfunction be given individual psychotherapy focused on the lack of basic trust and psychological conflicts that these authors regard as the underlying psychopathology. They offer theoretical explanations for both the pleasure and intimacy dysfunctions within a framework of ego psychology, but however one conceptualizes these problems they are observed in clients seeking or undergoing programmes of direct treatment for sexual dysfunction and can present very real difficulties in such treatment.

Sexual variations

Unconventional forms of sexual behaviour, such as transvestism, sado-masochism, homosexuality, or fetishism, sometimes co-exist with sexual inadequacy either in the same individual or within a partnership and the implications of this for treatment need to be considered.

There are a number of client situations in which sexual variation and sexual dysfunction may occur together and only a few illustrative examples are discussed here.

For instance, a homosexually oriented client might complain that he suffers from an erectile or ejaculatory problem during sexual encounters with his regular homosexual partner. In fact, perhaps because of their distrust of the health professions and their low expectation of effective help, very few clients seem to be present with problems of inadequacy in a homosexual relationship, so there is only limited clinical experience of treatment in such circumstances. However, it seems likely that many of the procedures discussed in Part 3 in the context of heterosexual relationships, would be equally applicable with partners of the same sex, but this assumption remains to be evaluated.

Another homosexually oriented man may complain that he is unable to respond or perform sexually with women, and ask for treatment to enable him to establish and enjoy an adequate sexual relationship with a regular partner of the opposite sex. To promote his sexual adequacy with women he might be treated with any of the procedures that were described in an earlier section as being at least partially feasible for clients who lack a regular partner, and these procedures will in many such cases need to be accompanied by suitable training in the social skills required to establish and maintain relationships with potential heterosexual partners. Sometimes this kind of treatment approach is sufficiently successful in itself, so that there is no need for any direct attempt to reduce the client's homosexual preferences and activities, but in other cases it is necessary to try to do this perhaps by means of procedures such as covert sensitization and self-regulation. These procedures, and the kind of comprehensive treatment approach outlined in this paragraph, are reviewed by Annon (1975a), Bancroft (1974), Barlow (1974), Barlow and Abel (1976), and Marks (1976).

Finally, let us consider a situation where a sexual variation and dysfunction co-exist within a heterosexual partnership. The husband can only become aroused and perform satisfactorily if his wife wears plastic bags on her feet during their lovemaking. For her part, she cannot respond sexually, perhaps as a specific consequence of this fetishistic condition or because of the discord it causes between the partners. In such circumstances, the couple will probably need therapeutic help to clarify and decide whether they would like to be able to accept and accommodate the husband's unconventional behaviour within their sexual and general relationship, or if they would prefer this behaviour to be discontinued; in either case, with both partners being able to respond adequately and to experience pleasure during their sexual activities. In such circumstances, many couples do decide to live with the unconventional behaviour, in which case they might be offered a treatment programme with a strong emphasis on the provision of information and the modification of attitudes relating to the sexual variation, although other procedures to promote adequate sexual functioning would probably be included. The latter type of procedure would feature strongly in an alternative kind of treatment programme that might be offered if the couple had decided to try to discontinue the unconventional behaviour, and some direct attempt to achieve this might well be made by means of procedures such as covert sensitization and self-regulation that were referred to in the previous paragraph.

The upshot of these few examples for the purposes of this book, is that the existence of a sexual variation in an individual or a couple who are seeking treatment for sexual dysfunction, does have considerable implications for the treatment of the latter, and these will need to be assessed and taken into accout when planning such treatment. The same point applies, of course, if treatment is originally sought for the sexual variation but is also required for sexual dysfunction.

Professional resources

We turn now to the third category of resources to be appraised, those relating to the therapist and the services at his disposal. The availability of sufficient therapeutic time from an individual therapist or a co-therapy team needs to be ascertained, together with their possession of the knowledge, attitudes, and skills that are necessary for the treatment of the client's problem, and these topics are considered further in the next chapter in context of treatment planning.

It is necessary also to consider the availability and efficacy of suitable procedures for the treatment of the client's problem. The available pool from which these might be drawn is outlined in Part 3, their selection for particular clients is discussed in the next chapter, and the evidence on their efficacy with specific dysfunctions is evaluated in Part 5. At this stage therefore, we merely note the need to assess the professional resources for treatment.

BEHAVIOURAL FORMULATION

An assessment of the problem and the resources available for treatment along the lines just described, provides data for a behavioural formulation of the client's problem situation, which includes the specification of his dysfunctional behaviour, some hyotheses about the contemporary conditions that influence its initiation and maintenance, and an appraisal of the available therapeutic resources.

For the reasons discussed in Chapter 8, this causal explanation of the problem and the associated rationale for treatment are shared with the client and his partner, and their understanding and acceptance of these are important prerequisites for the successful implementation and outcome of treatment. For instance, a couple is unlikely to collaborate in or complete satisfactorily any programme of psychological treatment if they remain convinced that a dysfunction is entirely due to some organic condition. On the basis of this shared formulation the goals of treatment are negotiated with the couple and a treatment plan is drawn up and agreed with them. These two processes are discussed in the next chapter.

12

Selecting Goals and Planning Treatment

A preliminary point to be considered and decided with the client and his partner is whether or not a programme of behavioural treatment focused upon the sexual dysfunction is the most appropriate therapeutic strategy. For instance, if this problem co-exists with a physical illness or as a side-effect of prescribed medication, then it may be more appropriate to obtain any necessary medical treatment or a change of prescription, instead of proceeding immediately to a psychological intervention. If serious discord exists between the partners, then marital therapy focused upon their general relationship may be the treatment of choice. Where sexual dysfunction is accompanied by a psychiatric syndrome, it is sometimes essential or preferable to give therapeutic priority to the latter problem. With clients who are undergoing non-sexual stresses, perhaps of an occupational or financial nature, it may be more appropriate to obtain help for them with these problems. Finally, some socially inadequate clients who lack partners, may best be helped at least initially by a programme of training focused upon the promotion of their heterosocial skills. Thus, a direct attempt to treat the sexual dysfunction is not always the most suitable therapeutic strategy.

GOALS OF TREATMENT

Nature of goals

When such treatment is appropriate, then it is focused directly upon the alleviation of the sexual dysfunction; its goals geing formally conceptualized as the reduction of problematic responses and the promotion of more acceptable alternatives, in specified sexual situations.

The responses to be changed might be of an overt, emotional, or cognitive kind. For instance, a goal might be to reduce any of the stress reactions discussed in Chapter 4, such as the physical avoidance of sexual activities, performance anxiety, or cognitive monitoring. On the positive side, one might aim to promote a client's capacity to obtain an erection or orgasm, to experience sexual excitement and pleasure, and to judge his sexual functioning as acceptable rather than inadequate.

As discussed in Chapter 5, the problematic or acceptable nature of the client's responses has to be considered in relation to specific sexual situations. An inability to become aroused or to reach orgasm would not necessarily be judged a problem if it is restricted to situations involving insufficient foreplay, or if it occurs only with a partner towards whom the client feels hostile, or in a setting that is uncomfortable or lacking in privacy. Similarly, acceptable sexual functioning does not imply an ability to perform perfectly, on every occasion, with any partner, and in any circumstances.

This leads to the general point that the goals of behavioural treatment do not entail any absolute norm or standard of sexual performance, rather they reflect the judgements of adequacy in sexual functioning made by the couple concerned, according to the kind of criteria discussed in Chapter 5. Thus, it is these subjective and individual judgements that determine the goals of treatment, and not any definitive or normative criteria such as a certain frequency of intercourse, its prolongation for a certain period of time before ejaculation, the attainment of orgasm on a certain proportion of occasions, or a couples willingness to engage in certain practices such as oral sex.

Selection of goals

It follows that the goals of treatment are chosen largely by the client and his partner in accordance with their own wishes and values, although in consultation with the therapist. The major contribution of behavioural treatment *per se* is to provide effective ways of achieving these goals only after they have been selected on personal, social and ethical grounds.

The aim is to negotiate a therapeutic contract in which mutually agreeable goals are specified. However, this is not always possible, the partners may not be able to agree on goals between themselves, or their selection may not be acceptable to the therapist in the light of his own values or professional knowledge. An example of the former situation arose with a married couple who presented for treatment together because the wife could not become aroused or reach orgasm. The husband's goal was for her to be able to respond more adequately in their joint sexual relationship, but she disclosed in an individual interview that she did not want to respond better with her husband, although she would like to be able to do so with several boyfriends. This was the purpose of treatment from her point of view, and she saw the involvement of her husband as simply being a vehicle towards this end. Thus, these partners had discrepant goals and there was not even a possibility of reconciling them because of the wife's refusal to disclose her own wishes to her husband.

This situation was also one in which the therapists could not accept the goals proposed by either partner. It was felt that there was virtually no chance of these being achieved in view of the wife's attitude, and that it would be improper to involve the husband in treatment on false pretences. It was suggested to the couple that they might consider marital therapy, but the wife did not wish to pursue this alternative. Another would have been for her to have sought treatment on an individual basis at some stage, with the initial goal of being able to respond and reach orgasm under conditions of self-stimulation.

Other instances of the therapist being unable to accept a client's goals may arise when these do not accord with the physical limitations imposed on sexual functioning by the aging process or an illness. Thus, if an older man wanted to regain his earlier ability to perform intercourse several times with only short intervals, this might be quite unrealistic in the light of his more prolonged refractory period, and the therapist could not properly agree to this goal. Similarly, it would be unrealistic to accept the goal of normal ejaculation for a patient suffering from retrograde ejaculation due to some irreversible organic cause.

In any of these or similar circumstances, the therapist will explain his reasons for not being able to accept the goals proposed by either partner, while respecting their wishes concerning the non-disclosure of certain information to the other. Whenever possible the therapist will suggest alternative goals for the direct treatment of sexual dysfunction, but if these cannot be satisfactorily negotiated and agreed, then it is not possible for the therapist to offer such treatment. In appropriate cases, he might offer another form of threatment, such as marital therapy, or he could offer to refer a client to another therapist.

Specification of goals

Having selected the goals of treatment it is necessary to specify them very precisely in terms of the responses desired in particular situations. This specification serves to clarify the goals for both the clients and the therapists, to guide the choice of treatment procedures, and to facilitate the assessment of progress and outcome in treatment.

In order to enhance the precision and reliability of this ongoing assessment process, the goals are operationalized in terms of observable behaviour and in considerable detail. This applies equally to the overt, emotional, and cognitive aspects of these goals. Thus, the overt aspects might be specified in terms of engagement in sexual activities, either with adequate erectile and ejaculatory responses, or with adequate vaginal lubrication and orgastic contractions. The emotional aspects might be specified in terms of the client's verbal reports of reduced apprehension concerning his sexual performance, and of enhanced excitement and pleasure during sexual encounters. Similarly, the cognitive aspects of the goals might be specified in terms of similar reports indicating that the client is no longer monitoring his own sexual responses, and that he now has more realistic standards of sexual performance so that he no longer judges his own to be inadequate. It should be noted that although the overt, emotional, and cognitive aspects of the goals are discussed in rather broad terms in this paragraph, in practice each of these is defined in much greater detail, including their form, frequency, and timing, as well as the situations in which they should occur.

PLANNING TREATMENT

The next stage is to draw up a treatment plan that reflects the behavioural formulation and the selection of goals. This requires decisions concerning the provision of therapists, the setting and timing of treatment, and the choice of procedures to be employed in certain combinations and sequences.

Therapists

Dual sex teams

Masters and Johnson insist that the treatment should be conducted by a team comprising a cotherapist of each sex, and a number of arguments are advanced in support of this practice by these authors and others (Masters and Johnson, 1970; Roman and Meltzer, 1977). One such argument, which led to the original recruitment of Virginia Johnson by William Masters, is that it is impossible for anyone to really understand and empathize with the subjective sexual experiences of the opposite gender; for instance, a man cannot understand what orgasm means to a woman, and she cannot grasp his experience of ejaculation. This view is to some extent challenged by Kaplan (1974) who believes that it is possible to train therapists to become sufficiently sensitive and empathic towards the sexual responses of clients belonging to a different gender from their own, for these therapists to be able to treat such clients quite satisfactorily in many cases.

Another argument is that the availability of both a male and female therapist means that each partner has 'a friend at court' and an 'interpreter' of the same sex. Some clients may be able to relate and communicate more easily with a therapist of their own sex, and this therapist can also support and explain that client's point of view to the other partner as well as to the cotherapist. A related point is that a dual sex team may reduce the risk of getting biased information from one partner, who may be embarrassed or feel the need to maintain a front when giving information to a therapist of the opposite sex. However, in this context, it should be noted that Rosen et al. (1974) found that both male and female clients awaiting treatment, expressed equal readiness to discuss specific sexual matters with therapists of the same or of the opposite sex.

A dual sex team may also reduce the risk of one partner feeling that his or her viewpoint is being neglected or submerged by a partner and a therapist who both belong to the opposite sex; for instance, a wife might feel that she is being misunderstood and pressured by a male therapist who appears to be siding with husband, so that they seem to be 'ganging up' on her.

Another possible risk reduced by a dual sex team is that of a strong emotional relationship developing between one of the partners and a therapist of the opposite sex. Any such special or exclusive affinity, particularly if it has an erotic connotation, will militate against the kind of communication and relationship which it is desirable to promote between the partners. An undesirable client–therapist relationship is probably less likely to develop when there is a therapist of each sex, but if an incipient affinity does occur then Masters and Johnson suggest that it can be rapidly extinguished by each therapist communicating only with the client of the same sex, so that there is little opportunity for the continuation or extension of the cross-sex relationship. Incidentally, the presence of a cotherapist is also likely to reduce the possibility of a therapist slipping into a position of rivalry with the partner of the same sex, in which they might have become competitors for the attention, admiration, and sexual interest of the other partner.

A dual sex team also provides each partner with a therapist of the same sex who can model positive sexual attitudes and behaviour, which that partner may then imitate or identify with. Similarly, it should provide a model of a relationship between two people of opposite sexes who interact and communicate with each other in an open, egalitarian, and rewarding manner. Clearly, the effectiveness of each therapist and the team as models will reflect their capacities to demonstrate the desirable behaviour, a point we return to in discussing the background of therapists and the cotherapy relationship.

It is not only the presence of a therapist of the same sex that may have therapeutic value, this may also be derived from the involvement of a therapist of the opposite sex. For instance, any anxiety that a client experiences in his or her relationships with the opposite sex may be alleviated, and much needed accurate information may be acquired about the sexual attitudes and experiences of that sex. An example of such corrective relationships occurred in the context of the group treatment of dysfunctional men without partners, which is reported by Zilbergeld (1975). All the group members, without exception, agreed on the desirability of having a female co-leader in such groups, with whom the members could share their sexual feelings, often for the first time with a woman, and who could tell them about her own sexual feelings and experiences in order to rectify their ignorance and misapprehensions about these matters. An illustration is cited of prematurely ejaculating man who could not accept that a woman would tolerate any brief interruption of lovemaking to assist his control, until the female co-leader assured him that such short breaks were quite usual and acceptable in her own sexual relationships.

The arguments in favour of dual sex teams reviewed so far have related primarily to the sex rather than the number of the therapists, and there are certain other arguments that stem mainly from the fact that more than one therapist is involved in treatment. This can widen the range of perceptiveness, experience, and professional expertise that is brought to bear on the assessment and treatment of the dysfunction. The impact of two therapists on a client may also be greater than that of an individual therapist, so that greater weight is lent to explanations and advice from the therapists, and the client is more stimulated and motivated to collaborate and progress in treatment. A further possibility is that the presence of two therapists constitutes a more secure situation, in which a client may feel safer when discussing highly sensitive and emotionally charged sexual matters of an intimate nature.

There may also be some advantages accruing to the cotherapists in being able to share the responsibilities of treatment. One of them can passively monitor the verbal and non-verbal interactions between the partners and the other therapist who is actively conducting the interview at that stage. Thus, one therapist is free to concentrate on observing the couple's reactions to the cotherapist and to each other, and in the light of these, the observer can take over the more active role in order to support or clarify the points being made, to change topics, or to present material which it is especially appropriate for a man or a woman to discuss, while the cotherapist shifts into the observer role. For this and other reasons, the strain of conducting therapeutic sessions is often reduced when it is shared, and working with a congenial colleague with whom one can discuss clients who are known at first hand to each therapist, can be a most stimulating and rewarding experience. The extent to which this opportunity is realized depends of course on the quality of the relationship between the therapists, and we return to this topic later.

Finally, the co-therapy situation constitutes an excellent training opportunity, whereby a less experienced therapist can work with someone who is more experienced, although again as we see later, it is important to be wary of the possible implications of this for the egality of the relationship that is being modelled for the clients (Siddall and Bosma, 1976).

To counterbalance these numerous supporting arguments for the dual sex team, we must note certain disadvantages and limitations that may be entailed. One of these is that two therapists working individually may be more cost-effective than if they work as a team, and in the current shortage of good facilities for the treatment of sexual dysfunction this is not an unimportant consideration. Another possible limitation is that a suitable cotherapist may simply not be available, and a decision has to be made between treatment by an individual therapist or no treatment at all. Moreover, any attempt to work in a co-therapy relationship that is insufficiently compatible or egalitarian, is likely to be stressful and unrewarding for the therapists, and quite possibly damaging to the clients.

Several authors have attempted to delineate the desirable elements of a co-therapy relationship, and although none of them have directly addressed this issue in the context of dual sex teams for the treatment of sexual dysfunction, nevertheless their comments do seem apposite. For example, Weinstein (1971) suggests that for psychotherapy to be effective, the co-therapists must trust each other, understand and recognize their individual differences, and have equal real or potential ability as psychotherapists, in that order of importance. Similarly, Getty and Shannon (1969) propose three essential ingredients; acceptance of each other, shared mutual responsibility, and equal participation. The desirability of an egalitarian relationship is strongly emphasized in these and other papers.

Clearly, there are numerous possible sources of threat to this and other desirable aspects of the co-therapy relationship. Apart from individual incompatibility, conflicts and barriers may arise from clashes of values between the therapists; from differences in their therapeutic styles or theoretical orientations; from a discrepancy in their levels of experience, especially when the role of the less experienced therapist is not clearly defined; and from professional stereotypes, role expectations, and status differences (Roman and Meltzer, 1977). Problems may arise also from discrepancies in the gender role expectations of each therapist in relation to the other; or from the transfer of conflicts from the personal relationship between them into the therapeutic situation, especially when they are married or sexually involved with each other, although this is not to deny some possible advantages of treatment being undertaken by co-therapists who share a stable partnership, such as their potentially superior modelling capacity (Belleville *et al.*, 1969, Dunn and Dickes, 1977; Golden and Golden, 1976; Rice and Rice, 1975; Rosenthal and Rosenthal, 1975; Zentner and Povyat, 1978). Finally, some strain may be imposed on the cotherapy relationship, if the uninvolved spouse of one of the therapists feels threatened by that relationship and his or her exclusion from it (Brown, 1976).

All these arguments for and against the dual sex team are either *a priori* or based upon unsystematic clinical experience, and there is very little research evidence bearing upon questions such as the relative effectiveness of these teams in comparison with individual therapists, the extent to which any differences in process or outcome between these two modalities are due to the number of therapists involved or to the sexual composition of the team, and whether there are any such differences associated with the sex of a therapist who is working individually. One unique study at the present time is reported by Mathews *et al.* (1976), and discussed in detail later in this book. Among the variables investigated was the deployment of the same six therapists either in dual sex teams or on an individual basis, with different randomly allocated groups of patients. The use of teams did appear to enhance the outcome of the Masters and Johnson approach in treatment, but not those of other programmes in which either systematic desensitization or postal instruction was the major distinguishing feature.

In the light of this early study, together with what appears to be the weight of the arguments reviewed above, it seems reasonable at present to establish dual sex teams whenever it is possible to do so, but otherwise to be prepared to work individually rather than denying treatment to those who seek it.

Qualifications and competence

It is clear from the literature and from personal knowledge, that the direct treatment of sexual dysfunction has been undertaken by therapists from a wide variety of professions and specialities, including counsellors, family doctors, gynaecologists, nurses, physicians, psychiatrists, psychologists, social workers, and urologists. At present, there is no systematic evidence to indicate the relative superiority of any of these groups in conducting such treatment, although *prima facie* arguments have been advanced in favour of each of them, usually by members of the profession or speciality concerned. It is of course essential to have the particular expertise of each group available when it is required; for example, a suitably qualified medical practitioner to undertake the necessary screening for any relevant organic conditions, or someone trained in behaviour therapy to implement specific procedures such as desensitization.

Ideally, if particular expertise is needed to undertake some component of treatment that is a major feature in the programme, then it may be preferable for a competent exponent of that expertise to act either as an individual therapist or as one member of a dual sex team. We have already noted that one advantage of these teams is that they can widen the range of professional expertise available within the team and thus reduce the need for outside referral. However, such ideal arrangements are not always feasible, in which case it is essential to have ready access to any necessary external expertise, and in practice this seems to be a viable method of working.

Probably more important than the particular professional discipline of the therapist, are the attitudes, knowledge and skills that he brings to the treatment of sexual dysfunction (Kaplan, 1977; Lo Piccolo, 1978; Waggoner et al., 1973; World Health Organization, 1975). These attributes are fundamentally similar to those acquired and exercised in the profession to which the therapist belongs, but they may well require some extension and refinement for this particular therapeutic task. While again, there is no systematic evidence available about the respective influences of certain attitudes, knowledge, and skills on the process and outcome of the direct treatment of sexual dysfunction, it seems highly probable that a therapist will need to understand and accept his own sexuality, to exhibit positive attitudes towards sex, and to be tolerant of a wide range of sexual behaviour, if his communications and relationships with dysfunctional clients are not to be inhibited of distorted. Clearly, he will need to be generally well informed about the whole sphere of sexual behaviour, and more especially knowledgeable about the causation, assessment and treatment of sexual dysfunction. Finally, he must possess the clinical skills to undertake these assessment and treatment tasks. Such skills are reviewed in the present part of this book, as well as in Part 3; in addition to the ability to implement the more specific procedures, they include the basic capacities to establish a therapeutic relationship, to formulate an acceptable explanation of the dysfunction, to enhance prognostic expectancies, and to communicate easily and effectively with clients about sexual matters.

Treatment settings

A second area requiring decisions in treatment planning concerns the settings where this is to be conducted. We have seen that one important aspect of treatment, namely the sexual assignments, are undertaken by the clients themselves in their own private accommodation. This has the advantage of to some extent circumventing the common clinical problem of generalizing beneficial change from the clinic to the client's ordinary life situation, but it is also subject to the adverse influences of avoidance reactions, low motivation and poor organizational capacity on the part of the clients concerned.

Given that the clients are going to undertake the assignments in their own accommodation, there remains the questions of where this is to be during treatment, and where they are going to meet with the therapists. As far as the first of these questions is concerned, Masters and Johnson (1970) advocate that couples should leave their own home environments and live elsewhere during treatment. Some 90% of their patients came to St. Louis for treatment from other places, and these couple lived in hotels during two week programmes. The remaining couples continued to live in their homes in St. Louis, and were asked to allow three weeks for treatment. Masters and Johnson prefer the former arrangement because it gives couples an opportunity to work intensively together on their sexual relationship, without being distracted by the usual familial, social, domestic, and occupational demands of their everyday lives. However desirable this arrangement may be, it is likely to be impracticable for many clients and clinical facilities, so that treatment has to be provided on an out-patient basis while the clients continue to live in their own homes and to fulfil their usual responsibilities. Undoubtedly, this does sometimes entail difficulties, in implementing the assignments or in regularly keeping appointments with the therapists, and real impediments of this kind are to be distinguished from the avoidance of treatment commitments as a stress reaction although the latter are often superimposed on some more concrete difficulty. On the other hand, it can be argued that if couples can learn to manage and enjoy their sexual relationship as part of their everyday lives during the treatment programme, then there is a greater chance of any improvement being maintained after the programme ends. The comparative merits of these arguments are at present speculative (Williams and Orsmond, 1977), for no controlled investigation has been conducted into the relative effects of living away from home or of remaining there, on the process and outcome of treatment.

Lastly, some thought needs to be given to the selection of a suitable place for the therapists to conduct treatment sessions with sexually dysfunctional clients (Devaneson *et al.* 1976). The range of possibilities is so wide that it is impossible to propose any firm guidelines, but it may be wise to avoid using a local psychiatric hospital in order to reduce the risk of such clients thinking that they are suffering from a mental illness. It may be preferable to provide teatment for them in a general or day hospital, or perhaps even better in a health-oriented facility such as a family planning clinic.

Timing of treatment

This aspect of treatment planning concerns such matters as the number, length, and spacing of the clients' meetings with the therapists, as well as the overall duration of the programme. Masters and Johnson (1970) operated an intensive programme usually lasting two weeks, during which the couple met the therapists at least once on every day, as well as devoting substantial periods of time to the sexual assignments. A major advantage claimed for this system is that it enables the therapists to deal promptly with any obstacles or difficulties encountered in the assignments, before these are compounded by increasing performance anxiety and distress for the couple concerned.

Despite this and other possible advantages of such intensive programmes (Williams and Orsmond, 1977), they are not a feasible proposition for many clients and therapists. Therefore, it is more usual to follow a treatment format consisting of a series of out-patient sessions on a once or twice weekly basis, each lasting about an hour; although the spacing and length of the sessions are varied according to treatment needs at particular times, and the therapists usually make themselves available to clients by telephone if difficulties should arise in the assignments.

Using this kind of format, Kaplan (1974) reports that the average number of sessions taken to treat premature ejaculation was 6.5, over a period of 3 to 6 weeks; while the comparable figures for vaginismus were 10 sessions over 6 weeks. Similarly, Brown (1976) reports average durations of 14.2 and 14.3 weeks for treatment undertaken by dual sex teams and individual therapists respectively. The range for male dysfunctions was from 12 to 28 weeks, and for female dysfunctions from 9 to 21 weeks; there being no statistically significant differences between particular dysfunctions in the number of sessions required for their treatment, although the largest averages in males and females respectively were for retarded ejaculation with 18 sessions and vaginismus with 14 sessions.

No controlled studies have yet been conducted into the relative effectiveness of very intensive versus more prolonged programmes, and unless and until there is strong evidence favouring the former, it seems likely that the practical considerations affecting most clients and therapists will prevail to support the spacing of treatment over longer periods of time, perhaps typically of the order of 10 to 20 weeks.

Treatment programmes

In the course of their work, Masters and Johnson (1970) developed several standardized treatment programmes, the first part of each being common to all types of dysfunction, and the latter part to particular dysfunctions. The first part commences with an initial interview, during which the therapists explain the programme to the clients, and a ban is placed on their sexual activities. Two assessment interviews are then conducted with each partner separately, one by the therapist of the same sex, and the second by the other co-therapist. A medical examination is also conducted with each client. The findings from these interviews and examinations and their implications for treatment, are shared with the couple in a roundtable discussion, and they are instructed to attempt sensate focus assignments. When these are proceeding satisfactorily, the couple move on to the second part of the programme which is specifically designed for their particular dysfunction. Briefly, this part centres upon the squeeze technique for premature ejaculation; upon intensive stimulation with successive approximations to ejaculation in the vagina, in cases of retarded ejaculation; upon non-demand coitus for impotence and female orgastic dysfunction; and upon the use of graded dilators for vaginismus. In each case, of course, these assignments are accompanied by interviews with the therapists, and although the components of the programmes are standardized, they are applied with great sensitivity to characteristics and reactions of individual couples.

Nevertheless, the Masters and Johnson programmes are standardized for each dysfunction, and in this respect the approach of these authors does differ significantly from that adopted by most behaviour therapists, who place great emphasis on the individual composition of programmes to suit particular clients. They may present with similar problems, and perhaps even with similar goals, but their other personal characteristics and their life situations will differ in many ways, and these differences necessitate unique treatment programmes that are individually tailored to suit each client. A second, and less fundamental difference between the Masters and Johnson and behaviour therapy programmes is that the latter are at present drawn from a wider range of component procedures and assignments. There is no basic reason why Masters and Johnson should not broaden their programmes, but so long as the components of these remain standardized for particular dysfunctions, their approach will differ from that of most behaviour therapists.

We now look at the planning of individualized programmes in the general categories of the initiation of treatment, the selection and sequencing of its components, the maintenance of treatment effects and the possibility of offering some part of treatment on a group basis.

Initiation of treatment

One quite fundamental task in initiating treatment is to promote the kind of therapeutic relationship that is discussed in Chapter 8. Another, also discussed in that chapter, is to work out a mutually acceptable causal explanation of the dysfunction with the clients. In particular, it is often useful to counteract their common misconception that such difficulties indicate that they are neurotic or mentally ill. A third introductory task is to review the possible treatment programme with the clients, to explain its rationale, and to negotiate a contract for its implementation. This review will cover the components of the programme and its timing, the respective roles of the clients and therapists, and some indication of its likely progress and outcome.

The selection of components is considered in the next section, and the timing of treatment will be decided in the light of the factors discussed in the previous section. Several important points need to be made with clients concerning their own roles and those of the therapists in treatment. If this is to be conjoint, then the willing and committed involvement of both partners is essential, and the reasons for this are explained along the lines of the discussion in the previous chapter. Similarly, if treatment is to be provided by a dual sex team, then the reasons for this arrangement are explained to the clients. Their responsibility for the organization and implementation of the sexual assignments is emphasized, and the crucial nature of these in the treatment programme is stressed. It is sometimes useful to use the analogy of the therapists as coaches who can motivate, facilitate, guide, and encourage, while the clients are the players who actually win or lose the game on the field. Such active and necessary participation in their own treatment, may be contrasted with the more usual conceptualization of the patient role as that of a relatively passive recipient of professionally administered treatment.

As far as the progress and outcome of treatment are concerned, clients should be warned that it is unlikely to follow a completely smooth course or to produce an extremely rapid cure. Instead, obstacles and reversals in progress will probably be encountered and do not necessarily signify that treatment has failed; they can more usefully be regarded as opportunities for the clients to learn about their sexual difficulties and how they can best be overcome. At the same time, as discussed in Chapter 8, every effort should be made to promote a realistic expectation of effective help from treatment, towards the achievement of those goals that have been selected and specified in the negotiations between the clients and the therapists.

The results of such negotiations concerning these goals, the components of the programme designed to achieve them, the respective responsibilities of the clients and the therapists, and any other relevant conditions of treatment, are sometimes set down in a formal written contract that is signed by all parties, otherwise these agreed features are left at an implicit level. Although the use of more explicit contracts is not widespread at the present time, it may have the potential advantages of enhancing the clarification, specification and negotiation of all these aspects of treatment, and of promoting compliance with them. Whether implicitly or explicitly stated, it is important for therapists to establish and operate a therapeutic contract with their clients, and there is no reason why such contracts should not be of a short-term exploratory nature, with subsequent revision by agreement as treatment progresses.

Selection of components

The selection of components for an individualized treatment programme may be made in the light of their *suitability* for a therapeutic task, their *acceptability* to the clients and therapists, their *feasibility* in terms of the available therapeutic resources, their probable *efficacy* in achieving the goals of treatment, and their *efficiency* in utilizing therapeutic resources.

We see above, that the goals of treatment are formally conceptualized in terms of the reduction of problematic responses, and the promotion of more acceptable alternatives, in specified sexual situations. Furthermore, in Part 4, it is noted that certain possible components of treatment are particularly suitable for one of these therapeutic tasks, although usually with some spillover into the other; while some components appear to have a significant contribution to both tasks. Thus, the reduction of problematic responses, such as stress reactions, may be achieved by means of relaxation training, desensitization, flooding, and vaginal dilatation. More adequate sexual responses may be promoted by means of classical conditioning, biofeedback, phantasy training, hypnosis, vaginal muscle exercises, facilitative medication for the disabled, and certain prosthetic or mechanical aids. Both therapeutic tasks may be served by the provision of information, the modification of attitudes and various sexual assignments. Within these broad guidelines, certain components may be especially suitable for more specific therapeutic tasks; for instance, relaxation training when a great deal of muscular tension is experienced during sexual activities, vaginal dilatation in cases of vaginismus, self-stimulation to relieve primary orgastic dysfunction, and the squeeze or stop-start techniques for premature ejaculation.

Turning now to the *acceptability* of possible components, these are selected with due regard for the wishes and values of the clients and the therapists. For instance, a client's genuine belief that masturbation is sinful would be of primary importance when considering the prescription of genital stimulation assignments in cases of primary orgastic dysfunction or retarded or absent ejaculation. Similarly, the therapists might have ethical objections to the use of surrogate partners. As indicated earlier, in some cases the unacceptability of certain components does have implications for the feasibility of treatment, either generally or by particular therapists.

This leads to the issue of the *feasibility* of the possible components of treatment, which has to be considered in the light of the assessment of resources discussed in the previous chapter. For example, the assignments of general pleasuring or non-demand coitus are clearly impossible for a client who does not have a partner. Similarly, some neurologically disordered clients are physically incapable of implementing masturbatory assignments. In addition to such situational or personal constraints on the choice of procedures, this may also be restricted by certain limitations in the professional resources available; for example, the therapists may not have the knowledge, skills, or equipment required for biofeedback procedures.

Obviously, the *efficacy* of the possible procedures is another important criterion for their selection, and this is considered in the light of the available evidence on the outcome of certain forms of treatment that is reviewed in later chapters.

Likewise, these chapters include discussion of the scant evidence available on the *efficiency* of the components under consideration, so that their relative cost-effectiveness can be taken into account in the selection process.

Sequencing of components

Having selected the components, it is necessary to plan the sequence of treatment. Often an important aspect of this is the arrangement of a series of intermediate steps to the ultimate goal of treatment. Sexual situations that instigate stress reactions may be introduced into the programme in a graded manner, so that the client is not traumatized, or precipitated into avoidance or escape reactions. Thus, a couple who have long discontinued any attempt at sexual activity, might be started on general pleasuring, and then perhaps progress through genital pleasuring and non-demand coitus to full intercourse. Similarly, while the ultimate goal of the selected sexual behaviour may be beyond a client's current capacity, it can be very helpful to establish a series of intermediate goals so that the achievement of these will minimize the experience of failure and optimize the contingent reinforcement received by the client. Thus, a woman who cannot reach climax during intercourse with her husband, might consecutively achieve the goals of being able to do so by self-stimulation, during genital stimulation from her husband, during intercourse with accompanying direct stimulation of the clitoris, and finally by the movement of his penis in her vagina alone. Likewise, a client suffering from retarded or absent ejaculation, might progress from masturbating himself to ejaculation, followed by his wife being able to do this for him, with increasing approximation to her vagina, until he is able to ejaculate inside her during intercourse.

Maintenance of treatment effects

The maintenance of more adequate sexual behaviour after the specific treatment intervention ends, has been given virtually no attention in the literature on the treatment of sexual dysfunction. It is presumably assumed that the performance of such behaviour is intrinsically rewarding, so that it is constantly reinforced and thus maintained.

However, relapses undoubtedly do occur as we see in later chapters, and much more consideration could usefully be given to their prevention. It should be emphasized during treatment that fluctuations in sexual interest and capacity are a normal experience and do not necessarily herald a relapse. Accordingly, the clients may be more prepared to accept such fluctuations with equanimity, and not to react to them with stress reactions such as performance anxiety, that might produce an escalation of a temporary low patch into a more serious and persistent dysfunction.

Similarly, clients might usefully be oriented to regard their experiences during treatment as a training in managing their own sexual relationships, so that if an incipient relapse does occur they will apply the knowledge and skills they have learned to prevent it worsening. This 'self-management' approach, and a number of other behavioural procedures that might usefully be investigated for their potential in maintaining the effects of treatment for sexual dysfunction, are reviewed by Marholin et al. (1976). One particular aspect of the self-management approach is the training of clients during treatment to monitor and record their sexual activities, so that these are less likely to slip imperceptively to a very low frequency, perhaps with a subsequent 're-entry problem' of starting them up again.

One component that is commonly employed to promote the maintenance of treatment effects is a series of follow-up interviews with the therapists, usually at gradually lengthening intervals. In this way it is hoped to ensure that the recently acquired more adequate sexual behaviour becomes sufficiently well established for it to be self-reinforcing, and that the therapists are available to help clients with any initial difficulties they may encounter during this process. It is possible that some particularly vulnerable clients might need follow-up support over a very prolonged period, so that the therapeutic interviews might be conceptualized as a prosthetic environment for such clients. This, and many other aspects of the maintenance issue, remain to be systematically investigated in the area of sexual dysfunction.

Group treatment

Finally, in planning a treatment programme, consideration can usefully be given to the possibility of providing some part of it in a group context. This is one of the growing points in the behavioural treatment of sexual dysfunction (see review by Burbank, 1976), and the nature and efficacy of some group programmes are considered in later chapters. In most of these programmes, it was the interview components of the provision of information, the modification of attitudes and the management of sexual assignments that were provided on a group basis, but some specific behavioural procedures, such as desensitization, have also been conducted with groups of clients. Clearly, this has the advantages of conserving scarce professional resources, and of being less expensive for clients who have to pay for their treatment. Furthermore, it is a feasible modality for those clients who are unable to undertake treatment with a partner.

Many other potential advantages may accrue from the therapeutic influence of the group itself (Burbank, 1976; Lieberman, 1975; Sadock and Spitz, 1975). It can provide understanding and support from peers suffering from similar problems, so that they are able to comfort and reassure each other when they are ashamed or anxious about their sexual functioning. When strong feelings of cohesion and closeness do develop in a group, this may be of particular therapeutic value to those clients suffering from what were referred to earlier as 'intimacy dysfunctions'. Meeting with others who share similar problems can also relieve a client's sense of isolation or alienation, that springs from his feelings of being different from other people and not understood by them. From its supportive and cohesive base, a group can stimulate and reinforce therapeutic progress in its members. If one of these appears to be overcoming his difficulties, then this can inculcate hope in the others, and the group may constitute a powerful source of encouragement and approval for the efforts and successes of its members in working on their problems.

More particularly, a group can accept and sanction certain thoughts, feelings, and activities of a sexual kind that have previously evoked anxiety or inhibition in a client, so that he may become increasingly able to engage in a range of sexual phantasies and activities with excitement and pleasure. Helpful information may be exchanged between members; for instance, a comparison of their sexual behaviour and experiences may reduce an individual's concern about some aspect of his own sexual functioning and suggest more effective ways of coping in his sexual relationships. Such vicarious learning opportunities may lead to a client imitating the more adequate behaviour of another member, and the group may provide a range of such potential models from which an individual can select one or more who seem likely to be helpful to him. The group can promote the capacities of its members to communicate easily and effectively about sexual matters, and particularly to talk about their own feelings and experiences in this area. For some clients, this will be the first time that they have been able to express and disclose themselves in this way, and the understanding and accepting reactions of other group members may serve to change a client's perception of his sexual functioning, to alleviate the distress it causes him, and to enhance the openness and honesty of his communications with a sexual partner. This is just one of many possible examples of the provision of innovative experiences for individual clients in the context of a treatment group. The support and security this affords to is members often enables them to try out new ways of behaving in a protected environment. A final potential advantage of group treatment is the opportunities it provides for clients to help others as well as to receive help themselves, often with consequent improvement in their confidence and self-esteem.

Turning now to some potential disadvantages of group treatment, the demand this places on members to disclose very private and intimate sexual matters in the presence of strangers may well deter some clients from consenting to this form of treatment, or cause them severe embarrassment and distress if they do undertake it. Furthermore, in contrast to the positive group influences discussed above, these may be of a negative kind for particular clients or in certain groups. For instance, while the progress of another member may inculcate hope of similar improvement in some clients, for others it may be a source of considerable discouragement because they have not been able to achieve as much themselves. Similarly, certain groups may develop anti-therapeutic norms, so that the members model and reinforce inappropriate behaviour for each other. Lastly, treatment in a group may entail some diminution of the attention given to the individual problems and progress of each member. There is a risk of this happening despite the selection of such treatment as appropriate for each client to whom it is offered, and although it is only part of an overall programme, the remainder of which is conducted on an individual basis.

Many questions concerning the composition of groups for the treatment of sexual dysfunction remain to be systematically investigated as a basis for clinical decisions. For instance, whether groups should focus on clients presenting with a particular dysfunction, or include those exhibiting a variety of dysfunctions, it can be argued that the former arrangement makes the group more directly applicable to all its members, but that it also makes progress more competitive and thus discourages those who are less successful. Another potential advantage claimed for the mixed dysfunction group is that it widens the range of sexual experience from which members can draw information and models; for example, a woman who has never experienced orgasm may learn what it is like to do so from another woman who is able to reach climax but is suffering from vaginismus, while she in return may receive some reassurance about the experience of penetration from the first client. A further issue concerning the composition of groups is whether it is better to conduct these on a single sex basis, or to include both partners whenever this is possible. At present, there are no firm guidelines to resolve these and many other similar issues, but their investigation has commenced (e.g. Leiblum et al., 1976; McGovern et al., 1978).

ASSESSMENT OF TREATMENT

Having planned a programme of treatment, its progress and outcome are systematically monitored and evaluated on a continuous basis throughout the implementation and follow-up periods. This provides feedback to the client on his progress, and reveals any necessity for a revision of the treatment plan. As noted earlier, the reliability of this whole assessment process is facilitated by the detailed specification in operational terms of the dysfunctional behaviour and the goals of treatment.

In the longer term, such assessment of the treatment of individual clients, may provide data for evaluating the efficacy of the programmes used, so that they can be repeated, improved, or abandoned in the interests of future clients. More specifically, the assessment may contribute to the identification of the crucial therapeutic ingredients in the programme, thus providing a basis for its refinement and increased efficiency. Both the efficacy of treatment programmes and their crucial ingredients can be established only by properly controlled studies using appropriate research designs (see reviews by Hersen and Barlow, 1976; Yates, 1976). The availability and findings of such studies in the field of sexual dysfunction are considered in later chapters.

13

Methods of Data Collection

The topics on which information needs to be gathered throughout the assessment and planning process are considered in the previous two chapters, and we turn now to the methods available for collecting this information. These are discussed in the general categories of the interview, questionnaires, self-monitoring, physiological techniques, and medical examination. Each of these has certain strengths and weaknesses in terms of coverage, reliability, and validity, therefore it is preferable to employ some suitable combination of methods in order to achieve a balanced and comprehensive assessment. This may still contain discrepant and conflicting information, but such imperfect agreement is to be expected in view of the variation in objectivity and subjectivity across methods and the differences in the areas of information they are able to tap. For example, a self-report method, such as an interview or questionnaire, will generate subjective data about how the informant *perceives* his own behaviour and experiences, as well as the situations in which they occur, while physiological techniques will yield relatively more objective information about certain aspects of the client's physical responses to particular stimuli.

As in the case of treatment programmes, the assessment scheme will be suitably varied for individual clients. For instance, when a lack of social skills, a psychotic condition, or some relevant organic pathology might be present, then appropriate methods of investigation would be included to screen for these particular conditions.

ASSESSMENT INTERVIEWS

Interviews are the most frequently used methods of assessment in the field of sexual dysfunction. They have the advantage of not infringing the privacy traditionally afforded to sexual activities in our society, which usually precludes the use of direct observation on both ethical and therapeutic grounds. Another strength of the interview is its flexibility and breadth. The therapist can ask, for example, about the client's responses in a wide range of situations, and can follow up any promising leads with more detailed questioning.

The responses described by the client will include his thoughts and feelings, as well as his overt behaviour, and the relevance of such covert reactions in defining, explaining and treating sexual dysfunction is noted earlier in this book. The most direct sources of information available to the therapist about these important covert reactions are the client's self-reports, made either in interviews, or in reply to questionnaires, or in systematic records maintained by the client of his own responses in particular circumstances.

There is however, the problem of the uncertain validity of client self-reports as accurate accounts of events as they actually occurred. For instance, a client may never have been aware of certain aspects of his behaviour or experiences, or he may have forgotten them, or for various reasons he may distort or omit information, or he may be unable to make the perceptual and verbal discriminations that are necessary to yield the type of detailed accounts that are required in a behavioural assessment.

In addition to eliciting self-report data, the therapist can also observe a client's behaviour in an interview, and from this the therapist may make certain inferences about the client's behaviour in real life situations outside the consulting room. Thus, if a client's voice is tremulous, if he is restless, or if he blushes or sweats profusely, when talking about sexual matters, then the therapist may infer that he will be anxious in corresponding sexual situations. The problem is of course that the therapist's inferences may or may not be valid.

Nevertheless, despite the uncertain validity of both client self-reports and of therapist inferences in interviews, these do constitute valuable assessment tools as long as their limitations are recognized and the information derived from them is checked against other sources whenever possible.

Conduct of interviews

The conduct of assessment interviews in the field of sexual dysfunction is essentially the same as for any other type of psychological problem (see reviews by Korchin, 1976; Linehan, 1977; Morganstern, 1976; Wiens, 1976), and only a few points requiring particular emphasis are discussed in this section. Clearly, it is vital for the therapist to conduct the interview without embarrassment and in a non-judgemental manner, otherwise the client's anxiety is likely to be increased rather than alleviated, and he will not be willing to disclose relevant matters that he fears may evoke disapproval from the therapist.

Similarly, it is important to conduct interviews in the kind of language that ensures clear communication between the client and therapist, and which both of them feel comfortable in using. Some clients may not understand certain medical or scientific terms and it is necessary either to explain these or to continue the interview in the vernacular. The latter course may be perfectly easy and natural for some clients, while others may be embarrassed by the use of street language and feel that the therapist is talking down to them. Ideally, therapists should be familiar and comfortable with a wide ranging sexual vocabulary, so that they can select terms that are understandable and acceptable to individual clients.

Interviewing couples

The literature contains some conflict of opinion about how best to arrange interviews when both partners are involved in treatment with a dual sex team, and there is no systematic evidence available to resolve this issue. It is fairly generally agreed that an introductory meeting should take place, at which both partners and both therapists are present. After this, Masters and Johnson (1970) advocate two assessment interviews with each partner separately, the first being conducted by the therapist of the same sex, and the second by the opposite sex therapist. In contrast, Hartman and Fithian (1974) claim that they achieve better results by reversing this order, the first interview being with the opposite sex therapist, followed by a brief second interview with the other therapist. As a third variation, Brown (1976) argues in favour of each partner being interviewed separately by both therapists. This is said to enhance and equalize their direct familiarity with the material produced by both clients, as well as being less time-consuming than the subsequent communication of this information between individual interviewers. At present, the choice of one of these arrangements, or of some other, can only be decided according to their apparent suitability for particular couples and the individual preferences of the clients and therapists concerned.

Seeing each partner separately does provide an opportunity for them to give relatively independent accounts of the problem and other related matters, and to disclose any information that they have not revealed to their partner, perhaps about an extra-marital affair or an earlier experience of an incestuous or homosexual nature. Both partners are told beforehand that any such confidences disclosed in the individual interviews will be respected and not passed on to the other partner by the therapists, although they may encourage the client concerned to tell the partner if this is indicated on therapeutic grounds, and in some cases a refusal to do so may mean that treatment is not a feasible proposition. The fact that each partner knows that the other is being interviewed separately may also discourage the deliberate omission or distortion of relevant information known to both of them, and a comparison of the material from each informant does provide a useful check on its validity. To facilitate this, clients are usually asked not to discuss their individual assessment interviews with each other, before they do so jointly with the therapists in what Masters and Johnson (1970) call the 'roundtable discussion'. Any discrepancies in the two accounts can then be resolved with the couple, or be regarded as useful clues to matters that should be followed up in treatment. A particular advantage of separate interviews being conducted by a male and female therapist respectively, is that this provides an opportunity for each client to discuss certain matters with a member of either sex, whichever is easier for the client, and this will not necessarily be the therapist of the same sex.

In listing these potential advantages of separate interviews, it is of course assumed that they will be accompanied by some conjoint interviews. These provide the therapists with immediate feedback on the reactions of one partner by the other, as well as an opportunity to observe the nature of the interaction between the partners. As we see in Chapter 8, they can also learn to communicate more effectively with each other in such joint interviews.

Content of interviews

The topics to be covered in assessment interviews are discussed in the previous two chapters, and detailed outlines have been published by several authors including Annon (1975a), Brown (1976), Group for the Advancement of Psychiatry (1973), Hartman and Fithian (1974), Lobitz and Lobitz (1978), Lo Piccolo and Heiman (1978), and Masters and Johnson (1970). The present writer finds it convenient and flexible to select and sequence certain topics from the checklist shown in an Appendix to this book, in order to formulate interview plans that are appropriate for particular informants.

QUESTIONNAIRES

The completion of written questionnaires by clients shares those advantages and limitations of self-reports in interviews that are discussed above. One additional advantage is that it is a method of collecting comprehensive information with relatively little expenditure of time by the therapist. Another, is that some, though not all, clients find it easier initially to disclose embarrassing material in writing rather than during a face-to-face meeting with a therapist. The method is flexible in that questionnaires can be selected to investigate particular assessment problems in individual clients, such as the level of their social skills or the quality of the general relationship between partners. Moreover, the use of questionnaires with acceptable levels of reliability does yield comparable data across occasions, clients, and therapists, therefore such instruments can be used to monitor the therapeutic progress of individual clients as well as in research studies involving groups of clients or therapists.

It should be noted that in a behavioural assessment the client's replies to questionnaires are regarded as *samples* of his reactions in particular situations, rather than as *signs* of hypothetical personality traits that are presumed to have a general influence on his behaviour in a broad range of situations. Thus, if he reports that he would experience strong anxiety as a reaction to a particular sexual situation that is postulated in a questionnaire, then this reply is taken to indicate that he is likely to react with anxiety in the actual situation, and not as a sign that he has a high level of trait anxiety which will cause him to be anxious not only in that situation but in very many others as well. The focus is on what the client *does* in specific circumstances, rather than on what he *has* in terms of traits, dispositions, characteristics, or motives, of a general kind (Goldfried and Kent, 1972; Mischel, 1968).

As far as the administration of questionnaires is concerned, clients may be asked to complete them either in the clinic or at home, and their replies are usually discussed with them, so that the therapist can seek clarification and expansion, and the client can raise any difficulties he had in understanding and answering the questions. When questionnaires are given to both partners, they are usually asked to complete them independently, and their replies may be discussed in separate interviews with each partner in order to respect their confidences. The remainder of this section is devoted to a selected review of some questionnaires that may be useful in the assessment of sexually dysfunctional clients and their partners. These instruments are considered in the general categories of personal and family background, sexual behaviour, general relationship between partners, heterosocial competence, and depression.

Personal and family background

Information in this category is more commonly gathered by means of interviews rather than questionnaires, but two recent instruments that have been used for this purpose are the Life History Questionnaire designed by Annon (1975a) and the Behavioural Analysis History Questionnaire published in Cautela and Upper (1976). Each covers similar topics to those listed under this sub-heading on the check-list in the Appendix to this book.

Sexual behaviour

Some questionnaires to gather information about various aspects of this broad area are considered below in the categories of sexual information, attitudes, experience, arousal, anxiety, relationships, and variations.

Sexual information

Questionnaires to ascertain the respondent's knowledge of sexual matters have been published by Lief and Reed (1972), Gough (1974), and McHugh (1955), but none of these instruments offers very suitable coverage of the kind of information that is most relevant for sexually dysfunctional clients, and there are no group norms available that would be appropriate for such clients. All the questionnaires mentioned were designed and used primarily to test the levels of sexual knowledge in various academic and professional groups, often before and after some programme of instruction in human sexuality (Lief and Karlen, 1976). Their major use with clients at the present time is to identify some areas of ignorance or misunderstanding so that these can be rectified in treatment.

Sexual attitudes

In addition to assessing sexual information, the Sexual Knowledge and Attitude Scale by Lief and Reed (1972) also contains a 5-point Likert scale comprising 35 items designed to assess the respondent's attitudes towards pre- and extramarital heterosexual relations, abortion, and masturbation, as well as his acceptance or rejection of some commonly held sexual myths or misconceptions. There does not appear to be any report on the reliability or validity of this scale and there are no norms that would be relevant for sexually dysfunctional clients (Lief and Karlen, 1976).

These limitations apply also to two Heterosexual Attitude Scales developed by Robinson and Annon (1975a, 1975b), for men and women clients respectively. Each instrument contains 77 items and is designed to elicit on a 7-point Likert scale, the client's attitudes towards a wide range of individual and conjoint sexual activities and experiences.

A more narrowly focused questionnaire to assess attitudes towards mastur- bation, was developed by Abramson and Mosher (1975). It comprises 30 items, and subjects are asked to respond on a 5-point Likert scale. With groups of 96 male and 102 female undergraduate students, the questionnaire had good reliability, and the significant correlations between the respective scores of these groups on the instrument and their reported actual frequencies of masturbation does constitute some preliminary evidence of its validity. The results from these two groups are the only norms that are currently available.

A semantic differential method for assessing sexual preferences is described in a later section on sexual variation. This method was developed originally by Marks and Sartorius (1968), and it has been revised recently by Whitehead and Mathews (1977) in order to assess certain attitudes among sexually dysfunctional clients. The original 'general evaluation' and 'anxiety' components were retained, but the original 'sexual evaluation' factor was subdivided into three factors designated 'loving' (loving–unloving, warm–cold, affectionate–un- affectionate), 'sexually attractive' (sexually attractive–unattractive, seductive– repulsive), 'easy to arouse' (easy to arouse sexually–hard to arouse, erotic– frigid). This revision yielded 11 bipolar adjectival scales, on which the clients were asked to rate the concepts 'Myself', 'My Partner', 'Ideal Self', and 'Ideal Partner'. Their ratings on the first two concepts changed systematically during treatment, and the pre-treatment rating of the partner on the sexually attractive–unattractive scale proved predictive of treatment outcome.

Sexual experience

Questionnaires to assess the range of heterosexual behaviour engaged in by male and female informants respectively have been compiled by Bentler (1968a, 1968) Zuckerman (1975;) and Joe and Brown (1975). These instruments are all very similar, each being in the form of a Guttman ordinal scale developed from the responses of college students. It should be noted that none of these respondents were married in the Zuckerman samples, and only a small proportion were married in those studied by Bentler. The Zuckerman scales each consist of 12 items, and the full Bentler scales comprise 21 items, although there are shorter 10 item versions that correlate very highly with the full scales. The reliability of all the scales is very satisfactory.

The 77 items in the Heterosexual Attitude Scales by Robinson and Annon (1975a, 1975b), are also utilized in their Heterosexual Behaviour Inventories for male and female clients respectively (Robinson and Annon, 1975c, 1975d). These inventories are designed to assess the range and frequency of a client's sexual practices either alone or with a partner, but no data or their reliability or validity is available and there are no norms.

Sexual arousal

Hoon, Hoon, and Wincze (1976) have developed a Sexual Arousability Inventory for women. Respondents are asked to rate 28 sexual activities and situations on a 7-point Likert scale ranging from 'adversely affects arousal'; unthinkable, repulsive, distracting to 'always causes sexual arousal; extremely arousing'. The instrument can also be used in alternate forms with 14 items in each. It has been shown to have good reliability and validity, and norms are available from a population of educated middle and upper-middle class North American women. The mean score of a group of 15 dysfunctional women fell at the 5th percentile on these norms, and there is some evidence that scores rise during successful treatment so that the instrument may well be a suitable measure of outcome.

Sexual Pleasure Inventories for males and females respectively have been published by Annon (1975b, 1975c). Each consists of 130 sexually related items, to which respondents are asked to indicate on a 5-point Likert scale the degree of arousal and pleasure evoked by each of the activities or situations described. No data is available on the reliability or validity of these inventories, and no norms have been reported.

Sexual anxiety

Annon (1975d, 1975e) has used the same two sets of 130 items from his Sexual Pleasure Inventories in his Sexual Fear Inventories for males and females respectively. In these instruments, the respondent is asked to indicate on a 5-Point Likert scale the degree of fear or other unpleasant feelings evoked by each activity or situation. Again, the reliability and validity of these inventories have not been reported, but some normative data is available from college undergraduates only (Annon, 1975a).

A card sort method for assessing sexual anxiety is reported by Caird and Wincze (1974). Situations and activities that are potential sources of anxiety for an individual client are described on cards, and he or she is asked to sort them into 5 categories ranging from '0 = no anxiety' to '4 = very much anxiety'. This task can be repeated throughout therapy in order to monitor changes in anxiety both generally and in relation to particular cards. There is some evidence that the method is reactive to treatment effects, and thus may be a suitable measure of outcome.

Sexual relationships

Lo Piccolo and Steger have developed a Sexual Interaction Inventory for assessing sexual adjustment and sexual satisfaction in heterosexual couples (Lo

Piccolo and Steger, 1974; Lo Piccolo, 1977; McCoy and D'Agostino, 1977). This consists of a 17 item list of sexual activities, and six questions are asked about each of these which are answered separately by the male and female partner on a 6-point rating scale. Their responses are used to derive scores on 11 scales which measure respectively:

1, 2   each partner's degree of dissatisfaction with the frequency of the sexual activities,

3, 4   the extent of each partner's self-acceptance of the pleasure he or she derives from the activities,

5, 6   mean scores for the actual amount of pleasure derived from the activities by each partner,

7, 8   the accuracy of each partner's perceptions of which particular activities are pleasurable for the other partner,

9,10   each partner's degree of acceptance of the responsiveness and pleasure of the other partner during the activities,

11   a summary scale indicating the total disharmony and dissatisfaction in the sexual relationship.

The reliability and validity of the Sexual Interaction Inventory are satisfactory, and it does discriminate between sexually dysfunctional and non-dysfunctional couples. It also has the additional clinical advantages of pinpointing those aspects of a couple's sexual relationship that require therapeutic attention, and of being a suitable measure of treatment outcome.

Another available measure of a couple's sexual relationship is the Sexual Compatibility Test developed by Foster (1974, 1976, 1977). The first part includes 55 questions, organized into 12 scales, covering general bodily caressing, nudity, variety of sexual behaviour, intercourse positions, embracing, loving verbalizations, manual–genital caressing, oral–genital caressing, breast stimulation, and kissing activities. Respondents are asked to answer each question in six different ways according to (1) how frequently the activity occurred during the past year, (2) how frequently he or she would like it to have occurred, (3) how pleasant it was for the respondent, (4) how pleasant the respondent thinks it was for his or her mate, (5) how pleasant the respondent would like it to be, and (6) how pleasant the respondent would like his or her mate to find it.

The respondents answers can be interpreted in the light of the normative data which is available from the replies of a representative sample of the U.S. Population to this part of the test. Each respondent's answers to it, as well as to certain questions in the second part, can also be analysed to yield scores for:

1. sexual activity level
2. desired activity level
3. pleasure from sexual activities
4. estimate of mate's pleasure
5. desired pleasure

6. desire for mate's pleasure
7. dissonance respondent feels from mate in ability to take pleasure from sexual activities
8. perceptual accuracy in estimating mates pleasure
9. desire for increased pleasure
10. desire for mate's increased pleasure
11. problem solving, as a measure of the frequency with which the couple verbally express sexual dissatisfactions at the time they occur.

These scores can be profiled for each partner, and a comparison made between them as an index of the couples sexual satisfaction with each other.

A second part of the test includes 23 questions, each requiring a single answer, and these are organized into eight scales to assess (1) female discomfort or pain during intercourse, (2) impotence, (3) ejaculatory incompetence, (4) premature ejaculation, (5) orgasmic insufficiency, (6) overall sexual satisfaction, (7) deception or lying when completing the test, and (8) problem-solving verbalizations between the partners. The client's score on each of these scales can be interpreted in the light of data derived from the representative sample of the U.S. population.

The reliability and validity of the Sexual Compatibility Test are satisfactory; as already mentioned, normative data is available from a representative sample of the U.S. population; and there is some preliminary evidence for the value of the instrument in predicting response to behavioural treatment for sexual dysfunction. Overall, this test appears to be a promising contribution to the literature, and it merits further investigation and application.

Sexual variation

Several authors have recently presented comprehensive reviews of the assessment of sexual variation (Abed, 1976; Bancroft, 1974; Barlow, 1977), and any detailed consideration of the topic in this book would be both unnecessarily repetitive and tangential to its main theme. Therefore, discussion is restricted to only a few selected instruments that may be particularly useful in ascertaining the nature and degree of any sexual variation in certain clients who are seeking treatment for some inadequacy in their sexual functioning with a partner of the opposite sex.

Marks and Sartorius (1968) have developed a convenient and flexible method of assessing a wide range of *sexual preferences*, based upon Osgood's semantic differential technique (Osgood *et al.*, 1957). Certain deviant and non-deviant sexual concepts are selected, either in standardized form or to suit individual clients. For male clients, the deviant concepts might include: 'brassieres', to tap fetishistic tendencies; 'wearing women's panties', as an indication of transvestism; and 'seeing a man in the nude' as one measure of homosexuality. An example of a non-deviant concept would be 'sexual intercourse with an attractive woman'. The client is asked to rate each concept on a series of 7-point bipolar adjectival scales which sample his general evaluation of the concept (pleasant–unpleasant, good–bad, kind–cruel), his perception of its approachability (friendly–unfriendly, approachable–distant, warm–cold), his sexual evaluation of the concept (seductive–repulsive, sexy–sexless, exciting–dull, erotic–frigid), and how anxiety evoking it is for him (placid–jittery, calm–anxious, relaxed–tense). The instrument is easily scored to yield a profile of the client's sexual preferences, and it has been shown to have satisfactory reliability and to reflect changes during treatment. Its major disadvantage is the possibility of the client 'faking good' in his responses. This problem is common to all self-report measures but it may be particularly important in the field of sexual variation.

Among the instruments available to assess *gender identity* and *gender role behaviour* are the inventories developed by Freund *et al.* (1974, 1977) and Bem (1974). The first of these is designed for males, and consists of questions about such matters as the client's preferences for 'boys' or 'girls' play activities and whether he has worn women's clothing. The reliability and validity of the instrument are satisfactory, and norms are available for a variety of groups including homosexuals, paedophiliacs, and heterosexual men. The Bem inventory is not specifically designed for clients who may be deviant in their gender role behaviour, but it does yield estimates of masculinity, femininity, and androgyny, for both male and female subjects. The first two of these dimensions are treated independently of each other in the instrument, rather than as polar opposites, and the androgyny score represents what are considered to be the positive aspects of both sexes. The major limitation of these and similar instruments is their dependence upon the prevailing definitions of gender roles in particular cultures at particular times.

Paitch *et al.* (1977) have reported very recently on their development of a clinical sex history questionnaire for males, entitled the Clark SHQ. This consists of 225 items which sample the respondent's performance of a wide range of deviant sexual activities and his emotional reactions to these. Among the behaviour and preferences covered are homosexuality, transvestism, paedophilia, voyeurism, obscene telephone calls, exhibitionism, and rape. The reliability and validity of the instrument are good, and norms are available from a variety of relevant clinical groups.

General relationship between partners

Turning now from sexual behaviour to the general relationship between partners, there are a number of recent, comprehensive reviews of the range of methods and questionnaires used to assess such relationships (Cromwell *et al.*, 1976; Gambrill, 1977; Glick and Gross, 1975; Jacob, 1976; Weiss and Margolin, 1977), therefore the present discussion is restricted to a single instrument which appears to be the most sophisticated and convenient of those currently available, for use with couples who are seeking treatment for sexual dysfunction. This is the Dyadic Adjustment Scale, developed by Spanier (1976). The full scale consists of 32 items, to which subjects are asked to rate their responses, and there are four sub-scales that measure satisfaction, consensus, cohesion, and affectional expression in the dyad. All scales have good reliability and validity, and norms are available from 218 married and 94 divorced people who were drawn from a fairly representative North American population. The Dyadic Adjustment Scale was designed to be appropriate for unmarried as well as married couples, and it is intended to investigate its applicability with the former group.

Heterosocial competence

It is apparent from recent reviews of the assessment of heterosocial anxiety and skills (Barlow, 1977; Eisler, 1976; Hersen and Bellack, 1977), that there are few psychometrically adequate questionnaires available in this area. Perhaps the most suitable of these for screening sexually dysfunctional males, is the Survey of Heterosexual Interactions developed by Twentyman and McFall (1975) as a measure of the extent to which the respondent avoids heterosexual social situations. This consists of four questions about his past dating behaviour; followed by 20 items concerning his ability to initiate and conduct interactions with women in certain specified social situations, to which he is asked to respond on a 7-point scale, ranging from 1 (unable to respond) to 7 (able to carry out the interaction). The instrument has been validated, and norms are available from a large group of college students.

Depression

There is a substantial literature on the behavioural assessment of neurotic and psychotic conditions (e.g. see reviews by Alevizos and Callahan, 1977; Borkovec et al., 1977; Lick and Katkin, 1976; Pehm, 1976; Tasto, 1977; Wallace, 1976), but depression is likely to be the most relevant of these among sexually dysfunctional clients. This discussion is restricted therefore, to two questionnaires that are particularly suitable for use in screening such clients for depression.

The first of these instruments is the Beck Depression Inventory (Beck, 1972; Beck et al., 1961). It consists of 21 items covering a range of cognitive, physiological, and overt symptoms of depression, each accompanied by a ranked list of 4 or 5 statements describing varying degrees of severity for the symptom. The respondent is asked to endorse the statement which most nearly describes his or her present state. The reliability and validity of the BDI are very satisfactory, and norms are available from both clinical and non-clinical groups.

The second instrument is the Lubin Depression Adjective Check List (Levitt and Lubin, 1975; Lubin, 1965, 1967; Lubin and Himelstein, 1976). It was designed as a measure of depressive affect, and thus taps a narrower range of symptoms than the BDI. The DACL is available in seven different forms, each consisting of 32 or 34 synonyms and antonyms for 'depressed', therefore repeated administration at short intervals is quite feasible. The respondent is asked to indicate whether or not each adjective is applicable to him or her. Both reliability and validity are good for this instrument, and excellent norms are available from a large sample of the general population in the U.S., as well as for depressed and non-depressed patient groups.

SELF-MONITORING

In this method of assessment, the client is asked to observe and record specific aspects of his own behaviour and its surrounding circumstances, in a systematic manner (see reviews by Ciminero *et al.*, 1977; Kazdin, 1974; Mahoney 1977; McFall 1977; Nelson 1977; Thoresen and Mahoney, 1974). These records can be used for several purposes. Before any specific therapeutic programme is implemented, they are a means of obtaining information about the nature, frequency and timing of the dysfunctional behaviour, thus providing a baseline against which the subsequent effects of treatment can be assessed. The records can also yield information about those circumstances that immediately precede or follow the dysfunctional behaviour and which may be influencing its occurrence. Once treatment has commenced, then the client's records are a valuable means of assessing its efficacy in producing beneficial changes in his behaviour, and of identifying any problems that may arise in implementing the programme, such as any failure to carry out the sexual assignment as prescribed.

Individual clients are asked to monitor those aspects of their behaviour and its surrounding circumstances that are particularly relevant in assessing their problem and progress. This behaviour may well include the client's thoughts and feelings, as well as his overt responses, and he will record certain selected features of these reactions, such as their nature, frequency, duration, or magnitude. For instance, an inorgastic woman who is undertaking a masturbation programme might be asked to record the parts of her genitals that she touches and the ways in which she does this, together with any erotic thoughts or feelings of pleasure that she experiences. She might also record when the assignments were carried out, for how long on each occasion, and with what degree of arousal.

The circumstances surrounding the behaviour that are to be monitored may similarly include the client's thoughts, feelings and overt activities, as well as certain situational factors such as the time, the place and the behaviour of the partner. Thus, an impotent man might note that he lost an erection after thinking that he would not be able to sustain it during intromission, and feeling very anxious about this anticipated failure. He might note also, that his loss of erection was followed by critical and angry comments from his partner. All the observations made by a client of his own behaviour and its surrounding circumstances may be recorded in a behavioural diary or on a suitable form, and it is important to minimize the onerousness of this task in order to facilitate its satisfactory performance.

Self-monitoring has a number of advantages as a method of assessment. The need for precise definition of the problem and its surrounding circumstances is indicated earlier, and the observation and recording of these events by the client requires the prior formulation of such precise definitions. Furthermore, when clients are asked in interviews or questionnaires to describe these events retrospectively, they are often unable to do so with sufficient accuracy and precision, while the compilation of systematic and specific records on an ongoing basis may go some way towards remedying these limitations. Similarly, such records may well provide better indices of therapeutic progress and obstacles than the global and impressionistic judgements that are often relied upon for these purposes. Self-monitoring is also a means of systematically observing overt sexual behaviour that would not normally be open to observation by others, because of the therapeutic and ethical objections this would entail. Similarly, only the client himself can observe his own thoughts and feelings in sexual situations. Finally, in addition to these strengths as a method of assessment, self-monitoring may have certain therapeutic effects. It can increase the client's awareness of the nature of his dysfunctional behaviour and of the circumstances which influence its occurrence, and more particularly it may reduce any misapprehension that he is suffering from a generalized disease process or personality defect rather than a specific impairment of his sexual response in particular situations. There is also evidence, which is reviewed in the sources cited above, that self-monitoring is sometimes accompanied by beneficial changes in the behaviour that is being observed and recorded by the client, although why this may happen is not yet clear.

This therapeutic effect of self-monitoring also constitutes one of its major limitations as a method of assessment. The reactivity of the method means that the data gathered does not necessarily represent an accurate pre-intervention baseline for the behaviour concerned, and it is often difficult to distinguish the extent to which any changes in this behaviour during treatment are due to the self-monitoring or to other more specifically therapeutic components in the programme. However, this limitation is less important from a purely clinical point of view, than in research investigations into the efficacy and crucial ingredients of particular forms of treatment, and in such investigations it is possible to employ designs that facilitate the correct attribution of therapeutic change.

A second potential problem with self-monitoring is its variable accuracy across individual clients, the responses concerned, the circumstances in which these occur, and the recording techniques used. The reviews cited above, contain evidence that the accuracy of a client's records is often enhanced if he is aware that another observer is making comparable recordings. Thus, it may be desirable to ask each partner to compile an independent record, and this will have the additional advantage of yielding some estimate of the accuracy of the records from examination of their consistency across partners. Unfortunately, this check on accuracy cannot be applied to records of thoughts and feelings, these being accessible only to self-observation by the partner concerned.

PHYSIOLOGICAL TECHNIQUES

Currently, the major use of these techniques in the assessment of sexually dysfunctional clients is to measure directly the physiological aspects of their sexual arousal, by means of penile or vaginal plethysmography (Geer, 1976, 1977). The data gathered in these ways complements, but does not replace, the self-reports of arousal obtained in interviews, on questionnaires, or through client records; for the direct measures of physiological arousal and the self-reports of subjective arousal are not always in agreement, and neither is necessarily an accurate index of the other. This fact, together with the special equipment and expertise required for physiological measurement, are probably its major limitations in clinical practice.

Penile plethysmography

The techniques and instruments available for the measurement of erectile responses in the male, are reviewed in the papers by Geer cited in the previous paragraph as well as by Abel and Blanchard (1976), Barlow (1977) and Freund (1976). They fall largely into two major categories, according to whether they measure penile volume or penile circumference. An example from the former category is the widely used apparatus developed by Freund (Freund et al., 1965). This consists of a glass cylinder with a rubber cuff at one end. The penis is inserted into this and measurements are taken of the amounts of air displaced from the cylinder as erection occurs, thus providing a quantitative measure of the total volume of the penis. In contrast, only the circumference of the penis is measured by those instruments in the second category. An example of these is the device developed by Barlow et al. (1970), comprising a thin, metal ring, open at one side, with one or more strain gauges at the base. This device is fitted around the penis, and as erection occurs the open side becomes wider which causes a slight bending of the strain gauge and produces a measurable increase in electrical output.

Both the volumetric and the circumferential devices have their respective advantages and disadvantages. The former are relatively more sensitive and can pick up levels of arousal down to about 10% of a full erection, whereas the circumferential devices are responsive to levels of about 25% upwards. However, both kinds of device can pick up penile changes of which the subject himself is unaware, and the circumferential devices can cover the range of arousal that is of major clinical significance. Moreover, the circumferential devices are easily positioned by the subject and comfortable to wear, as well as being less expensive than the volumetric devices which are also more cumbersome and difficult to work with.

The techniques of penile plethysmography can be used to assess a client's degree of physiological arousal to a wide range of erotic stimulation, and an interesting recent development is their application during sleep to differentiate cases of organic impotence from those of psychogenic or mixed origin (Fisher et al., 1975, Karacan, 1978a, b; Karacan et al., 1975, 1977). This work is based on the findings that people generally have four or five periods of dreaming sleep, during which they display rapid eye movements (REMs), amounting to about 25% of an average night's sleep; and that these periods of REM sleep are typically associated with full penile erections. In adolescence and young adulthood, some 90% or more of REM periods are associated with full erection; in middle-aged subjects, the incidence of such erections drops to about 60%; while in elderly subjects, aged over 71 years, it commonly falls to about 26%. The preliminary findings reported in the two studies cited above, suggest that erectile responses during REM sleep may be normal for the client's age group in cases of impotence of psychogenic origin, but not among those of organic origin. Thus, a marked discrepancy may exist between erectile capacity during sleep and in the walking state in cases of psychogenic impotence, while no such discrepancy may appear in those with an organic aetiology.

Vaginal plethysmography

Vaginal photoplethysmographic devices have been developed recently by Geer and his colleagues (Geer et al., 1974; Sintchak and Geer, 1975), and by Hoon and his coworkers (Hoon, Wincze, and Hoon, 1976). In each case, the device consists essentially of a vaginal probe with a light source at one end, and a photodetector cell on the side. This measures the amount of light reflected from the walls of the vagina, which varies with the degree of vasocongestion occurring during sexual arousal. The probe can easily be inserted and removed by the client herself, and it causes no discomfort when *in situ*.

There is evidence that such devices are capable of discriminating between sexual arousal and other arousal states (Hoon, Wencze, and Hoon, 1976), and that the physiological measure of arousal they provide does correlate highly with self-reports of cognitive arousal in many, but not all, subjects (Wincze et al., 1977). Some early studies using the probe, have indicated that sexually dysfunctional women tend to achieve lower levels of vasocongestion than others (see review by Barlow, 1977).

Vaginal blood volume is not the only measure of physiological arousal in women that is being investigated. There are some early reports available concerning at least two alternatives, one being vaginal pulse amplitude (Heiman, 1976, 1977, 1978) and another labial temperature (Henson et al., 1978, Henson and Rubin, 1978).

MEDICAL EXAMINATION

We end this chapter by again emphasizing the importance of arranging a medical examination as part of a comprehensive assessment for clients complaining of sexual dysfunction. As we have seen, this may arise directly or indirectly, from an illness, as a side effect of a surgical or obstetrical intervention, or as a result of the ingestion of prescribed or non-prescribed drugs, and it is essential to identify any such organic contributory factors so that suitable medical treatment can be provided when indicated. Both Brown (1976) and Masters and Johnson (1970) have published outline forms for the general medical examination of sexually dysfunctional patients, and further more specific investigations may need to be carried out when relevant pathology is suspected or ascertained.

Part 5

Outcome of Treatment

14

Programmes for Male and Female Dysfunctions

This part of the book consists of a selective review of the evidence available on the outcome of behavioural programmes for the treatment of sexual dysfunction. In choosing studies for discussion, much weight was attached to the degree of their approximation to certain widely accepted standards for the evaluation of therapeutic interventions.

One such standard requires a thorough description of the clients treated in the study, in terms of those characteristics that may influence outcome. A number of possible examples of such prognostic variables are listed in the Appendix, but they remain to be identified, and the reporting of relevant information about clients provides a necessary basis for such investigation. It also reduces the risk of unjustified over generalization of results obtained with particular groups of clients. For instance, the processes of referral and selection may yield a group of clients who enjoy a harmonious general relationship with their partners, and certain treatment programmes may be shown to be effective with this group. However, one cannot safely assume that these programmes will be equally successful in cases where serious discord exists, and sufficient knowledge of the composition of the original group will militate against such unwarranted extrapolation.

Similarly, the precise conditions of the treatment provided need to be comprehensively described, in terms of those variables that may influence its outcome. These also require much further investigation, but they may well include many of the factors discussed in Chapter 12 in the sections on therapist characteristics and the setting, timing and composition of treatment. Clearly, a full description of such conditions is necessary if the treatment programme is to be properly replicated. It also reduces the risk of outcome results obtained under particular treatment conditions being invalidly generalized to other programmes where these conditions do not apply. Thus, it is not safe to assume that the results obtained by very experienced therapists will necessarily be achieved by others who are just beginning work in this field, and adequate information about the therapists concerned will help to avoid such unjustified assumptions and to ensure that they are tested empirically.

Next, the criteria of outcome should be clearly specified in ways that permit the valid and reliable assessment of their attainment. It is not sufficient to rely on subjective allocation to global categories with labels such as 'cured', 'improved', 'not improved', or 'failure', for which precise definitions are not provided.

It follows that valid and reliable methods of data collection are required in order to assess the achievement of the outcome criteria, and the strengths and limitations of many existing techniques and instruments are discussed in Chapter 13. The desirability of employing a variety of methods in suitable combinations to ensure a balanced and comprehensive assessment is also noted, and it is preferable for this to be broad enough to ascertain any changes in a client's psychological functioning and life situation that may accompany treatment for sexual dysfunction. For instance, some change might occur in a client's level of self-esteem or in the general relationship between partners, and it is important to reveal such side effects of behavioural programmes focused upon the treatment of sexual dysfunction.

Lastly, all evaluative studies should be designed so that it is possible to distinguish the relative outcome of different treatment programmes when compared to each other or to no-treatment control conditions. Some studies are specially designed to elicit the crucial ingredients in a programme by identifying the respective contributions to the outcome of its various components and conditions, and/or to reveal the respective influences on outcome of relevant client characteristics. A variety of experimental designs using single subjects or control groups can be employed in these tasks (Hersen and Barlow, 1976; Yates, 1976), and an adequate design will include not only pre- and post-treatment assessments, but also an adequate follow up in order to ascertain the course of change after the specific treatment intervention is terminated.

Few, if any, of the outcome studies reviewed below meet all these requirements, but they are selected from among those that most nearly approach this desirable level, and their strengths and limitations are indicated in the discussion. The remainder of this chapter is devoted to those studies in which both male and female dysfunctions were treated, leaving those that were focused on either male or female dysfunctions for discussion in the following two chapters.

MASTERS AND JOHNSON (1970)

The innovative and now classic treatment programme conducted by these authors is described in Parts 3 and 4 of this book and in the present section we consider the characteristics of their patients and the outcome of their interventions.

Over an 11 year period between 1959 and 1969 a total of 790 dysfunctional patients were treated. There were 448 males and 342 females, ranging in age from 23 to 76 years. Those who were married and participated in treatment with the spouse numbered 733, while the remaining 57 unmarried patients were treated with a surrogate or other partner. As a result of the referral and selection processes, the group was biased towards the higher socioeconomic and educational levels, the patients were highly motivated, and 52.3% of them had previously undergone psychotherapy for their sexual dysfunction.

Masters and Johnson present their results in terms of the number of patients who were judged to be treatment failures either at the end of treatment or on follow up five years later. An initial failure is defined as 'an indication that the two-week rapid treatment phase has failed to initiate reversal of the basic symptomatology of sexual dysfunction . . . ' (Masters and Johnson, 1970, pp. 352/3). According to this criterion, there were 142 (18%) initial failures out of the 790 patients treated.

The results of a five year follow up on patients treated between 1959 and 1964 are also reported. There was a total of 313 such patients, but 56 of these were initial failures and were not included in the follow up in case this should be harmful, while a further 31 patients could not be traced. Thus, 226 patients were followed up, of whom 16 (5.7%) were judged to be treatment failures in that they had reverted to prior patterns of sexual inadequacy. These relapsed patients when added to those who failed initially yield an overall failure rate of 25.5% after five years.

No significant differences were found between males and females in either the initial or the overall failure rates, and the breakdown of these rates according to the particular dysfunction treated is deferred until later sections on each of these.

The series of sexually dysfunctional patients in this study is the largest ever reported, and the proportions of successful cases at the end of treatment (82%) and after five years (74.5%) are remarkably impressive. Being an uncontrolled study it is not possible to determine the extent to which this outcome is attributable to the treatment given or to other factors, but the fact that over half the patients had not gained equal benefit from previous psychotherapy for their dysfunction does provide some indication of the efficacy of the Masters and Johnson programme. Again because of the lack of suitable control, it is not possible to distinguish the crucial ingredients in the total treatment package and some of the studies reviewed below are designed to throw light on this issue. Two final points should be noted in this discussion of the Masters and Johnson study. One is that the criteria for initial and subsequent failure are rather imprecisely stated, and the reliability of the subjective allocation to these categories is unknown. Secondly because of the selection biases reported by the authors, it is necessary to exercise considerable caution in generalizing their excellent results to other patient groups.

MATHEWS et al. (1976)

This study involved the deployment of a modified Masters and Johnson programme in the setting of a British National Health Service clinic. It was specifically designed with two aims in view. One of these was to distinguish the contributions to outcome of what the investigators term the 'directed practice' and 'counselling' components in that programme or what are referred to in this book as the 'sexual assignment' and 'interview' components. The second aim was to compare the results obtained by dual sex therapy teams as advocated by Masters and Johnson, with those attained by the same therapists working on an individual basis.

The patients were allocated randomly to one of three treatment programmes, and to either a dual sex team or an individual therapist. One programme consisted of systematic desensitization plus counselling, and it included the *in vivo* practice of items already desensitized in imagination. This programme was included in the design because it was considered impractical to use counselling alone. A second programme combined directed practice and counselling, and represented the modified Masters and Johnson approach in the study. The third programme comprised directed practice with minimal therapist contact, so that the counselling component was thereby markedly reduced. After the initial assessment interviews, the couples in this group were seen at the clinic only twice, in the middle and at the end of treatment, when the focus was upon the implementation of assignments rather than more general sexual counselling. Otherwise their assignments were prescribed and managed by means of letters sent at weekly intervals, to accord with the weekly clinic meetings between the therapists and the couples in the first two programmes. All three programmes lasted for a period of ten weeks, and a four month follow up was conducted.

There were three male and three female therapists, all either clinical psychologists or psychiatrists. Half the couples were treated by these therapists working in dual sex teams, while the remaining half were treated by the same therapists working individually. In the latter cases, the couples were allocated so that the sex of the therapist and of the main complainant were the same.

Couples were referred to the clinic by general practitioners, other physicians and psychiatrists, Family Planning Clinics and the Marriage Guidance Council. On referral they were screened by an independent psychiatrist who assessed and rated their sexual difficulties, and ensured that the selection criteria were met. This process resulted in the exclusion of 9 couples who were considered unsuitable or refused treatment, in most cases because their primary problem was partner discord or psychiatric disorder rather than sexual dysfunction. A further 7 couples started but did not complete treatment, usually because they separated or found difficulty in undertaking the assignments. These 16 couples were not included among those who comprised the study group.

This consisted of 36 couples, in 18 of which the problem was primarily on the male side, while in the other 18 couples the female partner was the main complainant. The mean ages of the male and female main complainants respectively were 38.3 and 28.0 years. Their presenting problems included erectile dysfunction, premature ejaculation, retarded or absent ejaculation, orgastic dysfunction, vaginismus, and inadequate interest and arousal.

We turn now to the results of the study. One measure of outcome was a set of ratings of the satisfactoriness of each couple's general and sexual relationships, completed by the independent psychiatrist, the therapist(s), and the partners themselves. These ratings were obtained during the initial assessment, at the end of treatment, and on follow up. No significant differences between the treatment programmes were found on these measures, and considerable individual variation in response occurred within the directed practice with counselling and directed practice with minimal contact groups, the last treatment in particular being associated with a greater number of couples who deteriorated or relapsed in their general and sexual relationships. Additionally, the ratings of these relationships were not found to be significantly associated with the conduct of treatment by a dual sex team or an individual therapist. However, the investigators do report some non-significant but consistent trends in the data which suggest that the outcome of directed practice with counselling is enhanced by use of a dual sex team, although the same cannot be said for the other two programmes.

The therapists also rated the satisfactoriness of certain specific aspects of sexual functioning in the patients, but an analysis of this data yielded only one significant association. This was between type of treatment and female enjoyment of sexual contact, the most improvement being associated with directed practice plus counselling and the least with desensitization plus counselling.

The semantic differential scales completed by the patients are described in Chapter 13, and an analysis of this data is reported in a further paper from the same group of investigators (Whitehead and Mathews, 1977). In the first place, this shows that improvements in sexual behaviour were accompanied by positive changes in attitude both towards the respondents themselves and towards their partners. Another finding, of considerable importance, is that directed practice plus counselling was significantly superior to the other two treatments in producing positive attitude change. Moreover, the directed practice with minimal contact type of treatment was associated with a widening of the gap between actual and ideal ease of arousal as perceived by the respondents.

A general point to be noted in discussing these results is that global ratings of satisfactoriness are somewhat imprecise measures of outcome, even though these ratings reach acceptable levels of reliability. For instance, the authors draw attention to the fact that although the ratings of sexual relationship improved in the female complainant couples, only 2 women showed an improvement in orgastic response on follow up out of the 13 who were impaired in this respect at the commencement of treatment. Thus, some clearer specification and assessment of outcome criteria might have facilitated more discriminating and informative data on treatment results.

The only evidence for the superiority of a dual sex team compared to an individual therapist related to the directed practice plus counselling type of treatment, and the authors do not consider this to amount to an overwhelming case for the employment of two therapists.

Taken togehter, the outcome data provides some support for the superiority of the combination of sexual assignments and therapeutic interviews in the directed practice plus counselling type of treatment, similar to that advocated by Masters and Johnson. Although this was not significantly associated with greater improvement in the ratings of general and sexual relationships, it did produce the most beneficial changes on these measures when compared with the other two treatments. Directed practice with counselling was also associated with the most improvement in female enjoyment of sexual contact on the therapists' ratings of specific sexual functions, and with the greatest positive changes in attitudes on the semantic differential scales completed by the patients.

In contrast, the prescription of sexual assignments alone in the directed practice with minimal contact programme, seemed to be the least effective of the three treatments. It was associated with the widest variation in outcome, and with a relatively high incidence of deterioration and relapse, on the ratings of general and sexual relationships. It was also accompanied by a widening gap between actual and ideal ease of arousal on the semantic differential scale. The authors suggest that while the performance of sexual assignments alone may help some patients, it can also be ineffective or damaging with others, perhaps because no provision is made for resolving any problems that arise in implementing the assignments. Thus, it is important to try to identify the characteristics of patients for whom a largely self-administered form of treatment is helpful or harmful.

There is no evidence in the study to suggest that systematic desensitization plus counselling is to be preferred to the modified Masters and Johnson programme, but the efficacy of desensitization procedures in the treatment of sexual dysfunction is considered further in the next and some subsequent sections.

OBLER (1973)

The study was conducted in the United States, with the main aim of comparing the outcome of a desensitization treatment package with those of psycho-dynamically oriented group therapy and of a no-treatment control condition.

The 64 subjects were selected from a population of 225 who ageed to be referred to the study from various professional and other sources of help in New York universities. The main criteria for selection were (a) the presence of premature ejaculation, retarded or absent ejaculation, or secondary impotence in males, and of primary or secondary orgastic dysfunction in females, (b) the absence of a related psychiatric or organic disorder, (c) high motivation for treatment, and (d) average or above intelligence, with at least one year's attendance at college. Those individuals who met these criteria and consented to treatment comprised 37 females and 27 males. They were matched on the nature and duration of the dysfunction, and on their marital status, before being allocated to one of three groups (a) desensitization therapy, (b) group therapy, and (c) no-treatment control.

Desensitization therapy was conducted by the investigator, and consisted of 15 individual sessions held at weekly intervals and each lasting 45 minutes. The imaginal presentation of anxiety evoking items was supplemented by the graphic presentation on film or slides of those items that the subject found difficult to imagine; for instance a male's failure to maintain an eretion. From the sixth session onwards, these subjects were given assertive training (Salter, 1949) and confidence training (Susskind, 1970) to reduce heterosocial anxiety.

Group therapy was conducted by two experienced therapists who described their approach as Neo-Freudian, and who were unaware of the aims of the study. Two groups, each of 10 subjects, had 10 weekly meetings lasting $1\frac{1}{2}$ hours on each occasion. To ensure their equivalent exposure to the graphic materials these subjects were shown the same items as the desensitization subjects, and these were discussed in the therapeutic sessions.

The no-treatment control group subjects participated in similar assessment procedures to the desensitization and group therapy subjects, at the beginning and end of a 15 week period, but the control subjects were not otherwise involved in the research study.

A range of behavioural, physiological, and cognitive measures of outcome were employed in this investigation. The behvioural measure consisted of records of successful and unsuccessful sexual experiences, according to given criteria, that were completed independently by subjects and their partners. Although it is mentioned that the ratios of successful to total experiences were approximately the same across groups at the beginning of treatment, these ratios are not reported, so that it is not possible to evaluate any changes in them over the period of the study. However, the ratios of successes to experiences at the end of treatment, and for females and males respectively, were 42% and 61% for the desensitization subjects, 3% and 3% for those in group therapy, and 2% and 3% in the no-treatment control group. These differences in outcome between desensitization and the other two conditions are all statistically significant.

The physiological measures of outcome consisted of galvanic skin responses and heart rates during exposure to sexual and heterosocial stimuli of an anxiety evoking kind. These measures were obtained for the desensitization and group therapy subjects before treatment started, and for all three groups when it ended. The pre-treatment rates for the desensitization and group therapy subjects were essentially similar, but the former had achieved significantly greater reductions in both GSR and HR by the end of treatment. At that time, the desensitization subjects had significantly lower rates than both the group therapy and no-treatment control subjects.

The cognitive measures of outcome included two scales for the assessment of anxiety reactions in certain specific situations. These were completed at the beginning and end of the study period by subjects in all three groups. The Sexual Anxiety Scale was developed by Obler for this investigation, and it assessed the intensity of the anxiety experienced by each respondent during certain sexual and heterosocial encounters. On this scale, the desensitization subjects achieved significantly greater reductions in anxiety than both the group therapy and no-treatment control subjects. Similar superior results for the desensitization subjects were obtained on the Anxiety Differential Scale (Alexander and Husek, 1962), which was used to assess anxiety reactions to a film depicting sexual stresses, such as woman's inability to achieve orgasm.

The results of this study, on the behavioural, physiological and cognitive measures used, are consistent in showing the superiority of the desensitization package. Moreover, Obler adds that 18 (80%) out of the 22 subjects in this group became sexually functional, and that they did not regress during a one and half year follow up. He does not specify his criteria for being 'sexually functional', nor does he report any systematic follow-up data. The psychodynamically oriented group did not apparently achieve any better outcome than the no-treatment group which participated only in the assessment procedures. However, in comparing the outcome of desensitization and group therapy it is important to note that the former was implemented on an individual basis, and that it was conducted by the investigator who was aware of the aims and design of the study.

The desensitization package included the specific components of imaginal and graphic desensitization together with assertive and confidence training, and the respective contributions to outcome of these and other ingredients in the package cannot be distinguished in this study.

Some more general conclusions on the three studies reviewed in this chapter are offered at the end of this part of the book, after we have examined the outcome of some programmes focused specifically on male or female dysfunctions respectively.

15

Programmes for Male Dysfunctions

Apart from a few uncontrolled case reports, there is no information available on the outcome of behavioural programmes focused upon the treatment of inadequate interest, retrograde ejaculation, inadequate pleasure, or dyspareunia in male clients. Therefore, the studies reviewed in this chapter are selected from those in which erectile dysfunction, premature ejaculation, or retarded or absent ejaculation was the focus of treatment.

ERECTILE DYSFUNCTION

Masters and Johnson (1970)

These authors describe the treatment of primary, erectile dysfunction as their 'clinical disaster area' (Masters and Johnson, 1970, p. 358). They treated 32 cases in this category, of whom 13 (40.6%) were initial failures, and as there were no relapses during the follow up period the overall failure rate remains the same.

Rather lower but still relatively high failure rates are reported for the 213 cases of secondary erectile dysfunction treated in the study. The initial failure rate was 56 (26.3%), and the addition of 10 relapses yielded an overall failure rate of 66 (30.9%).

Ansari (1976)

A relatively disappointing outcome for a modified Masters and Johnson approach in the treatment of erectile dysfunction is also reported by this investigator. He compared the outcome of this approach with those of chemotherapy and a no-treatment control condition, in the setting of a psychiatric out-patient department in the British National Health Service.

The modified Masters and Johnson approach was similar to that used in the study by Mathews *et al.* (1976) which is discussed above. Patients in the chemotherapy group were prescribed oxazepam, for its anxiety reducing properties. Those in the no-treatment control condition participated in the same assessment procedures as the two treatment groups, but were not given any specific therapy. However, their attendance at the clinic was similar to the patients being treated, and what occurred on these occasions other than assessment is not reported.

All patient contacts were with an individual therapist, and they occurred at approximately two-weekly intervals, on 12 to 14 occasions, over a period of 6 to 8 months. The patients were followed up for a further period of eight months, during which they were seen on 2 or 3 occasions.

The patients in the modified Masters and Johnson programme were treated with their partners, while those in the chemotherapy and no-treatment groups were treated individually, although their partners were interviewed for assessment purposes whenever they were available and agreed to attend. The allocation of patients to the three groups was not random, for those who lacked a regular partner or whose partner was unwilling to participate could not be assigned to the Masters and Johnson treatment.

A total of 65 patients were originally allocated to the three groups, but 10 of these discontinued participation after attending only a few sessions, and the outcome in these cases is unknown. The outcome for the remaining 55 patients is expressed in terms of the categories 'recovered', improved, and 'no change'. The first category comprises those patients 'who were completely satisfied with their sexual performance and considered themselves recovered', while the patients in the improved category 'were able to perform coitus more often . . . but they experienced occasional failure and were considerably less satisfied than the recovered group' (Ansari, 1976, pp. 195/6).

There were no significant differences in outcome between the three groups either at the end of treatment or on follow up. The proportions in the Masters and Johnson group who were categorized as recovered or improved were 67% at termination and 33% on follow up.

However, significant differences in outcome are reported between certain aetiological patient groupings that are described by the same investigator in an earlier paper (Ansari, 1975) and discussed in Chapter 6. To recapitulate briefly; Group 1 comprised those patients whose erectile dysfunction was of acute onset and triggered off by psychological or physical trauma; in Group 2 the dysfunction had an insidious onset due to long term psychological or physical factors, often involving partner discord; while the Group 3 patients had experienced an insidious onset without any discernible psychological or physical causal factors. The outcomes for patients in Groups 1 or 2 were significantly better than for those in Group 3.

Ansari concludes that the prognosis for erectile dysfunction is related to the clinical features of the patients rather than the form of treatment. However, there are several limitations in the design and conduct of his study that suggest the need for further more rigorous investigation before this conclusion is accepted. Information about the sexual functioning of the patients before treatment commenced is limited to the statement that they suffered from 'erectile impotence'. Their allocation to the treatment or no-treatment groups was not random, although the availability and willingness of a partner to participate in treatment might have been expected to favour the Masters and Johnson programme. No data is presented on the reliability of the allocation of patients either to the aetiological groups or to the outcome categories, and the latter suffer from the usual lack of precision in such global classifications.

Kockott *et al.* (1975)

This study was conducted in West Germany with the aim of evaluating the effectiveness of systematic desensitization as a treatment for erectile dysfunction.

The subjects were 24 men with a mean age of 31 years, who had suffered for at least six months with a problem of erectile dysfunction that made intromission impossible. An initial screening had excluded from the study those patients whose dysfunction was due to organic disturbance, sexual deviation, endogenous depression, or partner discord.

After matching on certain characteristics, including the primary or secondary nature of their dysfunction, the subjects were allocated to one of three equal sized groups. One of these received 14 sessions of systematic desensitization, and was also instructed initially not to attempt intercourse, on the assumption that it would be possible to lift this ban as treatment progressed. However, only 2 of the 8 patients in this group improved sufficiently for this to be done. A routine therapy group was seen by psychiatrists on four occasions at intervals of 3 to 5 weeks, and was given the standardized advice and medication that constituted the routine treatment of erectile dysfunction in private medical practice. The subjects in the third group were placed on a waiting list for treatment for an average of 16 weeks, so that they constituted a control for the two treatment programmes.

A range of behavioural, subjective, and physiological assessment measures was administered twice before, once during, and once at the end of the treatment or waiting list period. No follow up is reported.

The behavioural measure consisted of a semi-structured interview during which the quality and quantity of certain aspects of the patient's sexual behaviour were ascertained, and subsequently rated by the interviewer, as well as by two independent psychiatrists from a tape of the interview. No clear differences appeared between the three groups on this measure of outcome.

As a subjective measure the patients were asked to rate 32 anxiety related adjectives according to how well they would describe their feelings in two standardized situations that the patients imagined. One of these situations involved the patient having intercourse with his own partner, and the other involved him in an invitation to have intercourse with an attractive woman whom he has just met at a party. At the end of the treatment or waiting list periods, this latter imagined situation evoked significantly less reported anxiety in the desensitization patients compared to those in the other two groups.

Plethysmographic recordings of erections were obtained from only 10 of the 24 subjects, while they imagined the two standardized situations described above. No clear results were obtained on this physiological measure of outcome.

Finally, the patients were rated clinically at the end of the study period. They were rated as 'cured' if erection was maintained for at least one minute after intromission with intravaginal ejaculation before loss of erection; and as 'improved' if erection was maintained for one minute after intromission, with or without ejaculation, the point being that intromission was then possible whereas it was not possible at the commencement of the study. The numbers in the desensitization group who were considered to be cured, improved or not improved, were 2, 1, and 5 respectively. The corresponding figures for the routine therapy group were identical to those for the desensitization group. In the waiting list group, the criterion for a cure was achieved by 1 patient, and the remaining 7 were unimproved.

Thus, the only evidence of a superior outcome for desensitization in this study is on the subjective measure of experienced anxiety in an imagined situation, and the investigators conclude that this form of treatment used alone is of very limited effectiveness with cases of erectile dysfunction. They attribute this to the fact that desensitization was deployed in their study to reduce sexual anxiety, whereas many other factors contributed to the patients' erectile difficulties, including unrealistic sexual standards, a limited range of sexual behaviour, negative sexual attitudes, and partner discord.

Consequently after the study was ended, those patients who had not improved during it were given further treatment using the Masters and Johnson approach. The outcome of this is not reported in detail, but at the time the paper was written there were 12 patients who had been treated in this way, of whom 8 are cured or improved according to the criteria given above, 3 patients did not improve, and 1 relapsed shortly after therapy ended. The authors say that they are impressed by the apparent superiority of these results over those obtained with desensitization, but they cannot say to what extent these results should be attributed to the Masters and Johnson approach specifically because of the uncontrolled nature of the data.

Auerbach and Kilmann (1977)

The aim of this American study was to evaluate the efficacy of systematic desensitization when administered on a group basis, in the treatment of erectile dysfunction. The subjects in the desensitization group progressed through a composite hierarchy of anxiety-evoking situations in imagination while relaxed. Another group engaged in relaxation training only, and this was conceived as constituting an attention—placebo control condition. Any subjects who did not improve sufficiently to their own satisfaction during the course of the relaxation group, were given desensitization treatment after the study was completed. Both groups were conducted by a senior male doctoral student in clinical psychology, and each met three times a week for five weeks, a total of 15 sessions. For the first one and a half weeks of treatment they were asked not to attempt intercourse, after which this ban was lifted.

The 24 subjects were recruited by means of advertisement, questionnaires, and referrals, from the university and surrounding area, and they represented a middle to upper-middle class population. They were screened to ensure that they were unable to achieve and/or maintain full intromission on at least 15% of their coital encounters, and this difficulty was of a secondary nature in all cases, although this was not a planned feature of the study. After matching on a number of factors, the subjects were allocated to one of two equal sized groups. At an early stage of treatment there were four drop outs from each group, leaving eight subjects in each who completed treatment.

The outcome for these subjects was assessed in several ways. The success/experience ratio utilized by Obler (1973) and described in the previous chapter, was ascertained from the subjects and their partners during the pre-treatment, post-treatment and three month follow up assessments. On this measure the desensitization group achieved a significantly better outcome than the relaxation group at the termination of treatment. The pre- and post-treatment ratios were 35/123 (28.45%) and 57/83 (68.67%) for the desensitization group, and 43/136 (31.62%) and 27/78 (34.62%) for the relaxation group. Thus, the desensitization group had increased its ratio of successes by over 40%, and this improvement was maintained during the three month follow up period. A direct comparison could not be made between the two groups at follow up because a number of subjects in the relaxation group had been crossed over to de-sensitization treatment during that period.

Two inventories were developed by the investigators in order to assess the non-sexual and sexual relationships of the subjects and their partners. On the non-sexual inventory they were asked to rate their satisfaction with areas such as communication, decision-making, and non-sexual displays of affection. The sexual relationship inventory elicited similar ratings in respect of specific aspects of sexual functioning such as foreplay, intercourse, frequency of sex, and variety of sexual experience. All the subjects completed both inventories in respect of the pre- and post-treatment and follow up periods. Their partners were also asked to provide this information but only 4 of the 8 partners in each group complied with this request, so that their data is not adequate. As far as the subjects' ratings are concerned, on both inventories there was a significant difference towards greater satisfaction in favour of the desensitization group.

Thus, the outcome for this group was superior on all measures, including the inventory of the non-sexual relationship between the partners, and there is evidence that this improvement was maintained during the three month follow up period. Some caution is indicated concerning the 68.67% success/experience ratio achieved by the desensitization group at the end of treatment, for a failure of erection on something like a third of coital encounters could still be judged to be a significant problem by some patients and their partners, and it may serve to maintain performance anxiety so that the risk of relapse is enhanced. In short, the statistically significant superiority of systematic desensitization on this measure of outcome, does not obviate the possibility of a clinically significant residual problem.

As both the desensitization and relaxation groups participated in the same assessment procedures, were given equivalent amounts of therapeutic time and similar prognostic expectancies, and were trained in relaxation, it seems likely that the additional imaginal exposure to the hierarchy items was a crucial ingredient in the achievement of a better outcome from desensitization treatment.

Conclusions

Because of the differences in the outcome criteria and assessment methods used in the studies reviewed, it is not possible to make valid direct comparisons of outcome. There is reasonable accordance between the post-treatment success rates achieved by Masters and Johnson, of approximately 59% for primary cases and 74% for secondary cases, and the cured/improved figure of 67% reported by Ansari for a modified Masters and Johnson approach. A similar 66% cured/improved rate is reported by Kockott et al. in respect of those patients who were crossed over to Masters and Johnson treatment after failing to improve during desensitization. However, whereas the success achieved by Masters and Johnson was generally maintained over a five year follow up period, the Ansari figure dropped to 33% during an eight month follow up, and there is no obvious explanation for this discrepancy.

The outcome of the modified Masters and Johnson approach was not found to be significantly different from those of chemotherapy or a no-treatment control condition in the Ansari study, and this investigator attributes individual differences in outcome to patient characteristics such as the nature of the onset of their dysfunction, an insidious onset without discernible cause having a worse prognosis. Similarly, Masters and Johnson report a poorer outcome for primary cases of erectile dysfunction compared to those of a secondary nature.

Turning to the two studies of systematic desensitization, in the first of these conducted by Kockott et al., only one significant difference on the outcome measures used was found between the outcome of this form of treatment and those of routine medical treatment or a waiting list control condition. The investigators conclude that the use of systematic desensitization alone is too narrow an approach to the complex problem of erectile dysfunction, and this view would accord with the advocacy of more comprehensive treatment programmes in this book.

In the second study of systematic desensitization by Auerbach and Kilmann, this treatment was administered on a group basis, and it achieved a significantly better outcome compared to the attention–placebo control condition involving relaxation training. The comparison of these two treatments suggests that exposure to the anxiety hierarchy is a crucial ingredient contributing to the superior outcome of desensitization.

It is not clear why Auerbach and Kilmann were able to achieve better results than Kockott et al., although there are differences between their studies, such as the inclusion of primary cases among those treated by Kockott et al. and their absence from the Auerbach and Kilmann groups; the administration of treatment on an individual or group basis respectively; and the variation in outcome criteria and assessment methods across the two studies.

PREMATURE EJACULATION

Masters and Johnson (1970)

These investigators consider a man to be suffering from premature ejaculation if he cannot control his ejaculation for a sufficient length of time during vaginal containment to satisfy his partner on at least 50% of occasions, always providing that she is not inorgastic for reasons other than the man's rapid ejaculation.

Among the 186 men meeting this definition, who were treated by Masters and Johnson, there were 4 (2.2%) who were initial failures and 1 who relapsed during the five year follow up period, yielding an overall failure rate of 2.7%.

Yulis (1976)

This investigator also used the Masters and Johnson programme for premature ejaculation, but in appropriate cases he also provided assertive training for heterosocial situations. The clients were all treated with their partner, and the couples were seen by a dual sex therapy team, on a three times a week basis, for up to 18 sessions.

The 37 clients were either self referred or referred by a psychiatrist or psychologist. Their mean age was 26.6 years and the mean duration of the premature ejaculation was 8.4 years. The group was predominantly middle or upper class, and well educated.

The outcome of the study is reported in terms of the proportion of clients who achieved control of ejaculation during at least 80% of their sexual encounters. This information was obtained from the clients themselves, and in the majority of cases it was substantiated by their partner. At six months follow up, the criterion was achieved by 33 (89%) of the clients.

A particularly interesting feature of this study is that information was gathered about 'the generalization of therapeutic gains from sexual encounters with the treatment partner to those with non-treatment partners. Among the 37 clients, there were 23 who reported encounters with a non-treatment partner, and 22 of these had difficulty in exercising adequate ejaculatory control during their initial experience with such a partner. However, 14 subsequently achieved adequate control, while 9 failed to do so. A statistically significant association was found between participation in the assertion training component of the programme and successful generalization of therapeutic gains.

This investigation has a number of methodological limitations, including a lack of pre-treatment data on ejaculatory control, heavy reliance on client self-reports in assessing both outcome at follow up and generalization to non-treatment partners, and an uncontrolled design that does not permit the distinction of the contributions to outcome either of the total treatment package or of any of its various components.

Lowe and Mikulas (1975)

The aim of this study was to ascertain the outcome of a Masters and Johnson approach in the treatment of premature ejaculation when this is presented largely in written form.

Ten couples were selected as subjects on the criteria (a) that the man ejaculated before, during, or within three minutes of, intromission, (b) that his partner was willing to participate in treatment, and (c) that serious discord did not exist between them. All subjects were volunteers, 4 having been referred, and 6 having responded to a newspaper advertisement. Their education levels were fairly high.

Five of the couples were allocated to an immediate treatment group and asked to work their way through an 80 page manual. This included an orientation to the problem of premature ejaculation and the proposed treatment, instructions for the sexual assignments, quizzes for the subjects to test their comprehension of these instructions before implementing them, and further instructions on how to proceed through the assignments in the light of the progress being made.

The remaining five couples were placed on a waiting list for treatment, and thus constituted a control group. As the average time taken to complete the manual was three weeks, after an equivalent period had elapsed the waiting list couples were also asked to work through the manual and thus become a second treatment group.

All couples, including those on the waiting list, were telephoned twice a week to monitor and encourage their participation and progress. They could also contact their therapist whenever they encountered problems.

Before and after treatment, the male subjects were asked to estimate the length of time between the onset of sexual stimulation and the completion of the ejaculatory reflex in their own sexual functioning. The pre-treatment means for the original treatment and control groups were 1.8 and 1.4 minutes respectively, and their post-treatment means were 39.0 and 1.4 minutes. Thus, the control group had not increased their ejaculatory control, while the treatment group had done so to a statistically significant degree. When the control group became the second treatment group, it also significantly increased its mean ejaculatory control from 1.4 to 20.0 minutes.

The investigators point out the heavy reliance in their study on the subjects' estimates of the duration of ejaculatory control, and the uncertain accuracy and reliability of these. Moreover, even though this control did increase significantly statistically, there might still be a residual problem of premature ejaculation at a clinically significant level. For example, a man may no longer ejaculate at the onset of sexual stimulation, but he might still do so whenever intromission is attempted or shortly afterwards, and this may still be judged inadequate by the couple concerned. It is not suggested that this happened among the subjects in the Lowe and Mikulas study, but there is nothing in their report to refute the possibility. Subject to these limitations their study does suggest that the written presentation of the Masters and Johnson programme, with some therapist support, may be quite an effective and efficient way of treating premature ejaculation in certain selected groups of clients. In this respect, it should be remembered that the subjects in this study were volunteers and presumably well motivated, that partners were available and willing to participate in treatment, and that serious discord did not exist between them.

Zeiss *et al.* (1978)

In this study the male clients were seen on a group basis but they were expected to convey the information gained in the group to their partner, who participated in the sexual assignments.

The subjects were six consecutive referrals for premature ejaculation. Their mean age was 28.2 years, and their relationships had existed for a mean duration of eight years and were assessed as being of a positive nature.

Intake interviews were held with each couple for assessment purposes, to explain the programme, and to obtain the co-operation of the female partner.

The six men were then divided into groups of equal size, each of which met with two male therapists for six sessions at weekly intervals. Between these sessions, the therapists telephoned the clients to monitor progress and to maintain contact with the female partner. Follow up sessions were conducted after eight weeks for the first group, and after 4 and 8 weeks for the second group. The post-treatment assessments were undertaken just before the last follow-up session.

Basically, a Masters and Johnson approach was used in treatment, as it included a ban on intercourse, sensate focus, and the squeeze technique. However, the stop-start technique was also taught, and either this or the squeeze was used initially during male masturbation, then in mutual manual stimulation, and finally in intercourse. Additionally, talking assignments were prescribed to promote sharing of intimate feelings.

Three main measures were used to assess outcome in the study (a) the latency between intromission and ejaculation as recorded on a stop watch by the couple (b) their subjective estimates of this latency, and (c) their reports of the frequency of premature ejaculation during sexual activity.

The recorded and estimated ejaculatory latencies increased after treatment in 4 of the 6 couples, but a further eight month follow up revealed that 1 of these had relapsed.

The frequency of premature ejaculation was reported to have decreased after treatment by 4 couples, but it still occurred on a relatively high proportion of occasions in 3 of these, the post-treatment rates being 50%, 10%, 50–75%, and 50–75% respectively.

The authors suggest that these high reported rates may reflect the couples' somewhat unrealistic expectations of an adequate ejaculatory latency, for the actual timed post-treatment latencies were not unduly low in these 4 couples, ranging from 3 minutes 41 seconds to 13 minutes 6 seconds. However, the limited success of their approach is recognized by the investigators, who recommend that clinicians should be prepared to offer the standard Masters and Johnson programme to individual couples who are unable to succeed in group treatment. They cite one of their own couples who was unable to collaborate in the sexual assignments when the husband was attending a group, but were subsequently successfully treated in an individual programme that was specifically tailored to their needs. Finally, the whole of this discussion is fraught with the problem of the unknown validity and reliability of the latency and frequency measures of outcome.

Conclusions

Masters and Johnson consider that premature ejaculation is the easiest of the male sexual dysfunctions to treat effectively, and their success rate of 97.3% at the end of a five year follow up period certainly supports this statement. It is also in accordance with the 89% success rate reported by Yulis for a similar treatment approach, although the improvement in ejaculatory control did not always generalized to sexual activity with partners who had not been involved in treatment. Some specific components may need to be included in treatment programmes to facilitate such generalization if it is desired, and it is interesting that assertive training was associated with successful generalization in the Yulis study.

Both the Lowe and Mikulas and the Zeiss et al. studies, use changes in the latency of ejaculation to assess outcome, and the lack of data on the validity and reliability of this measure is noted above, although clearly there are both ethical and methodological difficulties involved in correcting these deficiencies. Subject to these and other limitations discussed above, the study by Low and Mikulas does indicate that with selected couples, a Masters and Johnson approach can be effective when it is presented largely in written form but with some direct therapist support, and the study by Zeiss et al. achieved more limited success when an extended Masters and Johnson approach has provided on a male-only group basis. At present, no systematic evidence is available about any patient characteristics that may influence outcome, or on the crucial ingredients of the Masters and Johnson package for the treatment of premature ejaculation.

RETARDED OR ABSENT EJACULATION

Masters and Johnson (1970)

Only 17 patients with this dysfunction were treated by these authors, who report identical initial and overall failure rates of 3 (17.6%) for this series.

Geboes et al. (1975b)

A larger series of 72 patients is reported by Geboes et al. from their Belgian clinic. None of these patients had ever ejaculated during masturbation or intercourse, but nocturnal emissions had occurred in all cases, and a possible organic basis for the dysfunction was found in only 4 patients. The average age in the series was 28 years, with a range of 17 to 68 years, and it was drawn from all social and educational levels.

Four types of treatment were offered for retarded or absent ejaculation in the clinic (a) sexual education to teach patients how to masturbate, (b) psychotherapy, (c) high doses of hormones, and (d) the use of an electrovibrator. The report does not state that the patients were allocated randomly to these different treatments, and only small numbers were given one of the first three listed.

The results are stated simply in terms of the proportions of patients who achieved 'positive results', and the criteria for this are unspecified. Such results were achieved by all 4 (100%) patients who were given sexual education, by 4 (57%) out of the 7 given psychotherapy, by 3 (50%) of the 6 to whom hormones were administered, and by 41 (75%) of the 55 who used a vibrator.

Methodologically this study is extremely weak, but it does report the largest series to date, and is suggestive of the efficacy of a vibrator in the treatment of retarded or absent ejaculation.

Schellen (1968)

Some further support for this conclusion is provided by Schellen's report on the treatment of 21 patients from a clinic in the Netherlands. None of them could ejaculate during either masturbation or intercourse, but the occurrence of nocturnal emissions was established in most cases. No organic basis was found for the dysfunction in any of these patients. They ranged in age from 25 to 47 years, and all had experienced previous unsuccessful treatment attempts, including the prescription of hormones or sedatives, urological procedures, and psychotherapy.

The use of a vibrator is reported to have produced ejaculation in 17 (81%) of the 21 patients, although how many became able to ejaculate during intercourse is not altogether clear. Schellen states that 4 were able to do so shortly after achieving ejaculation with a vibrator, but he also says that 12 of the wives became pregnant, and there is no indication that this was by means of artificial insemination.

Conclusions

The lack of control and rigour in the studies reviewed prevent any firm conclusions being drawn from them. The most that can be said is that they do provide some preliminary indication of quite high rates of success in achieving ejaculation both from the Masters and Johnson programme, and the use of a vibrator. However, the proportion of patients who became able to ejaculate intravaginally remains uncertain.

This concludes the review of studies on the outcome of programmes with a main focus on male sexual dysfunctions, and we turn now to those that are primarily concerned with female dysfunctions, before drawing some general conclusions on the outcome of treatment at the end of this part of the book.

16

Programmes for Female Dysfunctions

With the exception of some uncontrolled case reports, no information is available on the outcome of behavioural approaches to the treatment of inadequate interest, inadequate pleasure, or dyspareunia in female clients, nor is such evidence available in respect of vasocongestive dysfunction as it is defined in Chapter 7, although many women with this problem are among those included in reports on the treatment of orgastic dysfunction. Thus, it is this last condition and that of vaginismus that are considered in this chapter.

VAGINISMUS

Masters and Johnson (1970) treated 29 women with this problem and all of them became able to engage in intercourse without relapse over a five-year period.

A similar high success rate is reported by Dawkins and Taylor (1961) using either digital and/or artificial vaginal dilatation. None of the 44 patients had been able to consummate their marriage because of vaginismus, but 40 (91%) became able to engage in intercourse after treatment.

Fuchs et al. (1973) investigated two methods of treatment, both involving hypnosis. The first of these was imaginal desensitization under hypnosis, and 6 (66%) of the 9 women treated in this way are reported as 'cured'. The second method involved in vivo desensitization, in that graded glass dilators were inserted while the patient was hypnotized, and this was accompanied by a 'cure' in 31 (91%) of the 34 women treated in this way. All the patients who were successfully treated by either method maintained their improvement over follow up periods ranging from 1 to 5 years.

These three reports can only be regarded as preliminary communications, but they do indicate relatively high success rates in the treatment of vaginismus, as well as the probably important contribution of vaginal dilatation to these results.

ORGASTIC DYSFUNCTION

Masters and Johnson (1970)

These authors define primary orgastic dysfunction as an inability to attain orgasm by any physical means throughout the entire lifespan, although orgasm may have occurred during dreams. They treated 193 women with this problem and report an initial failure rate of 32 (16.6%), to which 2 relapses were added during the five year follow up period, yielding overall failure rate of 34 (17.6%).

Patients suffering from situational orgastic dysfunction have experienced at least one orgasm produced by any form of physical stimulation, and Masters and Johnson break this category down further into masturbatory, coital, and random orgastic-inadequacy. Masturbatory orgastic-inadequacy occurs when a woman can reach orgasm during intercourse but not by any other physical means. Coital orgastic-inadequacy refers to the opposite situation of women who cannot reach orgasm during intercourse but are able to do so in response to other forms of physical stimulation. Patients suffering from random orgastic-inadequacy have reached orgasm by coital and by other means on at least one occasion in each case, but they are currently rarely orgastic and usually have a very low level of sexual interest.

The initial and overall failure rates for the 149 situationally inorgastic women treated by Masters and Johnson are 34 (22.8%) and 37 (24.8%). Only initial failure rates are reported for the sub-categories, and these are 1/11 (9.1%) for masturbatory orgastic-inadequacy, 21/106 (19.8%) for coital orgastic-inadequacy, and 12/32 (37.5%) for random orgastic-inadequacy. Thus, as Masters and Johnson observe, it is the last group that has proved a stumbling block in their treatment for orgastic dysfunction, and it contributes substantially to the higher failure rates for situational compared to primary orgastic dysfunction.

Munjack et al. (1976)

In this investigation the outcome of individually tailored behavioural programmes for inorgastic women is compared to that of a waiting list control group.

The mean age of the 22 subjects was 26 years, and they had been married for an average of 6.6 years. All were currently living with their husbands, and cases of serious discord were excluded from the sample as far as possible. The women were white, middle to upper class, and non-psychotic. Following the definitions proposed by Masters and Johnson, 12 were primarily inorgastic, and 10 were situationally inorgastic, the mean symptom duration of the latter group being 4.2 years. In the previous year none of the patients had reached orgasm by any means with any partner, although how many of the situationally orgastic had done so by masturbation is not reported.

After a very full assessment of the patients and their partners by two independent evaluations, including the requirement of a recent gynaecological examination, the couples were randomly assigned either to an immediate treatment group, or to a waiting list control group which was promised treatment in not more than 10 weeks.

A behavioural assessment was undertaken for each couple in the immediate treatment group and an individually tailored treatment programme was formulated. The components of these programmes included the provision of information and attitude modification in interviews; specific procedures such as systematic desensitization and social skills training; and sexual assignments, although it is noteworthy that masturbation training was only occasionally employed.

These programmes were conducted by three therapists, a male psychiatrist, a male psychologist, and a female psychologist, each of whom worked individually. They saw the patients weekly for an average of 22 sessions, and the partner concerned attended on only about 25% of these occasions.

After the immediate treatment group had completed 20 weekly sessions, and the control group had been on a waiting list for 10 weeks, each was reassessed; and this was repeated at the end of an average follow up period of nine months. These assessments were conducted with the patients and their partners by the two independent evaluators, who were unaware of the groups to which the patients had been allocated.

A wide range of measures was used to assess the outcome in the two groups only some of which are discussed here. One criterion was the subject's report on the achievement of orgasm during intercourse, whether or not this was accompanied by direct clitoral stimulation. In this respect, a statistically significant pre-post-treatment improvement occurred in the treatment group, whereas there was no change in the control group. Approximately one-third of the treatment group reached the criterion at the post-treatment assessment, and this improvement was maintained during the follow up period.

A similar significant improvement occurred in the ratings of sexual satisfaction completed by the treatment subjects, but not in those by the controls. At the initial assessment, only one-sixth of the subjects in both groups expressed themselves as being satisfied in at least 50% of their sexual relations, while two-thirds of the treated subjects reached this criterion at the post-treatment assessment and this improvement was maintained on follow up.

The subjects were also asked to rate their feelings towards a variety of sexually stimulating situations and activities. Compared to the control group, the treatment subjects reported a greater number of statistically significant pre-post-treatment changes in a favourable direction.

The outcome of treatment differed between the primarily inorgastic and situationally inorgastic patients. At the post-treatment assessment, the criterion of orgasm on 50% of sexual relations was achieved by 22% of the primary patients and by 40% of the situational patients. At follow up the proportion of the latter who reached the criterion had risen to 60%, while the proportion of the primary patients who did so had declined to zero.

Similarly, in the initial assessment, 18% of the primary and 20% of the situational patients rated themselves as being satisfied in at least 50% of their sexual relations. At the end of treatment, the equivalent proportions were 80% for the primarily inorgastic and 70% for the situationally inorgastic, but at follow up the proportion in the primary group had dropped to 40%, while it had increased to 100% in the situational group.

The inferior outcome for the primarily inorgastic patients is somewhat unusual in the literature, and the authors suggest two possible reasons for it. One of these is the small size of the sample, and the other is an excess of partner discord in the primary group that was not revealed in the initial assessment. Such discord could not be dealt with adequately in a programme focused upon the sexual dysfunction and of limited duration, especially when the wives were seen alone in 75% of the sessions. Another possible reason for the atypical findings, is the only occasional employment of masturbatory training which is particularly efficacious in the treatment of primary orgastic dysfunction.

Munjack *et al.* raise the point that the treatment group were re-assessed after 20 weeks, while this was done after 10 weeks for the control group. However, they cite some evidence to suggest that only a very small proportion of inorgastic women would be expected to become orgastic without treatment during a 12 week period, so that any improvement in the treated subjects over the last 12 weeks of their treatment is likely to be due to the therapeutic experience rather than spontaneous remission.

The results of this controlled and fairly rigorous study do support the efficacy of individually tailored programmes for orgastic dysfunction; and we see below that an even better outcome might have been achieved if more use had been made of masturbatory training, although this is of course quite speculative.

Kohlenberg (1974)

In this study, masturbatory training was utilized in the treatment of three primarily inorgastic women. They and their husbands had been participating in a modified Masters and Johnson programme, but when there was no improvement after 8, 12, and 24 weeks of treatment respectively, the couples were switched to a masturbation programme very similar to that proposed by Lo Piccolo and Lobitz (1972a) and described in Chapter 9. Additionally, the husbands followed a parallel masturbation programme, and the couples were instructed to engage in at least three joint sexual encounters a week, which could comprise general pleasuring, genital pleasuring or intercourse at their own discretion and mutual agreement. The couples met with the therapists usually at weekly intervals, in one case with a dual sex team and in the other two cases with a male therapist working on an individual basis.

Before the commencement of the masturbation programmes, none of the women had experienced orgasm either by self-stimulation or during intercourse. All three reported achieving orgasm by self-stimulation after 3, 4, and 6 weeks respectively in the masturbation programme. Several weeks later, they all reached orgasm during intercourse, and monthly follow ups for at least six months after treatment ended revealed that this continued to occur in at least 50% of coital experiences. Comparable improvement is reported in the women's ratings of their own arousal during self-stimulation and sexual encounters.

This is an early uncontrolled study, but the successful outcome after the subjects' previous lack of progress in a modified Masters and Johnson programme is suggestive of the efficacy of masturbatory assignments in the treatment of primary orgastic dysfunction. However, the author emphasizes that these assignments were only one component in a more comprehensive programme, and he considers therapeutic interviews to be essential.

McGovern et al., (1975)

In this paper, the outcome of a treatment programme that included masturbatory assignments is reported for primarily and situationally inorgastic women respectively, and some possible explanations are advanced for the differential responsiveness of the two categories to this form of therapy.

Gynaecological examination revealed no organic basis for the dysfunctions of the six subjects in each category, and the mean ages and duration of marriage were 27.7 and 4.83 years for the primary group, and 26.6 and 4.67 years for the situational group. All patients had completed the Lo Piccolo and Lobitz (1972a) programme which included the masturbatory assignments described in Chapter 9, and the outcome of this is reported in terms of orgastic attainment, heterosexual satisfaction, and general marital adjustment.

Before treatment, none of the primarily inorgastic patients had ever experienced orgasm by any physical means. At termination, all 6 of them were able to do so during intercourse on between 25% and 75% of occasions. Additionally, 5 (83%) could reach orgasm by self-stimulation and 4 (66%) were able to do so when receiving manual stimulation of the genitals from the partner.

In contrast, before treatment all 6 of the situationally inorgastic patients could reach orgasm very frequently by self-stimulation, 3 (50%) could do so by partner stimulation, and 2 (33%) were able to climax during intercourse on 50% of occasions. After treatment, the numbers who could attain orgasm during self-stimulation, partner stimulation, or intercourse, remained the same, but the frequency of orgasm during intercourse had declined in 1 patient from 50% to 25% of occasions.

Thus, the programme was followed by greater improvement in the primary compared to the situational patients, although it is important to remember that more of the latter could already achieve orgasm in various sexual activities, so that they had less scope for improvement. Nevertheless, at the termination of treatment, all 6 primary patients were able to attain orgasm during intercourse whereas none had been able to do so before, while the number of situational patients who reached this criterion remained unchanged from the pre-treatment level of 2 (33%) out of 6.

The degree of sexual satisfaction in each couple's relationship was assessed on the Sexual Interaction Inventory (Lo Piccolo and Steger, 1974) which is discussed in Chapter 13. No significant differences were found between the primary and situational groups on this instrument either before or after treatment, although both groups achieved significant pre-post-treatment improvements on several scales. Thus, the investigators conclude that the programme did improve the sexual compatibility of the situationally inorgastic patients and their partners, although it did not increase the attainment of orgasm by these patients.

The general relationship between the partners was assessed by means of the Locke–Wallace Marital Adjustment Test (Locke and Wallace, 1959), and the results indicate that before treatment, the situationally inorgastic women and their partners were more dissatisfied in this respect than the primarily inorgastic women and their partners. After treatment, both the situationally dysfunctional couples, and the primarily inorgastic women, had achieved a significant degree of improvement in their general relationships. However, a similar improvement did not occur among the partners of the primarily inorgastic women, and the investigators suggest that this could have been due to the fact that the programme had been strongly focused on the female partner in the primarily dysfunctional couples.

Thus, as far as the situationally inorgastic women are concerned, their sexual satisfaction and general marital relationships improved following therapy, but their attainment of orgasm did not. The investigators suggest two possible reasons for this outcome. One of these refers to the finding of more general marital dissatisfaction among the situationally dysfunctional compared to the primarily dysfunctional couples at the commencement of treatment. This necessitated a larger proportion of therapeutic time in the 15 session programme being devoted to the resolution of non-sexual marital problems, with correspondingly less being available for work focused specifically upon the attainment of orgasm. Consequently, the authors recommend that situationally dysfunctional couples with a serious degree of partner discord either receive marital therapy before entering a programme aimed directly at the achievement of orgasm, or that the latter be sufficiently lengthy to allow both problem areas to be dealt with satisfactorily.

The second possible reason advance for the absence of orgastic improvement among the situationally dysfunctional women, is that the majority of them had a long history of masturbating to orgasm in a very constrained way, and this tight stimulus control had to be loosened during treatment before the attainment of orgasm could be generalized to intercourse. Only the situationally inorgastic women were faced with this task of 'unlearning' a restricted response pattern, for the primarily inorgastic women had never acquired such a response, and this difference might have contributed to the poorer outcome in the former group. The investigators suggest some techniques for breaking the excessively narrow stimulus control of orgasm in some situationally inorgastic women, and the successful outcome of a case in which one of these techniques was applied together with marital therapy is reported in a further paper from the same group of investigators (Snyder et al., 1975).

Wallace and Barbach (1974)

These authors report the outcome of a programme of group treatment for primarily inorgastic women, which emphasized self-stimulation assignments.

The 17 subjects were from an unselected series of women seeking treatment for this problem, and represented a wide variety of educational and occupational backgrounds. Their mean age was 27 years, with a range from 19 to 34 years. Fourteen of them were married or in a stable partnership.

The treatment programme followed is very fully described by Barbach (1974, 1975), and it centred around a modified version of the Lo Piccolo and Lobitz (1972a) masturbatory assignments described in Chapter 9. These were prescribed, monitored and discussed in a series of group meetings comprising six clients and two co-counsellors, which took place twice a week for five weeks. Male partners were not included in the meetings, although they did participate in some of the sexual assignments, and intercourse was not restricted at any time during the programme.

Only some of the wide range of outcome measures used are discussed here. All 17 women could achieve orgasm by masturbation at the end of five weeks treatment, and this improvement was maintained at an 8 month follow up. Moreover, at that time, over 87% of the women were orgastic in 'partner-related activities', and for 68% of them this occurred in 75% of occasions. The nature of the partner-related activities is not specified in the paper, but significant pre-post-treatment improvements occurred in the attainment of orgasm both during partner stimulation and intercourse. Similar significant improvement are reported in client ratings of their enjoyment of intercourse and their sexual satisfaction.

The uncontrolled nature of this study precludes determination of the extent to which the outcome is properly attributable to the treatment programme, and more particularly to certain of its ingredients. Nevertheless, further support is provided for the efficacy of programmes with a strong emphasis on self-stimulation assignment in the treatment of primary orgastic dysfunction, and the feasibility of delivering these programmes in a group context is demonstrated. Some additional evidence is available in another paper by Barbach (1974) who reports that among the first 83 women who participated in groups, there were 91.6% who could reach orgasm by masturbation at the end of five weeks treatment, but no corresponding figure is given for partner-related activities.

Conclusions

Again because of variation in outcome criteria and assessment methods it is impossible to make valid direct comparisons across studies. However if one takes the proportion of clients who were able to attain orgasm during intercourse at the latest point of assessment in each study, then the appropriate figures for those suffering from primary orgastic dysfunction are probably as follows:

Masters and Johnson	92.4%
Munjack et al.	0.0%
Kohlenberg	100.0%
McGovern et al.	100.0%
Wallace and Barbach	87.0%

Thus, both the Masters and Johnson programme that did not include masturbatory assignments, and the last three studies which emphasized such assignments as part of the Lo Piccolo and Lobitz (1972a) programme, all achieved similar high rates of success on this particular criterion. The odd man out is the study of individually tailored behavioural programmes by Munjack et al. which has a markedly discrepant success rate. The investigators attribute this to an excess of general marital discord among the primary patients and their partners, but another possible reason is the only occasional use of masturbatory assignments with these patients. However, a similar gap in the Masters and Johnson programme was not accompanied by a low success rate, so it may be that this is attributable to the marital discord as suggested by the investigators and discussed further below.

Turning now to the outcome for the situationally inorgastic patients on the same criterion, the appropriate figures appear to be as follows:

Masters and Johnson	75.2%
Munjack et al.	60.0%
McGovern et al.	33.0%

Thus, these success rates are lower than those for the primarily inorgastic patients in the studies by Masters and Johnson and McGovern et al, and higher in that by Munjack et al. We see above that a substantial contribution to the lower figure in the Masters and Johnson study is made by the random orgasmic-dysfunction group, in which low sexual interest is a common feature. In the study by McGovern et al., the lower figure is attributed mainly to the greater prevalence of marital discord among the situationally inorgastic compared to the primarily inorgastic patients. In the study by Munjack et al., such discord was commoner among the primary than the situational patients, and it was advanced as a major reason for the poorer outcome in the former group. Thus, it may be that serious discord between the partners impedes successful treatment in the type of programme reported, whether the discord occurs in primarily or situationally dysfunctional couples, although it may be more prevalent among the latter.

The only study among those reviewed that included a no-treatment control group is that by Munjack et al., in which a superior outcome is reported for the individually tailored behavioural programmes compared to the control condition. The contribution of treatment to outcome cannot be determined in the remaining four studies, and in none of five reviewed is it possible to distinguish the influence on outcome of particular components in the treatment packages.

The differences in outcome between the primary and situational patients in the studies by Masters and Johnson, Munjack *et al.* and McGovern *et al.* do indicate a patient variable of some prognostic importance, and other such variables may be low sexual interest as exhibited among the randomly orgasmic dysfunctional patients in the Masters and Johnson study, and serious partner discord as discussed above.

Finally, the choice of orgasm during intercourse as the criterion for the comparison of outcome across studies in this section, is not meant to imply that it is the only appropriate criterion, or necessarily the best among those used. Clearly, a couple's degree of sexual satisfaction and general marital happiness, are also very important considerations in evaluating a treatment intervention, as is a woman's ability to reach orgasm by means of self-stimulation. However, the inclusion and definition of such other criteria varied so much across studies that comparison is more difficult than in the case of orgasm during intercourse. Not that the specification of even this criterion is identical across studies; for instance, it is not precisely specified by Masters and Johnson; it requires the attainment of orgasm on at least 50% of occasions, with or without direct clitoral stimulation, in the study by Munjack *et al.* both Kohlenberg and McGovern *et al.* refer simply to reaching orgasm during intercourse; and Wallace and Barbach use the term 'partner-related activities' without further specification. These differences need to be borne in mind throughout this section, as well as the variable periods after the completion of treatment that the latest assessment was made, varying from 6 months in the Kohlenberg study to 5 years in that by Masters and Johnson.

GENERAL CONCLUSIONS

In this concluding section, some points of a more general nature are made about the studies reviewed throughout this part of the book, in the light of the desirable standards for the evaluation of therapeutic interventions that are discussed at the beginning of Chapter 14.

Client variables

The reports on these studies generally include a reasonable description of the clients although not a great deal of progress has been made in identifying those characteristics that influence the outcome of treatment. The client variable that has received most attention is the nature of the presenting problem; and it seems clear that some dysfunctions such as premature ejaculation and vaginismus, have been more successfully treated than others such as primary erectile dysfunction. There is also some evidence to suggest that the primary or secondary nature of the problem may be of prognostic significance. For instance, the outcome for primary erectile dysfunction appears to be worse than for secondary erectile dysfunction, while that for primary orgastic dysfunction is generally better than for situational orgastic dysfunction. The possible relevance of marital discord in explaining the differential outcome between primary and situational orgastic dysfunction is discussed above, and mention is made of the contribution by the randomly inorgastic group, characterized by low sexual interest, to the poorer outcome among the situationally inorgastic patients treated by Masters and Johnson.

Despite this attention to the influence of certain problems on the outcome of treatment, there are others which have not yet been systematically investigated from this point of view, including inadequate interest, inadequate pleasure, and dyspareunia, in both sexes. Similarly, among the many other client variables that require further investigation in order to ascertain their possible influence on outcome are level of motivation, religious and moral beliefs, organic conditions, psychiatric syndromes, sexual variations, the availability of a regular partner, the general relationship between partners, and the existence of sexual dysfunction in both partners.

Treatment variables

Although descriptions of treatment conditions are provided in varying degrees of detail in the studies reviewed, very little information is available about the influence of these conditions on the outcome of treatment, and some of this information is contradictory.

In their report on the treatment of heterogeneous male and female dysfunctions, Mathews et al. found some evidence for a superior outcome from a combination of sexual assignments and therapeutic interviews in a modified Masters and Johnson programme, in comparison with the outcomes whene each of these components was delivered separately. Another finding in this study concerned the provision of treatment through a dual sex team or an individual therapist, the former having some slight superiority in the delivery of the modified Masters and Johnson programme.

In another study with clients suffering from heterogeneous male and female dysfunctions, Obler reported a superior outcome from an individually delivered desensitization package compared to psychodynamically oriented group therapy and a no-treatment control condition. This indicates that the specific behavioural components in the desensitization package produced beneficial effects over and above those arising either from the specific psychodynamic components in the group therapy, or from the non-specific and extra-therapeutic factors operating to some extent in all three groups.

Similarly, in the treatment of secondary erectile dysfunction, any effects of such non-specific and extra-therapeutic factors appear to have been exceeded by the specific components in the group desensitization programme reported by Auerbach and Kilmann. However, their findings may conflict with those of Kockott et al. who found no significant differences in outcome between individual desensitization, routine medical treatment, and a no-treatment control condition, although their clients included cases of primary as well as secondary erectile dysfunction. With a similar mixed group of cases, Ansari reported no significant differences in outcome between a modified Masters and

Johnson programme, a chemotherapeutic regime, and a no-treatment control condition.

Lastly, in the treatment of orgastic dysfunction, the study by Munjack *et al.* appears to demonstrate that individually tailored behavioural programmes added something to any beneficial effects accruing from the non-specific and extra-therapeutic factors operating in the no-treatment control condition as well as the treatment group.

This inadequate and somewhat confused state of knowledge concerning the influence of certain components of treatment on its outcome, clearly requires supplementation and clarification through further investigation. Equally obvious is the need for investigation into the influence of many other treatment variables, including the characteristics of the therapists, the nature of the treatment setting, and the timing of therapy.

In conducting such research it is important to ensure that the treatment conditions studied are representative of those pertaining in good clinical practice, otherwise the results of the investigation will not be generalizable from the research to the clinical setting. For instance, there is little point in evaluating the effectiveness of systematic desensitization as an isolated procedure if it is customarily used as only one component in a more comprehensive treatment programme, perhaps to reduce some specific anxiety reaction that is impeding therapeutic progress. Similarly, if the timing of treatment is standardized in order to control the temporal variables in a research study, then the results may not be generalizable to clinical practice where the intervals between sessions, their duration, and their number, are varied in accordance with the current needs of particular clients. In short, attention needs to be paid both to the internal validity of investigations, so that it is possible to distinguish the effects of various treatment variables, and to their external validity, so that the findings from a particular investigation can be properly generalized to other treatment situations (Campbell and Stanley, 1966).

Criteria of outcome

These criteria are stated with varying degrees of precision in the studies reviewed, ranging from poorly defined global classifications of outcome through to more exactly specified standards for the performance of certain sexual responses such as erection or orgasm. Many studies utilize more than one criterion, often including not only the capacity to perform certain sexual responses up to specified standards, but also the degrees of satisfaction experienced by clients and their partners in the sexual and non-sexual aspects of their relationships.

Both the more precise specification of outcome criteria, and the use of multiple criteria, are desirable features to be included and developed in future studies of outcome. It would also be advantageous if the same criteria with identical definitions were more widely adopted in such studies, in order to facilitate comparison between them. In formulating criteria, attention should be paid to their clinical significance, for as mentioned above, while a statistically significant improvement may occur in some aspect of sexual functioning, this may still leave a residual problem of considerable clinical significance because of the distress it continues to cause to the client and his or her partner.

Methods of data collection

A regrettable number of the methods of assessment used in the studies reviewed are lacking in information about their validity and reliability. Such psychometric data should be gathered and reported in future investigations, and this could be facilitated by use of some of the better instruments and techniques discussed in Chapter 13.

More widespread use of these and other methods in different studies, would also facilitate the comparison of outcomes, the difficulty of doing this at the present time having been noted several times in the earlier discussion.

The employment of a variety of methods in order to achieve a comprehensive and balanced assessment of outcome, is a valuable feature of some of the studies reviewed, which merits emulation and development in future investigations.

Similarly, these should extend the start that has been made in assessing any changes in the broader psychological functioning and life situations of clients that accompany their behavioural treatment for sexual dysfunction.

Design of investigations

Most of the studies reviewed do include pre- and post-treatment assessments with follow ups at varying intervals after the termination of treatment. However, a general prolongation of follow up periods with assessments at more frequent intervals would improve the quality of the outcome data that becomes available in future.

Much less satisfactory is the provision for suitable control over relevant variables in the designs of very many studies. This scarcity of adequately controlled investigations is a very significant impediment to the evaluation of outcome, for we see above that it is difficult or impossible to distinguish the influence of many client and treatment variables. To cite just one example, although Masters and Johnson achieved commendably high success rates with the largest series of sexually dysfunctional patients ever reported, we do not know how well these patients would have fared if they had received certain other forms of treatment or no systematic treatment at all. Nor do we know the extent to which the various components in the Masters and Johnson programme contributed to its outcome, and only slightly more information is available about some of the characteristics of the patients which influenced their response to treatment.

Clearly more controlled investigations are called for, and some of these might usefully employ the kind of single subject experimental designs advocated by Hersen and Barlow (1976). Although these designs have many advantages and have been used successfully in investigations of the outcome of treatment with a wide range of psychological problems, including sexual variations, they are relatively unexploited in the field of sexual dysfunction. It is not suggested that they completely replace group control designs, only that the considerable potential of single subject experimental designs be better recognized and utilized in this field.

Whatever designs may be selected, there can be no doubt about the necessity for further more rigorous and controlled investigation into the outcome of the behavioural treatment of sexual dysfunction. Only in this way can its efficacy be evaluated and improved, so that clients and their partners can be helped more effectively. Fortunately, we see in Chapter 1 that a commitment to the empirical investigation of outcome is a strong feature of the behavioural approach, so that it is reasonable to expect such progress to be made.

Appendix

Checklist of Topics For Assessment Interviews with Sexually Dysfunctional Clients and Partners

It is intended that therapists will select and sequence items from this checklist to suit individual clients and their partners, rather than using it in a rigid or chronological fashion.

DESCRIPTION OF PROBLEM(S)

1. Nature
2. Frequency
3. Timing
4. Surrounding circumstances (see also 8, 9, and 10 below)
5. Duration
6. Onset
7. Course

CONTEMPORARY INFLUENCES ON PROBLEM(S)

8. Situational antecedents
   e.g. (a) sexual stresses
   (b) deficient or inappropriate stimulation
   (c) relationship with partner
   (d) timing and setting of encounter
   (e) concomitant non-sexual stresses
9. Organismic variables
   (a) thought processes
   e.g. (i) cognitive avoidance
   (ii) cognitive monitoring
   (iii) deficient or false information
   (b) emotional reactions
   e.g. (i) anxiety
   (ii) guilt
   (iii) depression
   (iv) anger

        (c) organic states
           e.g. (i) aging
               (ii) illness
              (iii) surgery
              (iv) drugs

10. Situational consequences
     e.g. (a) partner's reactions
           (b) absence of sexual relationships, due to avoidance reactions

PERSONAL AND FAMILY BACKGROUNDS

11. Both partners
       (a) age
       (b) sex
       (c) marital status and history
       (d) occupation
       (e) education
       (f) ethnic background
       (g) religion and moral beliefs
       (h) leisure activities
       (i) friendship pattern
       (j) health (including *inter alia* venereal disease, infertility, pregnancies, abortions, menstruation, menopause, use of alcohol or illicit drugs, and psychiatric disorders).

12. Partner's parents
       (a) year of birth
       (b) year and cause of death
       (c) marital status and history
       (d) occupation
       (e) education
       (f) ethnic background
       (g) religion and moral beliefs
       (h) health
       (i) relationship between parents
       (j) relationships between each partner and (i) own parents (ii) parents-in-law

13. Partners' siblings
       (a) age
       (b) sex
       (c) marital status and history
       (d) occupation
       (e) education
       (f) health
       (g) relationship with parents
       (h) relationship with eath partner

14. Children
       (a) age
       (b) sex
       (c) education
       (d) occupation
       (e) health
       (f) relationship with eath partner

CHILDHOOD AND PUBERTY

15. Family attitudes towards sex
16. Learning about sex
17. Sexual activities
18. Traumatic sexual experiences
19. Puberty
       (a) menstruation or first emissions
       (b) secondary sexual characteristics

SEXUAL EXPERIENCE BEFORE CURRENT PARTNERSHIP

20. Nocturnal emissions or orgasms
21. Masturbation
22. Sexual fantasies and dreams
23. Erotic literature, pictures, and films
24. Dating and previous partnerships
25. Petting
26. Intercourse
27. Frequency of orgasm from all outlets
28. Traumatic sexual experiences
29. Date of marriage or cohabitation
30. Engagement
31. Sexual experience with current partner before marriage or cohabitation
32. Honeymoon
33. Sexual relationship during marriage or cohabitation
34. Contraceptive methods and wishes concerning conception
35. General relationship between partners

SEXUAL EXPERIENCE OUTSIDE CURRENT PARTNERSHIP

36. Nocturnal emissions or orgasms
37. Masturbation
38. Sexual fantasies and dreams
39. Erotic literature, pictures, and films
40. Sexual partners
41. Petting

42. Intercourse
43. Traumatic sexual experiences

SEXUAL EXPERIENCE SINCE LAST PARTNERSHIP ENDED
(e.g. by death, separation, or divorce)

44. Nocturnal emissions or orgasms
45. Masturbation
46. Sexual fantasies and dreams
47. Erotic literature, pictures, or films
48. Sexual partners
49. Petting
50. Intercourse
51. Traumatic sexual experiences

SEXUAL VARIATION

52. Homosexuality
53. Bestiality
54. Paedophilia
55. Voyeurism
56. Exhibitionism
57. Fetishism
58. Transvestism
59. Transsexualism
60. Sadomasochism
61. Sexual assault and rape
62. Incestuous behaviour

SELF CONCEPT

63. Body image
64. Gender identity
65. Popularity and attractiveness
66. Self-esteem

ATTITUDES TOWARDS TREATMENT

67. Motivation
68. Organizational capacity
69. Prognostic expectancy
70. Desired outcome

References

Abel, G. G. (1976). 'Assessment of sexual deviation in the male'. In M. Hersen and A. S. Bellack (Eds.), *Behavioural Assessment: A Practical Handbook*, Pergamon, Oxford, 437–57.

Abel, G. G., and Blanchard, E. B. (1976). 'The measurement and generation of sexual arousal in male sexual deviates'. In M. Hersen, R. M. Eisler, and P. M. Miller (Eds.), *Progress in Behavior Modification*, Vol. 2, Academic Press, New York, 99–136.

Abram, H. S., Hester, L. R., Sheridan, W. F., and Epstein, G. M. (1975). 'Sexual functioning in patients with chronic renal failure', *Journal of Nervous and Mental Disease*, **160**, 220–6.

Abramson, P. R., and Mosher, D. L. (1975). 'Development of a measure of negative attitudes toward masturbation'. *Journal of Consulting and Clinical Psychology*, **43**, 485–90.

Agras, W. S. (1967). 'Transfer during systematic desensitization therapy'. *Behaviour Research and Therapy*, **5**, 193–9.

Alevizos, P. N., and Callahan, E. J. (1977). 'Assessment of psychotic behaviour'. In A. R. Ciminero, K. S. Calhoun, and H. E. Adams (Eds.), *Handbook of Behavioral Assessment*, Wiley, New York, 683–721.

Alexander, L. (1974). 'Treatment of impotency and anorgasmia by psychotherapy aided by hypnosis'. *American Journal of Clinical Hypnosis*, **17**, 33–43.

Alexander, S., and Husek, T. R. (1962) 'The anxiety differential: Initial steps in the development of a measure of situational anxiety'. *Educational and Psychological Measurement*, **22**, 325–48.

Annon, J. S. (1974). *The Behavioral Treatment of Sexual Problems. Vol. 1: Brief Therapy*, Enabling Systems, Honolulu.

Annon, J. S. (1975a). *The Behavioral Treatment of Sexual Problems. Vol. 2: Intensive Therapy*, Enabling Systems, Honolulu.

Annon, J. S. (1975b). *The Sexual Pleasure Inventory—Male Form*, Enabling Systems, Honolulu.

Annon, J. S. (1975c). *The Sexual Pleasure Inventory—Female Form*, Enabling Systems, Honolulu.

Annon, J. S. (1975d). *The Sexual Fear Inventory—Male Form*, Enabling Systems, Honolulu.

Annon, J. S. (1975e). *The Sexual Fear Inventory—Female Form*, Enabling Systems, Honolulu.

Ansari, J. M. A. (1975). 'A study of 65 impotent males'. *British Journal of Psychiatry*, **127**, 337–41.

Ansari, J. M. A. (1976). 'Impotence: Prognosis (a controlled study)'. *British Journal of Psychiatry*, **128**, 194–8.

Apfelbaum, B. (1977). 'The myth of the surrogate'. *Journal of Sex Research*, **13**, 238–49.

Apfelberg, D. B., Maser, M. R., and Lash, H. (1976). 'Surgical management of impotence: Progress report'. *American Journal of Surgery*, **132**, 336–7.

266

Asirdas, S., and Beech, H. R. (1975). 'The behavioural treatment of sexual inadequacy'. *Journal of Psychosomatic Research*, **19**, 345–53.

Astrup, C. (1974). 'Flooding therapy with hypnosis'. *Behavior Therapy*, **5**, 704–5.

Auerbach, R., and Kilmann, P. R. (1977). 'The effects of group systematic desensitization on secondary erectile failure'. *Behavior Therapy*, **8**, 330–9.

Azrin, N. H., Naster, B. J. and Jones, R. (1973). 'Reciprocity counseling: A rapid learning-based procedure for marital counseling'. *Behaviour Research and Therapy*, **11**, 365–82.

Bancroft, J. (1970). 'Disorders of sexual potency'. In O. W. Hill (Ed.), *Modern Trends in Psychosomatic Medicine*, Butterworths, London.

Bancroft, J. (1974). *Deviant Sexual Behaviour: Modification and Assessment*, Oxford University Press, London.

Bancroft, J., and Coles, L. (1976). 'Three years' experience in a sexual problems clinic'. *British Medical Journal*, **1**, 1575–7.

Bandura, A. (1969). *Principles of Behavior Modification*, Holt, Rinehart, and Winston, New York.

Bandura, A. (1973). *Aggression: A Social Learning Analysis*, Prentice-Hall, Englewood Cliffs, New Jersey.

Bandura, A., Blanchard, E. B., and Ritter, B. (1969). 'The relative efficacy of desensitization and modeling approaches for inducing behavioral, affective, and attitudinal changes'. *Journal of Personality and Social Psychology*, **13**, 173–99.

Barbach, L. G. (1974). 'Group treatment of preorgasmic women'. *Journal of Sex and Marital Therapy*, **1**, 139–45.

Barach, L. G. (1975). *For Yourself: The Fulfilment of Female Sexuality*, Doubleday, New York.

Bardwick, J. M. (1971). *Psychology of Women: A Study of Bio-cultural Conflicts*, Harper and Row, New York.

Barlow, D. H. (1974). 'The treatment of sexual deviation: Toward a comprehensive behavioral approach'. In K. S. Calhoun, H. E. Adams, and K. M. Mitchell (Eds.), *Innovative Treatment Methods in Psychopathology*, Wiley, New York, 121–48.

Barlow, D. H. (1977). 'Assessment of sexual behaviour'. In A. R. Ciminero, K. S. Calhoun, and H. E. Adams (Eds.), *Handbook of Behavioral Assessment*, Wiley, New York, 461–508.

Barlow, D. H., and Abel, G. G. (1976). 'Sexual deviation'. In W. E. Craighead, A. E. Kazdin, and M. J. Mahoney, *Behavior Modification: Principles, Issues, and Applications*, Houghton–Mifflin, Boston, 341–60.

Barlow, D. H., Abel, G. G., Blanchard, E. B., Bristow, A. R., and Young, L. D. (1977). 'A heterosocial skills behaviour checklist for males', *Behavior Therapy*, **8**, 229–39.

Barlow, D. H., Becker, R., Leitenberg, H., and Agras, W. S. (1970), 'A mechanical strain gauge for recording penile circumference change'. *Journal of Applied Behavior Analysis*, **3**, 73–6.

Bauer, H. G. (1959). 'Endocrine and metabolic conditions relating to the pathology of the hypothalamus'. *Journal of Nervous and Mental Diesease*, **128**, 323–38.

Beach, F. A., (1967). 'Cerebral and hormonal control of reflexive machanisms involved in copulatory behaviour'. *Physiological Review*, **47**, 289–316.

Beach, F. A., and Ford, C. S. (1975). *Patterns of Sexual Behaviour*, Methuen, London.

Beaumont, G. (1976). 'Untoward effects of drugs on sexuality'. In S. Crown (Ed.). *Psychosexual Problems: Psychotherapy, Counselling and Behavioural Modification*, Academic Press, London, 325–35.

Back, A. T. (1970). 'Cognitive therapy: Nature and relation to behavior therapy'. *Behavior Therapy*, **1**, 184–200.

Back, A. T. (1972). *Depression: Causes and Treatment*, University of Pennsylvania Press, Philadelphia.

Beck, A. T., Ward, C. H., Mendelsohn, M. Mock, J., and Enbraugh, J. (1961). 'An inventory for measuring depression'. *Archives of General Psychiatry*, **4**, 561–71.

Beck, D. F. (1975). 'Research findings on the outcomes of marital counseling'. *Social Casework*, **56**, 153–81

Bellville, T. P. Raths, O. N., and Belliville, C. J. (1969). 'Conjoint marriage therapy with a husband-and-wife team'. *American Journal of Orthopsychiatry*, **39**, 373–483.

Bem, S. L. (1974). 'The measurement of psychological androgyny', *Journal of Consulting and Clinical Psychology*, **42**, 155–62.

Bentler, P. M. (1968a). 'Heterosexual behaviour assessment—I. Males' *Behaviour Research and Therapy*, **6**, 21–5.

Bentler, P. M. (1968b). 'Heterosexual behaviour assessment—II. Females'. *Behaviour Research and Therapy*, **6**, 27–30.

Bergin, A. E. (1970). 'Cognitive therapy and behavior therapy: Foci for a multidimensional approach to treatment', *Behavior Therapy*, **1**, 205–12.

Bergin, A. E., and Suinn, R. M. (1975). 'Individual psychotherapy and behavior therapy'. *Annual Review of Psychology*, **26**, 509–56.

Bergner, R. M. (1977). 'The marital system of the hysterical individual'. *Family-Process*, **16**, 85–95.

Berman, E. M., and Lief, H. I. (1975). 'Marital therapy from a psychiatric perspective: An overview', *American Journal of Psychiatry*, **132**, 583–92.

Bernstein, D. A., and Borkovec, T. D. (1973). *Progressive Relaxation Training: A Manual for the Helping Professions*, Research Press, Champaign, Illinois.

Beumont, P. V. J., Bancroft, J. H. J., Beardwood, C. J., and Russell, G. F. M. (1972). 'Behavioural changes after treatment with testosterone: Case report'. *Psychological Medicine*, **2**, 70–2.

Birchler, G. R., Weiss, R. L., and Vincent, J. P. (1975). 'A multi-method analysis of social reinforcement exchange between maritally distressed and nondistressed spouse and stranger dyads'. *Journal of Personality and Social Psychology*, **31**, 349–60.

Blanchard, E. B., and Young, L. D. (1974). 'Clinical applications of biofeedback training: A review of evidence'. *Archives of General Psychiatry*, **30**, 573–89.

Bloch, A., Maeder, J. P., and Haissly, J. C. (1975). 'Sexual problems after myocardial infarction'. *American Heart Journal*, **90**, 536–7.

Borkovec, T. D. (1973). 'The role of expectancy and physiological feedback in fear research: A review with special reference to subject characteristics', *Behavior Therapy*, **4**, 491–505.

Borkovec, T. D., Weerts, T. C., and Bernstein, D. A. (1977). 'Assessment of anxiety'. In A. R. Ciminero, K. S. Calhoun, and H. E. Adams (Eds.). *Handbook of Behavioral Assessment*, Wiley, New York, 367–428.

Bors, E., and Comarr, A. E. (1960). 'Neurological disturbances of sexual function with Special reference to 529 patients with spinal cord injury'. *Urological Survey*, **10**, 191–222.

Brady, J. P. (1966). 'Brevital-relaxation treatment of frigidity'. *Behaviour Research and Therapy*, **4**, 71–7.

Brady, J. P. (1967). 'Comments on methohexitone-aided systematic desensitization'. *Behaviour Research and Therapy*, **5**, 259–60.

Brady, J. P. (1971). 'Brevital-aided systematic desensitization'. In R. D. Rubin, H. Fensterheim, A. A. Lazarus, and C. M. Franks (Eds.). *Advances in Behavior Therapy 1969*, Academic Press, New York, 79–83.

Brecher, R., and Brecher, E. (Eds.) (1968). *An Analysis of Human Sexual Response*, Panther, London.

Bregman, S. (1978). 'Sexual adjustment of spinal cord injured women'. *Sexuality and Disability*, **1**, 85–92.

Brehm, J. W. (1966). *A Theory of Psychological Reactance*, Academic Press, New York.

Brehm, J. W., and Cohen, A. R. (1962). *Explorations in Congnitive Dissonance*, Wiley, New York.

Briddell, D. W., and Wilson, G. T. (1976). 'Effects of alcohol and expectancy set on male sexual arousal'. *Journal of Abnormal Psychology*, **85**, 225–34.

British Medical Journal (1965). Editorial. 'Priapism', **2**, 401–2.

British Medical Journal (1974). Editorial. 'Diabetic autonomic neuropathy', **2**, 2–3.

Brown, P. R. (1976). Report to the Counselling Advisory Board of the National Marriage Guidance Council of the research work of the marital sexual dysfunction project. *Unpublished Manuscript*. National Marriage Guidance Council.

Brown, W. A., Monti, P. M., and Corriveau, D. P. (1978). 'Serum testosterone and sexual activity and interest in men'. *Archives of Sexual Behavior*, **7**, 97–103.

Burbank, F. (1976). 'The treatment of sexual problems by group therapy'. In S. Crown (Ed), *Psychosexual Problems: Psychotherapy, Counselling, and Behavioural modification*, Academic Press, London, 31–58.

Burnham, W. R., Lennard-Jones, J. E., and Brooke, B. N. (1976). 'Proceedings: The incidence and nature of sexual problems among married ileostomists', *Gut*, **17**, 391–2.

Butler, C. A. (1976). 'New data about female sexual response'. *Journal of Sex and Marital Therapy*, **2**, 40–6.

Caird, W. K., and Wincze, J. P. (1974). 'Videotaped desensitization of frigidity'. *Journal of Behavor Therapy and Experimental Psychiatry*, **5**, 175–8.

Campbell, D. T., and Stanley, J. C. (1966). *Experimental and Quasi-experimental Designs For Research*, Rand McNally, Chicago.

Canning, J. R., Bowers, L. M., Llyod, F. A., and Cottrell, T. L. C. (1963). 'Genital vascular insufficiency and impotence'. *Surgical Forum*, **14**, 298–9.

Carver, J. R. and Oaks, W. W. (1976). 'Sex and hypertension'. In W. W. Oaks, G. A. Melchiode, and I. Fecher (Eds.), *Sex and the Life Cycle*, Grune and Stratton, New York, 175–8.

Cassidy, W. L., Flangan, N. B., Spellman, M., and Cohen, M. E. (1957).'Clinical observations in manic–depressive disease'. *Journal of the American Medical Association*, **164**, 1535–46.

Cautela, J. R., and Upper, D. (1976). 'Behavioural inventory battery: The use of self-report measures in behavioural analysis and therapy'. In M. Hersen and A. S. Bellack (Eds.), *Behavioural Assessment: A Practical Handbook*, Pergamon, Oxford, 77–109.

Chapanis, N. P., and Chapanis, A. (1964). 'Cognitive dissonance: Five years later'. *Psychological Bulletin*, **61**, 1–23.

Cheek, D. B., (1976). 'Short-term hypnotherapy for frigidity using exploration for early life attitudes'. *American Journal of Clinical Hypnosis*, 19–20–7.

Christenson, C. V., and Gagnon, J. H. (1965). 'Sexual behavior in a group of older women'. *Journal of Gerontology*, **20**, 351–6.

Ciminero, A. R., Calhoun, K. S., and Adams, H. E. (Eds.) (1977a). *Handbook of Behavioral Assessment*, Wiley, New York.

Ciminero, A. R., Nelson, R. O., and Lipinski, D. P. (1977b). 'Self-monitoring procedures' In A. R. Ciminero, K. S. Calhoun, and H. E. Adams (Eds.). *Handbook of Behavioral Assessment*, Wiley, New York, 195–232.

Clifford, R., (1977). 'Women's responses to erectile failure'. *Medical Aspects of Human Sexuality*, **11**, 9, 43–4.

Clifford, R. E. (1978). 'Subjective sexual experience in college women'. *Archives of Sexual Behavior*, **7**, 183–97.

Cohen, A. R. (1964). *Attitude Change and Social Influence*, Basic Books, New York.

Cole, M. (1975). 'Human sex behaviour and sex therapy'. In S. Jacobson (Ed.), *Sexual Problems*, Paul Elek, London, 102–20.

Comarr, A. E. (1970). 'Sexual function among patients with spinal cord injury'. *Urologica Internationals*, **25**, 134–68.

Comfort, A. (1967). *The Anxiety Makers*, Delta, New York.

Cone, J. D., and Hawkins, R. P. (Eds.) (1977). *Behavioral Assessment: New Directions in Clinical Psychology*, Brunner/Mazel, New York.

Cooper, A. J. (1968a). 'Neurosis and disorders of sexual potency in the male', *Journal of Psychosomatic Research*, **12**, 141–4.

Cooper, A. J., (1968b). 'A factual study of male potency disorders', *British Journal of Psychiatry*, **114**, 719–31.

Cooper, A. J., (1969a). 'A clinical study of coital anxiety in male potency disorders'. *Journal of Psychosomatic Research*, **13**, 143–7.

Cooper, A. J. (1969a) 'Clinical and therapeutic studies in premature ejaculation'. *Comprehensive Psychiatry*, **10**, 285–95.

Cooper, A. J. (1972). 'Diagnosis and management of "endocrine impotence"'. *British Medical Journal*, **2**, 34–6.

Cooper, A. J. (1974a). 'The place of testosterone in male sexuality'. *British Journal of Sexual Medicine*, **1**, 6–10.

Cooper, A. J., (1974b). 'A blind evaluation of a penile ring—a sex aid for impotent males'. *British Journal of Psychiatry*, **124**, 402–6.

Cooper, A. J. Smith, C. G., Ismail, A. A. A., and Loraine, J. A. (1973). 'A controlled trial of Potensan Forte ("Aphrodisiac" and testosterone combined) in impotence'. *Irish Journal of Medical Science*, **142**, 155–61.

Corsini, R. J. (1966). *Roleplaying in Psychotherapy: A Manual*, Aldine, Chicago.

Couper-Smartt, J. D., and Rodham, R. (1973). 'A technique for surveying side-effects of tricylic drugs with reference to reported sexual effects'. *Journal of International Medical Research*, **1**, 473–6.

Crasilneck, H. B., and Hall, J. A. (1975). *Clinical Hypnosis: Principles and Applications*. Grune and Stratton, New York.

Croft, H. A. (1975). 'The sexual information examination.' *Journal of Sex and Marital Therapy*, **1**, 319–25.

Cromwell, R. E., Olson, D. H. L., and Fournier, D. G. (1976). 'Tools and techniques for diagnosis and evaluation in marital and family therapy'. *Family Process*, **15**, 1–49.

Csillag, E. R. (1976). 'Modification of penile erectile responses'. *Journal of Behavior Therapy and Experimental Psychiatry*, **7**, 27–9.

Cummings, V. (1975). 'Amputees and sexual dysfunction'. *Archives of Physical and Medical Rehabilitation*, **56**, 12–3.

Curran, J. P. (1977). 'Skills training as an approach to the treatment of heterosexual-social anxiety: A review'. *Psychological Bulletin*, **84**, 140–57.

Cushman, P. (1972). 'Sexual behavior in heroin addiction and methadone maintenance'. *New York State Journal of Medicine*, **72**, 1261–5.

Davison, G. C. (1973). 'Counter control in behavior modification'. In L. A. Hamerlynck, L. C. Handy, and E. J. Marsh (Eds.), *Behavior Change: Methodology, Concepts and Practice*. Research Press, Champaign, Illinois, 153–67.

Davison, G. C., and Wilson, G. T. (1972). 'Critique of "Desensitization": Social and cognitive factors underlying the effectiveness of Wolpe's procedure"'. *Psychological Bulletin*, **78**, 28–31.

Davison, G. C., and Wilson, G. T. (1973). 'Processes of fear-reduction in systematic desensitization: Cognitive and social reinforcement factors in humans'. *Behavior Therapy*, **4**, 1–21.

Dawkins, S., and Taylor, R. (1961). 'Non-consummation of marriage: A survey of seventy cases'. *Lancet*, **2**, 1029–30.

Deabler, H. L. (1976). 'Hypnotherapy of impotence'. *American Journal of Clinical Hypnosis*, **19**, 9–12.

Dearborn, L. W. (1967). 'Autoeroticism'. In A. Ellis and A. Arbanel (Eds.). *The Encyclopedia of Sexual Behavior*, Hawthron, New York, 204–15.

Deutsch, R. M. (1973). *The Key to Feminine Response in Marriage*, Ballantine Books, New York.

Devanesan, M., Tiku, J., Massler, D., Calderwood, M. D., Samuals, R. M., and

Kaminetzky, H. A. (1976). 'Changing attendance patterns to sex therapy programs as a function of location and personnel'. *Journal of Sex and Marital Therapy*, **2**, 309–14.

Divita, E. C., and Olsson, P. A. (1975). 'The use of sex therapy in a patient with a penile prosthesis'. *Journal of Sex and Marital Therapy*, **1**, 305–11.

Dmowski, W. P., Luna, M., and Scommegna, A. (1974). 'Hormonal aspects of female sexual response'. *Medical Aspects of Human Sexuality*, **8**(6), 92–113.

Dormont, P. (1975). 'Ejaculatory anhedonia'. *Medical Aspects of Human Sexuality*, **9**(2), 32–48.

Duddle, M. (1977). 'Etiological factors in the unconsummated marriage'. *Journal of Psychosomatic Research*, **21**, 157–60.

Dunn, M. E., and Dickes, R. (1977). 'Erotic issues in cotherapy'. *Journal of Sex and Marital Therapy*, **3**, 205–11.

Easley, E. B. (1974). 'Atrophic vaginitis and sexual relations'. *Medical Aspects of Human Sexuality*, **8**(11), 32–58.

Eisler, R. M. (1976) 'Behavioural assessment of social skills'. In M. Hersen and A. S. Bellack (Eds.), *Behavioural Assessment: A Practical Handbook*, Pergamon, Oxford, 369–95.

Ellenberg, M. (1977). 'Sex and the female diabetic'. *Medical Aspects of Human Sexuality*, **11** (12), 30–8.

Ellenberg, M., and Webber, H. (1966). 'Retrograde ejaculation in diabetic neuropathy'. *Annals of Internal Medicine*, **65**, 1237–46.

Ellis, A. (1962). *Reason and Emotion in Psychotherapy*, Stuart, New York.

Ellis, A. (1969). 'A cognitive approach to behavior therapy'. *International Journal of Psychotherapy*, **8**, 896–900.

Ellis, A. (1973). 'Are cognitive behavior therapy and rational therapy synonymous?' *Rational Living*, **8**, 8–11.

Ellis, A. (1975). 'The rational–emotive approach to sex therapy'. *Counseling Psychologist*, **5**, 14–22.

Ellison, C. (1972). 'Vaginismus', *Medical Aspects of Human Sexuality*, **6**(8), 34–54.

Escamilla, R. F. (1976). 'Therapy of organic sexual dysfunctions'. *Current Psychiatric Therapies*, **16**, 117–25.

Fabbri, R. (1976). 'Hypnosis and behavior therapy: A coordinated approach to the treatment of sexual disorders'. *American Journal of Clinical Hypnosis*, **19**, 4–8.

Farkas, G. M., and Rosen, R. C. (1976). 'Effects of alcohol on elicited male sexual response'. *Journal of Studies on Alcohol*, **37**, 265–72.

Fellman, S. L., Kupperman, H. S., and Miller, W. W. (1975). 'Should androgens be used to treat impotence in men over 50?'. *Medical Aspects of Human Sexuality*, **9**(7), 32–43.

Festinger, L. (1937). *A Theory of Cognitive Dissonance*, Stanford University Press, Stanford, California.

Fish, J. M. (1973). *Placebo Therapy*, Jossey Bass, San Francisco.

Fishbein, M. (1967). 'Attitudes and the prediction of behavior'. In M. Fishbein (Ed.), *Readings in Attitude Theory and Measurement*, Wiley, New York, 477–92.

Fisher, C., Schiavi, R., Lear, H., Edwards, A., Davis, D. M., and Witkin, A. P. (1975). 'The assessment of noctural REM erection in the differential diagnosis of sexual impotence'. *Journal of Sex and Marital Therapy*, **1**, 277–89.

Fisher, S. (1973). *The Female Orgasm: Psychology, Physiology, Fantasy*. Allen Lane, London.

Fitting, M. D., Salisbury, S., Davies, N. H., and Mayclin, D. K. (1978). 'Self-concept and sexuality of spinal cord injured women'. *Archives of Sexual Behavior*, **7**, 143–56.

Flowers, J. V., and Booream, C. D. (1975). 'Imagination training in the treatment of sexual dysfunction'. *Counseling Psychologist*, **5**, 50–1.

Fordney-Settlage, D. S., (1975). 'Clitoral abnormalities'. *Medical Aspects of Human Sexuality*, **9**(5), 183–4.

Foster, A. L. (1974). *Sexual Compatibility Test*, Phoenix Institute, Los Gatos, California.

Foster, A. L. (1976). *Manual for the Sexual Compatibility Test*, Phoenix Institute, Los Gatos, California.

Foster, A. L. (1977). 'The Sexual Compatibility Test', *Journal of Consulting and Clinical Psychology*, **45**, 332–3.

Fox, C. A. (1970). 'Reduction in the rise of systolic blood pressure during human coitus by a beta-adrenergic blocking agent, propranolol'. *Journal of Reproduction and Fertility*, **22**, 587–90.

Fox, C. A., Ismail, A. A. A., Love, D. N., Kirkham, K. E., and Loraine, J. A. (1972). 'Studies on the relationship between plasma testosterone levels and human sexual activity'. *Journal of Endocrinology*, **52**, 51–8.

Frank, D., Dornbush, R. L. Webster, S. K., and Kolodny, R. C. (1978). 'Mastectomy and Sexual behavior: A pilot study'. *Sexuality and Disability*, **1**, 16–26.

Frank, E., Anderson, C., and Kupfer, D. J. (1976). 'Profiles of couples seeking sex therapy and marital therapy'. *American Journal of Psychiatry*, **133**, 559–62.

Frank, J. D. (1973). *Persuasion and Healing: A Comparative Study of Psychotherapy*, Revised Edition, John Hopkins University Press, Baltimore.

Frank, J. D., Gliedman, L. W., Imber, S. D., Stone, A. R., and Nash, E. W. Jr. (1959). 'Patients' expectancies and relearning as factors determining improvement in psychotherapy'. *American Journal of Psychiatry*, **115**, 961–8.

Freeman, W., and Meyer, R. G. (1975). 'A behavioral alternation of sexual preferences in the human male'. *Behavior Therapy*, **6**, 206–12.

Freund, K. (1976). 'Assessment of anomalous erotic preferences in situational impotence'. *Journal of Sex and Marital Therapy*, **2**, 173–83.

Freund, K., Langevin, R., Satterberg, J., and Steiner, B. (1977). 'Extension of the Gender Identity Scale for Males'. *Archives of Sexual Behavior*, **6**, 507–19.

Freund, K., Nagler, E., Langevin, R., Zojac, A., and Steiner, B. (1974). 'Measuring feminine gender identity in homosexual males'. *Archives of Sexual Behavior*, **3**, 249–61.

Freund, K., Sedlack, J., and Knob, K. (1965). 'A simple transducer for mechanical plethysmography of the male genital'. *Journal of the Experimental Analysis of Behavior*, **8**, 169–70.

Friedman, D. E. (1966). 'A new technique for the systematic desensitization of phobic patients'. *Behaviour Research and Therapy*, **4**, 139–40.

Friedman, D. E. (1968). 'The treatment of impotence by Brietal relaxation therapy'. *Behaviour Research and Therapy*, **6**, 257–61.

Friedman, D. E., and Lipsedge, M. S. (1971). 'Treatment of phobic anxiety and psychogenic impotence by systematic desensitization employing methohexitone-induced relaxation'. *British Journal of Psychiatry*, **118**, 87–90.

Friedman, H. J. (1963). 'Patient-expectancy and symptom reduction'. *Archives of General Psychiatry*, **8**, 61–7.

Friedman, J. M. (1978). 'Sexual adjustment of the post-coronary male'. In J. Lo Piccolo and L. Lo Piccolo (Eds.), *Handbook of Sex Therapy*, Plenum, New York, 373–86.

Friedman, L. J. (1962). *Virgin Wives*, Tavistock, London.

Fuchs, K., Abramovici, H., Hoch, Z., Timor-Tritsch, I., and Kleinhaus, M. (1975). 'Vaginismus—the hypno-therapeutic approach'. *Journal of Sex Research*, **11**, 39–45.

Fuchs, K., Hoch, Z., Paldi, E., Abramovici, H., Brandes, J., Timor-Tritsch, I., and Kleinhasu, M. (1973). 'Hypno-desensitization therapy of vaginismus. I. "*In vitro* method". II. "*In vivo* method".' *International Journal of Clinical and Experimental Hypnosis*, **21**, 144–56.

Gambrill, E. D. (1977). *Behavior Modification: Handbook of Assessment, Intervention, and Evaluation*, Jossey–Bass, San Francisco.

Gauthier, J., and Marshall, W. L. (1977). 'The determination of optimal exposure to phobic stimuli in flooding therapy'. *Behaviour Research and Therapy*, **15**, 403–10.

Geboes, K., Steeno, O., and DeMoor, P. (1975a). 'Sexual impotence in men'. *Andrologia*, **7**, 217–27.

Geboes, K., Steeno, O., and De Moor, P. (1975b). 'Primary an ejaculation: Diagnosis and therapy'. *Fertility and Sterility*, **26**, 1018–20.

Geer, J. H. (1976). 'Genital measures: Comments on their role in understanding human sexuality'. *Journal of Sex and Marital Therapy*, **2**, 165–72.

Geer, J. H. (1977). 'Sexual functioning: Some data and speculations on psychophysiological assessment'. In J. D. Cone and R. P. Hawkins (Eds.), *Behavioral Assessment: New Directions in Clinical Psychology*, Brunner/Mazel, New York, 196–209.

Geer, J. H., and Fuhr, R. (1976). 'Cognitive factors in sexual arousal: The role of distraction'. *Journal of Consulting and Clinical Psychology*, **44**, 238–43.

Geer, J., Morokoff, P., and Greenwood, P. (1974). 'Sexual arousal in women: The development of a measurement device for vaginal blood volume'. *Archives of Sexual Behavior*, **3**, 559–64.

Getty, C., and Shannon, A. (1969). 'Co-therapy as an egalitarian relationship'. *American Journal of Nursing*, **69**, 767–71.

Gill, H., and Temperley, J. (1974). 'Time-limited marital treatment in a foursome'. *British Journal of Medical Psychology*, **47**, 153–61.

Ginsberg, G. L., French, W. A., and Shapiro, T. (1972). 'The new impotence'. *Archives of General Psychiatry*, **26**, 218–20.

Glass, D. D. (1976). 'Sexuality and the spinal cord injured patient'. In W. W. Oaks, G. A. Melchiode, and I. Filcher (Eds.), *Sex and the Life Cycle*, Grune and Stration, New York, 179–90.

Glick, B. R., and Gross, S. J. (1975). 'Marital interaction and marital conflict: A critical evaluation of current research strategies'. *Journal of Marriage and the Family*, **37**, 505–12.

Glisson, D. H. (1976). 'A review of behavioral marital counseling: Has practice tuned out theory?. *Psychological Record*, **26**, 95–104.

Goldberg, M. (1977). 'The merging of love and passion'. *Medical Aspects of Human Sexuality*, **11**(2), 100–10.

Golden, J. S., and Golden, M. A. (1976) 'You know who and what's her name: The woman's role in sex therapy'. *Journal of Sex and Marital Therapy*, **2**, 6–16.

Goldfried, M. R. (1971). 'Systematic desensitization as a training in self-control', *Journal of Consulting and Clinical Psychology*, **37**, 228–34.

Goldfried, M. R. (1973). 'Reduction of generalized anxiety through a variant of systematic desensitization'. In M. R. Goldfried and M. Merbaum (Eds.), *Behaviour Change Through Self Control*, Holt, Reinhart, and Winston, New York, 297–304.

Goldfried, M. R. (1976). 'Behavioral assessment'. In I. B. Weiner (Ed.), *Clinical Methods and Psychology*, Wiley, New York, 281–330.

Goldfried, M. R., Decenteo, E. T., and Weinberg, L. (1974). 'Systematic rational restructuring as a self-control technique', *Behavior Therapy*, **5**, 247–54.

Goldfried, M. R., and Kent, R. N. (1972). 'Traditional vs behavioral assessment: A comparison of methodological and theoretical assumptions'. *Psychological Bulletin*, **77**, 409–20.

Goldfried, M. R., and Sobocinski, D. (1975). 'Effect of irrational beliefs on emotional arousal'. *Journal of Consulting and Clinical Psychology*, **43**, 504–10.

Goldstein, A. P. (1962). *Therapist—Patient Expectancies in Psychotherapy*, Pergamon, New York.

Goldstein, A. P. (1971). *Psychotherapeutic Attraction*, Pergamon, New York.

Goldstein, A. P., and Simonson, N. R. (1971). 'Social psychological approaches to psychotherapy research'. In A. E. Bergin and S. L. Garfield (Eds.), *Handbook of Psychotherapy and Behavior Change: An Empirical Analysis*, Wiley, New York, 154–95.

Gorer, G. (1971). *Sex and Marriage in England Today*, Nelson, London.

Gough, H. G. (1974). 'A 24-item version of the Miller-Fisk Sexual Knowledge Questionnaire', *Journal of Psychology*, **87**, 183–92.

Grabstald, H., and Goodwin, W. E. (1973). 'Devices and surgical procedures in the treatment of organic impotence', *Medical Aspects of Human Sexuality*, 7(12), 113–20.

Greenberg, J. S., and Archambault, F. X. (1973). 'Masturbation, self-esteem, and other variables', *Journal of Sex Research*, 9, 41–51.

Greenblatt, R. B., Jungck, E. C., and Blum, H. (1972). 'Endocrinology of sexual behaviour', *Medical Aspects of Human Sexuality*, 6(1), 110–31.

Greene, L. F., and Kelalis, P. P. (1968). 'Retrograde ejaculation of semen due to diabetic neuropathy', *Journal of Urology*, 98, 696.

Geer, B. E. (1975) 'Painful coitus due to hymenal problems', *Medical Aspects of Human Sexuality*, 9(2), 160–9.

Greer, S., and D'Zurilla, T. J. (1976). 'Behavioral approaches to marital discord and conflict'. In C. M. Franks, and G. T. Wilson (Eds.), *Annual Review of Behavior Therapy: Theory and Practice*, Vol. 4, Brunner/Mazel, New, York, 793–816.

Griffith, E. R., Tomoko, M. A., and Timms, R. J. (1973). 'Sexual function in spinal cord injured patients: a review'. *Archives of Physical and Medical Rehabilitation*, 54, 539–43.

Griffith, E. R., and Trieschman, R. B. (1975). 'Sexual functioning in women with spinal cord injury'. *Archives of Physical and Medical Rehabilitation*, 56, 18–21.

Groth, N. A., and Burgess, A. W. (1977). 'Sexual dysfunction during rape'. *New England Journal of Medicine*, 297(14), 764–6.

Group for the Advancement of Psychiatry (1973). *Assessment of Sexual Function: A Guide to Interviewing*, Group for the Advancement of Psychiatry, New York.

Gurman, A. S. (1977). 'The patient's perception of the therapeutic relationship'. In A. S. Gurman and A. M. Razin (Eds.), *Effective Psychotherapy: A Handbook of Research*, Pergamon, Oxford, 503–43.

Gurman, A. S., and Rice, D. G. (Eds.) (1975). *Couples in Conflict: New Directions in Marital Therapy*, Aronson, New York.

Hamilton, A. (1975a). 'Sex and arthritis'. *British Journal of Sexual Medicine*, 2(1), 27–33.

Hamilton, A. (1975b). 'Problems of the arthritic'. *British Journal of Sexual Medicine*, 2(2), 28–32.

Harbin, H. T., and Gamble, B. (1977). 'Sexual conflicts related to dominance and submission'. *Medical Aspects of Human Sexuality*, 11(1), 84–9.

Hare, E. H. (1962). 'Masturbatory insanity: The history of an idea'. *Journal of Mental Science*, 108, 2–25.

Hartland, J. (1966). *Medical and Dental Hypnosis*, Williams and Wilkins, Baltimore.

Hartman, W. E., and Fithian, M. A. (1974). *Treatment of Sexual Dysfunction*, Aronson, New York.

Heiman, J. R. (1976). 'Issues in the use of psychophysiology to assess female sexual dysfunction', *Journal of Sex and Marital Therapy*, 2, 197–204.

Heiman, J. R. (1977). 'A psychophysiological exploration of sexual arousal patterns in females and males', *Psychophysiology*, 14, 266–74.

Heiman, J. R. (1978). 'Uses of psychophysiology in the assessment of treatment of sexual dysfunction'. In J. Lo Piccolo and L. Lo Piccolo (Eds.), *Handbook of Sex Therapy*, Plenum, New York, 123–35.

Heiman, J., Lo Piccolo, L., and Lo Piccolo, J. (1976). *Becoming Orgasmic: A Sexual Growth Program for Women*, Prentice-Hall, Englewood Cliffs, N. J.

Heimberg, R. G., Montgomery, D., Madsen, C. H., and Heimberg, J. S. (1977). 'Assertion training: A review of the literature'. *Behaviour Therapy*, 8, 953–71.

Hellerstein, H. K. and Friedman, E. H. (1970). 'Sexual activity and the post-coronary patient'. *Archives of Internal Medicine*, 125, 987–99.

Henson, D. E., and Rubin, H. B. (1978). 'A comparison of two objective measures of sexual arousal in women'. *Behaviour Research and Therapy*, 16, 143–51.

Henson, D. E., Rubin, H. B., and Henson, C. (1978). 'Consistency of the labial temperature change measure of human female eroticism'. *Behaviour Research and Therapy*, 16, 125–9.

Henton, C. L. (1976). 'Nocturnal orgasm in college women: Its relation to dreams and anxiety associated with sexual factors', *Journal of Genetic Psychology*, **129**, 245–51.

Herman, S. H., Barlow, D. H., and Agras W. S. (1974). 'An experimental analysis of classical conditioning as a method of increasing heterosexual arousal in homosexuals'. *Behaviour Therapy*, **5**, 33–47.

Hersen, M., and Barlow, D. H. (1976). *Single-case Experimental Designs: Strategies for Studying Behavior Change*, Pergamon, New York.

Hersen, M., and Bellack, A. S. (Eds.) (1976). *Behavioural Assessment: A Practical Handbook*, Pergamon, Oxford.

Hersen, M., and Bellack, A. S. (1977). 'Assessment of social skills'. In A. R. Ciminero, K. S. Calhoun, and H. E. Adams (Eds.), *Handbook of Behavioral Assessment*, Wiley, New York, 509–54.

Hersen, M., and Eisler, R. M., (1976). 'Social skills training'. In W. E. Craighead, A. E. Kazdin, and M. J. Mahoney (Eds.) *Behavior Modification: Principles, Issues, and Applications*, Houghton–Mifflin, Boston, 361–75.

Hessellund, H. (1976). 'Masturbation and sexual fantasies in married couples'. *Archives of Sexual Behavior*, **5**, 133–47.

Higgins, G. E. (1978). 'Aspects of sexual response in adults with spinal-cord injury: A review of the literature'. In J. Lo Piccolo and L. Lo Piccolo (Eds.), *Handbook of Sex Therapy*, Plenum, New York, 387–409.

Hogan, R. A. (1975). 'Frigidity and implosive therapy', *Psychology*, **12**, 39–45.

Hoon, E. F., Hoon, P. W., and Wincze, J. P. (1976). 'An inventory for the measurement of female sexual arousability: The SAI'. *Archives of Sexual Behavior*, **5**, 291–300.

Hoon, P., Wincze, J., and Hoon, E. (1976). 'Physiological assessment of sexual arousal in women'. *Psychophysiology*, **13**, 196–204.

Hoon, P. W., Wincze, J. P., and Hoon, E. F. (1977a). 'A test of reciprocal inhibition: Are anxiety and sexual arousal in women mutually inhibitory?'. *Journal of Abnormal Psychology*, **86**, 65–74.

Hoon, P. W., Wincze, J. P., and Hoon, E. F. (1977b). 'The effects of biofeedback and cognitive mediation upon vaginal blood volume'. *Behavior Therapy*, **8**, 694–702.

Hops, H. (1976). 'Behavioral treatment of marital problems'. In W. E. Craighead, A. E. Kazdin, and M. J. Mahoney, *Behavior Modification: Principles, Issues and Applications*, Houghton-Mifflin, Boston, 431–46.

Hovland, C. I., Janis, I. L., and Kelley, H. H. (1953). *Communication and Persuasion: Psychological Studies of Opinion Change*, Yale University Press, New Haven.

Hunt, M. (1974). *Sexual Behavior in the 1970's*, Playboy Press, Chicago.

Jacob, T. (1976). 'Assessment of marital dysfunction'. In M. Hersen and A. S. Bellack (Eds.), *Behavioural Assessment: A Practical Handbook*. Pergamon, Oxford, 297–417.

Jacobs, M., Thompson, L. A., and Truxaw, P. (1975). 'The use of sexual surrogates in counseling'. *Counseling Psychologist*, **5**, 73–7.

Jacobson, E. (1938). *Progressive Relaxation*. University of Chicago Press, Chicago.

Jacobson, E. (1964). *Anxiety and Tension Control*, Lippincott, Philadelphia.

Jacobson N. S., and Martin B. (1976). 'Behavioral marriage therapy: Current status'. *Psychological Bulletin*, **83**, 540–56.

Janis, I. L., and Gilmore, J. B. (1965). 'The influence of incentive conditions on the success of roleplaying in modifying attitudes'. *Journal of Personality and Social Psychology*, **1**, 1–27.

Jehu, D., Hardiker, P., Yelloly, M., and Shaw, M. (1972). *Behaviour Modification in Social Work*, Wiley, London.

Jehu, D., Morgan, R. T. T., Turner, R. K., and Jones, A. (1977). 'A controlled trial of the treatment of nocturnal enuresis in residential homes for children'. *Behaviour Research and Therapy*, **15**, 1–16.

Joe, V. C., and Brown, C. (1975). 'A test of the Zuckerman heterosexual scales'. *Journal of Personality Assessment*, **39**, 271–2.

Johnson, J. (1965). 'Sexual impotence and the limbic system', *British Journal of Psychiatry*, **111**, 300–3.

Johnson, J. (1968). *Disorders of Sexual Potency in the Male*, Pergamon, Oxford.

Johnson, J. (1975). 'Importance'. In T. Silverstone and B. Barraclough (Eds.), *Contemporary Psychiatry: Selected Reviews from the British Journal of Hospital Medicine*, Headley Brothers, Ashford, 206–11.

Jones, E. E., Kanouse, D. E., Kelley, H. H. Nisbett, R. E., Valins, S., and Weiner, B. (Eds.) (1971). *Attribution: Perceiving the Causes of Behavior*, General Learning Press, Morristown, N. J.

Jourard, S. M. (1964). *The Transparent Self*, Van Nostrand, Princeton, N. J.

Kanin, E. J., and Howard, D. H. (1958). 'Postmarital consequences of premarital sex adjustments'. *American Sociological Review*, **23**, 556–62.

Kaplan, H. S. (1974). *The New Sex Therapy: Active Treatment of Sexual Dysfunctions*, Bailliere Tindall, London.

Kaplan, H. S. (1975). *The Illustrated Manual of Sex Therapy*, Quadrangle, New York.

Kaplan, H. S. (1977a). 'Training of sex therapists'. In W. H. Masters, V. E. Johnson, and R. C. Kolodny (Eds.), *Ethical Issues in Sex Therapy and Research*, Little, Brown and Co., Boston, 182–205.

Kaplan, H. S. (1977b). 'Hypoactive sexual desire'. *Journal of Sex and Marital Therapy*, **3**, 3–9.

Karacan, I., Williams, R. L., Thornby, J. I., and Salis, P. J. (1975). 'Sleep-related penile tumescence as a function of age'. *American Journal of Psychiatry*, **132**, 932–7.

Karacan, I., Scott, F. B., Salis, P. J., Attia, S. L., Ware, J. C., Altinel, A., and Williams, R. L. (1977). 'Nocturnal erections, differential diagnosis of impotence and diabetes', *Biological Psychiatry*, **12**, 373–80.

Karacan, I. (1978a). 'Advances in the psychophysiological evaluation of male erectile impotence'. In J. Lo Piccolo and L. Lo Piccolo (Eds.). *Handbook of Sex Therapy*, Plenum, New York, 132–45.

Karacan, I. (1978b). 'Advances in the diagnosis of erectile impotence'. *Medical Aspects of Human Sexuality*, **12**(5), 85–97.

Kazdin, A. E. (1974). 'Self-monitoring and behavior change'. In M. J. Mahoney and C. E. Thoresen (Eds.), *Self-Control: Power to the Person*, Brooks/Cole, Monterey, California, 218–46.

Kazdin, A. R., and Wilcoxon, L. A. (1976). 'Systematic desensitization and nonspecific treatment effects: A methodological evaluation'. *Psychological Bulletin*, **83**, 729–58.

Keefe, F. J., Kopel, S. A., and Gordon, S. B. (Eds.) (1978). *A Practical Guide to Behavioral Assessment*, Springer, New York.

Kegel, A. H. (1952). 'Sexual functions of the puboccygeus muscle'. *Western Journal of Surgery, Obstetrics, and Gynaecology*, **60**, 521–4.

Kerckhoff, A. (1974). 'Social class differences in sexual attitudes and behavior'. *Medical Aspects of Human Sexuality*, **8**(11), 10–25.

Kinsey, A. C., Pomeroy, W. B., and Martin, C. E. (1948). *Sexual Behavior in the Human Male*, Saunders, Philadelphia.

Kinsey, A. C., Pomeroy, W. B., Martin, C. E., and Gebhard, P. H. (1953). *Sexual Behavior in the Human Female*, Saunders, Philadelphia.

Klebanow, D., and MacLeod, J. (1960). 'Semen quality and certain disturbances of reproduction in diabetic men'. *Fertility and Sterility*, **11**, 255–61.

Kline-Graber, G., and Graber, G. (1978). 'Diagnosis and treatment of pubococcygeal deficiencies in women'. In J. Lo Piccolo and L. Lo Piccolo (Eds.), *Handbook of Sex Therapy*, Plenum, New York, 227–39.

Kockott, G., Dittman, F., and Nusselt, L. (1975). 'Systematic desensitization of erectile impotence: A controlled study'. *Archives of Sexual Behavior*, **4**, 493–9.

Kohlenberg, R. J. (1974). 'Directed masturbation and the treatment of primary orgasmic dysfunction'. *Archives of Sexual Behavior*, **3**, 349–56.

Koncz, L., and Balodimus, M. C. (1970). 'Impotence in diabetes mellitus'. *Medical Times*, **98**, 159–70.

Korchin, S. J. (1976). *Modern Clinical Psychology*, Basic Books, New York.

Kotin, J., Wilbert, D. E., Verburg, D., and Soldinger, S. M. (1976). 'Thioridazine and sexual dysfunction'. *American Journal of Psychiatry*, **133**, 82–5.

Kraemer, H. C., Becker, H. B., Brodie, K. H., Doering, C. H. Moos, R. H., and Hamburg, D. A. (1976). 'Orgasmic frequency and plasma testosterone levels in normal human males'. *Archives of Sexual Behavior*, **5**, 125–32.

Kraft, M., and Al-Issa (1968). 'The use of methohexitone sodium in the systematic desensitization of premature ejaculation'. *British Journal of Psychiatry*, **114**, 351–2.

Kolodny, R. C., (1971). 'Sexual dysfunction in diabetic females'. *Diabetes*, **20**, 557–9.

Kolodny, R. C., Kahn, C. B., Goldstein, H. H., and Barnett, D. M. (1974). 'Sexual dysfunction in diabetic men'. *Diabetes*, **23**, 306–9.

Kreuz, L. E., Rose, R. M., and Jennings, J. R. (1972). 'Suppression of plasma testosterone levels and psychological stress'. *Archives of General Psychiatry*, **26**, 479–82.

Lacey, J. I. (1950). 'Individual differences in somatic response patterns'. *Journal of Comparative and Physiological Psychology*, **43**, 338–50.

Lacey, J. I., Bateman, D. E., and Van Lehn, R. (1953). 'Autonomic response specificity: An experimental study'. *Psychosomatic Medicine*, **15**, 8–12.

Lacey, J. I., and Lacey, B. C. (1958).'Verification and extension of the principle of autonomic response stereotype'. *American Journal of Psychology*, **71**, 50–73.

Lallemand, M. (1847). *Practical Treatise on Spermatorrhoea*, translated H. J. McDougall. John Churchill, London.

Landis, J., Poffenberger, T., and Poffenberger, S. (1950). 'The effects of first pregnancy upon the sexual adjustment of 212 couples'. *American Sociological Review*, **15**, 767–72.

Langevin, R., and Martin, M. (1975). 'Can erotic responses be classically conditioned?'. *Behavior Therapy*, **6**, 350–5.

Langmyhr, G. J. (1977). 'Reciprocity of sexual problems between partners'. *Medical Aspects of Human Sexuality*, **11**(9), 7–21.

Lash, H. (1968). 'Silicone implant for impotence'. *Journal of Urology*, **100**, 709–10.

Lazarus, A. A. (1963). 'The treatment of chronic frigidity by systematic desensitization'. *Journal of Nervous and Mental Disease*, **136**, 272–8.

Lazarus, A. A. (1971). *Behavior Therapy and Beyond*, McGraw-Hill, New York.

Lazarus, R. S. (1966). *Psychological Stress and the Coping Process*, McGraw-Hill, New York.

Leiblum, S. R., Rosen, R. C., and Pierce, D. (1976). 'Group treatment format: Mixed sexual dysfunctions'. *Archives of Sexual Behavior*, **5**, 313–22.

Leitenberg, H., Agras, W. S., Barlow, D. H., and Oliveau, D. C. (1969). 'Contributions of selective positive reinforcement and therapeutic instructions in systematic desensitization therapy'. *Journal of Abnormal Psychology*, **74**, 113–8.

LeRoy, D. H. (1972). 'The potential criminal liability in human sex clinics and their patients'. *St. Louis University Law Journal*, **16**, 586–603.

Levay, A. N., and Kagle, A. (1977). 'Ego deficiencies in areas of pleasure, intimacy, and cooperation: Guidelines in the diagnosis and treatment of sexual dysfunctions'. *Journal of Sex and Marital Therapy*, **3**, 10–8.

Levine, S. B. (1975). 'Premature ejaculation: Some thoughts about its pathogenesis'. *Journal of Sex and Marital Therapy*, **1**, 326–34.

Levine, S. B., and Yost, M. A. (1976), 'Frequency of sexual dysfunction in a general gynaecological clinic: An epidemological approach'. *Archives of Sexual Behavior*, **5**, 229–38.

Levis, D. J. (1974). 'Implosive therapy: A critical analysis of Morganstern's review'. *Psychological Bulletin*, **81**, 155–8.

Levit, H. I. (1971). 'Marital crisis intervention: Hypnosis in impotence/frigidity cases'. *American Journal of Clinical Hypnosis*, **14**, 56–60.

Levitt, E. E., and Lubin, B. L. (1975). *Depression: Concepts, Controversies and Some New Facts*, Springer, New York.

Levy, N. B. (1973). 'Sexual adjustment to maintenance hemodialysis and renal transplantation: National survey by questionnaire: Preliminary report', *Transactions of the American Society for Artificial Internal Organs*, **19**, 138–43.

Libby, R. W. (1977), 'Today's changing sexual mores'. In J. Money and H. Musaph (Eds.) *Handbook of Sexology*, Elsevier/North-Holland Biomedical Press, Amsterdam, 563–76.

Liberman, R. P., King, L. W., DeRisi, W. J., and McCann, M. (1975). *Personal Effectiveness: Guiding People to Assert Themselves and Improve Their Social Skills*, Research Press, Champaign, Illinois.

Lick, J. R., and Katkin, E. S. (1976). 'Assessment of anxiety and fear'. In M. Hersen and A. S. Bellack (Eds.), *Behavioural Assessment: A Practical Handbook*, Pergamon, Oxford, 175–206.

Leberman, M. A. (1975). 'Group methods'. In Kanfer, F. H., and Goldstein, A. P. (Eds.), *Helping People Change: A Textbook of Methods*, Pergamon, New York, 433–85.

Lief, H. I. (1977a). 'Inhibited sexual desire'. *Medical Aspects of Human Sexuality*, **11**(7), 94–5.

Lief, H. I. (1977b). 'Sexual desire and responsivity during pregnancy', *Medical Aspects of Human Sexuality*, **11**(12), 51–7.

Lief, H. I. (1977c). 'Sexual survey no. 5: Current thinking on sex and depression', *Medical Aspects of Human Sexuality*, **11**(12), 22–3.

Lief, H. I. and Karlen, A. (Eds.) (1976). *Sex Education in Medicine*, Spectrum, New York.

Lief, H. I., and Reed, D. M. (1972). *Sexual Knowledge and Attitude Test (S.K.A.T.)* (2nd ed)., Centre for the Study of Sex Education in Medicine, University of Pennsylvania.

Linehan, M. M. (1977). 'Issues in behavioral interviewing'. In J.D. Cone and R.P. Hawkins (Eds.), *Behavioral Assessment: New Directions in Clinical Psychology*, Brunner/Mazel, New York, 30–51.

Lobitz, W. C., and Lobitz, G. K. (1978). 'Clinical assessment in the treatment of sexual dysfunctions'. In J. Lo Piccolo, and L. Lo Piccolo (Eds.), *Handbook of Sex Therapy*, Plenum, New York, 85–102.

Lobitz, W. C., Lopiccolo, J., Lobitz, G. K., and Brockway, J. (1967). 'A closer look at "simplistic" behaviour therapy for sexual dysfunction: Two case studies'. In H. J. Eysenck (Ed.), *Case Studies in Behavior Therapy*, Routledge and Kegan Paul, London, 237–71.

Locke, H. J., and Wallace, K. (1959). 'Short marital adjustment and prediction tests: Their reliability and prediction'. *Marriage and Family Living*, **21**, 251–5.

Loeffler, R. A., and Iverson, R. E. (1976). 'Surgical treatment of impotence in the male: A 18 year experience with 250 patients'. *Plastic and Reconstructive Surgery*, **58**, 292–7.

Loeffler, R. A., and Sayegh, E. S. (1960). 'Perforated acrylic implants in management of organic impotence'. *Journal of Urology*, **84**, 559–61.

Lo Piccolo, J. (1977). 'A reply to McCoy and D'Agostino'. *Archives of Sexual Behavior*, **6**, 169–71.

Lo Picolo, J. (1978). 'The professionalization of sex therapy: Issues and problems'. In J. Lo Piccolo and L. Lo Piccolo (Eds.), *Handbook of Sex Therapy*, Plenum, New York, 511–26.

Lo Piccolo, J., and Lobitz, W. C. (1972a). 'The role of masturbation in the treatment of orgasmic dysfunction'. *Archives of Sexual Behavior*, **2**, 163–71.

Lo Piccolo, J., and Lobitz, W. C. (1972b). 'Behavior therapy of sexual dysfunction'. In L. A. Hamerlynck, L. C. Handy, and E. J. Mash (Eds.), *Behavior Change: Methodology, Concepts and Practice*, Research Press, Champaign, Illinois, 343–58.

Lo Piccolo, L., and Heiman, J. R. (1978). 'Sexual assessment and history interview'. In J. Lo Piccolo and L. Lo Piccolo (Eds.), *Handbook of Sex Therapy*, Plenum, New York, 103–22.

Lo Piccolo, J., and Steger, J. C. (1974). 'The Sexual Interaction Inventory: A new instrument for assessment of sexual dysfunction'. *Archives of Sexual Behavior*, **3**, 585–95.

Lowe, J. C., and Mikulas, W. L. (1975). 'Use of written material in learning self-control of premature ejaculation'. *Psychological Reports*, **37**, 295–8.

Lowndes Sevely, J., and Bennett, J. A. (1978). 'Concerning female ejaculation and the female prostate'. *Journal of Sex Research*, **14**, 1–20.

Lubin, B. L. (1965). 'Adjective checklists for measurement of depression'. *Archives of General Psychiatry*, **12**, 57–62.

Lubin, B. L. (1967). *Manual for the Depression Adjective Checklists*, Educational and Industrial Testing Service, San Diego.

Lubin, B., and Himelstein, P. (1976). 'Reliability of the Depression Adjective Check Lists'. *Perceptual and Motor Skills*, **43**, 1037–8.

Luttge, W. C. (1971). 'The role of gonadal hormones in the sexual behavior of the rhesus monkey and human'. *Archives of Sexual Behavior*, **1**, 61–88.

Mack, W. (1964). 'Ruminations on the testis'. *Proceedings of the Royal Society of Medicine*, **57**, 47–51.

MacLean, P. D. (1975). 'Brain mechanisms of elemental sexual functions'. In A. M. Freedman, H. I. Kaplan, and B. J. Sadock (Eds.), *Comprehensive Textbook of Psychiatry*, Vol. II (2nd edn.), Williams and Wilkins, Baltimore, 1386–92.

Maddison, J. (1974). 'Sex hormone replacement therapy in men'. *British Journal of Sexual Medicine*, **1**, 41–3.

Maddock, J. W. (1975). 'Initiation problems and time structuring in brief sex therapy'. *Journal of Sex and Marital Therapy*, **1**, 190–7.

Madsen, C. H., and Ullman, L. P. (1967). 'Innovations in the desensitization of frigidity'. *Behaviour Research and Therapy*, **5**, 67–8.

Mahoney, M. J. (1974). *Cognition and Behavior Modification*, Ballinger, Cambridge, Massachusetts.

Mahoney, M. J. (1977). 'Some applied issues in self-monitoring'. In J. D. Cone and R. P. Hawkins (Eds.), *Behavioral Assessment: New Directions in Clinical Psychology*, Brunner/Mazel, New York, 241–54.

Malamuth, N., Wanderer, Z. W., Sayner, R. B., and Durnell, D. (1976). 'Utilization of surrogate partners: A survey of health professionals'. *Journal of Behavior Therapy and Experimental Psychiatry*, **7**, 149–50.

Marholin, D. II., Siegel, L. J., and Phillips, D. (1976). 'Treatment and transfer: A search for empirical procedures'. In M. Hersen, R. M. Eisler, P. M. Miller (Eds.), *Progress in Behavior Modification*, Vol. 3, Academic Press, New York, 293–342.

Marks, I. (1972) 'Perspective on flooding'. *Seminars in Psychiatry*, **4**, 129–38.

Marks, I. (1975). 'Behavioral treatments of phobic and obsessive–compulsive disorders: A critical appraisal'. In M. Hersen, R. M. Eisler, and P. M. Miller (Eds.), *Progress in Behavior Modification*, Vol, 1, Academic Press, New York, 65–158.

Marks, I. M. (1976). 'Management of sexual disorders'. In H. Leitenberg (Ed.), *Handbook of Behavior Modification and Behavior Therapy*, Prentice-Hall, Englewood Cliffs, N.J., 255–302.

Marks, I. M., and Sartorius, N. H. (1968). 'A contribution to the measurement of sexual attitude'. *Journal of Nervous and Mental Disease*, **145**, 441–51.

Marston, E. D. (1871). *Brain and Spinal System*, Trubner, London.

Martin, C. E. (1977). 'Sexual activity in the aging male'. In J. Money and H. Musaph (Eds.), *Handbook of Sexology*, Elsevier, North-Holland Biomedical Press, Amsterdam, 813–24.

Martin, P. A. (1977). 'The happy sexless marriage'. *Medical Aspects of Human Sexuality*, **11**(5), 75–85.

Masters, W. H., and Johnson, V. E. (1966). *Human Sexual Response*, Little, Brown and Co., Boston.

Masters, W. H., and Johnson, V. E. (1970). *Human Sexual Inadequacy*, Little, Brown and Co., Boston.

Masters, W. H., Johnson, V. E., and Kolodny, R. C. (Eds.) (1977). *Ethical Issues in Sex Therapy and Research*, Little, Brown and Co., Boston.

Mathews, A. M. (1971). 'Psychophysiological approaches to the investigation of desensitization and related procedures'. *Psychological Bulletin*, **76**, 73–91.

Mathews, A., Bancroft, J., Whitehead, A., Hackmann, A., Julier, D., Bancroft, J., Gath, D., and Shaw, P. (1976). 'The behavioural treatment of sexual inadequacy: a comparative study'. *Behaviour Research and Therapy*, **14**, 427–36.

Maurice, W. L., and Guze, S. B. (1970). 'Sexual dysfunction and associated psychiatric disorders'. *Comprehensive Psychiatry*, **11**, 539–43.

Mawson, A. B. (1970). 'Methohexitone-assisted desensitization in treatment of phobias', *Lancet*, **1**, 1084–6.

May, J. R., and Johnson, H. J. (1973). 'Physiological activity to internally elicited arousal and inhibitory thoughts'. *Journal of Abnormal Psychology*, **82**, 239–45.

McConaghy, N. (1975). 'Aversive and positive conditioning treatments of homosexuality'. *Behaviour Research and Therapy*, **13**, 309–19.

McCoy, N. N., and D'Agostino, P. A. (1977). 'Factor analysis of the Sexual Interaction Inventory'. *Archives of Sexual Behavior*, **6**, 25–35.

McFall, R. M. (1977). 'Parameters of self-monitoring'. In R. B. Stuart (Ed.), *Behavioral Self-Management: Strategies, Techniques and Outcomes*, Brunner/Mazel, New York, 186–214.

McGovern, K. B., Stewart, R. C., and Lo Piccolo, J. (1975). 'Secondary orgasmic dysfunction. I. analysis and strategies for treatment'. *Archives of Sexual Behavior*, **4**, 265–75.

McGovern, K. B., Kirkpatrick, C. C., and Lo Piccolo, J. (1978). 'A behavioral group treatment program for sexually dysfunctional couples'. In J. Lo Piccolo and L. Lo Piccolo (Eds.), *Handbook of Sex Therapy*, Plenum, New York, 459–66.

McHugh, G. (1955). *Sexual Knowledge Inventory: Vocabulary and Anatomy*, Family Life Publications, Saluda, North Carolina.

Medical Aspects of Human Sexuality (1975). 'Do women always know when they have had an orgasm?'. **9**(12), 32–44.

Medical Aspects of Human Sexuality (1977a). 'Painful intercourse caused by severe penile curvature'. **11**(11), 23.

Medical Aspects of Human Sexuality (1977b). 'Vascular diseases causing sexual dysfunction by interfering with penile blood supply'. **11**(6), 103.

Medical Aspects of Human Sexuality (1978). 'Pelvic congestion resulting from sexual frustration'. **12**(4), 76.

Meichenbaum, D. H. (1972). 'Ways of modifying what clients say to themselves'. *Rational Living*, **7**, 23–7.

Meichenbaum, D. H. (1973). 'Cognitive factors in behavior modification: Modifying what clients say to themselves. In C. M. Franks and G. T. Wilson (Eds.), *Annual Review of Behavior Therapy: Theory and Practice*, Brunner/Mazel, New York, 416–31.

Meichenbaum, D. H. (1974). *Cognitive Behavior Modification*. General Learning Press, Morristown, N. J.

Meikle, S. (1977). 'The psychological effects of hysterectomy'. *Canadian Psychological Review*, **18**, 128–41.

Miller, W. R., and Lief, H. I. (1976). 'Masturbatory attitudes, knowledge, and experience: Data from Sex Knowledge and Attitude Test (SKAT)'. *Archives of Sexual Behavior*, **5**, 447–67.

Mills, L. C. (1975). 'Drug-induced impotence'. *American Family Physician*, **12**, 104–6.

Mills, L. C. (1976) 'Sexual disorders in the diabetic patient'. In W. W. Oaks,

280

G. A. Melchiode, and I. Ficher (Eds.), *Sex and the Life Cycle*, Grune and Stratton, New York, 163–78.

Mischel, W. (1968). *Personality and Assessment*, Wiley, New York.

Mitchell, K. M., Bozarth, J. D., and Krauft, C. C. (1977). 'A re-appraisal of the therapeutic effectiveness of accurate empathy, nonpossessive warmth, and genuineness'. In A. S. Gurman and A. M. Razin (Eds.), *Effective Psychotherapy: A Handbook of Research*, Pergamon, Oxford, 482–502.

Morganstern, K. P. (1973). 'Implosive therapy and flooding procedures: A review'. *Psychological Bulletin*, **79**, 318–34.

Morganstern, K. P. (1974). 'Issues in implosive therapy: Reply to Levis'. *Psychological Bulletin*, **81**, 380–2.

Morganstern, K. P. (1976). 'Behavioural interviewing: The initial stages of assessment'. In M. Hersen and A. S. Bellack (Eds.), *Behavioural Assessment: A Practical Handbook*, Pergamon, Oxford, 51–76.

Mourad, M., and Chiu, W. S. (1974). 'Marital–sexual adjustment of amputees'. *Medical Aspects of Human Sexuality*, **8**(2), 47–51.

Munjack, D., Cristol, A., Goldstein, A., Phillips, D., Goldberg, A., Whipple, K., Staples, F., and Kanno, P. (1976). 'Behavioural treatment of orgasmic dysfunction: A controlled Study'. *British Journal of Psychiatry*, **129**, 497–502.

Munjack, D. J., and Oziel, L. J. (1978). 'Resistance in the behavioral treatment of sexual dysfunctions'. *Journal of Sex and Marital Therapy*, **4**, 122–38.

Munjack, D. J., and Staples, F. R. (1976). 'Psychological characteristics of women with sexual inhibition (frigidity) in sex clinics'. *Journal of Nervous and Mental Disease*, **163**, 117–23.

Murray, L. (1976). 'The conjoint physical'. *British Journal of Sexual Medicine*, **3**, 9–13.

Musaph, H., Haspels, A. A. (Eds.) (1977). *Dyspareumia: Aspects of Painful Coitus*, Bohn, Scheltema, and Holkema, Utrecht.

Nawas, M. M. (1970). 'Wherefore cognitive therapy?: A critical scrutiny of three papers by Beck, Bergin, and Ullman'. *Behavior Therapy*, **1**, 359–70.

Nelson, R. O. (1977). 'Methodological issues in assessment via self-monitoring'. In J. D. Cone and R. P. Hawkins (Eds.), *Behavioral Assessment: New Directions in Clinical Psychology*, Brunner/Mazel, New York, 217–40.

Obler, M. (1973). 'Systematic desensitization in sexual disorders'. *Journal of Behavior Therapy and Experimental Psychiatry*, **4**, 93–101.

O'Brien, K. M., Rawl, J., Binkley, L., and Stone, W. J. (1975). 'Sexual dysfunction in uremia'. *Proceedings of the Clinic Dialysis Transplant Forum*, **5**, 98–101.

O'Connor, J. F. (1976) 'Sexual problems, therapy, and prognostic factors'. In J. K. Meyer (Ed.), *Clinical Management of Sexual Disorders*, Williams and Wilkins, Baltimore, 74–98.

O'Connor, J. F., and Stern, L. O. (1972). 'Developmental factors in functional sexual disorders', *New York State Journal of Medicine*, **72**, 1838–43.

Offit, A. K. (1977). 'Common causes of female orgasm problems'. *Medical Aspects of Human Sexuality*, **11**(8), 40–8.

Osgood, C. E., Suci, G. J., and Tannenbaum, P. H. (1957). *The Measurement of Meaning*, University of Illinois Press, Urbana.

Page, L. B. (1975). 'Advising hypertensive patients about sex'. *Medical Aspects of Human Sexuality*, **9**(1), 103–4.

Paitch, D., Langevin, R., Freeman, R., Mann, K., and Handy, L. (1977). 'The Clark SHQ: A clinical sex history questionnaire for males'. *Archives of Sexual Behavior*, **6**, 421–36.

Paquin, M. J. (1977). 'The status of family and marital therapy outcomes: Methodological and substantive considerations'. *Canadian Psychological Review*, **18**, 221–32.

Patterson, G. R., and Hops, H. (1972). 'Coercion, a game for two: Intervention techniques for marital conflict'. In R. E. Ulrich and P. Mountjoy (Eds.), *The Experimental Analysis of Social Behavior*, Appleton-Century-Crofts, New York, 424–40.

Patterson, G. R., and Reid, J. B. (1970). 'Reciprocity and coercion: two facets of social systems'. In C. Neuringer and J. Michael (Eds.), *Behavior Modification in Clinical Psychology*, Appleton-Century-Crofts, New York, 133–77.

Patterson, G. R., Weiss, R. L. and Hops, H. (1976). 'Training of Marital skills: Some problems and concepts'. In H. Leitenberg (Ed.), *Handbook of Behavior Therapy and Behavior Modification*, Prentice-Hall, Englewood Cliffs, N. J. 242–54.

Paul, G. L. (1969a). 'Outcome of systematic desensitization I: Background and procedures and uncontrolled reports of individual treatments. In C. M. Franks (Ed.), *Behavior Therapy: Appraisal and Status*, McGraw-Hill, New York, 63–104.

Paul, G. L. (1969b). 'Outcome of systematic desensitization II: Controlled investigations of individual treatment, technique variations, and current status. In C. M. Franks (Ed.), *Behavior Therapy: Appraisal and Status*, McGraw-Hill, New York, 105–59.

Pearman, R. O. (1967). 'Treatment of organic impotence by implantation of a penile prosthesis'. *Journal of Urology*, **97**, 716–9.

Pehm, L. P. (1976). 'Assessment of depression'. In M. Hersen and A. S. Bellack (Eds.), *Behavioral Assessment: A Practical Handbook*, Pergamon, Oxford, 233–59.

Pfeiffer, E. (1974). 'Sexuality in the aging individual'. *Journal of the American Geriatrics Society*, **22**, 481–4.

Pfeiffer, E. (1975). 'Sexual behaviour'. In J. G. Howells (Ed.), *Modern Perspectives in the Psychiatry of Old Age*, Churchill Livingstone, London, 133–25.

Phares, E. J. (1973). *Locus of Control: A Personality Determinant of Behaviour*, General Learning Press, Morristown, N.J.

Piemme, T.E. (1976). 'Sex and illicit drugs'. *Medical Aspects of Human Sexuality*, **10**(1), 85–6.

Pieroni, A., De Giorgi, E., and Guidice, P. A. (1963). 'Sexual impotence in aortic obliteration'. *Archives of Scientific Medicine (Torino)*, **116**, 395–401.

Pinderhughes, C. A., Grace, E. B., and Reyna, L. G. (1972). 'Psychiatric disorders and sexual functioning'. *American Journal of Psychiatry*, **128**, 1276–82.

Polivy, J. (1977). 'Psychological effects of mastectomy on a woman's feminine self-concept'. *Journal of Nervous and Mental Disease*, **164**, 77–87.

Purtell, J. J., Robins, E., and Cohen, M. E. (1951). 'Observations on clinical aspects of hysteria'. *Journal of the American Medical Association*, **146**, 902–9.

Raboch, J., and Bartak, V. (1968a). 'A contribution to the study of the anesthetic—frigid syndrome in women'. *Ceskoslovenska Psychiatrie*, **64**, 230–5.

Raboch, J., and Bartak V. (1968b). 'The sexual life of frigid women'. *Psychiatrie, Neurologie, and Medizinische Psychologie*, **20**, 368–73.

Rainwater, L. (1960). *And the Poor Get Children*, Quandrangle, Chicago.

Rainwater, L. (1965). *Family Design: Marital Sexuality, Family Size and Contraception*, Aldine, Chicago.

Ray, C. (1977). 'Psychological implications of mastectomy'. *British Journal of Social and Clinical Psychology*, **16**, 373–7.

Rees, W. L. (1976). 'Stress, distress and disease'. *British Journal of Psychiatry*, **128**, 3–18.

Regestein, Q. R., and Horn, H. R. (1978). 'Coitus in patients with cardiac arrythmias'. *Medical Aspects of Human Sexuality*, **12**(2), 108–25.

Reiss, I. L. (1977). 'Changing sexual mores'. In J. Money and H. Musaph (Eds.), *Handbook of Sexology*, Elsevier/North-Holland Biomedical Press, Amsterdam, 563–76.

Renshaw, D. C. (1978). 'Diabetic impotence: A need for further evaluation'. *Medical Aspects of Human Sexuality*, **12**(4), 19–25.

Rice, J. K., and Rice, D. G. (1975). 'Status and sex role issues in co-therapy'. In A. S. Gurman and D. G. Rice (Eds.), *Couples in Conflict: New Directions in Marital Therapy*, Jason Aronson, New York, 145–50.

Rimm, D. C., and Litvak, S. B. (1969). 'Self-verbalization and emotional arousal'. *Journal of Abnormal Psychology*, **74**, 181–7.

Robbins, M. B., and Jensen, G. D. (1978). 'Multiple orgasm in males'. *Journal of Sex Research*, **14**, 21–6.

Roberts, C. D., and Sloboda, W. (1974). 'Afrodex *vs.* placebo in the treatment of male impotence: Statistical analysis of two double-blind crossover studies. *Current Therapeutic Research*, **16**, 96–9.

Robinson, C. H., and Annon, J. S. (1975a). *The Heterosexual Attitude Scale—Female From*, Enabling Systems Inc., Honolulu.

Robinson, C. H., and Annon, J. S. (1975b). *The Heterosexual Attitude Scale—Male Form*, Enabling Systems Inc., Honolulu.

Robinson, C. H., and Annon, J. S. (1975c). *The Heterosexual Behaviour Inventory—Female Form*, Enabling Systems Inc., Honolulu.

Robinson, C. H., and Annon, J. S. (1975d). *The Heterosexual Behaviour Inventory—Male Form*, Enabling Systems Inc., Honolulu.

Roman, M., and Meltzer, B. (1977). 'Co-therapy: A review of current literature (with special reference to therapeutic outcome)'. *Journal of Sex and Marital Therapy*, **3**, 63–77.

Rosen, A., Duehn, W. D., and Connaway, R. S. (1974). 'Content classification system for sexual counseling: Method and application'. *Journal of Sex and Marital Therapy*, **1**, 53–62.

Rosen, R. C. (1976). 'Genital blood flow measurement: Feedback application in sexual therapy'. *Journal of Sex and Marital Therapy*, **2**, 184–96.

Rosen, R. C. (1977). 'Operant control of sexual responses in man'. In G. E. Schwartz and J. Beatty (Eds.), *Biofeedback: Theory and Research*, Academic Press, New York, 301–12.

Rosen, R. C., Shapiro, D., and Schwartz, G. E. (1975). 'Voluntary control of penile tumescence'. *Psychosomatic Medicine*, **37**, 479–83.

Rosenblum, J. A. (1974). 'Human sexuality and the cerebral cortex'. *Diseases of the Nervous System*, **35**, 268–71.

Rosenthal, S. H., and Rosenthal, C. F. (1975). 'Joint sexual counseling: Results and follow up'. *Southern Medical Journal*, **68**, 46–8.

Ross, L. D., Rodin, J., and Zimbardo, P. G. (1969). 'Toward an attribution therapy: The reduction of fear through induced cognitive–emotional misattribution'. *Journal of Personality and Social Psychology*, **62**, 356–63.

Royal College of General Practitioners (1974). *Oral Contraceptives and Health: An Interim Report*, Pitman Medical, London.

Rubin, H. B., and Henson, D. E. (1975). 'Voluntary enhancement of penile erection'. *Bulletin of the Psychonomic Society*, **6**, 158–60.

Russell, P. C., and Brandsma, J. M. (1974). 'A theoretical and empirical integration of the rational-emotive and classical conditioning theories'. *Journal of Consulting and Clinical Clinical Psychology*, **42**, 234–9.

Sadock, B. J., and Spitz, H. I. (1975). 'Group psychotherapy of sexual disorders'. In A. M. Freedman, H. I. Kaplan, and B. J. Sadock (Eds.), *Comprehensive Textbook of Psychology*, Vol. II (2nd edn.), Williams and Wilkins, Baltimore, 1569–75.

Segar, C. J. (1974). 'Sexual dysfunctions and marital discord'. In Kaplan, H. S., *The New Sex Therapy: Active Treatment of Sexual Dysfunctions*, Bailliere Tindall, London, 501–18.

Salter, A. (1949). *Conditioned Reflex Therapy*, Capricorn Books, New York.

Salvatierra, O., Fortmann, J. L., and Belzer, F. O. (1975). 'Sexual function in males before and after renal transplantation'. *Urology*, **5**, 74–6.

Schapiro, B. (1943). 'Premature ejaculation: Review of 1130 cases'. *Journal of Urology* (Baltimore), **50**, 374–80.

Scheig, R. (1975). 'Changes in sexual performance due to liver disease'. *Medical Aspects of Human Sexuality*, **9**(4), 67–79.

Schellen, M. C. M. (1968). 'Further results with induction of ejaculation by electrovibration'. *Bulletin Society. R. Blege. Gynecology and Obstetrics*, **38**, 301–5.

Schiavi, R. C., and White, D. (1976). 'Androgens and male sexual dysfunction: A review of human studies'. *Journal of Sex and Marital Therapy*, **2**, 214–28.

Schneider, M. D., and Julian, D. G. (1974). 'Myocardial infarction and disturbed sexual behaviour'. *British Journal of Sexual Medicine*, **1**, 24–6.

Schofield, M. (1965). *The Sexual Behavior of Young People*, Longmans, London.

Schofield, M. (1973). *The Sexual Behaviour of Young Adults*, Allen Lane, London.

Scott, F. B., Bradley, W.E., and Timm, G. W. (1973). 'Management of erectile impotence: Use of implantable inflatable prosthesis'. *Urology*, **2**, 80–2.

Semans, J. (1956). 'Premature ejaculation: A new approach', *Southern Medical Journal*, **49**, 353–8.

Shapiro, A. K. (1971). 'Placebo effects in medicine, psychotherapy and psychoanalysis'. In A. E. Bergin and S. L. Garfield (Eds.), *Handbook of Psychotherapy and Behavior Change: An Empirical analysis*. Wiley, New York, 439–73.

Sharpe, R., and Meyer, V. (1973). 'Modification of "cognitive sexual pain" by the spouse under supervision'. *Behavior Therapy*, **4**, 285–7.

Sherman, A. R. (1972). 'Real-life exposure as a primary therapeutic factor in the desensitization of treatment of fear'. *Journal of Abnormal Psychology*, **79**, 19–28.

Siddall, L. B., and Bosma, B. J. (1976). 'Co-therapy as a training process'. *Psychotherapy: Theory, Research and Practice*, **13**, 209–13.

Simpson, G. M., Blair, J. H., and Amuso, D. (1965). 'Effects of anti-depressants on genito-urinary function'. *Diseases of the Nervous System*, **20**, 787–9.

Singer, J., and Singer, I. (1978). 'Types of female orgasm'. In J. Lo Piccolo and L. Lo Piccolo (Eds.), *Handbook of Sex Therapy*, Plenum, New York, 175–86.

Sintchak, G. and Geer, J. (1975). 'A vaginal plethysmograph system'. *Psychophysiology*, **12**, 13–5.

Skynner, A. C. R. (1976a). 'A comment on the conjoint physical'. *British Journal of Sexual Medicine*, **3**, 13–4.

Skynner, A. C. R., (1976b). *One Flesh: Separate Persons: Principles on Family and Marital Therapy*, Constable, London.

Sloane, R. B., Staples, F. R., Whipple, K., and Cristol, A. H. (1977). 'Patients' attitudes toward behavior therapy and psychotherapy'. *American Journal of Psychiatry*, **133**, 134–7.

Smith, H. D. (1975). 'The use of hypnosis in treating inorgasmic sexual response in women: Report of five cases'. *Journal of the American Institute of Hypnosis*, **16**, 119–25.

Snyder, A., Lo Piccolo, L., and Lo Piccolo, J. (1975). 'Secondary orgasmic dysfunction. II. case study'. *Archives of Sexual Behavior*, **4**, 277–83.

Sobrero, A. J., Stearns, H. E., and Blair, J. H. (1965). 'Technic for the induction of ejaculation in humans'. *Fertility and Sterility*, **16**, 765–7.

Solnick, R. L., and Birren, J. E. (1977). 'Age and male erectile responsiveness'. *Archives of Sexual Behavior*, **6**, 1–9.

Sorensen, R. C. (1973). *Adolescent Sexuality in Contemporary America (The Sorensen Report)*. World Publishing, New York.

Spanier, G. B. (1976). 'Measuring dyadic adjustment: New scales for assessing the quality of marriage and similar dyads'. *Journal of Marriage and the Family*, **38**, 15–28.

Spencer, R. F., and Raft, D. (1977). 'Depression and diminished sexual desire'. *Medical Aspects of Human Sexuality*, **11**(8), 51–61.

Spitz, C. J., Gold, A. R., and Adams, D. B. (1975). 'Cognitive and hormonal factors affecting coital frequency'. *Archives of Sexual Behavior*, **4**, 249–63.

Stamphl, T. G. (1967). 'Implosive therapy: The theory, the sub-human analogue, the strategy, and the technique: Part 1. The Theory'. In S. G. Armitage (Ed.), *Behavior Modification Techniques in the Treatment of Emotional Disorders*, V. A. Publication, Battle Creek, Michigan, 22–37.

Stamphl, T. G., and Levis, D. J. (1967). 'Essentials of implosive therapy: A learning-

284

theory-based psychodynamic behavioral therapy'. *Journal of Abnormal Psychology*, **72**, 496–503.

Steele, T. E., Finkelstein, S. H., and Finkelstein, F. O. (1976). 'Hemodialysis patients and spouses: marital discord, sexual problems, and depression'. *The Journal of Nervous and Mental Disease*, **162**, 225–37.

Stewart, T. D., and Gerson, S. N. (1976). 'Penile prosthesis: Psychological factors'. *Urology*, **7**, 400–2.

Stewart, W. F. R. (1975). *Sex and the Physically Handicapped*, National Fund for Research in Crippling Disease, Horsham.

Story, N. L. (1974). 'Sexual dysfunction resulting from drug side effects'. *Journal of Sex Research*, **10**, 132–49.

Strong, S. R., and Schmidt. L. D. (1970). 'Expertness and influence in counseling'. *Journal of Counseling Psychology*. **17**, 81–7.

Stuart, R. B. (1969). 'Operant-interpersonal treatment for marital discord'. *Journal of Consulting and Clinical Psychology*, **33**, 675–82.

Susskind, D. J. (1970). 'The idealized self-image: A new technique in confidence training'. *Behavior Therapy*, **1**, 538–41.

Tasto, D. L. (1977). 'Self-report schedules and inventories'. In A. R. Ciminero, K. S. Calhoun, and H. E. Adams (Eds.), *Handbook of Behavioral Assessment*, Wiley, New York, 153–93.

Tauber, E. S. (1940). 'The effects of castration upon the sexuality of the adult male'. *Psychosomatic Medicine*, **2**, 74–87.

Taylor, G. R. (1959). *Sex in History* (Rev. ed.), Thames and Hudson, London.

Taylor Segraves, R. (1977). 'Pharmacological agents causing sexual dysfunction'. *Journal of Sex and Marital Therapy*, **3**, 157–76.

Terman, L. M. (1938). *Psychological Factors in Marital Happiness*, McGraw-Hill, New York.

Terman, L. M. (1951). 'Correlates of orgasm adequacy in a group of 556 wives'. *Journal of Psychology*, **32**, 115–72.

Thomas, E. J. (1976). *Marital Communication and Decision Making: Analysis, Assessment and Change*, Free Press, New York.

Thoresen, C. E., and Mahoney, M. J. (1974). *Behavioral Self-Control*, Holt, Rinehart, and Winston, New York.

Thurm, J. (1975). 'Sexual potency of patients on chronic hemodialysis'. *Urology*, **5**, 60–2.

Toussieng, P. W. (1977). 'Men's fear of having too small a penis'. *Medical Aspects of Human Sexuality*, **11**(5), 62–70.

Trimmer, E. (1978). 'Reducing the side effects of the pill'. *British Journal of Sexual Medicine*, **5**(33), 3.

Truax, C. B., and Carkhuff, R. R. (1967). *Toward Effective Counseling and Psychotherapy: Training and Practice*, Aldine, Chicago.

Truax, C. B., and Mitchell, K. M. (1971). 'Research on certain therapist interpersonal skills in relation to process and outcome'. In A. E. Bergin and S. L. Garfield (Eds.), *Handbook of Psychotherapy and Behavior Change: An Empirical Analysis*, Wiley, New York, 271–344.

Tudoriu, T. (1977a). 'Penile implants'. *British Journal of Sexual Medicine*, **5**(24), 11–4.

Tudoriu, T. (1977b). 'Penile implants: Part II'. *British Journal of Sexual Medicine*, **5**(25), 27–8.

Twentyman, G. T., and McFall, R. M. (1975). 'Behavioral training of social skills in shy males'. *Journal of Counsulting and Clinical Psychology*, **43**, 384–95.

Uddenberg, N. (1974). 'Psychological aspects of sexual inadequacy in women'. *Journal of Psychosomatic Research*, **18**, 33–47.

Ullman, L. P. (1970). 'On cognitions and behavior therapy'. *Behavior Therapy*, **1**, 201–4.

Valins, S., and Nisbett, R. E. (1971). *Attribution Processes in the Development and Treatment of Emotional Disorders*, General Learning Press, Morristown, N. J.

Valins, S., and Ray, A. A. (1967). 'Effects of cognitive desensitization and avoidence behavior'. *Journal of Personality and Social Psychology*, 7, 345–50.

Van Egeren L. F. (1970). 'Psychophysiology of systematic desensitization: The habituation model'. *Journal of Behavior Therapy and Experimental Psychiatry*, 1, 249–55.

Van Egeren, L. F. (1971). 'Psychophysiological aspects of systematic desensitization: Some outstanding issues'. *Behaviour Research and Therapy*, 9, 65–77.

Van Egeren, L. F., Feather, B. W., and Hein, P. L. (1971). 'Desensitization of phobias: Some psychophysiological propositions'. *Psychophysiology*, 8, 213–28.

Van Keef, P. A., and Gregory, A. (1977). 'Sexual relations in the aging female'. In J. Money, and H. Husaph (Eds.), *Handbook of Sexology*, Elsevier/North-Holland Biomedical Press, Amsterdam, 839–46.

Van Thiel, D. H. (1976). 'Liver disease and sexual functioning'. *Medical Aspects of Human Sexuality*, 13(3), 117–8.

Van Thiel, D. H., and Lester, R. (1977). 'Therapy of sexual dysfunction in alcohol abusers. A Pandora's Box,' *Gastroenterology*, 71, 1354–6.

Velten, E. (1968). 'A laboratory task for induction of mood states'. *Behaviour Research and Therapy*, 6, 473–82.

Vincent, J. P., Weiss, R. L., and Birchler, G. R. (1975). 'A behavioral analysis of problem solving in distressed and nondistressed married and stranger dyads'. *Behavior Therapy*, 6, 475–87

Wabrek, A. J., and Wabrek, C. J. (1975). 'Dyspareunia'. *Journal of Sex and Marital Therapy*, 1, 234–41.

Waggoner, R. W., Mudd, E. H., and Shearer, M. L. (1973). 'Training dual sex teams for rapid treatment of sexual dysfunction: A pilot program'. *Psychiatric Annals*, 3, 61–76.

Wagner, N. N. (1977). 'Sexual behaviour and the cardiac patient'. In J. Money and H. Musaph (Eds.), *Handbook of Sexology*, Elsevier/North-Holland Biomedical Press, Amsterdam, 959–67.

Wallace, C. J. (1976). 'Assessment of psychotic behaviour'. In M. Hersen and A. S. Bellack (Eds.), *Behavioural Assessment: A Practical Handbook*, Pergamon, Oxford, 261–303

Wallace, D. H., and Barbach, L. G. (1974). 'Preorgasmic group treatment'. *Journal of Sex and Marital Therapy*, 1, 146–54.

Wallin, P. (1960). 'A study of orgasm as a condition of woman's enjoyment of intercourse'. *Journal of Social Psychology*, 51, 191–8.

Wallin, P., and Clark, A. L. (1963). 'A study of orgasm as a condition of women's enjoyment of coitus in the middle years of marriage'. *Human Biology*, 2, 131–9.

Wear, J. B. (1976). 'Causes of dyspareunia in men'. *Medical Aspects of Human Sexuality*, 10(5), 140–53.

Weinstein, L. (1971). 'Guidelines on the choice of a co-therapist'. *Psychotherapy: Theory, Research, and Practice*, 8, 301–3.

Weiss, A. J., and Diamond, M. D. (1966). 'Sexual adjustment, identification, and attitudes of patients with myelopathy.' *Archives of Physical Medicine and Rehabilitation*, 47, 245–50.

Weiss, H. D. (1972). 'The physiology of human penile erection'. *Annals of Internal Medicine*, 76, 793–9.

Weiss, R. L., and Margolin, G. (1977). 'Assessment of marital conflict and accord'. In A. R. Ciminero, K. S. Calhoun, and H. E. Adams (Eds.), *Handbook of Behavioral Assessment*, Wiley, New York, 555–602.

Weitzenhoffer, A. M. (1957). *General Techniques of Hypnotism*, Grune and Stratton, New York.

Whalen, R. E. (1966). 'Sexual motivation'. *Psychological Review*, 73, 151–63.

286

Whitehead, A., and Mathews, A. (1977). 'Attitude change during behavioural treatment for sexual inadequacy'. *British Journal of Social and Clinical Psychology*, **16**, 275–81.

Wicker, A. W. (1969). 'Attitudes *versus* actions: The relationship of verbal and overt behavioral responses to attitude objects'. *Journal of Social Issues*, **25**, 41–78.

Wiens, A. N. (1976). 'The assessment interview'. In I. B. Weiner (Ed.), *Clinical Methods in Psychology*, Wiley, New York, 3–60.

Wilkins, W. (1971). 'Desensitization: Social and cognitive factors underlying the effectiveness of Wolpe's procedure'. *Psychological Bulletin*, **76**, 311–7.

Wilkins, W. (1972). 'Desensitization: Getting it together with Davison and Wilson'. *Psychological Bulletin*, **78**, 32–6.

Wilkins, W. (1973). 'Expectancy of therapeutic gain: A empirical and conceptual critique'. *Journal of Consulting and Clinical Psychology*, **40**, 69–77.

Williams, W., and Orsmond, A. (1977). 'Rapid impatient treatment of severe female sexual dysfunction'. *Australian and New Zealand Journal of Psychiatry*, **11**, 61–4.

Wilson, G. T. (1973). 'Innovations in the modification of phobic behaviour in two clinical cases'. *Behavior Therapy*, **4**, 426–30.

Wilson, G. T. (1977). 'Alcohol and human sexual behaviour'. *Behaviour Research and Therapy*, **15**, 239–52.

Wilson, G. T., and Davison, G. C. (1971). 'Processes of fear reduction in systematic desensitization: Animal studies'. *Psychological Bulletin*, **76**, 1–14.

Wilson, G. T., and Evans, I. M. (1976). 'Adult behavior therapy and the therapist–client relationship'. In C. M. Franks and G. T. Wilson (Eds.), *Annual Review of Behavior Therapy Theory and Practice*, Vol. 4, Brunner-Mazel, New York, 771–92.

Wilson, G. T., and Evans, I. (1977). 'The therapist–client relationship in behaviour threapy'. In A. S. Gurman and A. M. Razin (Eds.), *Effective Psychotherapy: A Handbook of Research*, Pergamon, Oxford, 544–65.

Wince, J. P., and Caird, W. K. (1976). 'The effects of systematic desensitization and video desensitization in the treatment of essential sexual dysfunction in women'. *Behavior Therapy*, **7**, 335–42.

Wincze, J. P., Hoon, P., and Hoon, E. F. (1977). 'Sexual arousal in women: A comparison of cognitive and physiological responses by continuous measurement'. *Archives of Sexual Behavior*, **6**, 121–33.

Winokur, G., Guze, S. B., and Pfeiffer, E. (1959). "Developmental and sexual factors in women: A comparison between control, neurotic, and psychotic groups'. *American Journal of Psychiatry*, **115**, 1097–100.

Winokur, G., and Holeman, E. (1963). 'Chronic anxiety neurosis: clinical and sexual aspects'. *Acta Psychiatrica Scandinavica*, **39**, 384–412.

Winokur, G., and Leonard, C. (1963). 'Sexual life in patients with hysteria'. *Diseases of the Nervous System*, **24**, 337–43.

Wolberg, L. R. (1948). *Medical Hypnosis*, Vols. 1 and 2, Grune and Stratton, New York.

Wolberg, L. R. (1967). *The Technique of Psychotherapy*, Heinemann, London.

Wolfe, L. (1978). 'The question of surrogates in sex therapy'. In J. Lo Piccolo and L. Lo Piccolo (Eds.), *Handbook of Sex Therapy*, Plenum, New York, 491–7.

Wolpe, J. (1958). *Psychotherapy by Reciprocal Inhibition*, Stanford University Press, Stanford.

Wolpe, J. (1969). *The Practice of Behaviour Therapy*, Pergamon, Oxford.

Wolpe, J., Brady, J. P., Serber, M., Agras, S., and Liberman, R. P. (1973). 'The current status of systematic desensitization', *American Journal of Psychiatry*, **130**, 961–4.

World Health Organization (1975). *Education and Treatment in Human Sexuality: The Training of Health Professionals*, World Health Organization, Geneva.

Yates, A. J. (1975). *Theory and Practice of Behavior Therapy*, Wiley, New York.

Yates, A. J. (1976). 'Research methods in behavior modification: A comparative evaluation'. In M. Hersen, R. M. Eisler, and P. M. Miller (Eds.), *Progress in Behavior Modification*, Vol. 2, Academic Press, New York, 279–306.

Yulis, S. (1976). Generalization of therapeutic gain in the treatment of premature ejaculation'. *Behavior Therapy*, **7**, 355–8.

Zeiss, R. A., Christensen A., and Levine, A. G. (1978). 'Treatment of premature ejaculation through male-only groups'. *Journal of Sex and Marital Therapy*, **4**, 139–43.

Zentner, E. B., and Pouyat, S. B. (1978). 'The erotic factor as a complication in the dual-sex therapy team's effective functioning'. *Journal of Sex and Marital Therapy*, **4**, 114–21.

Zilbergeld, B. (1975). 'Group treatment of sexual dysfunction in men without partners'. *Journal of Sex and Marital Therapy*, **1**, 204–14.

Zimbardo, P. G., (Ed.) (1969). *The Cognitive Control of Motivation*, Scott Foresman, Glenview, Illinois.

Zinsser, H. H. (1975). 'Sex and surgical procedures in the male'. In A. M. Freedman, H. I. Kaplan, and B. J. Sadock (Eds.), *Comprehensive Textbook of Psychiatry*, Vol. II (2nd edn.), Williams and Wilkins, Baltimore, 1474–7.

Zuckerman, M. (1973). 'Scale for sex experience for males and females'. *Journal of Consulting and Psychology*, **41**, 27–9.

Zuckerman, M. (1976). 'Sexual behavior of college students'. In W. W. Oaks, G. A. Melchiode, and I. Ficher (Eds.), *Sex and the Life Cycle*, Grune and Stratton, New York, 67–79.

Additional references added in proof

Belliveau, F., and Richter, L. (1970). *Understanding Human Sexual Inadequacy*. Hodder and Stoughton, London.

Edwards, A. E., and Husted, J. R. (1976). 'Penile sensitivity, age and sexual behavior'. *Journal of Clinical Psychology*, **32**, 697–700.

Weisberg, M. (1977). 'Vaginal anaesthesia'. *Medical Aspects of Human Sexuality*, **11** (3) 81–9.

Author Index

Abel, G. G., 191, 219, 224, 265, 266
Abram, H. S., 20, 21, 265
Abramovici, H. 271
Abramson, P. R., 216, 265
Adams, D. B., 283
Adams, H. E., 268
Agras, W. S., 157, 265, 266, 274, 276, 286
Alevizos, P. N., 221, 265
Alexander, L., 164, 165, 265
Alexander, S., 235, 265
Al-Issa, 155, 276
Altinel, A., 275
Amuso, D., 283
Anderson, C., 271
Annon, J. S., 138, 149, 151, 166, 167, 191, 214, 215, 216, 217, 265, 282
Ansari, J. M. A., 83, 84, 85, 86, 237, 238, 242, 257, 265
Apfelbaum, B, 184, 265
Apfelberg, D. B. 169, 265
Archambault, F. X., 143, 273
Asirdas, S., 161, 162, 266
Astrup, C., 164, 266
Attia, S. L., 275
Auerbach, R., 240, 242, 243, 257, 266
Azrin, N. H., 50, 51, 266

Balodimus, M. C., 24, 276
Bancroft, John, 45, 104, 106, 191, 219, 266, 267, 279
Bancroft, Judy, 279
Bandura, A., 54, 134, 266
Barbach, L. G., 146, 254, 255, 256, 266, 285
Bardwick, J. M., 144, 266
Barlow, D. H., 185, 191, 210, 219, 221, 224, 225, 230, 259, 266, 274, 276
Barnett, D. M., 276
Bartak, V., 62, 281
Bateman, D. E., 276

Bauer, H. G., 23, 266
Beach, F. A., 26, 266
Beardwood, C. J., 267
Beaumont, G., 28, 266
Beck, A. T., 131, 221, 266, 267
Beck, D. F., 180
Becker, H. B., 276
Becker, R., 266
Beech, H. R., 161, 162, 266
Bellack, A. S., 5, 221, 274
Belliveau, F., 183, 287
Bellville, C. J., 267
Bellville, T. P., 200, 267
Belzer, F. O., 282
Bem, S. L., 220, 267
Bennett, J. A., 15, 278
Bentler, P. M., 216, 267
Bergin, A. E., 126, 131, 158, 159, 267
Bergner, R. M., 63, 267
Berman, E. M., 180, 267
Bernstein, D. A., 152, 153, 154, 267
Beumont, P. V. J., 167, 267
Binkley, L., 280
Birchler, G. R., 50, 51, 267, 285
Birren, J. E., 17, 283
Blair, J. H., 283
Blanchard, E. B., 134, 162, 224, 265, 266, 267
Bloch, A., 19, 267
Blum, H., 273
Booraem, C. D., 163, 270
Borkovec, T. D., 152, 153, 154, 159, 221, 267
Bors, E., 22, 24, 267
Bosma, B. J., 199, 283
Bowers, L. M., 268
Bozarth, J. D., 280
Bradley, W. E., 283
Brady, J. P., 155, 267, 286
Brandes, J., 271

Brandsma, J. M., 131, 282
Brecher, E., 12, 267
Brecher, R., 12, 267
Bregman, S., 24, 267
Brehm, J. W., 132, 133, 267
Briddell, D. W., 28, 267
Bristow, A. R., 266
Brockway, J., 277
Brodie, K. H., 276
Brooke, B. N., 268
Brown, C., 216, 274
Brown, P. R., 181, 200, 203, 213, 214,
    225, 268
Brown, W. A., 27, 268
Burbank, F., 208, 268
Burgess, A. W., 94, 273
Burnham. W. R., 28, 268
Butler, C. A., 109, 110, 111, 268

Caird, W. K., 158, 217, 268, 286
Calderwood, M. D., 269
Calhoun, K. S., 268
Callahan, E. J., 221, 265
Campbell, D. T., 258, 268
Canning, J. R., 27, 268
Carkhuff, R. R., 126, 284
Carver, J. R., 29, 268
Cassidy, W. L., 62, 268
Cautela, J. R., 215, 268
Chapanis, A., 134, 268
Chapanis, N. P., 134, 268
Cheek, D. B., 164, 268
Chiu, W. S., 28, 280
Christensen, A., 287
Christenson, C. V., 55, 268
Ciminero, A. R., 5, 222, 268
Clark, A. L., 109, 285
Clifford, R., 16, 82, 99, 268
Cohen, A. R., 130, 132, 134, 267, 268
Cohen, M. E., 268, 281
Cole, M., 184, 268
Coles, L., 104, 106, 266
Comarr, A. E., 22, 24, 267, 268
Comfort, A., 142, 268
Cone, J. D., 5
Connaway, R. S., 282
Cooper, A. J., 27, 43, 61, 82, 84, 85, 86,
    88, 90, 167, 168, 269
Corriveau, D. P., 268
Corsini, R. J., 130, 269
Cottrell, T. L. C., 268
Couper-Smartt, J. D., 269
Crasilneck, H. B., 165, 269
Cristol, A., 280, 283

Croft, H. A., 125, 269
Cromwell, R. E., 220, 269
Csillag, E. R., 162, 269
Cummings, V., 28, 269
Curran, J. P., 185, 269
Cushman, P., 29, 269

D'Agostino, P. A., 218, 279
Davies, N. H., 270
Davis, D. M., 270
Davison, G. C., 132, 159, 269, 286
Dawkins, S., 248, 269
Deabler, H. L., 164, 269
Dearborn, L. W., 143, 269
Decenteo, E. T., 272
De Giorgi, E., 27, 281
De Moor, P., 271, 272
De Risi, W. J., 277
Deutsch, R. M., 166, 269
Devanesan, M., 202, 269
Diamond, M. D., 285
Dickes, R., 200, 270
Dittman, F., 275
Divita, E. C., 169, 270
Dmowski, W. P., 167, 270
Doering, C. H., 276
Dormont, P., 100, 270
Dornbush, R. L., 271
Duddle, M., 108, 109, 270
Duehn, W. D., 282
Dunn, M. E., 200
Durnell, D., 278
D'Zurrila, T. J., 180, 273

Easley, E. B., 26, 167, 270
Edwards, A., 270, 287
Edwards, A. E., 64, 65
Eisler, R. M., 185, 221, 270, 274
Ellenberg, M., 25, 270
Ellis, A., 131, 132, 270
Ellison, C., 106, 108, 270
Enbraugh, J., 266
Epstein, G. M., 265
Escamilla, R. F., 26, 270
Evans, I. M., 126, 286

Fabbri, R., 164, 270
Farkas, G. M., 28, 270
Feather, B. W., 285
Fellman, S. L., 167, 270
Festinger, L., 134, 270
Finkelstein, F. O., 284
Finkelstein, S. H., 284
Fislt, J. M., 128, 270

Fishbein, M., 134, 270
Fisher, C., 224, 270
Fisher, S., 33, 34, 35, 36, 49, 62, 110, 111, 113, 114, 270
Fithian, M. A., 151, 167, 213, 214, 273
Fitting, M. D., 59, 270
Flanagan, N. B., 268
Flowers, J. V., 163, 270
Ford, C. S., 26, 266
Fordney-Settlage, D. S., 22, 116, 270
Fortmann, J. L., 282
Foster, A. L., 218, 270, 271
Fournier, D. G., 269
Fox, C. A., 27, 168, 271
Frank, D., 59, 271
Frank, E., 49, 271
Frank, J. D., 127, 128, 271
Freeman, R., 280
Freeman, W., 161, 271
French, W. A., 272
Freund, K., 220, 224, 271
Friedman, D. E., 155, 271
Friedman, E. H., 18, 19, 273
Friedman, H. J., 128, 271
Friedman, J. M., 18, 271
Friedman, L. J., 106, 271
Fuchs, K., 164, 248, 271
Fuhr, R., 47, 272

Gagnon, J. H., 55, 268
Gamble, B., 52, 273
Gambrill, E. D., 180, 185, 220, 271
Gath, D., 279
Gauthier, J., 159, 271
Gebhard, P. H., 275
Geboes, K., 61, 77, 93, 246, 271, 272
Geer, J. H., 47, 224, 225, 272, 283
Gerson, S. N., 169, 284
Getty, C., 199, 272
Gill, H., 181, 272
Gilmore, J. B., 130, 274
Ginsberg, G. L., 73, 272
Glass, D. D., 24, 272
Glick, B. R., 220, 272
Gliedman, L. W., 271
Glisson, D. H., 180, 272
Gold, A. R., 283
Goldberg, A., 280
Goldberg, M., 80, 272
Golden, J. S., 200, 272
Golden, M. A., 200, 272
Goldfried, M. R., 131, 132, 158, 159, 188, 214, 272
Goldstein, A. P., 128, 129, 130, 272, 280

Goldstein, H. H., 276
Goodwin, W. E., 168, 273
Gordon, S. B., 275
Gorer, G., 71, 272
Gough, H. G., 215, 272
Graber, G., 167, 275
Grabstald, H., 168, 273
Grace, E. B., 281
Greenberg, J. S., 143, 273
Greenblatt, R. B., 167, 273
Greene, L. F., 25, 273
Greenwood, P., 272
Greer, B. E., 273
Greer, S., 22, 115, 180, 273
Gregory, A., 55, 285
Griffith, E. R., 24, 273
Gross, S. J., 220, 272
Groth, N. A., 94, 273
Guidice, P. A., 281
Gurman, A. S., 126, 180, 273
Guze, S. B., 61, 279, 286

Hackman, A., 279
Haissly, J. C., 267
Hall, J. A., 165, 269
Hamburg, D. A., 276
Hamilton, A., 21, 168, 273
Handy, L., 280
Harbin, H. T., 52, 273
Hardiker, P., 274
Hare, E. H., 142, 273
Hartland, J., 165, 273
Hartman, W. E., 151, 167, 213, 214, 273
Haspels, A. A., 115, 280
Hawkins, R. P., 5, 268
Heiman, J. R., 146, 214, 225, 273, 278
Heimberg, J. S., 273
Heimberg, R. G., 185, 273
Hein, P. L., 285
Hellerstein, H. K., 18, 19, 273
Henson, C., 273
Henson, D. E., 45, 225, 273, 282
Henton, C. L., 12, 274
Herman, S. H., 161, 274
Hersen, M., 5, 185, 210, 221, 230, 259, 274
Hessellund, H., 143, 274
Hester, L. R., 265
Higgins, G. E., 24, 274
Himelstein, P., 221, 278
Hoch, Z., 271
Hogan, R. A., 160, 274
Holeman, E., 62, 63, 116, 286
Hoon, E. F., 225, 274, 286

292

Hoon, P. W., 159, 162, 217, 225, 274, 286
Hops, H., 50, 180, 274, 280, 281
Horn, H. R., 18, 281
Hovland, C. I., 130, 274
Howard, D. H., 33, 275
Hunt, M., 111, 274
Husek, T. R., 235, 265
Husted, J. R., 64, 65, 287

Imber, S. D., 271
Ismail, A. A. A., 269, 271
Iverson, R. E., 169, 277

Jacob, T., 220, 274
Jacobs, M., 184, 274
Jacobson, E., 152, 153, 155, 274
Jacobson, N. S., 180, 274
Janis, I. L., 130, 274
Jehu, D., 36, 91, 274
Jennings, J. R., 276
Jensen, G. D., 14, 97, 282
Joe, V. C., 216, 274
Johnson, H. J., 131, 279
Johnson, J., 23, 26, 82, 84, 90, 93, 97, 167, 275
Johnson, V. E., 12, 13, 14, 15, 17, 18, 32, 33, 34, 43, 45, 47, 52, 61, 63, 64, 65, 82, 84, 85, 86, 88, 89, 90, 93, 94, 99, 106, 108, 109, 115, 124, 125, 135, 138, 139, 144, 147, 148, 149, 160, 161, 181, 183, 184, 186, 188, 189, 197, 200, 201, 202, 203, 204, 213, 214, 225, 230, 231, 232, 233, 234, 237, 238, 240, 242, 243, 244, 245, 246, 247, 248, 249, 251, 252, 255, 256, 257, 258, 259, 279
Jones, A., 274
Jones, E. E., 127, 275
Jones, R., 266
Jourard, S. M., 130, 275
Julian, D. G., 283
Julier, D., 279
Jungck, E. C., 273

Kagle, A., 80, 100, 190, 276
Kahn, C. B., 276
Kaminetzky, H. A., 270
Kanin, E. J., 33, 275
Kanno, P., 280
Kanouse, D. E., 275
Kaplan, H. S., 13, 14, 18, 28, 43, 49, 54, 77, 78, 91, 92 93, 96, 100, 103, 104, 110, 111, 112, 139, 146, 147, 148, 149, 150, 160, 161, 189, 190, 197, 201, 203, 275

Karacan, I., 224, 275
Karlen, A., 215, 216, 277
Katkin, E. S., 221, 277
Kazdin, A. E., 159, 222, 275
Keefe, F. J., 5, 275
Kegel, A. H., 166, 167, 275
Kelalis, P. P., 25, 273
Kelley, H. H., 274, 275
Kent, R. N., 214, 272
Kerckhoff, A., 88, 275
Kilmann, P. R., 240, 242, 243, 257, 266
King, L. W., 277
Kinsey, A. C., 34, 55, 63, 71, 81, 88, 110, 111, 142, 143, 144, 275
Kirkham, K. E., 271
Kirkpatrick, C. C., 279
Klebanow, D., 25, 275
Kleinhaus, M., 271
Kline-Graber, G., 167, 275
Knob, K., 271
Kockott, G., 239, 242, 257, 275
Kohlenberg, R. J., 251, 255, 256, 275
Kolodny, R. C., 24, 25, 271, 276, 279
Koncz, L., 24, 276
Kopel, S. A., 275
Korchin, S. J., 212, 276
Kotin, J., 29, 276
Kraemer, H. C., 27, 276
Kraft, M., 155, 276
Krauft, C. C., 280
Kreuz, L. E., 27, 276
Kupfer, D. J., 271
Kupperman, H. S., 270

Lacey, B. C., 48, 276
Lacey, J. I., 48, 276
Lallemand, M., 276
Landis, J., 43, 276
Langevin, R., 162, 271, 276, 280
Langmyhr, G. J., 186, 276
Lash, H., 169, 265, 276
Lazarus, A. A., 131, 155, 276
Lazarus, R. S., 42, 276
Lear, H., 270
Leiblum, S. R., 209, 276
Leitenberg, H., 159, 266, 276
Lennard-Jones, J. E., 268
Leonard, C., 63, 286
LeRoy, D. H., 184, 276
Lester, R., 28, 285
Levay, A. N., 80, 100, 190, 276
Levine, A. G., 287
Levine, S. B., 92, 104, 105, 276
Levis, D. J., 160, 276, 283

Levit, H. I., 164, 277
Levitt, E. E., 221, 277
Levy, N. B., 20, 277
Libby, R. W., 73, 277
Liberman, R. P., 185, 277, 286
Lick, J. R., 221, 277
Lieberman, M. A., 208, 277
Lief, H. I., 77, 79, 80, 143, 180, 215, 216, 267, 277, 279
Linehan, M. M., 212, 277
Lipinski, D. P., 268
Lipsedge, M. S., 155, 271
Litvak, S. B., 131, 281
Lloyd, F. A., 268
Lobitz, G. K., 214, 277
Lobitz, W. C., 145, 146, 148, 214, 251, 252, 254, 255, 277
Locke, H. J., 49, 253, 277
Loeffler, R. A., 169, 277
Lo Piccolo, J., 145, 146, 148, 201, 214, 217, 218, 251, 252, 253, 254, 255, 273, 277, 278, 279, 283
Lo Piccolo, L., 273, 278, 283
Loraine, J., 269
Love, D. N., 271
Lowe, J. C., 244, 246, 278
Lowndes Sevely, J., 15, 278
Lubin, B. L., 221, 277, 278
Luna, M., 270
Luttge, W. C., 26, 278

McCann, M., 277
McConaghy, N., 161, 279
McCoy, N. N., 218, 279
McFall, R. M., 221, 222, 279, 284
McGovern, K. B., 37, 49, 114, 209, 252, 255, 256, 279
McHugh, G., 215, 279
Mack, W., 26, 278
MacLean, P. D., 23, 278
MacLeod, J., 25, 275
Maddison, J., 167, 278
Maddock, J. W., 135, 278
Madsen, C. H., 157, 273, 278
Maeder, J. P., 267
Mahoney, M. J., 131, 222, 278, 284
Malamuth, N., 184, 278
Mann, K., 280
Margolin, G., 220, 285
Marholin, D., 207, 278
Marks, I., 157, 159, 160, 191, 216, 219, 278
Marshall, W. L., 159, 271
Marston, E. D., 88, 278

Martin, B., 180, 274
Martin, C. E., 275, 278
Martin, M., 162, 276
Martin, P. A., 55, 78, 278
Maser, M. R., 265
Massler, D., 269
Masters, W. H., 12, 13, 14, 15, 17, 18, 32, 33, 34, 43, 45, 47, 52, 61, 63, 64, 65, 82, 84, 85, 86, 88, 89, 90, 93, 94, 99, 106, 108, 109, 115, 124, 125, 135, 138, 139, 144, 147, 148, 149, 160, 161, 181, 183, 184, 186, 188, 189, 197, 200, 201, 202, 203, 204, 213, 214, 225, 230, 231, 232, 233, 234, 237, 238, 240, 242, 243, 244, 245, 246, 247, 248, 249, 251, 252, 255, 256, 257, 258, 259, 279
Mathews, A. M., 159, 182, 186, 200, 216, 231, 233, 237, 257, 279, 286
Maurice, W. L., 61, 279
Mawson, A. B., 155, 279
May, J. R., 131, 279
Mayclin, D. K., 270
Meichenbaum, D. H., 131, 158, 279
Meikle, S., 59, 279
Meltzer, B., 197, 199, 282
Mendelsohn, M., 266
Meyer, R. G., 161, 271
Meyer, V., 101, 283
Mikulas, W. L., 244, 246, 278
Miller, W. R., 143, 279
Miller, W. W., 270
Mills, L. C., 25, 28, 29, 279
Mischel, W., 214, 280
Mitchell, K. M., 126, 280, 284
Mock, J., 266
Montgomery, D., 273
Monti, P. M., 268
Moos, R. H., 276
Morgan, R. T. T., 274
Morganstern, K. P., 159, 160, 212, 280
Morokoff, P., 272
Mosher, D. L., 216, 265
Mourad, M., 28, 280
Mudd, E. H., 285
Munjack, D., 61, 137, 249, 251, 255, 256, 258, 280
Murray, L., 125, 280
Musaph, H., 115, 280

Nagler, E., 271
Nash, E. W., 271
Naster, B. J., 266
Nawas, M. M., 131, 280
Nelson, R. O., 268, 280

Nisbett, R. E., 127, 275, 284
Nusselt, L., 275

Oaks, W. W., 29, 268
Obler, M., 158, 234, 235, 241, 280
O'Brien, K. M., 20, 280
O'Connor, J. F., 32, 33, 35, 93, 280
Offit, A. K., 99, 280
Oliveau, D. C., 276
Olson, D. H. L., 269
Olsson, P. A., 169, 270
Orsmond, A., 202, 286
Osgood, C. E., 219, 280
Oziel, L. J., 137, 280

Page, L. B., 29, 280
Paitch, D., 220, 280
Paldi, E., 271
Paquin, M. J., 180, 280
Patterson, G. R., 50, 51, 180, 280, 281
Paul, G. L., 157, 159, 281
Pearman, R. O., 169, 281
Pehm, L. P., 221, 281
Pfeiffer, E., 55, 281, 286
Phares, E. J., 127, 281
Phillips, D., 278, 280
Piemme, T. E., 29, 281
Pierce, D., 276
Pieroni, A., 27, 281
Pinderhughes, C. A., 61, 281
Poffenberger, S., 276
Poffenberger, T., 276
Polivy, J., 59, 281
Pomeroy, W. B., 275
Pouyat, S. B., 200, 287
Purtell, J. J., 63, 100, 116, 281

Raboch, J., 62, 281
Raft, D., 80, 283
Rainwater, L., 43, 88, 281
Raths, O. N., 267
Rawl, J., 280
Ray, A, A., 285
Ray, C., 59, 159, 281
Reed, D. M., 215, 277
Rees, W. L., 48, 281
Regestein, Q. R., 18, 281
Reid, J. B., 51, 281
Reiss, I. L., 73, 281
Renshaw, D. C., 25, 281
Reyna, L. G., 281
Rice, D. G., 180, 200, 273, 281
Rice, J. K., 200, 281
Richter, L., 183, 287

Rimm, D. C., 131, 281
Ritter, B., 134, 266
Robbins, M. B., 14, 97, 282
Roberts, C. D., 167, 282
Robins, E., 281
Robinson, C. H., 216, 282
Rodham, R., 269
Rodin, J., 282
Roman, M., 197, 199, 282
Rose, R. M., 276
Rosen, A., 197, 282
Rosen, R. C., 28, 45, 162, 270, 276, 282
Rosenblum, J. A., 24, 282
Rosenthal, C. F., 200, 282
Rosenthal, S. H., 200, 282
Ross, L. D., 127, 282
Rubin, H. B., 45, 225, 273, 282
Russell, G. F. M., 267
Russell, P. C., 131, 282

Sadock, B. J., 208, 282
Sager, C. J., 182, 282
Salis, P. J., 275
Salisbury, S., 270
Salter, A., 234, 282
Salvatierra, O., 20, 282
Samuals, R. M., 269
Sartorius, N. H., 216, 219, 278
Satterberg, J., 271
Sayegh, E. S., 169, 277
Sayner, R. B., 278
Schapiro, B., 89, 90, 282
Scheig, R., 28, 282
Schellen, M. C. M., 247, 282
Schiavi, R., 27, 167, 270, 283
Schmidt, L. D., 129, 284
Schneider, M. D., 168, 283
Schofield, M., 32, 283
Schwartz, G. E., 282
Scommegna, A., 270
Scott, F. B., 169, 283
Sedlacek, J., 271
Semans, J., 147, 283
Serber, M., 286
Shannon, A., 199, 272
Shapiro, A. K., 128, 283
Shapiro, D., 282
Shapiro, T., 272
Sharpe, R., 101, 283
Shaw, M., 274
Shaw, P., 279
Shearer, M. L., 285
Sheridan, W. F., 265
Sherman, A. R., 157, 283

Siddall, L. B., 199, 283
Siegel, L. J., 278
Simonson, N. R., 130, 272
Simpson, G. M., 283
Singer, I., 16, 99, 283
Singer, J., 16, 99, 283
Sintchak, G., 225, 283
Skynner, A. C. R., 125, 180, 283
Sloane, R. B., 127, 283
Sloboda, W., 167, 282
Smith, C. G., 269
Smith, H. D., 164, 283
Snyder, A., 37, 146, 253, 283
Sobocinski, D., 131, 272
Sobrero, A. J., 23, 283
Soldinger, S. M., 276
Solnick, R. L., 17, 283
Sorensen, R. C., 143, 283
Spanier, G. B., 220, 283
Spellman, M., 268
Spencer, R. F., 80, 283
Spitz, C. J., 26, 283
Spitz, H. I., 208, 282
Stamphl, T. G., 160, 283
Stanley, J. C., 258, 268
Staples, F., 61, 280, 283
Stearns, H. E., 283
Steele, T. E., 20, 284
Steeno, O., 271, 272
Steger, J. C., 217, 218, 253, 278
Steiner, B., 271
Stern, L. O., 32, 33, 35, 280
Stewart, R. C., 279
Stewart, T. D., 169, 284
Stewart, W. F. R., 56, 57, 284
Stone, A. R., 271
Stone, W. J., 280
Story, N. L., 28, 29, 284
Strong, S. R., 129, 284
Stuart, R. B., 50, 284
Suci, G. J., 280
Suinn, R. M., 126, 158, 159, 267
Susskind, D. J., 234, 284

Tannenbaum, P. H., 280
Tasto, D. L., 221, 284
Tauber, E. S., 26, 284
Taylor, G. R., 73, 284
Taylor, R., 248, 269
Taylor Segraves, R., 28, 29, 284
Temperley, J., 181, 272
Terman, L. M., 33, 34, 43, 110, 111, 113, 284
Thomas, E. J., 180, 284

Thompson, L. A., 274
Thoresen, C. E., 222, 284
Thornby, J. I., 275
Thurm, J., 20, 284
Tiku, J., 269
Timm, G. W., 283
Timms, R. J., 273
Timor-Tritsch, I., 271
Tomko, M. A., 273
Toussieng, P. W., 64, 284
Trieschmann, R. B., 24, 273
Trimmer, E., 30, 284
Truax, C. B., 126, 284
Truxaw, P., 274
Tudoriu, T., 169, 284
Turner, R. K., 274
Twentyman, G. T., 221, 284

Uddenberg, N., 34, 35, 49, 62, 113, 114, 284
Ullman, L. P., 131, 157, 278, 284
Upper, D., 215, 268

Valins, S., 127, 159, 275, 284, 285
Van Egeren, L. F., 159, 285
Van Keep, P. A., 55, 285
Van Lehn, R., 276
Van Thiel, D. H., 28, 285
Velten, E., 131, 285
Verburg, D., 276
Vincent, J. P., 51, 267, 285

Wabrek, A. J., 27, 115, 285
Wabrek, C. J., 27, 115, 285
Waggoner, R. W., 201, 285
Wagner, N. N., 18, 285
Wallace, C. J., 221, 285
Wallace, D. H., 254, 255, 256, 285
Wallace, K., 49, 253, 277
Wallin, P., 109, 111, 285
Wanderer, Z. W., 278
Ward, C. H., 266
Ware, J. C., 275
Wear, J. B., 101, 285
Weber, H., 25, 270
Webster, S. K., 271
Weerts, T. C., 267
Weinberg, L., 272
Weiner, B., 275
Weinstein, L., 199, 285
Weisberg, M., 100, 287
Weiss, A. I., 285
Weiss, H. D., 22, 285
Weiss, R. L., 220, 267, 281, 285

Weitzenhoffer, A. M., 165, 285
Whalen, R. E., 285
Whipple, K., 280, 283
White, D., 27, 167, 283
Whitehead, A., 216, 233, 279, 286
Wicker, A. W., 134, 286
Wiens, A. N., 212, 286
Wilbert, D. E., 276
Wilcoxon, L. A., 159, 275
Wilkins, W., 128, 159, 286
Williams, R. L., 275
Williams, W., 202, 286
Wilson, G. T., 28, 126, 143, 159, 267, 269, 286
Wincze, J. P., 158, 217, 225, 268, 274, 286
Winokur, G., 61, 62, 63, 116, 286
Witkin, A. P., 270
Wolberg, L. R., 128, 166, 286

Wolfe, L., 184, 286
Wolpe, J., 152, 153, 154, 155, 157, 158, 159, 286

Yates, A. J., 162, 210, 230, 286
Yelloly, M., 274
Yost, M. A., 104, 105, 276
Young, L. D., 162, 267
Yulis, S., 243, 246, 287

Zeiss, R. A., 245, 246, 287
Zentner, E. B., 200, 287
Zilbergeld, B., 144, 198, 287
Zimbardo, P. G., 134, 282, 287
Zinsser, H. H., 27, 28, 287
Zojac, A., 271
Zuckerman, M., 73, 216, 287

Subject Index

Achievement orientation, 126, 140
Adrenal gland, 26, 27
Afrodex, 167
Aggression, 50, 54, 55, 64, 66, 86, 92, 96, 105, 114, 115, 140, 181, 187
Aging, 17, 18, 54, 55, 56, 57, 64, 65, 66, 73, 74, 79, 83, 86, 93, 119, 120, 122, 127, 129, 132, 167, 177, 179, 189, 196, 225
Alcohol, 28, 61, 71, 120, 127, 177
Allergic reactions, 101, 116
Amputations, 28, 59, 121
Androgens, 26, 27, 167
Anger, 43, 45, 53, 54, 66, 71, 72, 78, 79, 85, 86, 89, 91, 92, 96, 104, 105, 112, 113, 114, 116, 122, 126, 140, 179, 181, 222
Antidepressant drugs, 29, 58, 120
Antihypertensive drugs, 20, 29, 79, 84, 95, 98, 120
Anxiety, assessment of, 179, 212, 214, 217, 220, 222, 235, 239
  disorders, 62, 63
  hierachies, 155, 157, 158, 240, 242
  reactions, 19, 32, 33, 34, 36, 37, 43, 44, 45, 46, 52, 53, 55, 57, 58, 59, 60, 61, 64, 66, 70, 71, 78, 82, 83, 85, 86, 88, 89, 91, 92, 94, 96, 101, 105, 106, 107, 108, 112, 114, 122, 123, 124, 126, 131, 137, 140, 142, 144, 177, 189, 207, 212, 241
  reduction of, 137, 139, 141, 143, 144, 145, 147, 152, 155, 156, 159, 160, 165, 168, 169, 194, 196, 198, 208, 209, 234, 235, 237, 239, 240, 258
Aortic aneurysm surgery, 95, 98
Arthritic disorders, 18, 21, 58, 102, 115, 121, 168
Attitudes, assessment of, 215, 226
  modification of, 7, 119, 125, 126, 127,

128, 129, 130, 131, 132, 133, 134, 135, 142, 143, 162, 170, 171, 185, 188, 192, 205, 208, 233, 234, 250
  negative, 33, 34, 39, 125, 126, 142, 143, 178, 240
Autonomic disorder, 24
Avoidance conditioning, see Learning processes
Avoidance reactions, 36, 46, 51, 55, 57, 63, 142, 201, 206
  cognitive, 39, 47, 48, 66, 79, 85, 91, 99, 100, 105, 109, 141, 142, 148
  overt, 30, 32, 43, 46, 60, 64, 66, 78, 79, 82, 89, 92, 96, 101, 104, 107, 108, 112, 113, 114, 115, 124, 125, 131, 140, 189
  reduction of, 120, 137, 139, 160, 194

Balanitis, 102
Barbiturates, 28
Bartholin's glands, 115
Beck Depression Inventory, 221
Behavioral Analysis History Question-naire, 215
Behavioural approach, 1, 2, 3, 4, 5, 6, 7, 36, 41, 66, 126, 128, 138
  formulation, 6, 127, 128, 129, 137, 171, 192, 193, 196, 201, 204
  procedures, 7, 125, 134, 136, 141, 152, 153, 154, 155, 156, 157, 158, 159, 160, 161, 162, 163, 164, 165, 166, 170, 171, 200, 207, 208
  rehearsal, 133
Beta-adrenergic blocking agents, 29, 168
Biofeedback, 152, 162, 163, 170, 171, 185, 205, 206
Bladder control, 24, 59, 91, 113, 121
Bladder neck surgery, 98
Blakoe Suspensory Energiser Ring, 168
Bowel control, 24, 59, 113, 121

Brain disorders, 23, 28
Bridge manoeuvre, 147, 150, 151
Brietal (Brevital), 155
Butyrophenone drugs, 28

Cancer, 26, 116
Cardiac disorders, 18, 19, 20, 56, 58, 102, 115, 120, 121, 122, 168
Card sort method, 217
Castration, 26
Chemotherapy, see Drug therapy
Chordee, 22, 101
Clark Sexual History Questionnaire, 220
Classical conditioning treatment, 152, 161, 162, 170, 171, 185, 205
Clitoris, 15, 16, 18, 22, 64, 111, 112, 114, 116, 121, 142, 144, 149, 150, 168
Cognitive monitoring, 47, 55, 64, 66, 85, 89, 105, 114, 122, 123, 124, 137, 139, 141, 145, 147, 194, 196
Cognitive restructuring, 129, 131, 132, 133, 134, 171
Coitus reservatus, 97
Colectomy, see Ileostomy
Colostomy, 27, 58, 59, 79, 84
Constitutional factors, 79, 86
Conversion symptoms, see Hysterical disorders
Covert sensitization, 191, 192
Cushing's syndrome, 26, 79, 84
Cystectomy, 84

Depression, 19, 30, 45, 55, 58, 59, 61, 62, 63, 66, 71, 79, 80, 82, 83, 89, 126, 189, 239
  assessment of, 221, 222
Desensitization, 133, 134, 139, 143, 152, 154, 155, 156, 157, 158, 159, 160, 164, 170, 171, 185, 205, 208, 232, 234, 239, 240, 242, 248, 250, 257, 258
Diabetes mellitus, 24, 25, 84, 98, 105, 113, 120, 127
Disability, see Illness
Dissonance theory, 130, 133, 134, 135
Drugs, 4, 18, 28, 29, 30, 54, 58, 60, 61, 65, 66, 79, 83, 84, 95, 98, 120, 121, 122, 179, 189, 194, 225, 257
Drug therapy, 168, 170, 171, 205, 237, 239, 242, 258
Dry run orgasm, 93
Dyadic Adjustment Scale, 220
Dyspareunia, female, 43, 108
  assessment, 219

causation, 22, 28, 30, 39, 58, 61, 62, 63, 74, 75, 106, 107, 112, 115, 116
description, 71, 74, 113, 115
treatment, 167, 248, 257
Dyspareunia, male, causation, 39, 58
description, 71, 74, 75, 101
treatment, 237, 257

Educational level, 188, 231, 234, 243, 244, 247, 254
Ejaculation, 14, 16, 17, 23, 55, 87, 90, 91, 92, 97, 99, 101, 102, 120
  emission component, 14, 15, 16, 17, 23, 87, 93
  expulsion component, 14, 15, 17, 23, 87, 93
Ejaculatory incompetence, see Retarded or absent ejaculation
Endocrine disorders, 18, 25, 26, 27, 79, 84, 98
Endometriosis, 22, 116
Engagement, 79, 80, 82, 83
Episiotomy, 27, 101, 115
Epispadias, 84
Erectile dysfunction, 103
  assessment, 177, 182, 191, 219, 222, 224
  causation, 20, 21, 24, 25, 26, 27, 28, 29, 32, 34, 41, 42, 43, 44, 45, 47, 54, 55, 56, 61, 65, 81, 83, 84, 85, 86, 87, 89, 94, 97, 98, 100, 101, 107, 108
  description, 4, 39, 42, 44, 52, 57, 69, 70, 71, 72, 73, 74, 75, 77, 81, 82, 83, 86, 87, 90, 104, 186
  treatment, 120, 122, 124, 125, 127, 141, 142, 144, 148, 149, 150, 151, 161, 162, 165, 167, 168, 169, 181, 196, 203, 232, 234, 237, 238, 239, 240, 241, 242, 243, 256, 257
Erection, 13, 14, 15, 16, 17, 22, 23, 55, 64, 81, 97, 99, 101, 120, 162, 224
Escape, see Avoidance reactions, overt
Exhibitionism, 220
Expectancies, prognostic, 7, 126, 127, 128, 129, 133, 137, 171, 201, 205
  self-efficacy, 126, 127

Fear, see Anxiety
Fetishism, 86, 94, 191, 219
Flooding, 152, 159, 160, 164, 170, 171, 185, 205
Frigidity, see Inadequate sexual interest, Inadequate sexual pleasure, Orgastic

dysfunction, Vasocongestive
    dysfunction

Gender identity, 59, 72, 82
    assessment of, 220
Gender role behaviour, assessment of, 220
General sexual dysfunction, 103
Genital anaesthesia, see Avoidance reac-
    tions, cognitive
Genital disorders, 18, 21, 22, 58, 84, 95,
    115
Genital pleasuring, 141, 142, 149, 150,
    158, 206
Gonads, 25, 26, 84, 167
Gonorrhea, 95
Guanethidine sulphate, 29
Guilt, 33, 34, 44, 45, 55, 66, 70, 71, 80, 88,
    89, 126, 137, 140, 141, 142, 143, 179,
    188, 208

Handicap, see Illness
Hepatic cirrhosis, 26, 28, 84
Heroin, 29
Heterosexual Attitude Scales, 216
Heterosexual Behavior Inventories, 216
Homosexuality, 65, 70, 78, 80, 87, 94, 106,
    109, 161, 191, 213, 219, 220
Honeymoon, 33, 82
Hormones, 25, 26, 27
Hormone therapy, 167, 168, 170, 171
Hymen, 22, 108, 115
Hypnosis, 152, 155, 164, 165, 166, 170,
    171, 185, 205, 248
Hypospadias, 22, 84, 101
Hypothalamus, 23, 25, 80, 105
Hysterectomy, 59, 79, 116
Hysterical disorders, 63, 100, 116

Ileostomy, 27, 58, 59, 79, 84, 98
Iliac artery occlusion, 84
Illness, 4, 18, 19, 20, 21, 22, 23, 24, 25, 26,
    27, 54, 57, 58, 59, 60, 64, 65, 66, 72,
    74, 79, 82, 83, 84, 86, 95, 97, 102,
    115, 120, 121, 122, 125, 132, 168,
    169, 179, 189, 194, 225, 234, 239,
    247, 257
Implosion, see Flooding
Impotence, see Erectile dysfunction
Inadequate sexual interest, 77, 78, 79, 80,
    81, 83, 86, 103, 134
    assessment, 175
    causation, 19, 20, 25, 26, 28, 29, 30, 33,
        36, 37, 38, 56, 62, 63, 79, 80, 81,
        89, 97, 98, 100, 101, 104, 105, 112

description, 4, 71, 73, 74, 75, 77, 78, 79,
    81, 82, 83, 90, 97, 109, 113, 115,
    186, 249, 255, 256, 257
treatment, 76, 123, 127, 128, 160, 161,
    232, 237, 248, 257
Inadequate sexual pleasure, 89, 103, 115
    assessment, 175, 178, 182, 190
    causation, 33, 34, 35, 36, 47, 53, 54, 56,
        58, 61, 62, 63, 88, 100, 114, 115
    description, 4, 43, 45, 71, 73, 74, 75, 78,
        82, 91, 93, 98, 99, 100, 104, 109,
        186, 187
    treatment, 76, 124, 142, 149, 150, 160,
        161, 166, 169, 181, 196, 232, 234,
        237, 248, 254, 257
Incest, 32, 44, 85, 213
Interviews, assessment, 7, 203, 211, 212,
    213, 214, 215, 222, 239, 260, 261,
    262, 263, 264
    therapeutic, 7, 119, 120, 121, 122, 123,
        124, 125, 126, 127, 128, 129, 130,
        131, 132, 133, 134, 135, 136, 166,
        170, 171, 198, 207, 232, 252, 257
Intimacy dysfunctions, 36, 38, 39, 43, 63,
    80, 140, 178, 190, 191, 208
Intromission, inadequate, 75, 81, 82, 83,
    84, 85, 86, 87, 103, 104, 105, 106,
    107, 108, 109
In vivo desensitization, see desensitization
Ismelin, 29

Klinefelter's syndrome, 26

Labial temperature, 225
Law, 72, 74
Learning conditions, 4, 31, 32, 33, 34, 35,
    36, 90, 91
    adverse family relationships, 31, 34, 35,
        36, 39, 44, 63, 65, 66, 84, 113, 178
    restrictive upbringing, 31, 33, 34, 38, 39,
        63, 65, 66, 95, 96, 107, 113, 178
    traumatic experiences, 31, 32, 33, 39,
        43, 63, 65, 66, 84, 94, 95, 96, 101,
        107, 113, 164, 177, 238
Learning processes, 4, 31, 36, 37, 38, 39
    active avoidance conditioning, 37, 159
    classical aversive conditioning, 36, 38,
        101, 108
    cognitive learning, 39
    discrimination learning, 38
    instrumental punishment conditioning,
        36, 38, 101, 108
    negative reinforcement, 37
    observational learning, 38, 208, 209

Learning processes, *cont.*
  passive avoidance conditioning, 37, 159
  positive reinforcement, 37, 38, 46, 80,
      81, 91, 137, 179, 206, 208, 209
Leriche's syndrome, 27, 84
Libido, *see* Inadequate sexual interest
Life History Questionnaire, 215
Liver disease, 28
Lubin Depression Adjective Checklist, 221
Lubrication-swelling phase, 14, 15, 16, 17,
      23, 55, 99, 103, 104, 105, 120
Lumber sympathectomy, 27, 95, 98

Marital discord, *see* Partner discord
Marital therapy, 6, 49, 180, 182, 194, 253
Marriage, 79, 80, 82, 83, 105
Mastectomy, 59, 79
'Masters and Johnson' programmes, 124,
      135, 138, 139, 181, 183, 197, 200,
      201, 202, 203, 204, 213, 230, 231,
      232, 233, 234, 257, 259
  for erectile dysfunction, 148, 237, 238,
      240, 242, 257, 258
  for inadequate sexual pleasure, 149, 150
  for orgastic dysfunction, 249, 251, 252,
      255, 256, 257
  for premature ejaculation, 147, 148, 243,
      244, 245, 246
  for retarded or absent ejaculation, 246,
      247
  for vaginismus, 125, 160, 161, 248
  for vasocongestive dysfunction, 149, 150
Masturbation, 32, 33, 37, 38, 39, 78, 79,
      82, 89, 93, 94, 95, 96, 97, 100, 101,
      104, 111, 116, 121, 122, 142, 143,
      144, 146, 206, 215, 216, 253
Masturbatory training, *see* Sexual
      assignments, Genital stimulation
Medical examination, 7, 200, 203, 211
  conjoint, 125, 225
Medical treatment, 6, 194, 239, 242, 257
Mellaril, 29
Menopause, 15, 17, 26, 55, 83, 105, 115,
      116, 120
Menstruation, 71, 179
Methadone, 29
Methohexitone sodium, 155
Methyldopa, 29
Modelling, *see* Learning processes, obser-
      vational learning
Monoamine oxidase inhibitors, 29
Morality, *see* Religion
Morphine, 29
Multiple sclerosis, 24, 90

Myotonia, 13

Narcotic drugs, 29, 30, 84, 95
Neurological disorders, 18, 22, 23, 24, 25,
      28, 84, 90, 95, 98, 105, 120, 206
Neurosis, *see* Psychiatric syndromes
Nitroglycerine, 168
Nocturnal emissions, 32, 33, 39, 93, 95, 96
Non-demand coitus, 149, 151, 158, 203,
      206
Non-sexual stresses, 41, 45, 48, 66, 79, 84,
      85, 123, 178, 194

Obscene telephone calls, 220
Obsessive–compulsive disorders, 100
Obstetrics, *see* Surgery
Oestrogens, 26, 105, 115, 116, 167
Oral contraceptives, 30, 79
Orchitis, 102
Orgasm, female, 14, 15, 16, 18, 23, 55, 64,
      99, 103, 109, 111, 120, 121, 122, 144
Orgasm, male, 14, 16, 17, 81, 87, 90, 91,
      92, 93, 94, 97, 99
Orgastic dysfunction, 46
  assessment, 175, 177, 182, 219, 222
  causation, 20, 21, 25, 34, 35, 36, 37, 41,
      43, 44, 52, 61, 62, 63, 64, 65, 88,
      100, 105, 113, 114, 115, 123
  description, 3, 32, 33, 42, 43, 4', 49, 53,
      69, 70, 71, 72, 73, 74, 75, 78, 103,
      104, 109, 110, 111, 112, 113, 186,
      187, 249
  treatment, 46, 121, 122, 123, 124, 142,
      144, 145, 146, 150, 160, 166, 169,
      196, 203, 206, 209, 232, 233, 234,
      249, 250, 251, 252, 253, 254, 255,
      256
Ostomy, *see* Colostomy, Ileostomy
Ovaries, 26, 27, 28, 105

Paedophilia, 78, 161, 220
Pain, *see* Dyspareunia
Paranoia, 189
Parkinson's disease, 95
Partial ejaculatory incompetence, 93
Partner communication, 125, 137, 140,
      141, 142, 144, 181, 209
Partner discord, 5, 41, 44, 49, 50, 51, 52,
      53, 54, 59, 60, 61, 63, 64, 65, 66, 72,
      79, 83, 86, 92, 96, 104, 105, 112, 113,
      114, 116, 123, 126, 187, 191, 194,
      232, 238, 239, 240, 244, 245, 249,
      251, 253, 255, 256
  assessment of, 177, 178, 180, 181, 182,
      220, 221, 241, 253

deficient reinforcement, 50, 51, 52, 53, 54, 59
dominance–submission conflicts, 52, 53, 54, 92, 96, 105, 114, 187
  reduction of, 233, 234, 241, 253, 255, 258
  rejection, 52, 53, 57, 59, 61, 70, 72, 78, 79, 82, 86, 89, 94, 96, 97, 105, 106, 107, 110, 112, 113, 114, 122, 132, 140, 141, 178, 179
  sexually dysfunctional partner, 31, 52, 53, 56, 59, 89, 92, 108
Partners, general relationship, see Partner discord
Pelvic fractures, 98
Penile plethysmography, 162, 224, 225, 239
Penile sensitivity, 65, 86
Penile size, 64, 121
Penile splints, external, 168
  implants, 168, 169
Penile trauma, 101
Penis, artificial, 121, 169
Performance anxiety, see Anxiety, and Sexual stresses, anticipation of failure
Personal and family background, assessment of, 215
Peyronie's disease, 22, 84, 101
Phantasy stimulation, 12, 45, 65, 78, 80, 111, 122, 145, 147, 149, 162
Phantasy training, 152, 163, 164, 170, 171, 185, 205
Phenothiazine drugs, 28, 29
Phimosis, 22, 101
Physical treatment, ancillary, 7, 119, 136, 141, 166, 167, 168, 169, 170, 171, 185
Physiological techniques, of assessment, 7, 211, 223, 224, 225, 235, 239
Pituitary gland, 25, 26, 105
Pleasure dysfunctions, 100, 190
Portenson Forte, 167
Post-partum period, 71, 79, 179
Pregnancy, 71, 79, 94, 95, 96, 97, 107, 108, 122, 179, 187, 189
Premature ejaculation, 83, 85, 99
  assessment, 176, 191, 219
  causation, 32, 37, 43, 48, 52, 54, 90, 91, 92, 108
  description, 3, 53, 69, 70, 74, 75, 77, 87, 88, 89, 90, 186, 187
  treatment, 93, 142, 144, 147, 148, 151, 169, 196, 198, 203, 206, 232, 234, 243, 244, 245, 246, 256

Priapism, 84
Progesterone, 26
Propranolol, 168
Prostatectomy, 27, 58, 79, 84, 98, 120
Prostatitis, 22, 102
Prosthetic or mechanical aids, 64, 121, 168, 169, 170, 171, 205
Psychiatric syndromes, 5, 31, 61, 62, 63, 65, 66, 82, 194, 232, 234
  assessment of, 122, 189, 190, 191, 221, 249, 257
Psychodynamically oriented group therapy, 234, 257
Psychological reactions to organic factors, 5, 18, 19, 20, 21, 27, 30, 54, 55, 56, 57, 58, 59, 60, 61, 65, 66, 79, 83, 120, 177, 189
Psychological stress, 5, 41, 42, 43, 44, 45, 46, 47, 48, 49, 66, 71
  conditions, 42, 49, 50, 51, 52, 53, 54, 61, 64, 65, 66, 79, 91, 96, 100, 105, 113, 116, 144
  individual differences, 33, 34, 42, 48, 49, 55, 90, 96, 107, 113
  reactions, 36, 42, 45, 46, 47, 48, 53, 54, 66, 91, 97, 105, 116, 123, 124, 140, 207
  reduction of, 137, 139, 142, 143, 144, 146, 151, 152, 164, 171, 194, 205
Psychosis, see Psychiatric syndromes
Pubococcygeal muscles, 100, 166

Questionnaires, 7, 211, 214, 215, 216, 217, 218, 219, 220, 221, 222, 241, 250
Quiet vagina technique, 151

Radiation, 101, 116
Rape, see Sexual assault
Rational–emotional therapy, see Cognitive restructuring
Rational restructuring, see Cognitive restructuring
Rauwolfia alkaloids, 29
Refractory period, 14, 16, 17, 55, 71, 93
Relationship, therapeutic, 7, 126, 127, 129, 130, 133, 170, 201, 204
Relaxation training, 139, 152, 153, 154, 158, 164, 170, 171, 185, 205, 240, 242
Religion, 33, 34, 42, 44, 45, 66, 70, 72, 74, 85, 96, 108, 123, 125, 129, 143, 188, 206, 257
Renal disorders, 18, 20, 21, 58, 79, 84, 95, 113

Resolution phase, 14, 16, 17, 18
Retarded or absent ejaculation, 46, 109
    assessment, 176, 191, 219
    causation, 21, 24, 29, 30, 32, 37, 38, 42,
        54, 95, 96, 97, 101
    description, 3, 52, 70, 74, 75, 77, 93, 94,
        95, 187
    treatment, 146, 147, 151, 196, 203, 207,
        232, 234, 246, 247
Retrograde ejaculation, 93
    assessment, 191
    causation, 25, 27, 28, 29, 58, 95, 98
    description, 3, 74, 75, 77, 87, 97, 98
    treatment, 120, 196, 237
Retroperitoneal lymph node dissection, 98
Role playing, 129, 130, 131, 133, 145, 146,
    171
Roundtable discussion, see Sexual dysfunc-
    tion, treatment, initiation

Sadomasochism, 65, 78, 94, 191
Sanctioning, 129, 133, 171, 208
Schizophrenia, 189
Sedative drugs, 28, 84
Self-concept, 56, 59, 71, 72, 112, 190
    body image, 59
    gender identity, 59, 72, 82
    self-esteem, 59, 60, 72, 74, 82
Self-control desensitization, see
    Desensitization
Self-disclosure, 129, 130, 133, 171
Self-management, 207
Self-monitoring, 7, 188, 207, 211, 222,
    223, 235, 241, 243, 244, 245, 250
Self-recording, see Self-monitoring
Self-regulation, 191, 192
Semantic differential technique, 216, 219,
    233, 234
Seminal vesiculitis, 102
Sensate focus, see Sexual assignments,
    general pleasuring,
    genital stimulation
Sex education, 34, 108, 109
Sex therapy, 1, 49
Sexual anaesthesia, see Avoidance reac-
    tions, cognitive
Sexual anatomy or responses, 42, 43, 66,
    84, 121, 122, 142, 156, 178
Sexual Arousability Inventory, 217
Sexual arousal, 45, 47, 74, 75, 155, 158,
    233, 234
    assessment of, 217, 223, 224
    inadequate, 21, 26, 45, 47, 53, 64, 78,
        81, 82, 83, 84, 85, 86, 87, 96, 97,

        103, 104, 105, 106, 107, 108, 109
Sexual assault, 32, 43, 94, 107, 115, 220
Sexual assignments, 7, 119, 125, 133, 134,
    137, 138, 139, 140, 141, 142, 143,
    144, 145, 146, 147, 148, 149, 150,
    151, 158, 166, 170, 171, 181, 182,
    183, 188, 201, 205, 222, 231, 250,
    257
    general pleasuring, 7, 138, 139, 140,
        141, 149, 151, 158, 170, 171, 190,
        203, 206, 251
    genital stimulation, 7, 138, 139, 140,
        141, 142, 143, 144, 145, 146, 147,
        148, 149, 150, 160, 170, 171, 185,
        189, 190, 203, 206, 207, 222, 250,
        251, 252, 255
    management of, 7, 119, 135, 136, 154,
        170, 171, 188, 208, 254
    sexual intercourse, 7, 138, 146, 148,
        149, 150, 151, 158, 170, 171, 203,
        206, 207, 251
Sexual Compatibility Test, 218
Sexual desire, see Inadequate sexual
    interest
Sexual deviance, see Sexual variations
Sexual drive, see Inadequate sexual interest
Sexual dysfunction, assessment, 5, 6, 7,
    173, 174, 175, 176, 177, 178, 179,
    180, 181, 182, 183, 184, 185, 186,
    187, 188, 189, 190, 191, 192, 193,
    194, 195, 196, 197, 198, 199, 200,
    201, 202, 203, 204, 205, 206, 207,
    208, 209, 210, 210, 211, 212, 213,
    214, 215, 216, 217, 218, 219, 220,
    221, 222, 223, 224, 225
    methods, 7, 211, 212, 213, 214, 215,
        216, 217, 218, 219, 220, 221, 222,
        223, 224, 225, 230
    of problem, 6, 175, 176, 177, 178, 179,
        192, 222, 223, 260, 261, 262, 263,
        264
    of progress and outcome, 7, 196, 209,
        214, 222, 223, 259
    of resources, 6, 179, 180, 181, 182, 183,
        184, 185, 186, 187, 188, 189, 190,
        191, 192, 260, 261, 262, 263, 264
    process, 7, 175, 176, 177, 178, 179, 180,
        181, 182, 183, 184, 185, 186, 187,
        188, 189, 190, 191, 192, 193, 196,
        210
Sexual dysfunction, causation, 4, 5, 7, 65,
    66, 76, 127, 128, 133, 192, 193
    contemporary conditions, 4, 5, 31, 41,
        42, 43, 44, 45, 46, 47, 48, 49, 50,

51, 52, 53, 54, 55, 56, 57, 58, 59
60, 61, 62, 63, 64, 65, 66, 177,
178, 179
organic factors, 4, 11, 12, 13, 14, 15, 16,
17, 18, 19, 20, 21, 22, 23, 24, 25,
26, 27, 28, 29, 30, 31, 40, 41, 54,
55, 56, 57, 58, 59, 60, 61, 65, 66,
79, 83, 84, 90, 95, 98, 100, 101,
105, 107, 113, 115, 189, 224
previous learning experiences, 4, 31, 32,
33, 34, 35, 36, 37, 38, 39, 40, 41,
42, 65, 66, 84, 90, 95, 107, 113,
171, 177
Sexual dysfunction, classification, 75, 76
Sexual dysfunction, definition, 3, 4, 5, 41,
66, 69, 70, 71, 72, 73, 74, 76
Sexual dysfunction, treatment, 5, 7, 41,
117, 118, 119, 120, 121, 122, 123,
124, 125, 126, 127, 128, 129, 130,
131, 132, 133, 134, 135, 136, 137,
138, 139, 140, 141, 142, 143, 144,
145, 146, 147, 148, 149, 150, 151,
152, 153, 154, 155, 156, 157, 158,
159, 160, 161, 162, 163, 164, 165,
166, 167, 168, 169, 170, 171
client's motivation, 137, 187, 188, 201,
231, 234, 245, 257
Client's organizational capacity, 188,
201
client's role, 204, 205
components, 119, 129, 170, 171, 192,
204, 205, 206, 207
conjoint, 181, 209
contracts, 195, 204, 205
ethical issues, 184, 189, 195, 206, 223
goals, 6, 193, 194, 195, 196, 205
in groups, 198, 208, 209, 240, 243, 245,
246, 254
initiation, 204, 205, 213
maintenance of effects, 202, 207
of two dysfunctional partners, 186
outcome, 204, 205, 206, 227, 228, 229,
230, 231, 232, 233, 234, 235, 236,
237, 238, 239, 240, 241, 242, 243,
244, 245, 246, 247, 248, 249, 250,
251, 252, 253, 254, 255, 256, 257,
258, 259, 260
planning, 6, 7, 76, 171, 193, 196, 197,
198, 199, 200, 201, 202, 203, 204,
205, 206, 207, 208, 209, 210
programmes, 6, 76, 119, 134, 138, 145,
146, 171, 180, 192, 194, 203, 204,
205, 206, 207, 208, 209, 210, 230,
231, 232, 233, 234, 235, 236, 237,

238, 239, 240, 241, 242, 243, 244,
245, 246, 247, 248, 249, 250, 251,
252, 253, 254, 255, 256, 257, 258,
259, 260
settings, 6, 201, 202, 258
therapists, 6, 192, 197, 198, 199, 200,
201, 204, 205, 206, 232, 257,
258
timing, 6, 135, 138, 192, 202, 203, 204,
258
Sexual experience, assessment of, 216, 217
Sexual Fear Inventories, 217
Sexual information, assessment of, 215
deficient or inappropriate, 5, 33, 38, 63,
64, 65, 66, 108, 115, 134, 178, 188
provision of, 7, 119, 120, 121, 122, 123,
124, 125, 135, 141, 142, 143, 146,
170, 171, 185, 188, 192, 198, 205,
208, 209, 250
Sexual Interaction Inventory, 217, 253
Sexual intercourse, 32, 33, 37, 55, 64, 70,
73, 74, 79, 82, 83, 85, 87, 89, 90, 93,
100, 104, 107, 109, 110, 111, 121,
123, 144
assignments, see Sexual assignments,
sexual intercourse
frequency, 19, 20, 21, 46, 61, 63, 65, 69,
71, 72, 99, 100, 122
Sexual interest, 55, 207
inadequate, see Inadequate sexual
interest
Sexual Knowledge and Attitude Scale, 215
Sexual pleasure, 55, 92, 208, 217, 258
assessment of, 217, 218, 219
inadequate, see Inadequate sexual
pleasure
Sexual Pleasure Inventories, 217
Sexual relationship, assessment of, 217,
218, 219, 241, 252, 253
modification of, 233, 241, 252, 253, 256,
258
Sexual response, 12, 13, 14, 15, 16, 17, 18,
121, 207, 208, 240, 258
enhancement of, 137, 140, 152, 171,
194, 205
female, 15, 16, 17, 18
male, 13, 14, 15, 17
Sexual stimulation, 11, 12, 23, 24, 45, 46,
47, 64, 70, 85, 89, 99, 100, 101, 104,
106, 110, 111, 112, 116, 121, 144
deficient or inappropriate, 5, 52, 54, 64,
65, 66, 80, 83, 85, 86, 94, 97, 101,
106, 109, 114, 124, 134, 177, 178,
240

Sexual stimulation, *cont.*
  enhancement of, 137, 140, 142, 144,
    146, 152, 171
Sexual stresses, 41, 42, 43, 44, 45, 48, 66,
    79, 84, 91, 116
  anticipation of failure, 42, 43, 44, 45, 47,
    53, 55, 56, 57, 58, 60, 61, 64, 66,
    78, 79, 85, 86, 89, 91, 96, 108,
    113, 122, 123, 124, 131, 132, 140,
    142, 145, 165, 177, 178, 241
  anticipation of harm, 36, 38, 39, 42, 43,
    44, 57, 58, 66, 79, 84, 96, 101,
    106, 107, 108, 113, 116, 120, 122,
    131, 144, 145, 156, 177, 178
  moral or religious contraventions, *see*
    Religion
Sexual variations, 65, 74, 78, 80, 83, 86,
    87, 94, 97, 100, 106, 109, 124, 161,
    239, 257
  assessment of, 191, 192, 219, 220
Single clients, 46, 56, 59, 60, 72, 134, 143,
    183, 184, 185, 186, 187, 206, 257
Social norms, 72, 88, 134
Social skills, assessment of, 185, 221
  deficits, 185, 191
  training, 185, 186, 191, 194, 234, 236,
    243, 246, 250
Social status, 72
Socio-economic class, 88, 188, 230, 241,
    243, 247, 249, 254
Socio-economic resources for treatment,
    186, 187
Spectator role, *see* Cognitive monitoring
Spina bifida, 24
Spinal cord disorders, 24, 84, 90, 95, 98,
    120, 121, 127
Spinal fusion surgery, 95
Squeeze technique, 147, 148, 151, 203, 206
Stop–start technique, *see* Squeeze
    technique
Stress, *see* Psychological stress
Stuffing technique, 151
Surgery, 18, 26, 27, 28, 54, 57, 58, 59, 60,
    65, 66, 83, 95, 98, 101, 120, 121, 122,
    179, 189, 225, 257
Surrogate partners, 183, 206, 230
Survey of Heterosexual Interactions, 221
Sympathectomy, 84

Systematic desensitization, *see*
    Desensitization

Testes, 26, 27, 28
Therapists, *see* Sexual dysfunction, treat-
    ment, therapists
Thioridazine, 29
Thioxanthene drugs, 28
Tranquilizing drugs, 28, 29, 79, 84, 98, 120
Transvestism, 65, 86, 124, 191, 219, 220
Tricyclic drugs, 29

Unconventional sexual stimulation, *see*
    Sexual variations
Urethritis, 22, 102

Vaginal dilatation, 152, 160, 161, 164, 170,
    171, 185, 203, 205, 206, 248
Vaginal muscle exercises, 166, 167, 170,
    171, 205
Vaginal plethysmography, 224, 225
Vaginal pulse amplitude, 225
Vaginismus, 46
  causation, 43, 65, 107, 108, 109, 115
  description, 3, 69, 72, 75, 106, 107, 115,
    116
  treatment, 121, 125, 143, 156, 160, 203,
    206, 209, 232, 248, 256
Vaginitis, 22, 116
  atrophic, 26, 28, 116, 167
Vascular disorders, 18, 27, 84
Vasectomy, 83
Vasocongestion, 13, 14, 15, 16, 27, 81,
    116, 162, 225
Vasocongestive dysfunction, assessment,
    175, 178, 182
  causation, 27, 30, 32, 41, 43, 44, 45, 47,
    52, 100, 105, 106, 114, 115, 116,
    123
  description, 3, 53, 71, 74, 75, 101, 103,
    104, 105, 109, 116, 186, 187
  treatment, 124, 149, 150, 160, 166, 169,
    181, 196, 248
Venereal disease, 108
Vibrators, 64, 121, 145, 146, 147, 150,
    169, 247
Voyeurism, 220